Arizona State University
MTE301

PEARSON

ISBN 10: 1-269-80603-3
ISBN 13: 978-1-269-80603-9

Table of Contents

Table of Contents

An Introduction to Problem Solving

1 Mathematics and Problem Solving

2 Explorations with Patterns and Algebraic Thinking

Preliminary Problem

Jill received 10 boxes of coins, each box containing 10 identical looking coins. She knows that one box has 10 counterfeit coins, while all the other coins are genuine. She also knows that each fake coin weighs 1 ounce, while a real coin weighs 2 ounces. Jill has a scale and claims it is possible to determine which is the box with fake coins, in one weighing, as follows:

> "Number the boxes 1 through 10, and take 1 coin from the first box, 2 from the second, 3 from the third, and so on until 10 are taken from the last box. Next, I weigh all the coins taken out, and I can determine which box has the fake coins."

Explain why Jill's scheme would work.

If needed, see Hint before the Chapter Summary.

From Chapter 1 of *A Problem Solving Approach to Mathematics*, Twelfth Edition. Rick Billstein, Shlomo Libeskind, Johnny W. Lott, and Barbara Boschmans. Copyright © 2016 by Pearson Education, Inc. All rights reserved.

Problem solving has long been central in the learning of mathematics at all levels. George Pólya (1887–1985), a great mathematician of the twentieth century, is the father of mathematical problem solving. He pointed out that "solving a problem means finding a way out of difficulty, a way around an obstacle, attaining an aim which was not immediately attainable." (Pólya 1981, p. ix)

Polya developed a four-step problem solving process which has been adopted by many. A modified version is given here.

1. Understanding the problem
2. Devising a plan
3. Carrying out the plan
4. Looking back

 The *Common Core State Standards for Mathematics* (hereafter referred to as *Common Core Standards* and abbreviated as CCSS) were developed in 2010 through the work of the National Governors Association and the Council of Chief State School Officers. The *Common Core Standards* are built around its *Standards for Mathematical Practice* seen in Table 1.

Table 1

1. **Make sense of problems and persevere in solving them.**
   Mathematically proficient students start by explaining to themselves the meaning of a problem and looking for entry points to its solution. They analyze givens, constraints, relationships, and goals. They make conjectures about the form and meaning of the solution and plan a solution pathway rather than simply jumping in to a solution attempt.

2. **Reason abstractly and quantitatively.**
   Mathematically proficient students make sense of quantities and their relationships in problem situations.

3. **Construct viable arguments and critique the reasoning of others.**
   Mathematically proficient students understand and use stated assumptions, definitions, and previously established results in constructing arguments. They make conjectures and build a logical progression of statements to explore the truth of their conjectures. They are able to analyze situations by breaking them into cases, and can recognize and use counterexamples.

4. **Model with mathematics.**
   Mathematically proficient students can apply the mathematics they know to solve problems arising in everyday life, society, and the workplace. In early grades, this might be as simple as writing an addition equation to describe a situation. In middle grades, a student might apply proportional reasoning to plan a school event or analyze a problem in the community.

5. **Use appropriate tools strategically.**
   Mathematically proficient students consider the available tools when solving a mathematical problem. These tools might include pencil and paper, concrete models, a ruler, a protractor, a calculator, a spreadsheet, a computer algebra system, a statistical package, or dynamic geometry software.

6. **Attend to precision.**
   Mathematically proficient students try to communicate precisely to others. They try to use clear definitions in discussion with others and in their own reasoning. They state the meaning of the symbols they choose, including using the equal sign consistently and appropriately. They are careful about specifying units of measure, and labeling axes to clarify the correspondence with quantities in a problem.

7. **Look for and make use of structure.**
   Mathematically proficient students look closely to discern a pattern or structure. Young students, for example, might notice that three and seven more is the same amount as seven and three more, or they may sort a collection of shapes according to how many sides the shapes have. Later, students will see 7×8 equals the well remembered $7 \times 5 + 7 \times 3$, in preparation for learning about the distributive property. In the expression $x^2 + 9x + 14$, older students can see the 14 as 2×7 and the 9 as $2 + 7$.

8. **Look for and express regularity in repeated reasoning.**
   Mathematically proficient students notice if calculations are repeated, and look both for general methods and for shortcuts. Upper elementary students might notice when dividing 25 by 11 that they are repeating the same calculations over and over again, and conclude they have a repeating decimal.

The *Standards for Mathematical Practice* are used in this text to enhance Polya's four-step process as seen in Table 2.

Table 2

Expanded Four-Step Problem Solving Process with Input from *Standards for Mathematical Practice*

1. **Understanding the problem.**
   - Start by explaining the personal meaning of a problem.
   - Ask if the problem can be stated differently.
   - Analyze goals to identify what is to be found and what is needed.
   - Analyze the givens.
   - Analyze the constraints.
   - Ask what information is missing from the problem.
   - Ask about missing or unneeded information in the problem.
   - Make sense of quantities and their relationships in the problem situation.
   - Look for discernable patterns or structures.

2. **Devising a plan.**
   - Look for a pattern or a structure.
   - Examine related or analogous problems and determine whether the same techniques applied to them can be applied to the current problem.
   - Examine a simpler or special case of the problem to gain insight into the solution of the original problem.
   - Make a table or list.
   - Identify a subgoal.
   - Make a diagram.
   - Use guess and check.
   - Work backward.
   - Write an equation.
   - Abstract a given situation and represent it symbolically.
   - Plan a solution pathway.
   - Make assumptions and approximations to simplify a complicated situation.
   - Use clear definitions.

3. **Carrying out the plan.**
   - State the meaning of any symbols used.
   - Manipulate the representing symbols as if they have a life of their own.
   - Implement the strategy or strategies in step 2 and perform any necessary actions or computations.
   - Attend to the precision in language and mathematics used.
   - Apply the mathematics to solve problems.
   - Check each step of the plan along the way—this may be intuitive checking or formal proof of each step.
   - Keep an accurate record of all work.
   - Map relationships using such tools as diagrams, two-way tables, graphs, flowcharts and formulas.
   - Use appropriate tools strategically.
   - Look for general methods and for shortcuts to calculations.
   - Detect possible errors using estimation and other mathematical knowledge.
   - Specify units of measure.

4. **Looking back.**
   - Check the results in the original problem (in some cases this will require a proof).
   - Interpret the solution in terms of the original problem: Does the answer make sense? Does it answer the question that was asked?
   - Determine whether there is another method of finding the solution.
   - Improve the model if it has not served its purpose.
   - Maintain oversight of the process.
   - Evaluate the reasonableness of intermediate results.
   - Check answers with a different method.
   - Continually ask: "Does this make sense?"
   - Understand different approaches.
   - Identify correspondences among different approaches.
   - Justify conclusions.
   - Communicate conclusions to others.
   - Respond to arguments of others.
   - If possible, determine other related or more general problems for which the technique will work.

Students learn mathematics as a result of solving problems. *Exercises* are routine practice for skill building and serve a purpose in learning mathematics, but problem solving must be a focus of school mathematics. A reasonable amount of tension and discomfort improves problem-solving performance.

Mathematical problem solving may occur when:

1. Students are presented with a situation that they understand but do not know how to proceed directly to a solution.
2. Students are interested in finding the solution and attempt to do so.
3. Students are required to use mathematical ideas to solve the problem.

We present many opportunities in this text to solve problems. The chapter opens with a problem that can be solved using concepts developed in the chapter. We give a hint for the solution to the problem at the end of the chapter. Throughout the text, some problems are solved using a four-step process.

Working with others to solve problems enhances problem-solving ability and communication skills. We encourage *cooperative learning* and working in groups whenever possible. To encourage group work and help identify when cooperative learning could be useful, we identify activities and problems where group discussions are especially beneficial for learning mathematics.

1 Mathematics and Problem Solving

1 Objectives

Students will be able to understand and explain

- The four-step problem-solving process.
- How to solve problems using various problem-solving strategies.

If problems are approached in only one way, a mind-set may be formed. For example, consider the following:

Spell the word spot *three times out loud. "S-P-O-T! S-P-O-T! S-P-O-T!" Now answer the question "What do we do when we come to a green light?" Write an answer.*

If we answer "Stop," we may be guilty of having formed a mind-set. We do not stop at a *green* light.

Consider the following problem: "A shepherd had 36 sheep. All but 10 died. How many lived?" If we answer "10," we are ready to try some problems. If not, we probably did not understand the question by not reading it carefully. *Understanding the problem* is the first step in the four-step problem-solving process.

Strategies for Problem Solving

We next provide a variety of problems with different contexts to provide experience in problem solving. Strategies are used to discover or construct the means to achieve a solution. For each strategy described, we give an example that can be solved with that strategy. Often, problems can be solved in more than one way. There is no one best strategy to use.

In many of the examples, we use the set of **natural numbers**, 1, 2, 3, ... Note that the first three dots, an *ellipsis*, are used to represent missing terms. The expanded problem-solving steps highlighting some strategies are shown next.

(Historical Note)

George Pólya (1887–1985) was born in Hungary, moved to the United States in 1940, and after a brief stay at Brown University, joined the faculty at Stanford University. A preeminent mathematician, he also focused on mathematics education. He published 10 books, including *How To Solve It* (1945), which has been translated into 23 languages.

Strategy: Look for a Pattern

Problem Solving | Gauss's Problem

As a student, Carl Gauss and his fellow classmates were asked to find the sum of the first 100 natural numbers. The teacher expected to keep the class occupied for some time, but Gauss gave the answer almost immediately. How might he have done it?

Understanding the Problem The natural numbers are $1, 2, 3, 4, \ldots$. Thus, the problem is to find the sum $1 + 2 + 3 + 4 + \ldots + 100$.

Devising a Plan The strategy *look for a pattern* is useful here. One story about young Gauss reports that he listed the sum, and wrote the same sum backwards as in Figure 1. If $S = 1 + 2 + 3 + 4 + 5 + \ldots + 98 + 99 + 100$, then Gauss could have seen the following pattern.

$$\begin{array}{rcccccccccc}
S = & 1 + & 2 + & 3 + & 4 + & 5 + & \ldots + & 98 + & 99 + & 100 \\
+\ S = & 100 + & 99 + & 98 + & 97 + & 96 + & \ldots + & 3 + & 2 + & 1 \\
\hline
2S = & 101 + & 101 + & 101 + & 101 + & 101 + & \ldots + & 101 + & 101 + & 101
\end{array}$$

Figure 1

To discover the original sum from the last equation, Gauss could have divided the sum, $2S$, in Figure 1 by 2.

Carrying Out the Plan There are 100 sums of 101. Thus, $2S = 100 \cdot 101$ and $S = \dfrac{100 \cdot 101}{2} = 5050$.

Looking Back Note that the sum in each pair $(1, 100), (2, 99), (3, 98), \ldots, (100, 1)$ is always 101, and there are 100 pairs with this sum. This technique can be used to solve a more general problem of finding the sum of the first n natural numbers $1 + 2 + 3 + 4 + 5 + 6 + \ldots + n$. We use the same plan as before and notice the relationship in Figure 2. Because there are n sums of $n + 1$ we have $2S = n(n + 1)$ and $S = \dfrac{n(n + 1)}{2}$.

$$\begin{array}{rcccccc}
S = & 1 + & 2 + & 3 + & 4 + \ldots + & n \\
+\ S = & n + & (n - 1) + & (n - 2) + & (n - 3) + \ldots + & 1 \\
\hline
2S = & (n + 1) + & (n + 1) + & (n + 1) + & (n + 1) + \ldots + & (n + 1)
\end{array}$$

Figure 2

A different strategy for finding a sum of consecutive natural numbers involves the strategy of *making a diagram* and thinking of the sum geometrically as a stack of blocks. This alternative method is explored in exercise 2 of Assessment 1A.

▶ NOW TRY THIS 1

Explain whether the approach in Gauss's Problem of writing the sum backwards and applying the strategy "Look for a Pattern" will or will not work in finding the following sum: $1^2 + 2^2 + \ldots + 100^2$.

(Historical Note)

Carl Gauss (1777–1855), one of the greatest mathematicians of all time, was born to humble parents in Brunswick, Germany. He was an infant prodigy who later made contributions in many areas of science as well as mathematics. After Gauss's death, the King of Hanover honored him with a commemorative medal with the inscription "Prince of Mathematics." ●

Strategy: Examine a Related Problem

Problem Solving   Sums of Even Natural Numbers

Find the sum of the even natural numbers less than or equal to 100. Generalize the result.

Understanding the Problem Even natural numbers are $2, 4, 6, 8, 10, \ldots$. The problem is to find the sum of these numbers: $2 + 4 + 6 + 8 + \ldots + 100$.

Devising a Plan Recognizing that the sum can be *related to Gauss's original problem* helps us devise a plan. Consider the following:

$$2 + 4 + 6 + 8 + \ldots + 100 = 2 \cdot 1 + 2 \cdot 2 + 2 \cdot 3 + 2 \cdot 4 + \ldots + 2 \cdot 50$$
$$= 2(1 + 2 + 3 + 4 + \ldots + 50)$$

Thus, we can use Gauss's method to find the sum of the first 50 natural numbers and then double that result.

Carrying Out the Plan We carry out the plan as follows:

$$2 + 4 + 6 + 8 + \ldots + 100 = 2(1 + 2 + 3 + 4 + \ldots + 50)$$
$$= 2\left[\frac{50(50 + 1)}{2}\right]$$
$$= 2550$$

Thus, the sum of the even natural numbers less than or equal to 100 is 2550.

Looking Back A different way to approach this problem is to realize that there are 25 sums of 102, as shown in Figure 3. (Why are there 25 sums to consider, and why is the sum in each pair always 102?)

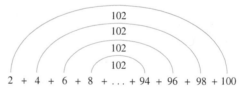

$$2 \;+\; 4 \;+\; 6 \;+\; 8 \;+\ldots+\; 94 \;+\; 96 \;+\; 98 \;+\; 100$$

Figure 3

Thus, the sum is $25 \cdot 102 = 2550$.

The numbers $2, 4, 6, 8, \ldots, 100$ are an example of an *arithmetic sequence*—an ordered list of numbers, or *terms*, in which each term starting from the second one differs from the previous term by the same amount—the common difference. The common difference in the above sequence is 2.

▶ NOW TRY THIS 2

Find the sum of consecutive natural numbers shown: $25 + 26 + 27 + \ldots + 120$. Solve this problem in two different ways.

▶ NOW TRY THIS 3

Each of 16 people in a round-robin handball tournament played each other person exactly once. How many games were played?

Strategies: Examine a Simpler Case; Make a Table

Often used strategies in problem solving are *examine a simpler case* and *make a table*. A table can be used to look for patterns that emerge in the problem, which in turn can lead to a solution. An example of these strategies is shown on the grade 4 student page below.

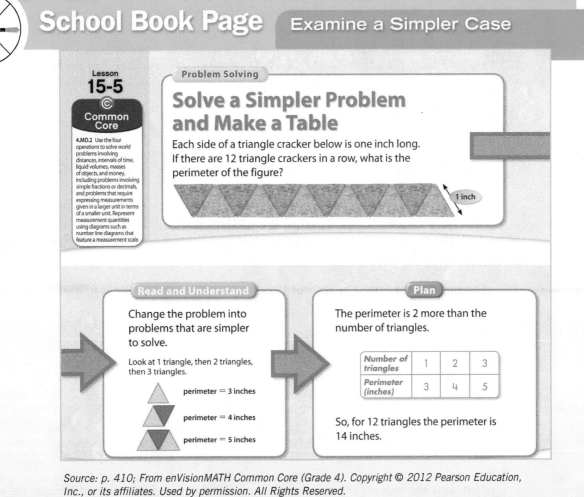

School Book Page Examine a Simpler Case

Lesson **15-5**

Common Core

4.MD.2 Use the four operations to solve world problems involving distances, intervals of time, liquid volumes, masses of objects, and money, including problems involving simple fractions or decimals, and problems that require expressing measurements given in a larger unit in terms of a smaller unit. Represent measurement quantities using diagrams such as number line diagrams that feature a measurement scale.

Problem Solving

Solve a Simpler Problem and Make a Table

Each side of a triangle cracker below is one inch long. If there are 12 triangle crackers in a row, what is the perimeter of the figure?

1 inch

Read and Understand

Change the problem into problems that are simpler to solve.

Look at 1 triangle, then 2 triangles, then 3 triangles.

perimeter = 3 inches

perimeter = 4 inches

perimeter = 5 inches

Plan

The perimeter is 2 more than the number of triangles.

Number of triangles	1	2	3
Perimeter (inches)	3	4	5

So, for 12 triangles the perimeter is 14 inches.

Source: p. 410; From enVisionMATH Common Core (Grade 4). Copyright © 2012 Pearson Education, Inc., or its affiliates. Used by permission. All Rights Reserved.

Strategy: Identify a Subgoal

In attempting to devise a plan for solving a problem, a solution to a somewhat easier or more familiar related problem could make it easier. In such a case, finding the solution to the easier problem may become a *subgoal*. The magic square problem on the next page shows an example of this.

Figure 4

Problem Solving A Magic Square

Arrange the numbers 1 through 9 into a square subdivided into nine smaller squares like the one shown in Figure 4 so that the sum of every row, column, and major diagonal is the same. The result is a *magic square*.

Understanding the Problem Each of the nine numbers $1, 2, 3, \ldots, 9$ must be placed in the small squares, a different number in each square, so that the sums of the numbers in each row, in each column, and in each of the two major diagonals are the same.

Devising a Plan If we knew the fixed sum of the numbers in each row, column, and diagonal, we would have a better idea of which numbers can appear together in a single row, column, or diagonal. Thus *the subgoal* is to find that fixed sum. The sum of the nine numbers, $1 + 2 + 3 + \ldots + 9$, equals 3 times the sum in one row. (Why?) Consequently, the fixed sum can be found using the process developed by Gauss. We have $\dfrac{1 + 2 + 3 + \ldots + 9}{3} = \dfrac{(9 \cdot 10) \div 2}{3} = 15$, so the sum in each row, column, and diagonal must be 15. Next, we need to decide what numbers could occupy the various squares. The number in the center space will appear in four sums, each adding to 15 (two diagonals, the second row, and the second column). Each number in the corners will appear in three sums of 15. (Why?) If we write 15 as a sum of three different numbers 1 through 9 in all possible ways, we could then count how many sums contain each of the numbers 1 through 9. The numbers that appear in at least four sums are candidates for placement in the center square, whereas the numbers that appear in at least three sums are candidates for the corner squares. Thus the new *subgoal* is to write 15 in as many ways as possible as a sum of three different numbers from $1, 2, 3, \ldots, 9$.

Carrying Out the Plan The sums of 15 can be written systematically as follows:

$$9 + 5 + 1$$
$$9 + 4 + 2$$
$$8 + 6 + 1$$
$$8 + 5 + 2$$
$$8 + 4 + 3$$
$$7 + 6 + 2$$
$$7 + 5 + 3$$
$$6 + 5 + 4$$

Note that the order of the numbers in sums like $9 + 5 + 1$ is irrelevant because the order in which additions are done does not matter. In the list, 1 appears in only two sums, 2 in three sums, 3 in two sums, and so on. Table 3 summarizes this information.

Table 3									
Number	1	2	3	4	5	6	7	8	9
Number of sums containing the number	2	3	2	3	4	3	2	3	2

The only number that appears in four sums is 5; hence, 5 must be in the center of the square. (Why?) Because 2, 4, 6, and 8 appear 3 times each, they must go in the corners. Suppose we choose 2 for the upper left corner. Then 8 must be in the lower right corner. This is shown in Figure 5(a). Now we could place 6 in the lower left corner or upper right corner. If we choose the upper right corner, we obtain the result in Figure 5(b). The magic square can now be completed, as shown in Figure 5(c).

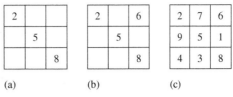

(a)   (b)   (c)

Figure 5

Looking Back We have seen that 5 was the only number among the given numbers that could appear in the center. However, we had various choices for a corner, and so it seems that the magic square we found is not the only one possible. Can you find all the others?

Another way to see that 5 could be in the center square is to consider the sums $1 + 9, 2 + 8, 3 + 7, 4 + 6$, as shown in Figure 6. We could add 5 to each to obtain 15.

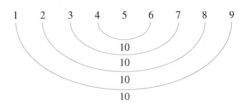

Figure 6

Strategy: Make a Diagram

In the following problem, *making a diagram* helps us to understand the problem and work toward a solution.

Problem Solving 50-m Race Problem

Bill and Jim ran a 50-m race three times. The speed of the runners did not vary. In the first race, Jim was at the 45-m mark when Bill crossed the finish line.

  a. In the second race, Jim started 5 m ahead of Bill, who lined up at the starting line. Who won?
  b. In the third race, Jim started at the starting line and Bill started 5 m behind. Who won?

Understanding the Problem When Bill and Jim ran a 50-m race, Bill won by 5 m; that is, whenever Bill covered 50 m, at the same time Jim covered only 45 m. If Bill started at the starting line and Jim started at the 5-m line or if Jim started at the starting line and Bill started 5 m behind, we are to determine who would win in each case.

Devising a Plan A strategy to determine the winner under each condition is to *make a diagram*. A diagram for the first 50-m race is given in Figure 7(a). In this case, Bill won by 5 m. In the second race, Jim had a 5-m head start and hence when Bill ran 50 m to the finish line, Jim ran only 45 m. Because Jim is 45 m from the finish line, he reached the finish line at the same time as Bill did. This is shown in Figure 7(b). In the third race, because Bill started 5 m behind, we use Figure 7(a) but move Bill back 5 m, as shown in Figure 7(c). From the diagram we determine the results in each case.

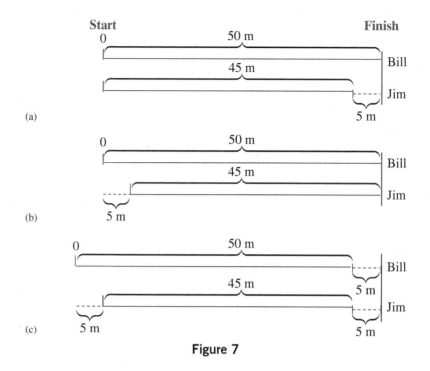

Figure 7

Carrying Out the Plan From Figure 7(b) we see that if Jim had a 5-m head start, then the race ends in a tie. If Bill started 5 m behind Jim, then at 45 m they would be tied. Because Bill is faster than Jim, Bill would cover the last 5 m faster than Jim and win the race.

Looking Back The diagrams show that the solution makes sense and is appropriate. Other problems can be investigated involving racing and handicaps. For example, if Bill and Jim run on a 50-m oval track, how many laps will it take for Bill to lead Jim by one full lap? (Assume the same speeds as earlier.)

▶ NOW TRY THIS 4

An elevator stopped at the middle floor of a building. It then moved up 4 floors, stopped, moved down 6 floors, stopped, and then moved up 10 floors and stopped. The elevator was now 3 floors from the top floor. How many floors does the building have?

Strategy: Use Guess and Check

In the strategy of *guess and check*, we first guess at an answer using as reasonable a guess as possible. Then we check to see whether the guess is correct. If not, the next step is to learn as much as possible about the answer based on the guess before making a next guess. This strategy can be regarded as a form of trial and error, in which the information about the error helps us choose what to try next. The guess-and-check strategy is often used when a student does not know how to solve the problem more efficiently or if the student does not yet have the tools to solve the problem in a faster way. Research has suggested that students in grades 1–3 rely primarily on a *guess-and-check* strategy when faced with a mathematical problem. In grades 6–12 this tendency decreases. Older students benefit more from the observed "errors" after a guess when formulating a new "trial."

The grade 4 student page shown on the next page gives an example of this strategy, referred to as "try, check, revise."

School Book Page — Try, Check, Revise

| Try, Check, Revise | Suzanne spent $27, not including tax, on dog supplies. She bought two of one item and one of another item. What did she buy?

$8 + $8 + $15 = $31
$7 + $7 + $12 = $26
$6 + $6 + $15 = $27 | Use Try, Check, Revise when quantities are being combined to find a total, but you don't know which quantities. |

Dog Supplies Sale!
Leash $8
Collar $6
Bowls $7
Medium Beds $15
Toys $12

Strategy: Work Backward

In some problems, it is easier to start with the result and to *work backward*. This is demonstrated on the grade 6 student page below.

School Book Page — Work Backward

 Test-Taking Strategies

Working Backward

The problem-solving strategy *Work Backward* is useful when taking multiple-choice tests. Work backward by testing each choice in the original problem. You will eliminate incorrect answers. Eventually you will find the correct answer.

EXAMPLE

A fruit stand is selling 8 bananas for $1.25. At this rate, how much will 24 bananas cost?

Ⓐ $1.50   Ⓑ $2.50   Ⓒ $3.75   Ⓓ $5.00

Use mental math to test the choices that are easy to use.

$2.50 is twice $1.25. Twice 8 is only 16, so choice B is not the answer.

$5.00 is four times $1.25. Three times 8 is 24, so choice D is not the correct answer.

Since 24 is between 16 and 32, the cost must be between $2.50 and $5.00. The correct answer is choice C.

Strategy: Write an Equation

Even though algebraic thinking is involved in the strategy *writing an equation* and may evoke thoughts of traditional algebra, a closer look reveals that algebraic thinking starts very early in students' school lives. For example, finding the missing subtrahend in a problem like

$$\begin{array}{r} 14 \\ -\square \\ \hline 3 \end{array}$$

could be thought of algebraically as $14 - \square = 3$, or as $3 + \square = 14$. In a traditional algebra course, this might be seen as $14 - x = 3$ or $3 + x = 14$ with 11 as a solution. We use such algebraic thinking long before formal algebra is taught.

A student example of *writing an equation* to solve a problem is seen on the grade 6 student page below.

School Book Page — Writing an Equation

GPS Guided Problem Solving

Writing Equations to Solve Problems

Around the World On March 4, 2005, Steve Fossett set a record by completing a nonstop solo jet flight around the world. He landed with 1,515 pounds of fuel. A fuel leak caused a loss of 2,600 pounds of fuel. He started with 18,100 pounds of fuel. How much fuel did the jet use on the flight?

What You Might Think

What do I know? What am I trying to find?

How can I show the main idea?

What equation can I write to show the problem?

How do I solve the problem?

What is the answer?

What You Might Write

- Fuel remaining = 1,515 pounds
- Fuel lost = 2,600 pounds
- Total fuel at start = 18,100 pounds
- How much fuel (in pounds) was actually used on the flight?

Draw a diagram.

18,100 lb		
1,515 lb	2,600 lb	x

$1,515 + 2,600 + x = 18,100$

$$4,115 + x = 18,100$$
$$4,115 - 4,115 + x = 18,100 - 4,115$$
$$x = 13,985$$

A total of 13,985 pounds of fuel was used on the flight.

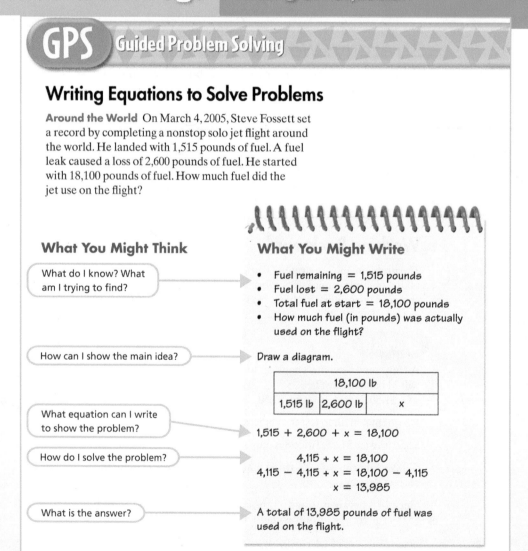

Source: p. 77; From MATHEMATICS Common Core (Course 1). Copyright © 2013 Pearson Education, Inc., or its affiliates. Used by permission. All Rights Reserved.

Assessment 1A

1. Use the approach in Gauss's Problem to find the following sums of arithmetic sequences (do not use formulas):
   a. $1 + 2 + 3 + 4 + \ldots + 99$
   b. $1 + 3 + 5 + 7 + \ldots + 1001$
   c. $3 + 6 + 9 + 12 + \ldots + 300$
   d. $4 + 8 + 12 + 13 + \ldots + 400$

2. Use the ideas in drawings (a) and (b) to find the solution to Gauss's Problem for the sum $1 + 2 + 3 + \ldots + n$. Explain your reasoning.

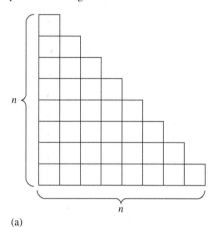

(a)

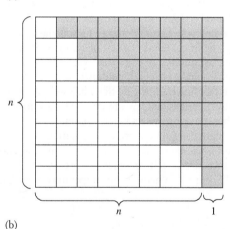

(b)

3. Find the sum $36 + 37 + 38 + 39 + \ldots + 146 + 147$.

4. Cookies are sold singly or in packages of 2 or 6. With this packaging, how many ways can you buy
   a. 10 cookies?
   b. a dozen cookies?

5. In a big, red box, there are 7 smaller blue boxes. In each of the blue boxes, there are 7 black boxes. In each of the black boxes, there are 7 yellow boxes. In each of those yellow boxes, there are 7 tiny, gold boxes. How many boxes are there altogether? Explain your answer.

6. How many triangles are in the following figure?

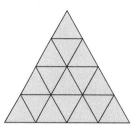

7. Without computing each sum of the arithmetic sequence, find which is greater, O or E, and by how much.
$$O = 1 + 3 + 5 + 7 + \ldots + 97$$
$$E = 2 + 4 + 6 + 8 + \ldots + 98$$

8. Alabama, Bubba, Cory, and Dandy are in a horse race. Bubba is the slowest; Cory is faster than Alabama but slower than Dandy. Name the finishing order of the horses.

9. How many ways can you make change for a $50 bill using $5, $10, and $20 bills?

10. The following is a magic square (all rows, columns, and diagonals sum to the same number). Find the value of each letter.

17	a	7
12	22	b
c	d	27

11. Debbie and Amy began reading a novel on the same day. Debbie reads 9 pages a day and Amy reads 6 pages a day. If Debbie is on page 72, on what page is Amy?

12. The 14 digits of a credit card are written in the boxes shown. If the sum of any three consecutive digits is 20, what is the value of A?

A		7									7		4

13. Three closed boxes (A, B, and C) of fruit arrive as a gift from a friend. Each box is mislabeled. How could you choose only one fruit from one box to decide how the boxes should be labeled?

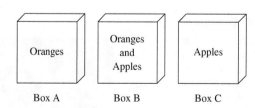

Oranges	Oranges and Apples	Apples
Box A	Box B	Box C

14. An electrician charges $50 per hour and spends $15 a day on gasoline. If she netted $1315 in 4 days, how many hours did she work?

15. Kathy stood on the middle rung of a ladder. She climbed up three rungs, moved down five rungs, and then climbed up seven rungs. Then she climbed up the remaining six rungs to the top of the ladder. How many rungs are there in the whole ladder?

Assessment 1B

1. Use the approach in Gauss's Problem to find the following sums of arithmetic sequences (do not use formulas):
   a. $1 + 2 + 3 + 4 + \ldots + 49$
   b. $1 + 3 + 5 + 7 + \ldots + 2009$
   c. $6 + 12 + 18 + \ldots + 600$
   d. $1000 + 995 + 990 + \ldots + 5$

2. Use the diagram below to explain how to find the sum of
   a. the first 100 natural numbers.

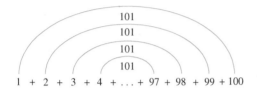

   b. $1 + 2 + 3 + 4 + \ldots + 201$

3. Find the sum of $58 + 59 + 60 + 61 + \ldots + 203$.

4. Eve Merriam* entitled her children's book *12 Ways to Get to 11* (1993). Using only addition and natural numbers, describe 12 ways that one can arrive at the sum of 11.

5. Explain why in a drawer containing only two different colors of socks one must draw only three socks to find a matching pair.

6. How many squares are in the following figure?

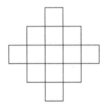

7. If $P = 1 + 3 + 5 + 7 + \ldots + 99$ and $Q = 5 + 7 + 9 + \ldots + 101$ are sums of arithmetic sequences, determine which is greater, P or Q, and by how much.

8. The sign says that you are leaving Missoula, Butte is 120 mi away, and Bozeman is 200 mi away. There is a rest stop halfway between Butte and Bozeman. How far is the rest stop from Missoula if both Butte and Bozeman are in the same direction?

9. Marc goes to the store with exactly $1.00 in change. He has at least one of each coin less than a half-dollar coin, but he does not have a half-dollar coin.
   a. What is the least number of coins he could have?
   b. What is the greatest number of coins he could have?

10. Find a 3-by-3 magic square using the numbers 3, 5, 7, 9, 11, 13, 15, 17, and 19.

11. Eight marbles look alike, but one is slightly heavier than the others. Using a balance scale, explain how you can determine the heavier one in exactly three weighings.

12. Recall the song "The Twelve Days of Christmas":

    On the first day of Christmas my true love gave to me a partridge in a pear tree.
    On the second day of Christmas my true love gave to me two turtle doves and a partridge in a pear tree.
    On the third day of Christmas my true love gave to me three French hens, two turtle doves, and a partridge in a pear tree.

    This pattern continues for 9 more days. After 12 days,
    a. which gifts did my true love give the most? (Yes, you have to remember the song.)
    b. how many total gifts did my true love give to me?

13. **a.** Suppose you have quarters, dimes, and pennies with a total value of $1.19. How many of each coin can you have without being able to make change for a dollar?
    b. Tell why one of the combinations of coin you have in part (a) is the least number of coins that you can have without being able to make change for a dollar.

14. Suppose you buy lunch for the math club. You have enough money to buy 20 salads or 15 sandwiches. The group wants 12 sandwiches. How many salads can you buy?

15. One winter night the temperature fell 15 degrees between midnight and 5 A.M. By 9 A.M., the temperature had doubled from what it was at 5 A.M. By noon, it had risen another 10 degrees to 32 degrees. What was the temperature at midnight?

Mathematical Connections 1

Reasoning

1. Create a 3-by-3 magic square using nine of the ten numbers 20, 21, 22, 23, 24, 25, 26, 27, 28, and 29. Explain your solution and reasoning. List the strategies you have used.

2. In the checkerboard, two squares on opposite corners have been removed. A domino can cover two adjacent squares on the

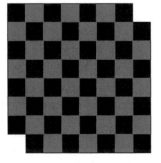

   board. Can dominoes be arranged in such a way that all the remaining squares on the board can be covered with no dominoes overlapping or hanging off the board? If not, why not? (Hint: Each domino must cover one black and one red square. Compare this with the number of each color of squares on the board.)

3. **a.** If 10 people shake hands with one another exactly once, how many handshakes take place?
   b. Find as many ways as possible to do the problem.
   c. Generalize the solution for n people.

4. Consider a game where you have two distinct piles of objects. Two players alternate moves, each player taking any number (not 0) of objects desired from a single pile. The player who

*Merriam, E. *12 Ways to Get to 11*. New York: Aladdin Paperbacks, 1993.

takes the last object (so nothing is left in either pile) is the winner. If there are a objects in one pile and b objects in the second, we write (a, b). Given the game $(1, 1)$, the first player loses because if she takes 1 from a pile, the second player takes 1 from the other pile. Answer the following:

a. Show that the first player can win the game $(1, 2)$ as well as $(1, 100)$.

b. Who will win the game $(1, a)$ if $a > 1$? Why?

c. Which player will win the games $(2, 2)$, $(3, 3)$, $(4, 4)$? Why?

d. Which games can the first player always win? Why?

5. Place a half-dollar, a quarter, and a nickel in position A as shown in the figure below. Try to move these coins, one at a time, to position C. At no time may a larger coin be placed on a smaller coin. Coins may be placed in position B.

a. How many moves does it take to get them to position C?

b. Now add a penny to the pile and see how many moves are required. This is a simple case of the famous Tower of Hanoi problem, in which ancient Brahman priests were required to move a pile of 64 disks of decreasing size, after which the world would end. How long would it take at a rate of one move per second?

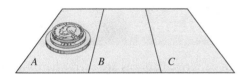

Open-Ended

6. Choose a problem-solving strategy and make up a problem that would use this strategy. Write the solution using Pólya's four-step approach.

7. The distance around the world is approximately 40,000 km. Approximately how many people of average size would it take to stretch around the world if they were holding hands?

Cooperative Learning

8. Work in pairs on the following versions of a game called NIM. A calculator is needed for each pair.

a. Player 1 presses $\boxed{1}$ and $\boxed{+}$ or $\boxed{2}$ and $\boxed{+}$. Player 2 does the same. The players take turns until the target number of 21 is reached. The first player to make the display read 21 is the winner. Determine a strategy for deciding who always wins.

b. Try a game of NIM using the digits 1, 2, 3, and 4, with a target number of 104. The first player to reach 104 wins. What is the winning strategy?

c. Try a game of NIM using the digits 3, 5, and 7, with a target number of 73. The first player to exceed 73 loses. What is the winning strategy?

d. Now play Reverse NIM with the keys $\boxed{1}$ and $\boxed{2}$. Instead of $\boxed{+}$, use $\boxed{-}$. Put 21 on the display. Let the target number be 0. Determine a strategy for winning Reverse NIM.

e. Try Reverse NIM using the digits 1, 2, and 3 and starting with 24 on the display. The target number is 0. What is the winning strategy?

f. Try Reverse NIM using the digits 3, 5, and 7 and starting with 73 on the display. The first player to display a negative number loses. What is the winning strategy?

Connecting Mathematics to the Classroom

9. John asks why the last step of Pólya's four-step problem-solving process, *looking back*, is necessary since he has already given the answer. What could you tell him?

10. A student asks why he just can't make "random guesses" rather than "intelligent guesses" when using the guess-and-check problem-solving strategy. How do you respond?

11. Rob says that it is possible to create a magic square with the numbers 1, 3, 4, 5, 6, 7, 8, 9, and 10. How do you respond?

National Assessments

National Assessment of Educational Progress (NAEP) Questions

1st	2nd	3rd	4th	5th	6th
1 dot	3 dots	6 dots	10 dots	___dots	___dots

A pattern of dots is shown above. How many dots would be in the 6th picture?

Answer: _____

Explain how you found your answer.
NAEP, Grade 4, 2009

Susie said, "I have 83¢ but fewer than 10 coins." Show in the chart how many of each coin she could have to total 83¢.

Total number of coins	25¢	10¢	5¢	1¢

NAEP, Grade 4, 2009

Ms. Kim has 45 stickers that she wants to give out to 6 students. The students are sitting in a circle. Ms. Kim gives out one sticker at a time and keeps going around the circle until all the stickers are gone. How many of the students will get more than 7 stickers?

A. 2
B. 3
C. 5
D. 6

NAEP, Grade 4, 2011

Sam folds a piece of paper in half once. There are 2 sections.

Sam folds the paper in half again. There are 4 sections.

Sam folds the paper in half again. There are 8 sections.

Sam folds the paper in half 2 more times.

Which list shows the number of sections each time Sam folds the paper?
A. 2, 4, 8, 10, 12
B. 2, 4, 8, 12, 24
C. 2, 4, 8, 16, 24
D. 2, 4, 8, 16, 32

NAEP, Grade 4, 2011

2 Explorations with Patterns

2 Objectives

Students will be able to understand and explain

- Finding patterns and determining if a pattern holds.

- Deductive and inductive reasoning and when to use them.

- Different types of sequences, such as arithmetic, geometric, and Fibonacci.

- Finding the nth term of certain sequences.

- Using differences to find a pattern for neither arithmetic nor geometric sequences.

Mathematics has been described as the study of patterns. Patterns are everywhere—in wallpaper, tiles, traffic, and even television schedules. Police investigators study case files to find the *modus operandi*, or pattern of operation, when a series of crimes are committed. Scientists look for patterns to isolate variables so that they can reach valid conclusions in their research.

Non-numerical patterns abound. For young children, a pattern could appear in non-numerical form as shown in Now Try This 5.

> ▶ NOW TRY THIS 5

a. Find three more terms to continue a pattern:

$$\bigcirc, \triangle, \triangle, \bigcirc, \triangle, \triangle, \bigcirc, \underline{}, \underline{}, \underline{}$$

b. Describe in words the pattern found in part (a).

Patterns can be surprising as seen in the following example.

Example 1

a. Describe any patterns seen in the following:

$$1 + 0 \cdot 9 = 1$$
$$2 + 1 \cdot 9 = 11$$
$$3 + 12 \cdot 9 = 111$$
$$4 + 123 \cdot 9 = 1111$$
$$5 + 1234 \cdot 9 = 11111$$

b. Do the patterns continue? Why or why not?

Solution

a. There are several possible patterns. For example, the numbers on the far left are natural numbers. The pattern starts with 1 and continues to the next greater natural number in each successive line. The numbers "in the middle" are products of two numbers, the second of which is 9; the left-most number in the first product is 0; after that the left-most number in each product is formed using successive natural numbers as digits, including an additional digit in each successive line. The five computations given above result in the numbers that are formed using 1s and include an additional 1 in each successive line.

b. The pattern in the complete equation appears to continue for a number of cases, but it does not continue in general; for example,

$$13 + 123456789101112 \cdot 9 = 1,111,111,101,910,021.$$

This pattern breaks down when the pattern of digits in the number being multiplied by 9 contains previously used digits.

As seen in Example 1, determining a pattern on the basis of a few cases is not reliable. For all patterns found, we should either show the pattern does not hold in general or justify that the pattern always works. Reasoning is used in both cases.

Reasoning

 Some books list various types of reasoning as a problem-solving strategies. However, we think that reasoning underlies problem solving. The *Common Core Standards for Mathematical Practice* lists the following:

- Reason abstractly and quantitatively.
- Construct viable arguments and critique the reasoning of others.
- Look for and express regularity in repeated reasoning. (p. 1)

For students to recognize reasoning and proof as fundamental aspects of mathematics, it is necessary that they use both reasoning and proof in their studies. However, it must be recognized that the level of use depends on the grade level of the students and their understanding of mathematics. For example, from very early ages, students use *inductive reasoning* to look for regularities in patterns based on a very few cases and to develop **conjectures**—statements or conclusions that have not been proven. **Inductive reasoning** is the method of making generalizations based on observations and patterns. Such reasoning may or may not be valid, and conjectures based on inductive reasoning may or may not be true. The validity, or truth, of conjectures in mathematics relies on **deductive reasoning**—the use of definitions, undefined terms, mathematical axioms that are assumed to be true, and previously proved theorems, together with logic to prove these conjectures.

Throughout mathematics, there is a fine interweaving of inductive reasoning and conjecturing to develop conclusions thought to be true. Deductive reasoning is required to prove those statements. In this section we show how inductive reasoning may lead to false conclusions or false conjectures. We show how deductive reasoning is used to prove true conjectures.

Inductive and Deductive Reasoning

Scientists make observations and propose general laws based on patterns. Statisticians use patterns when they draw conclusions based on collected data. This process of *inductive reasoning* may lead to new discoveries; its weakness is that conclusions are drawn only from the collected evidence. If not all cases have been checked, another case may prove the conclusion false. For example, considering only that $0^2 = 0$ and that $1^2 = 1$, we might conjecture that *every number squared is equal to itself*. However, $2^2 \neq 2$. Thus we found an example that contradicts the conjecture. Such an example is a **counterexample**; it shows that the conjecture is false. Sometimes finding a counterexample is difficult, but not finding one immediately does not prove a conjecture is true. A dramatic example of a conjecture that holds true for a very large number of cases but still fails to be true for all cases involves the concept of *perfect squares*. A natural number that is a square of some natural number is a perfect square. For example, 9 is a perfect square because $9 = 3^2$. The conjecture that $1 + 1141n^2$ is never a perfect square is true for every natural number n until $n = 30{,}693{,}385{,}322{,}765{,}657{,}197{,}397{,}208$ when it fails.

Next, consider a pattern that does work and helps solve a problem. How can you find the sum of three consecutive natural numbers without performing the addition? Three examples are given below.

$$14 + 15 + 16; \qquad \text{Sum} = 45$$
$$19 + 20 + 21; \qquad \text{Sum} = 60$$
$$99 + 100 + 101; \qquad \text{Sum} = 300$$

After studying the sums, a pattern of multiplying the middle number by 3 emerges. The pattern suggests other mathematical questions to consider. For example,

1. Does this work for any 3 consecutive natural numbers?
2. How can we find the sum of any odd number of consecutive natural numbers?
3. What happens if there is an even number of consecutive natural numbers?

To answer the first question, we give a proof showing that the sum of three consecutive natural numbers is equal to 3 times the middle number. This proof is an example of *deductive reasoning*.

Proof

Let n be the first of three consecutive natural numbers. Then the three numbers are $n, n + 1$, and $n + 2$. The sum of these three numbers is $n + (n + 1) + (n + 2) = 3n + 3 = 3(n + 1)$. Therefore, the sum of the three consecutive natural numbers is three times the middle number.

A somewhat different way is to let the middle number be m. Then the three consecutive numbers are $m - 1, m$ and $m + 1$. Their sum is $(m - 1) + m + (m + 1) = 3m$, that is, 3 times the middle number. ∎

The Danger of Making Conjectures Based on a Few Cases

The following discussion illustrates the danger of making a conjecture based on a few cases. In Figure 8, we choose points on a circle and connect them to form distinct, nonoverlapping regions. In this figure, 2 points determine 2 regions, 3 points determine 4 regions, and 4 points determine 8 regions. What is the maximum number of regions that would be determined by 10 points?

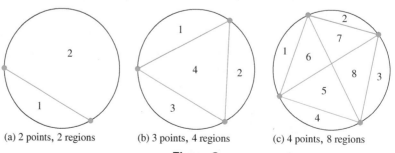

(a) 2 points, 2 regions   (b) 3 points, 4 regions   (c) 4 points, 8 regions

Figure 8

The data from Figure 8 are recorded in Table 4. It appears that each time the number of points increases by 1, the number of regions doubles. If this were true, then for 5 points we would have determined the number of regions by doubling the number of regions with 4 points, or $2 \cdot 8 = 16 = 2^4$, and so on. If we base our conjecture on this pattern, we might believe that for 10 points, we would have 2^9, or 512 regions. (Why?)

Table 4								
Number of points	2	3	4	5	6	...	10
Maximum number of regions	2	4	8				?

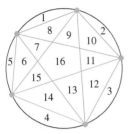

Figure 9

An initial check for this conjecture is to see whether we obtain 16 regions for 5 points. The diagram for 5 points in Figure 9 confirms our guess of 16 regions. For 6 points, the pattern predicts that the number of regions is 32. Choosing the points so that they are neither symmetrically arranged nor equally spaced and counting the regions carefully, we get 31 regions, not 32 as predicted. No matter how the points are located on the circle, the guess of 32 regions is not correct. This counterexample tells us that the doubling pattern is not correct. Note that it does not tell us whether there are 512 regions with 10 points; it tells us only that this conjecture is not true.

▶ **NOW TRY THIS 6**

A *prime number* is a natural number with exactly two distinct positive numbers, 1 and the number itself, that divide it with 0 remainder; for example, 2, 3, 5, 7, 11, and 13 are primes. One day Amy makes a *conjecture* that the formula $y = x^2 + x + 11$ will produce only prime numbers if she substitutes the natural numbers, $1, 2, 3, 4, 5, \ldots$ for x. She shows her work in Table 5 for $x = 1, 2, 3, 4$.

Table 5				
x	1	2	3	4
y	13	17	23	31

a. What type of reasoning is Amy using?
b. Try the next several natural numbers and see whether they seem to work.
c. Show that Amy's conjecture is false for $x = 11$.

Arithmetic Sequences

A **sequence** is an ordered arrangement of numbers, figures, or objects. A sequence has items or *terms* identified as *1st, 2nd, 3rd*, and so on. Often, sequences can be classified by their properties. For example, what property do the following first three sequences have that the fourth does not?

a. $1, 2, 3, 4, 5, 6, \ldots$
b. $0, 5, 10, 15, 20, 25, \ldots$
c. $2, 6, 10, 14, 18, 22, \ldots$
d. $1, 11, 111, 1111, 11111, 111111, \ldots$

In each of the first three sequences, each term—starting from the second term—is obtained from the preceding term by adding a fixed number, the **common difference** or **difference**. In part (a) the difference is 1, in part (b) the difference is 5, and in part (c) the difference is 4. Sequences such as the first three are arithmetic sequences. An **arithmetic sequence** is a sequence in which each successive term from the second term on is obtained from the previous term by the addition or subtraction of a fixed number. The sequence in part (d) is not arithmetic because there is no single fixed number that can be added to or subtracted from the previous term to obtain the next term.

It is convenient to denote the terms of a sequence by a single letter with a subscript. For example in the sequence (b) above $a_1 = 0$, $a_2 = 5$, $a_3 = 10$, and so on. Arithmetic sequences can be generated from objects, as shown in Example 2.

Example 2

Find a numerical pattern in the number of matchsticks required to continue the sequence shown in Figure 10 if each subsequent figure has one more square.

Figure 10

Solution Assume the matchsticks are arranged, so each figure has one more square on the right than the preceding figure. Note that the addition of a square to an arrangement requires the addition of three matchsticks each time. Thus, with this assumption, the numerical pattern obtained is 4, 7, 10, 13, 16, 19, . . . , an arithmetic sequence starting at 4 and having a difference of 3.

An informal description of an arithmetic sequence is one that can be described as an "add d" pattern, where d is the common difference. In Example 2, $d = 3$. In the language of children, the pattern in Example 2 is "add 3." This is an example of a **recursive pattern**. In a recursive pattern, after one or more consecutive terms are given, each successive term of the sequence is obtained from the previous term(s). For example, 11, 14, 17, . . . is another "add 3" sequence starting with 11.

A recursive pattern is typically used in a spreadsheet, as seen in Table 6, where the index column tracks the order of the terms. The headers for the columns are A, B, and so on. The first entry in the A column (in the A1 cell) is 4; to find the term in the A2 cell, we use the number in the A1 cell and add 3. The pattern is continued using the *Fill Down* command. In spreadsheet language, the formula = A1 + 3 finds any term after the first by adding 3 to the previous term and using *Fill Down*. A formula based on a recursive pattern is a **recursive formula**. (For more explicit directions on using a spreadsheet, see the Technology Manual, which can be found online at www.pearsonhighered.com/Billstein12einfo.)

Table 6

		A	B
Index → Column	1	4	
	2	7	
	3	10	
	4	13	
	5	16	
	6	19	
	7	22	
	8	25	
	9	28	
	10		
	11		
	12		
	13		

If we want to find the number of matchsticks in the 100th figure in Example 2, we use the spreadsheet or we find an explicit formula or a general rule for finding the number of matchsticks when given the position of the term, the term number. The problem-solving strategy *making a table* is again helpful here.

The spreadsheet in Table 6 provides an easy way to *make a table*. The index column gives the term numbers, and column A gives the terms of the sequence. If we are building such a table without a spreadsheet, it might look like Table 7. Notice that each term is a sum of 4 and a certain number of 3s. We see that the number of 3s is 1 less than the term number. This pattern should continue, since the first term is $4 + 0 \cdot 3$ and each time we increase the number of the term by 1, we add one *more* 3. Thus, it seems that the 100th term is $4 + (100 - 1)3$; and, in general, the **nth term** is $4 + (n - 1)3$. Note that $4 + (n - 1)3$ could be written as $3n + 1$.

Table 7

Term Number	Term
1	$4 = 4 + 0 \cdot 3$
2	$7 = 4 + 3 = 4 + 1 \cdot 3$
3	$10 = (4 + 1 \cdot 3) + 3 = 4 + 2 \cdot 3$
4	$13 = (4 + 2 \cdot 3) + 3 = 4 + 3 \cdot 3$
.	.
.	.
.	.
n	$4 + (n - 1)3 = 3n + 1$

Still a different approach to finding the number of matchsticks in the 100th term of Figure 10 might be as follows: If the matchstick figure has 100 squares, we could find the total number of matchsticks by adding the number of horizontal and vertical sticks. There are $2 \cdot 100$ placed horizontally. (Why?) Notice that in the first figure, there are 2 matchsticks placed vertically; in the second, 3; and in the third, 4. In the 100th figure, there should be $100 + 1$ vertical matchsticks. Altogether, there will be $2 \cdot 100 + (100 + 1)$, or 301, matchsticks in the 100th figure. Similarly, in the nth figure, there would be $2n$ horizontal and $n + 1$ vertical matchsticks, for a total of $3n + 1$. This discussion is summarized in Table 8.

Table 8

Term Number	Number of Matchsticks Horizontally	Number of Matchsticks Vertically	Total
1	2	2	4
2	4	3	7
3	6	4	10
4	8	5	13
.	.	.	.
.	.	.	.
.	.	.	.
100	200	101	301
.	.	.	.
.	.	.	.
.	.	.	.
n	$2n$	$n + 1$	$2n + (n + 1) = 3n + 1$

If we are given the value of the term, we can use the formula $3n + 1$ for the nth term in Table 8 to *work backward* and find the term number. For example, given the term 1798, we can write an equation: $3n + 1 = 1798$. Therefore, $3n = 1797$ and $n = 599$. Consequently, 1798 is the 599th term. We could obtain the same answer by solving $4 + (n - 1)3 = 1798$ for n.

In the matchstick problem, we found the nth term of a sequence. If the nth term of a sequence is given, we can find any term of the sequence, as shown in Example 3.

Example 3

Find the first four terms of a sequence, the nth term of which is given by the following, and determine whether the sequence seems to be arithmetic:

a. $4n + 3$ **b.** $n^2 - 1$

Solution

a.

Term Number	Term
1	$4 \cdot 1 + 3 = 7$
2	$4 \cdot 2 + 3 = 11$
3	$4 \cdot 3 + 3 = 15$
4	$4 \cdot 4 + 3 = 19$

Hence, the first four terms of the sequence are 7, 11, 15, 19. This sequence seems arithmetic, with difference 4.

b.

Term Number	Term
1	$1^2 - 1 = 0$
2	$2^2 - 1 = 3$
3	$3^2 - 1 = 8$
4	$4^2 - 1 = 15$

Thus, the first four terms of the sequence are 0, 3, 8, 15. This sequence is not arithmetic, because it has no common difference.

Example 4

The diagrams in Figure 11 show the molecular structure of alkanes, a class of hydrocarbons. C represents a carbon atom and H a hydrogen atom. A connecting segment shows a chemical bond.

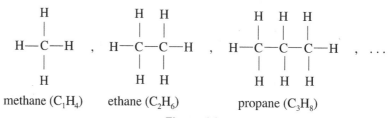

methane (C_1H_4)   ethane (C_2H_6)   propane (C_3H_8)

Figure 11

a. Hectane is an alkane with 100 carbon atoms. How many hydrogen atoms does it have?
b. Write a general rule for alkanes C_nH_m showing the relationship between m and n.

Solution

a. To determine the relationship between the number of carbon and hydrogen atoms, we first study the drawing of the alkanes and disregard the extreme left and right hydrogen atoms in each. With this restriction, we see that for every carbon atom, there are two hydrogen atoms. Therefore, there are twice as many hydrogen atoms as carbon atoms plus the two hydrogen atoms at the extremes. For example, when there are 3 carbon atoms, there are $(2 \cdot 3) + 2 = 8$ hydrogen atoms. This notion is summarized in Table 9. If we extend the table for 4 carbon atoms, we get $(2 \cdot 4) + 2$, or 10, hydrogen atoms. For 100 carbon atoms, there are $(2 \cdot 100) + 2$, or 202, hydrogen atoms.

Table 9

No. of Carbon Atoms	No. of Hydrogen Atoms
1	$2 \cdot 1 + 2 = 4$
2	$2 \cdot 2 + 2 = 6$
3	$2 \cdot 3 + 2 = 8$
.	.
.	.
.	.
100	$2 \cdot 100 + 2 = 202$
.	.
.	.
.	.
n	$2n + 2 = m$

b. In general, for n carbon atoms there would be n hydrogen atoms attached above, n attached below, and 2 attached on the sides. Hence, the total number of hydrogen atoms m would be $2n + 2$. It follows that the number of hydrogen atoms is $m = 2n + 2$.

Example 5

A theater is arranged so that there are 20 seats in the first row and 4 additional seats in each consecutive row to the back of the theater, where there are 144 seats. How many rows are there in the theater?

Solution Two strategies lend themselves to this problem. One is to *build a table* and to consider the entries as seen in Table 10.

Table 10

Row Number	Number of Seats
1	20
2	$20 + 4$
3	$20 + 2 \cdot 4$
4	$20 + 3 \cdot 4$
5	$20 + 4 \cdot 4$
.	.
.	.
.	.
n	$20 + (n - 1)4$

Observe that in Table 10 when we write the number of seats as 20 plus the number of additional 4 seats in consecutive rows, the number of 4s added is one less than the number of the row. We know that in the last row there are 144 seats. Thus, we have the following:

$144 = 20 + (n - 1)4$. Subtracting 20 from each side of the equation, we get
$$124 = (n - 1)4 \text{ or } n - 1 = 31.$$

Therefore, $n = 32$, and there are 32 rows in the theater.

A different way to solve the problem is to use a spreadsheet as seen in Table 11, where the number of the row is seen in the index column and the entry in cell A1 indicates 20 seats in that row. Filling down the A column by writing the recursive formula = A1 + 4 in cell A2 and using the *Fill Down* command, we find 144 seats in row 32. Thus, there are 32 rows in the theater.

Table 11

Spreadsheet continued.

	A	B
1	20	
2	24	
3	28	
4	32	
5	36	
6	40	
7	44	
8	48	
9	52	
10	56	
11	60	
12	64	
13	68	
14	72	
15	76	
16	80	
17	84	
18	88	

19	92	
20	96	
21	100	
22	104	
23	108	
24	112	
25	116	
26	120	
27	124	
28	128	
29	132	
30	136	
31	140	
32	144	
33	148	
34	152	
35	156	
36	160	
37	164	

Fibonacci Sequence

Dan Brown's popular book *The Da Vinci Code** brought renewed interest to one of the most famous sequences of all time, the ***Fibonacci sequence***.

The Fibonacci sequence is

$$1, 1, 2, 3, 5, 8, 13, 21, 34, 55, 89, 144, \ldots.$$

This sequence is not *arithmetic* as there is no fixed difference, *d*. The first two terms of the Fibonacci sequence are 1, 1 and each subsequent term is the sum of the previous two. If we denote the terms of the Fibonacci sequence by $F_1, F_2, F_3, \ldots$, we have

$$F_1 = F_2 = 1, F_3 = 2, F_4 = 3, F_5 = 5, F_6 = 8, \text{ and so on.}$$

Also $F_3 = F_2 + F_1, F_4 = F_3 + F_2, \ldots$, and in general $F_n = F_{n-1} + F_{n-2}$ for $n = 3, 4, 5, \ldots$. The numbers in the sequence are known as *Fibonacci numbers*.

*Brown, Dan. *The Da Vinci Code*. Doubleday, 2003.

Historical Note

Leonardo de Pisa was born around 1170. His real family name was Bonaccio but he preferred the nickname Fibonacci, derived from *filius Bonacci*, meaning "son of Bonacci." In his book *Liber Abaci* (1202) he described the now-famous rabbit problem, whose solution, the sequence $1, 1, 2, 3, 5, 8, 13, 21, \ldots$, became known as the *Fibonacci sequence*.

Example 6

Consider the two rows of hexagonal cells in Figure 12. The cells in the upper row are numbered by the even natural numbers and the ones in the lower row by the odd natural numbers. You can start at cell 1 or 2 and move to a neighboring cell with a higher number on it. How many different ways are possible to get from start to cell number 7?

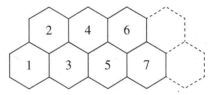

Figure 12

Solution   We first use the strategy of *solving a simpler problem*. Since we can start at cell 1 or cell 2, there is only one way to get to cell 1, but two ways to get to cell 2: by starting at cell 2 or via cell 1. There are three ways to get to cell 3: 1–3, 1–2–3, 2–3. There are five ways to cell 4: 2–4, 2–3–4, 1–2–3–4, 1–3–4, 1–2–4.

We can find the number of ways to get to other cells, record the results (see Table 12), and *search for a pattern*.

Table 12

Cell Number	Number of Ways to Get to the Cell
1	1
2	2
3	3
4	5
5	8
6	13

The pattern seems to be similar to the one in the Fibonacci sequence; that is, each term starting from the 3rd is the sum of the preceding two terms. If that is the case, then to reach cell number 7, the number of ways will be $8 + 13$ or 21.

But how can we be sure that the pattern exhibited in Table 12 continues as in the Fibonacci sequence? To reach any cell, for example cell 7 in Figure 12, we need to pass through either cell 5 or cell 6 (the two adjacent cells with lower numbers). Thus, the number of ways to reach cell 7 will be the number of ways to reach cell 5, that is, 8 ways, plus the number of ways to reach cell 6, that is, 13 ways. In general, to reach cell number n, we will have to go through cell number $n - 1$ or cell number $n - 2$, that is, we will add the number of ways to reach cell $n - 2$ to the number of ways to reach cell $n - 1$.

▶ **NOW TRY THIS 7**

In Figure 13, we want to know how many different paths there are from point A to point B if one is allowed to walk along the sides or on the indicated diagonals of the squares in the directions indicated by the arrows. Discover a pattern and explain why the pattern continues.

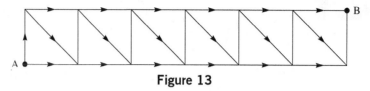

Figure 13

Geometric Sequences

A child has 2 biological parents, 4 grandparents, 8 great grandparents, 16 great-great grandparents, and so on. The number of generational ancestors form the **geometric sequence** $2, 4, 8, 16, 32, \ldots$. Each successive term of a geometric sequence is obtained from its predecessor by multiplying by a fixed nonzero number, the **ratio**. In this example, both the first term and the ratio are 2. (The ratio is 2 because each person has two parents.) To find the nth term examine the pattern in Table 13.

Table 13	
Term Number	**Term**
1	$2 = 2^1$
2	$4 = 2 \cdot 2 = 2^2$
3	$8 = (2 \cdot 2) \cdot 2 = 2^3$
4	$16 = (2 \cdot 2 \cdot 2) \cdot 2 = 2^4$
5	$32 = (2 \cdot 2 \cdot 2 \cdot 2) \cdot 2 = 2^5$
.	.
.	.
.	.

In Table 13, when the given term is written as a power of 2, the term number is the **exponent**. Following this pattern, the 10th term is 2^{10}, or 1024, the 100th term is 2^{100}, and the nth term is 2^n. Thus, the number of ancestors in the nth previous generation is 2^n. The notation used in Table 13 can be generalized as follows.

Definition of a^n

If n is a natural number, then $a^n = \overbrace{a \cdot a \cdot a \cdot \ldots \cdot a}^{n \text{ factors}}$.

If $n = 0$ and $a \neq 0$, then $a^0 = 1$.

Geometric sequences play an important role in everyday life. For example, suppose we have $1000 in a bank that pays 5% interest annually. (Note that 5% = 0.05.) If no money is added or withdrawn, then at the end of the first year we have all of the money we deposited plus 5% more.

Year 1: $\$1000 + 0.05(\$1000) = \$1000(1 + 0.05) = \$1000(1.05) = \$1050$

If no money is added or taken out, then at the end of the second year we would have 5% more money than the previous year.

Year 2: $\$1050 + 0.05(\$1050) = \$1050(1 + 0.05) = \$1050(1.05) = \$1102.50$

The amount of money in the account after any number of years can be found by noting that every dollar invested for one year becomes $1 + 0.05 \cdot 1$, or 1.05 dollars. Therefore, the amount in each year is obtained by multiplying the amount from the previous year by 1.05. The amounts in the bank after each year form a geometric sequence because the amount in each year (starting from year 2) is obtained by multiplying the amount in the previous year by the same number, 1.05. This is summarized in Table 14.

Table 14

Term Number (Year)	Term (Amount at the End of Each Year)
1	$\$1000(1.05)^1$
2	$\$1000(1.05)^2$
3	$\$1000(1.05)^3$
4	$\$1000(1.05)^4$
.	.
.	.
.	.
n	$\$1000(1.05)^n$

▶ **NOW TRY THIS 8**

a. Two bacteria are in a dish. The number of bacteria triples every hour. Following this pattern, find the number of bacteria in the dish after 10 hours and after n hours.

b. Suppose that instead of increasing geometrically as in part (a), the number of bacteria increases arithmetically by 3 each hour. Compare the growth after 10 hours and after n hours. Comment on the difference in growth of a geometric sequence versus an arithmetic sequence.

Other Sequences

Figurate numbers, based on geometrical patterns, provide examples of sequences that are neither arithmetic nor geometric. Such numbers can be represented by dots arranged in the shape of certain geometric figures. The number 1 is the beginning of most patterns involving figurate numbers. The arrays in Figure 14 represent the first four terms of the sequence of **triangular numbers**.

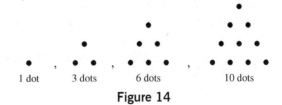

1 dot   3 dots   6 dots   10 dots

Figure 14

The triangular numbers can be written numerically as $1, 3, 6, 10, 15, \ldots$. The sequence $1, 3, 6, 10, 15, \ldots$ is not an arithmetic sequence because there is no common difference, as Figure 15 shows. It is not a geometric sequence because there is no common ratio. It is not the Fibonacci sequence.

$$1 \quad 3 \quad 6 \quad 10 \quad 15$$
(First difference) $\quad 2 \quad 3 \quad 4 \quad 5$

Figure 15

However, the sequence of differences, 2, 3, 4, 5, . . . , appears to form an arithmetic sequence with difference 1, as Figure 16 shows. The next successive terms for the original sequence are shown in color in Figure 16.

$$\begin{array}{ccccccc} 1 & 3 & 6 & 10 & 15 & 21 & 28 \end{array}$$

(First difference) $\quad 2 \quad 3 \quad 4 \quad 5 \quad 6 \quad 7$

(Second difference) $\quad 1 \quad 1 \quad 1 \quad 1 \quad 1$

Figure 16

Table 15 suggests a pattern for finding the next terms and the nth term for the triangular numbers. The second term is obtained from the first term by adding 2; the third term is obtained from the second term by adding 3; and so on.

Table 15

Term Number	Term
1	1
2	$3 = 1 + 2$
3	$6 = 1 + 2 + 3$
4	$10 = 1 + 2 + 3 + 4$
5	$15 = 1 + 2 + 3 + 4 + 5$
.	.
.	.
.	.
10	$55 = 1 + 2 + 3 + 4 + 5 + 6 + 7 + 8 + 9 + 10$

We could approach the problem differently without looking for differences. Because the nth triangular number has n dots in the nth row, it is equal to the sum of the dots in the previous triangular number (the $(n - 1)$st one) plus the n dots in the nth row. Following this pattern, the 10th term is $1 + 2 + 3 + 4 + 5 + 6 + 7 + 8 + 9 + 10$, or 55, and the nth term is $1 + 2 + 3 + 4 + 5 + \ldots + (n - 1) + n$. This problem is similar to Gauss's Problem in Section 1. Because of the work done in Section 1, we know that this sum can be expressed as

$$\frac{n(n + 1)}{2}.$$

Next consider the first four *square numbers* in Figure 17. These square numbers, 1, 4, 9, 16 can be written as $1^2, 2^2, 3^2, 4^2$. Continuing, the number of dots in the 10th array would be 10^2, the number of dots in the 100th array would be 100^2, and the number of dots in the nth array would be n^2. The sequence of square numbers is neither arithmetic nor geometric. Investigate whether the sequence of first differences is an arithmetic sequence and tell why.

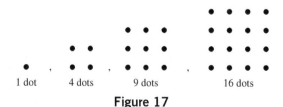

1 dot   4 dots   9 dots   16 dots

Figure 17

When asked to find a pattern for a given sequence, we first look for some easily recognizable pattern and determine whether the sequence is arithmetic or geometric. If a pattern is unclear, taking successive differences may help. *It is possible that none of the methods described reveals a pattern.*

> ▶ **NOW TRY THIS 9**

Consider the rectangular numbers in Figure 18 in which the number of columns and the number of rows increase by 1 with each successive "rectangle." What is the 10th rectangular number, and what is the nth rectangular number?

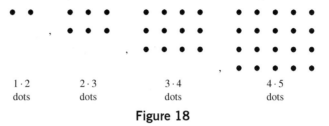

| $1 \cdot 2$ dots | $2 \cdot 3$ dots | $3 \cdot 4$ dots | $4 \cdot 5$ dots |

Figure 18

Example 7

Use differences to find a pattern. Then assuming that the pattern discovered continues, find the seventh term in each of the following sequences:

a. $5, 6, 14, 29, 51, 80, \ldots$ **b.** $2, 3, 9, 23, 48, 87, \ldots$

Solution

a. Figure 19 shows the sequence of first differences.

$$5 \quad 6 \quad 14 \quad 29 \quad 51 \quad 80$$
(First difference) $\quad 1 \quad 8 \quad 15 \quad 22 \quad 29$

Figure 19

To discover a pattern for the original sequence, we try to find a pattern for the sequence of differences $1, 8, 15, 22, 29, \ldots$. This sequence is an arithmetic sequence with fixed difference 7 as seen in Figure 20.

$$5 \quad 6 \quad 14 \quad 29 \quad 51 \quad 80$$
(First difference) $\quad 1 \quad 8 \quad 15 \quad 22 \quad 29$
(Second difference) $\quad 7 \quad 7 \quad 7 \quad 7$

Figure 20

Thus, the sixth term in the first difference row is $29 + 7$, or 36, and the seventh term in the original sequence is $80 + 36$, or 116. What number follows 116?

b. Because the second difference is not a fixed number, we go on to the third difference as in Figure 21.

$$2 \quad 3 \quad 9 \quad 23 \quad 48 \quad 87$$
(First difference) $\quad 1 \quad 6 \quad 14 \quad 25 \quad 39$
(Second difference) $\quad 5 \quad 8 \quad 11 \quad 14$
(Third difference) $\quad 3 \quad 3 \quad 3$

Figure 21

The third difference is a fixed number; therefore, the second difference is an arithmetic sequence. The fifth term in the second-difference sequence is $14 + 3$, or 17; the sixth term in the first-difference sequence is $39 + 17$, or 56; and the seventh term in the original sequence is $87 + 56$, or 143.

Example 8

Figure 22 shows the first three figures of arrays of matchsticks with the number of matchsticks written below the figures. If the next figure consists of a 4-by-4 square arrangement, and each subsequent figure has one more row and one more column of matchsticks squares than the preceding figure, without actually counting, find the number of matchsticks in

a. the 7th figure
b. the nth figure.

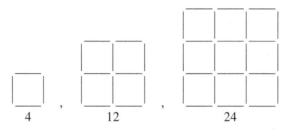

4   12   24

Figure 22

Solution

First Approach

Building the 4th and 5th figures, we find that the number of matchsticks in the figures is 40 and 60 correspondingly.

To discover a pattern for the original sequence, we use differences. Figure 23 shows first and second differences.

$$4 \quad 12 \quad 24 \quad 40 \quad 60$$

(First difference) $\qquad 8 \quad 12 \quad 16 \quad 20$

(Second difference) $\qquad 4 \quad 4 \quad 4$

Figure 23

Thus, the next two terms in the first difference are $20 + 4$ or 24 and $24 + 4 = 28$. Hence the next two terms in the original sequence are $60 + 24$ or 84 and $84 + 28$ or 112. Thus, the answer to part (a) is 112.

To answer part (b), we use the differences in Figure 21 to write the number of matchsticks in each figure in Table 16.

Table 16	
Figure Number	**Number of Matchsticks**
1	$4 \cdot 1$
2	$12 = 4 + 8 = 4(1 + 2)$
3	$24 = 4 + 8 + 12 = 4(1 + 2 + 3)$
4	$40 = 4 + 8 + 12 + 16 = 4(1 + 2 + 3 + 4)$
5	$60 = 4 + 8 + 12 + 16 + 20 = 4(1 + 2 + 3 + 4 + 5)$
$\vdots$	$\vdots$
n	$4(1 + 2 + 3 + 4 + 5 + \ldots + n)$

Now using Gauss's Problem, we find that the number of matchsticks in the nth figure is

$$4(1 + 2 + 3 + 4 + 5 + \ldots + n) = 4\frac{n(n + 1)}{2} = 2n(n + 1).$$

Notice that the above solution is based on *inductive reasoning*. Based on a few cases, we decided that the pattern of second differences continues and is always 4. However, we cannot be certain that the second differences continue to be 4. For that reason, we give another approach.

Second Approach

We count the matchsticks in rows and columns. Notice that the number of columns is the same as the number of rows. Thus, we will find the number of matchsticks in the rows and multiply the result by 2. In the first figure, we have 2 rows and 1 matchstick in each. Because we are adding one row and one column to get the subsequent figure, we can write the number of matchsticks in each figure as shown in Table 17.

Table 17

Figure Number	Number of Rows	Number in Each Row	Total in the Rows
1	2	1	$1 \cdot 2$
2	3	2	$2 \cdot 3$
3	4	3	$3 \cdot 4$
4	5	4	$4 \cdot 5$
5	6	5	$5 \cdot 6$
$\vdots$	$\vdots$	$\vdots$	$\vdots$
n	$n + 1$	n	$n(n + 1)$

Because the number of matchsticks in the columns is the same as in the rows, the total number is $2n(n + 1)$. If $n = 7$, then we have the answer for part (a) as $2 \cdot 7(7 + 1)$ or 112.

Assessment 2 A

1. For each of the following sequences of figures, determine a possible pattern and draw the next figure according to that pattern:

   a.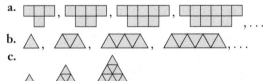

   , . . .

   b. $\triangle, \triangle\!\triangle, \triangle\!\triangle\!\triangle, \triangle\!\triangle\!\triangle\!\triangle, \ldots$

   c.

2. Each of the following sequences is either arithmetic or geometric. Identify the sequences and list the next three terms for each.

   a. $1, 5, 9, 13, \ldots$

   b. $70, 120, 170, \ldots$

   c. $1, 3, 9, \ldots$

   d. $10, 10^3, 10^5, 10^7, \ldots$

   e. $193 + 7 \cdot 2^{30}, 193 + 8 \cdot 2^{30}, 193 + 9 \cdot 2^{30}, \ldots$

3. Find the 100th term and the nth term for each of the sequences in exercise 2.

4. Use a traditional clock face to determine the next three terms in the following sequence.

$$1, 6, 11, 4, 9, \ldots$$

5. The pattern $1, 8, 27, 64, 125, \ldots$ is a cubic pattern named because $1 = 1 \cdot 1 \cdot 1$ or 1^3, $8 = 2 \cdot 2 \cdot 2$ or 2^3, and so on.

   a. What is the least 4-digit number greater than 1000 in this pattern?

   b. What is the greatest 3-digit number in this pattern?

   c. What is the greatest number in this pattern that is less than 10^4?

   d. If this pattern was produced in a normal spreadsheet, what is the number in cell A14?

6. The first windmill has 5 matchstick squares, the second has 9, and the third has 13, as shown. How many matchstick squares are in (a) the 10th windmill? (b) the nth windmill? (c) How many matchsticks will it take to build the nth windmill?

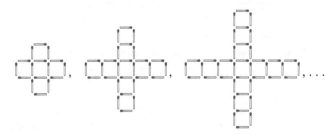

7. In the following sequence, the figures are made of cubes that are glued together. If the exposed surface needs to be painted, how many squares will be painted in (a) the 15th figure? (b) the nth figure?

8. The school population for a certain school is predicted to increase by 60 students per year for the next 12 years. If the current enrollment is 700 students, what will the enrollment be after 12 years?

9. Joe's annual income has been increasing each year by the same dollar amount. The first year his income was $24,000, and the ninth year his income was $31,680. In which year was his income $45,120?

10. The first difference of a sequence is the arithmetic sequence $2, 4, 6, 8, 10, \ldots$. Find the first six terms of the original sequence in each of the following cases:
    a. The first term of the original sequence is 3.
    b. The sum of the first two terms of the original sequence is 10.
    c. The fifth term of the original sequence is 35.

11. List the next three terms to continue a pattern in each of the following. (Finding differences may be helpful.)
    a. $5, 6, 14, 32, 64, 115, 191$
    b. $0, 2, 6, 12, 20, 30, 42$

12. How many terms are there in each of the following sequences?
    a. $51, 52, 53, 54, \ldots, 251$
    b. $1, 2, 2^2, 2^3, \ldots, 2^{60}$
    c. $10, 20, 30, 40, \ldots, 2000$
    d. $1, 2, 4, 8, 16, 32, \ldots, 1024$

13. Find the first five terms in sequences with the following nth terms.
    a. $n^2 + 2$
    b. $5n + 1$
    c. $10^n - 1$
    d. $3n - 2$

14. Find a counterexample for each of the following:
    a. If n is a natural number, then $(n + 5)/5 = n + 1$.
    b. If n is a natural number, then $(n + 4)^2 = n^2 + 16$.

15. Assume that the following patterns are built of square tiles and the pattern continues. Answer the questions that follow.

    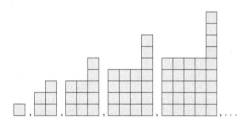

    a. How many square tiles are there in the sixth figure?
    b. How many square tiles are in the nth figure?
    c. Is there a figure that has exactly 1259 square tiles? If so, which one? (*Hint*: To determine if there is a figure in the sequence containing exactly 1259 square tiles, first think about the greatest square number less than 1259.)

16. Consider the sequences given in the table below. Find the least number, n, such that the nth term of the geometric sequence is greater than the corresponding term in the arithmetic sequence.

Term Number	1	2	3	4	5	6	...	n
Arithmetic	400	600	800	1000	1200	1400	...	
Geometric	2	4	8	16	32	64	...	

17. A sheet of paper is cut into 5 same-size parts. Each of the parts is then cut into 5 same-size parts and so on. Answer the following.
    a. After the 5th cut, how many of the smallest pieces of paper are there?
    b. After the nth cut, how many of the smallest pieces are there?

18. Each of the following sequences is labeled either arithmetic or geometric. In each part, find the missing terms.
    a. $\_\_, \underline{39}, \_\_, \_\_, \underline{69}$ (arithmetic)
    b. $\_\_, \underline{200}, \_\_, \_\_, \underline{800}$ (arithmetic)
    c. $\_\_, \underline{5^4}, \_\_, \_\_, \underline{5^{10}}$ (geometric)

19. A *Fibonacci-type sequence* is a sequence in which the first two terms are arbitrary and in which every term starting from the third is the sum of the two previous terms. Each of the following is a Fibonacci-type sequence. In each part, find the missing terms.
    a. $\_\_, \_\_, 1, 1, \_\_, \_\_, \_\_, \_\_$
    b. $\_\_, \_\_, \_\_, 10, 13, \_\_, 36, 59$
    c. $\underline{0}, \underline{2}, \_\_, \_\_, \_\_, \_\_, \_\_, \_\_$

20. Starting with 1 and 1 as the first two terms of the Fibonacci sequence, answer the following.
    a. Add the first three terms. The result is one less than which term?
    b. Add the first four terms. The result is one less than which term?
    c. Add the first five terms. The result is one less than which term?
    d. Write a conjecture regarding the sum of the first n terms of the sequence.
    e. Assuming that your conjecture in part (d) is true, what can you conclude about the sum of the first $n - 2$ terms of the sequence?

21. A new pair of tennis shoes cost $80. If the price increases each year by 5% of the previous year's price, find the following:
    a. The price after 5 years
    b. The price after n years

Assessment 2 B

1. In each of the following, determine a possible pattern and draw the next figure according to that pattern if the sequence continues.
    a.
    b.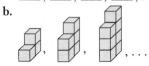

    c.

    2. Each of the following sequences is either arithmetic or geometric. Identify the sequences and list the next three terms for each.
    a. $2, 6, 10, 14, \ldots$ b. $0, 13, 26, \ldots$
    c. $4, 16, 64, \ldots$ d. $2^2, 2^6, 2^{10}, \ldots$
    e. $100 + 4 \cdot 2^{50}, 100 + 6 \cdot 2^{50}, 100 + 8 \cdot 2^{50}, \ldots$

3. Find the 100th term and the nth term for each of the sequences in exercise 2.

4. Use a traditional clock face to determine the next three terms in the following sequence:

$$1, 9, 5, 1, \ldots$$

5. Observe the following pattern:

$$1 + 3 = 2^2,$$
$$1 + 3 + 5 = 3^2,$$
$$1 + 3 + 5 + 7 = 4^2$$

   a. Conjecture a generalization based on this pattern.
   b. Based on the generalization in (a), find

$$1 + 3 + 5 + 7 + \ldots + 35.$$

6. In the following pattern, one hexagon takes 6 toothpicks to build, two hexagons take 11 toothpicks to build, and so on. How many toothpicks would it take to build
   a. 10 hexagons?
   b. n hexagons?

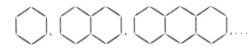

7. Each successive figure below is made of small triangles like the first one in the sequence. Conjecture the number of small triangles needed to make
   a. the 100th figure?
   b. the nth figure?

8. A tank contains 15,360 L of water. At the end of each subsequent day, half of the water is removed and not replaced. How much water is left in the tank after 10 days?

9. The Washington Middle School schedule is an arithmetic sequence. Each period is the same length and includes a 4th period lunch. The first three periods begin at 8:10 A.M., 9:00 A.M., and 9:50 A.M., respectively. At what time does the eighth period begin?

10. The first difference of a sequence is $3, 6, 9, 12, 15, \ldots$ Find the first six terms of the original sequence in each of the following cases:
   a. The first term of the original sequence is 3.
   b. The sum of the first two terms of the original sequence is 7.
   c. The fifth term of the original sequence is 34.

11. List the next three terms to continue a pattern in each of the following. (Finding differences may be helpful.)
   a. $3, 8, 15, 24, 35, 48, \ldots$
   b. $1, 7, 18, 37, 67, 111, \ldots$

12. How many terms are there in each of the following sequences?
   a. $1, 3, 3^2, 3^3, \ldots, 3^{99}$
   b. $9, 13, 17, 21, 25, \ldots, 353$
   c. $38, 39, 40, 41, \ldots, 238$

13. Find the first five terms in sequences with the following nth terms.
   a. $5n - 1$
   b. $6n - 2$
   c. $5n + 1$
   d. $n^2 - 1$

14. Find a counterexample for each of the following:
   a. If n is a natural number, then $(3 + n)/3 = n$.
   b. If n is a natural number, then $(n - 2)^2 = n^2 - 2^2$.

15. Assume the following pattern with terms built of square-tiles figures continues and answer the questions that follow.

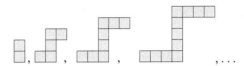

   a. How many square tiles are there in the seventh figure?
   b. How many square tiles are in the nth figure?
   c. Is there a figure that has exactly 449 square tiles? If so, which one?

16. Consider the sequences given in the table below. Find the least number, n, such that the nth term of the geometric sequence is greater than the corresponding term in the arithmetic sequence.

Term Number	1	2	3	4	5	6	...	n
Arithmetic	200	500	800	1100	1400	1700	...	
Geometric	1	3	9	27	81	243	...	

17. Female bees are born from fertilized eggs, and male bees are born from unfertilized eggs. This means that a male bee has only a mother, whereas a female bee has a mother and a father. If the ancestry of a male bee is traced 10 generations including the generation of the male bee, how many bees are there in all 10 generations? (*Hint:* The Fibonacci sequence might be helpful.)

18. Each of the following sequences is labeled either arithmetic or geometric. In each part, find the missing terms.
   a. __, 49, __, __, 64 (arithmetic)
   b. 1, __, __, __, 625 (geometric)
   c. __, 3^{10}, __, __, 3^{19} (geometric)
   d. a, __, __, __, $5a$ (arithmetic)

19. Each of the following sequences is a Fibonacci-type sequence (see problem 19 Assessment 2A). Find the missing terms.
   a. 1, __, __, $7, 11$
   b. __, 2, __, 4, __
   c. __, __, $3, 4$, __

20. Starting with 1 and 1 as the first two terms of the Fibonacci sequence, answer the following.
   a. Check that $F_1 + F_3 = F_4$
   b. Compute $F_1 + F_3 + F_5$. The sum is which term?
   c. Compute $F_1 + F_3 + F_5 + F_7$. The sum is which term?
   d. Write a conjecture based on the examples in parts (a), (b), and (c).

Mathematical Connections 2

Reasoning

1. a. If a fixed number is added to each term of an arithmetic sequence, is the resulting sequence an arithmetic sequence? Justify the answer.
   b. If each term of an arithmetic sequence is multiplied by a fixed number, will the resulting sequence always be an arithmetic sequence? Justify the answer.
   c. If the corresponding terms of two arithmetic sequences are added, is the resulting sequence arithmetic?

2. A student says she read that Thomas Robert Malthus (1766–1834), a renowned British economist and demographer, claimed that the increase of population will take place, if unchecked, in a geometric sequence, whereas the supply of food will increase in only an arithmetic sequence. This theory implies that population increases faster than food production. The student is wondering why. How do you respond?

3. Abby and Dan are preparing for a GRE (Graduate Record Exam) to take place in 5 months. Abby starts by studying 10 hours the first week and increases her study by 30 minutes per week. Dan starts at 6 hours per week, but increases his time every week by 45 minutes per week. Answer the following.
   a. How many hours did each student study in week 8?
   b. In which week will Dan first catch up with Abby in the number of hours spent studying per week?

4. The *arithmetic average* of two numbers x and y is $\dfrac{x+y}{2}$. Use *deductive reasoning* to explain why if three numbers $a, b,$ and c form an arithmetic sequence, then b is the arithmetic average of a and c.

5. The numbers $x, y,$ and z are in a Fibonacci-type sequence. If $z = x + y$, use deductive reasoning to find all triples $x, y,$ and z that make an arithmetic sequence as well as consecutive terms in a Fibonacci-type sequence.

6. The figure below shows the first three terms of a sequence of figures containing small square tiles. Some of the tiles are shaded. Notice that the first figure has one shaded tile. The second figure has $2 \cdot 2$, for 2^2, shaded tiles. The third figure has $3 \cdot 3$, or 3^2, shaded tiles. If this pattern of having shaded squares surrounded by white borders continues, answer the following:
   a. How many shaded tiles are there in the nth figure?
   b. How many white tiles are there in the nth figure?

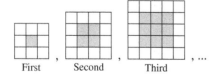

First , Second , Third , ...

Open-Ended

7. Patterns can be used to count the number of dots on the Chinese checkerboard; two patterns are shown here. Determine several other patterns to count the dots.

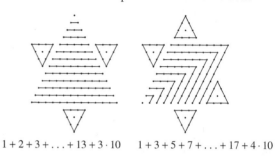

$$1 + 2 + 3 + \ldots + 13 + 3 \cdot 10 \qquad 1 + 3 + 5 + 7 + \ldots + 17 + 4 \cdot 10$$

8. Make up a pattern involving figurate numbers and find the number of dots in the 100th figure. Describe the pattern and how to find the 100th term.

9. A sequence that follows the same pattern as the Fibonacci sequence but in which the first two terms are any numbers is a Fibonacci type sequence. Choose a few such sequences and compare their behavior to the Fibonacci sequence.

10. Use online sources to find two problems involving the Fibonacci sequence appropriate for the 4th or 5th grades. State the problems and solve them, explaining your solutions in a way appropriate for that level.

Cooperative Learning

11. The following pattern is called *Pascal's triangle*. It was named for the mathematician Blaise Pascal (1623–1662).

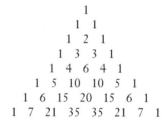

```
            1
          1   1
        1   2   1
      1   3   3   1
    1   4   6   4   1
  1   5  10  10   5   1
1   6  15  20  15   6   1
1  7  21  35  35  21  7  1
```

   a. Have each person in the group find four different patterns in the triangle and then share them with the rest of the group.
   b. Add the numbers in each horizontal row. Discuss the pattern that occurs.
   c. Use part (b) to find the sum in the 16th row.
   d. What is the sum of the numbers in the nth row?

12. If the following pattern continued indefinitely, the resulting figure would be called the *Sierpinski triangle*, or *Sierpinski gasket*.

In a group, determine each of the following. Discuss different counting strategies.

a. How many black triangles would be in the fifth figure?
b. How many white triangles would be in the fifth figure?
c. How many black triangles are in the nth figure?

Connecting Mathematics to the Classroom

13. Joey said that 4, 24, 44, and 64 all have remainder 0 when divided by 4, so all numbers that end in 4 must have 0 remainder when divided by 4. How do you respond?

14. Al and Betty were asked to extend the sequence 2, 4, 8, ... Al said his answer of 2, 4, 8, 16, 32, 64, . . . was the correct one. Betty said Al was wrong and it should be 2, 4, 8, 14, 22, 32, 44, ... What do you tell these students?

15. A student claims the sequence 1, 1, 1, 1, . . . is both arithmetic and geometric and would like to know if there are other such sequences. How do you respond?

16. A student claims that she has found an easy way to find the number of terms in an arithmetic sequence: "You take the difference between the last and first terms and divide by the common difference." How do you respond?

Review Problems

17. In a baseball league consisting of 10 teams, each team plays each of the other teams twice. How may games will be played?

18. How many ways can you make change for 40¢ using only nickels, dimes, and quarters?

19. Tents hold 2, 3, 5, 6, or 12 people. What combinations of tents are possible to sleep 26 people if all tents are fully occupied and only one 12-person tent is used?

National Assessments

National Assessment of Educational Progress (NAEP) Questions

The growing number pattern 3, 4, 6, 9, 13, . . . follows a rule. Explain the rule.

Write a new growing pattern beginning with 21 that follows the same rule. 21, _____, _____, _____, _____, _____

NAEP, Grade 4, 2013

Write the next two numbers in the number pattern.

1 6 4 9 7 12 10 ____ ____

Write the rule that you used to find the two numbers you wrote.
NAEP, Grade 4, 2009

A car can seat c adults. A van can seat 4 more than twice as many adults as the car can. In terms of c, how many adults can the van seat?
A. $c + 8$
B. $c + 12$
C. $2c - 4$
D. $2c + 4$
E. $4c + 2$
NAEP, Grade 8, 2013

Which of the following equations has the same solution as the equation $2x + 6 = 32$?
A. $2x = 38$
B. $x - 3 = 16$
C. $x + 6 = 16$
D. $2(x - 3) = 16$
E. $2(x + 3) = 32$
NAEP, Grade 8, 2009

Hint for Solving the Preliminary Problem

Show that if all the coins taken out were genuine, they would weigh 110 ounces. Also notice that if the first box contained all the fake coins, the weight of all the coins would be 109 ounces.

Chapter Summary

KEY CONCEPTS	DEFINITIONS, DESCRIPTIONS, AND THEOREMS
Section 1	
Four-step problem-solving process	• Understanding the problem • Carrying out the plan • Devising a plan • Looking Back
Natural numbers	The numbers 1, 2, 3, 4, 5, . . . The three dots above, called an *ellipsis*, indicate that the pattern of the numbers in the list continues.
Problem-solving strategies	• Look for a pattern • Make a diagram • Examine a related problem • Use guess and check • Examine a simpler case • Work backward • Make a table • Write an equation • Identify a subgoal
Section 2	
Conjecture	A statement thought to be true but has not been proven.
Inductive reasoning	Method of making generalizations based on observations and patterns, which may or may not be true.
Deductive reasoning	Method of proving the truth of conjectures through the use of axioms, theorems, undefined terms assumed to be true, and logic.
Counterexample	An example that shows a conjecture is false.
Sequence	An ordered arrangement of numbers, figures, or objects. The individual items of a sequence are the *terms* of the sequence. The *term number* indicates the position of the term in the sequence.
Arithmetic sequence	A sequence in which each successive term from the second term on is obtained from the previous term by adding a fixed number. The fixed number is the *common difference*, or *difference*. An arithmetic sequence involves a *recursive pattern*—each successive term of the sequence is obtained from the previous term(s).
Fibonacci sequence	The sequence in which the first two terms are both 1 and each subsequent term is the sum of the previous two terms: 1, 1, 2, 3, 5, 8, 13, 21, . . . In general, a sequence in which the first two terms are arbitrary and each subsequent term is the sum of the previous two terms in a *Fibonacci-type sequence*.
Geometric sequence	A sequence in which each successive term from the second term on is obtained from the previous term by multiplying by a fixed nonzero number. The fixed number is the *ratio*.
Exponentiation	If n is a natural number, then $a^n = \underbrace{a \cdot a \cdot a \cdot \ldots \cdot a}_{n \text{ factor}}$. If $n = 0$ and $a \neq 0$, then $a^0 = 1$.
Figurative numbers	Numbers that can be represented by dots arranged in the shape of geometric figures. Figurative numbers provide examples of sequences that are neither arithmetic nor geometric.
Finding common differences	A technique used to discover patterns in sequences.

Chapter Review

1. If today is Sunday, July 4, and next year is not a leap year, what day of the week will July 4 be on next year?
2. Jackie spent $40 on two items. If she spent $5.90 more on the more expensive item, how much did this item cost? What strategy have you used to solve this problem?
3. A nursery rhyme states:

    A diller, a dollar, a ten o'clock scholar!
    What makes you come so soon?
    You used to come at ten o'clock,
    But now you come at noon.

    Explain whether the rhyme makes sense mathematically.
4. List three more terms that complete a pattern in each of the following; explain your reasoning, and tell whether each sequence is arithmetic or geometric, or neither.
    a. 0, 1, 3, 6, 10, ____, ____, ____,
    b. 52, 47, 42, 37, ____, ____, ____,
    c. 6400, 3200, 1600, 800, ____, ____, ____,
    d. 1, 2, 3, 5, 8, 13, ____, ____, ____,
    e. 2, 5, 8, 11, 14, ____, ____, ____,
    f. 1, 4, 16, 64, ____, ____, ____,
    g. 0, 4, 8, 12, ____, ____, ____,
    h. 1, 8, 27, 64, ____, ____, ____,
5. Find a possible nth term in each of the following.
    a. 5, 8, 11, 14, ...
    b. 3, 9, 27, 81, 243, ...
    c. $2^2 - 1, 2^3 - 1, 2^4 - 1, 2^5 - 1, ...$
6. Find the first five terms of the sequences whose nth term is given as follows:
    a. $3n - 2$
    b. $n^2 + n$
    c. $4n - 1$
7. Find the following sums:
    a. $2 + 4 + 6 + 8 + 10 + ... + 200$
    b. $51 + 52 + 53 + 54 + ... + 151$
8. Produce a counterexample, if possible, to disprove each of the following. If a statement is true, justify it.
    a. If two odd numbers are added, then the sum is odd.
    b. If a number is odd, then it ends in a 1 or a 3.
    c. If two even numbers are added, then the sum is even.
9. Complete the following magic square; that is, complete the square so that the sum in each row, column, and diagonal is the same.

16	3	2	13
	10		
9		7	12
4		14	

10. How many people can be seated at 12 square tables lined up end to end if each table individually holds four persons?
11. Solve the following equations:
    a. $\boxed{} + 2^{60} = 2^{61}$ b. $\boxed{}^2 = 625$

12. If fence posts are to be placed in a row 5 m apart, how many posts are needed for 100 m of fence?
13. If a complete rotation of a car tire moves a car forward 6 ft, how many rotations of the tire occur before the tire goes off its 50,000 mi warranty?
14. The members of Mrs. Grant's class are standing in a circle; they are evenly spaced and are numbered in order. The student with number 7 is standing directly across from the student with number 17. How many students are in the class?
15. A carpenter has three large boxes. Inside each large box are two medium-sized boxes. Inside each medium-sized box are five small boxes. How many boxes are there altogether?
16. Use differences to find the next term in the following sequence:

$$5, 15, 37, 77, 141, \underline{}$$

17. An ant farm can hold 100,000 ants. If the farm held 1500 ants on the first day, 3000 ants on the second day, 6000 ants on the third day, and so on forming a geometric sequence, in how many days will the farm be full?
18. Toma's team entered a mathematics contest where teams of students compete by answering questions that are worth either 3 points or 5 points. No partial credit was given. Toma's team scored 44 points on 12 questions. How many 5-point questions did the team answer correctly?
19. Three pieces of wood are needed for a project. They are to be cut from a 90-cm-long piece of wood. The longest piece is to be 3 times as long as the middle-sized piece and the shortest piece is to be 10 cm shorter than the middle-sized piece. How long are the pieces?
20. How many four-digit numbers have the same digits as 1993?
21. If n and m are natural numbers and $n > m$, how many terms are in the arithmetic sequence $m, m + 1, m + 2, ... , n$? (Your answer should be in terms of n and m.) What strategy (or strategies) have you used to answer the question? Why?
22. We have two containers, one of which holds 7 cups and the other holds 4 cups. How can we measure exactly 5 cups of water, if we have an unlimited amount of water with which to start?
23. The following geometric arrays suggest a sequence of numbers: 2, 6, 12, 20, ...

    a. Find the next three terms.
    b. Find the 100th term.
    c. Find the nth term.

24. Each side of each pentagon below is 1 unit long.

    a. Draw a possible next figure in the sequence.
    b. What is the perimeter (distance around) of each of the first four figures?
    c. What is the perimeter of the 100th figure?
    d. What is the perimeter of the nth figure?

25. a. If every second term in an arithmetic sequence is circled, do the circled terms always constitute an arithmetic sequence? Justify your answer.
    b. Answer the question in part (a) again, but replace "arithmetic" by "geometric."

26. If for every natural number n, the sum of the first n terms of a certain sequence is $n^2 - n$, find the 4th term. Justify your answer.

27. Each of the following is a Fibonacci-type sequence. Find the missing terms. In part (c), your answer should be in terms of a. and b.
    a. 13 , ___ , ___ , 27
    b. 137, ___ , ___ , 163
    c. b , ___ , ___ , a

Answers to Problems

Answers to odd-numbered Mathematical Connections problems are available at www.pearsonhighered.com/mathstatsresources <http://www.pearsonhighered.com/mathstatsresources>.

Assessment 1A

1. a. 4950 **b.** 251,001 **c.** 15,150 **d.** 20,200 **2.** Building a staircase as seen in (a) gives a visual graphic of the sum $1 + 2 + \ldots + n$. Copying the staircase as in (b) and placing it as shown demonstrates that an array that is n units high and $n + 1$ units long is produced. There are $n(n + 1)$ units in (b) which is twice the number desired. So the sum $1 + 2 + \ldots + n$ must be $n(n + 1)/2$. Gauss's sum when $n = 100$ would be $100(100 + 1)/2$ or 5050. **3.** 10,248 **4. a.** 9 **b.** 12 **5.** 2801 **6.** 27 **7.** E is greater by 49. **8.** Dandy, Cory, Alababa, Bubba **9.** 12 **10.** $a = 42; b = 32; c = 37; d = 2$ **11.** 48 **12.** 9 **13.** Choose Box B and pull out a fruit. If you pull an apple then Box B must contain only apples (why?). Because Box A is mislabeled it can't be "Oranges," but it can't be "Apples" either (why?). So, it is "Oranges and Apples." Thus, Box C is "Oranges." If an orange is pulled the reasoning is similar. **14.** 27.5 hours **15.** 23

Assessment 2A

1. a. Each figure in the sequence adds one box each to the top and bottom rows. **b.** Each figure in the sequence adds one upright and one inverted triangle. **c.** Each figure in the sequence adds one box to the base and one row to the overall triangle.
2. a. arithmetic; 17, 21, 25 **b.** arithmetic; 220, 270, 320 **c.** geometric; 27, 81, 243 **d.** geometric; $10^9, 10^{11}, 10^{13}$ **e.** arithmetic; $193 + 10 \cdot 2^{30}, 193 + 11 \cdot 2^{30}, 193 + 12 \cdot 2^{30}$
3. a. $397; 4n - 3$ **b.** $5020; 50n + 20$ **c.** $3^{99}; 3^{n-1}$
d. $100^{199}; 10^{2n-1}$ **e.** $193 + 106 \cdot 2^{30}; 193 + (n + 6) \cdot 2^{30}$
4. 2, 7, 12 **5. a.** 1331 **b.** 729 **c.** 9261 **d.** 2744 **6. a.** 41
b. $4n + 1$ **c.** $12n + 4$ **7. a.** 62 **b.** $4n + 2$ **8.** 1420
9. 23rd **10. a.** 3, 5, 9, 15, 23, 33 **b.** 4, 6, 10, 16, 24, 34
c. 15, 17, 21, 27, 35, 45 **11. a.** 299, 447, 644 **b.** 56, 72, 90
12. a. 201 **b.** 61 **c.** 200 **d.** 11 **13. a.** 3, 6, 11, 18, 27
b. 6, 11, 16, 21, 26 **c.** 9, 99, 999, 9999, 99999 **d.** 1, 4, 7, 10, 13
14. a. Answers vary. For example, if $n = 5$, then $\frac{5 + 5}{5} \neq 5 + 1$.

b. Answers vary. For example, if $n = 2$, then $(2 + 4)^2 \neq 2^2 + 4^2$.
15. a. 41 **b.** $n^2 + n - 1$ **c.** 35th **16.** 12 **17. a.** 5^5
b. 5^n **18. a.** 29, 49, 59 **b.** 0, 400, 600 **c.** $5^2, 5^6, 5^8$
19. a. 1, 0, 2, 3, 5, 8 **b.** $^-4, 7, 3, 23$ **c.** 2, 4, 6, 10, 16, 26
20. a. 5 (the fifth Fibonacci term) **b.** 8 (the sixth Fibonacci term) **c.** 13 (the seventh Fibonacci term) **d.** $F_1 + F_2 + F_3 + \ldots + F_n = F_{n+2} - 1$ **e.** The sum of the first $n - 2$ terms of the Fibonacci sequence is one less than the nth term.
21. a. $102.10 **b.** $80 \cdot 1.05^n$

Chapter Review

1. Monday **2.** $22.95 **3.** The question "What makes you come so soon?" is asked when the scholar arrives two hours later than usual. This makes no sense *unless* the "ten o'clock" is at night.
4. a. 15, 21, 28; neither **b.** 32, 27, 22; arithmetic **c.** 400, 200, 100; geometric **d.** 21, 34, 55; neither **e.** 17, 20, 23; arithmetic
f. 256, 1024, 4096; geometric **g.** 16, 20, 24; arithmetic
h. 125, 216, 343; neither **5. a.** $3n + 2$ if the sequence is arithmetic with difference of 3. **b.** 3^n if the sequence is geometric with ratio 3. **c.** $2^{n+1} - 1$ **6. a.** 1, 4, 7, 10, 13

b. 2, 6, 12, 20, 30 **c.** 3, 7, 11, 15, 19 **7. a.** 10,100 **b.** 10,201
8. a. $5 + 3 = 8$; which is not odd. **b.** False; for example, 19 is odd and it ends in 9. **c.** True; the sum of any two even numbers, $2m$ and $2n$, is even because $2m + 2n = 2(m + n)$
9. Answers vary.

16	3	2	13
5	10	11	8
9	6	7	12
4	15	14	1

10. 26 **11. a.** 2^{60} **b.** 25

12. 21 posts **13.** 44,000,000 **14.** 20 **15.** 39 **16.** 235
17. Between the 7th and 8th day. **18.** 4 **19.** 10 cm, 20 cm, 60 cm
20. 12 **21.** $n - m + 1$, answers vary. **22.** Answers vary. For example, fill the 4-cup pot and empty it into the 7-cup pot. Repeat. There is now 1 cup in the 4-cup pot. Empty the 7-cup pot and pour the 1 cup into the 7-cup pot. Fill the 4-cup pot and empty it into the 7-cup pot. It will now contain 5 cups. **23.** $10,100; n(n + 1)$ **24. a.** A possible pattern is that each successive figure is constructed by adjoining another pentagon to the previous figure.

b. 5, 8, 11, 14 **c.** 302 **d.** $3n + 2$ **25. a.** The circled terms will constitute an arithmetic sequence because the common difference will be twice the difference in the original sequence.
b. The new sequence will be a geometric sequence because the ratio will be the square of the ratio of the original sequence. **26.** If the sequence is $a_1, a_2, a_3, a_4, \ldots$ to find the first term we substitute $n = 1$ and get $1^2 - 1$ or 0, so $a_1 = 0$. For $n = 2$, we get $2^2 - 2$ or 2. Thus, $a_1 + a_2 = 2$; hence $a_2 = 2$. For $n = 3, a_1 + a_2 + a_3 = 3^2 - 3 = 6$. Substituting for a_1 and a_2, we get $a_3 = 6 - 2 = 4$. For $n = 4, a_1 + a_2 + a_3 + a_4 = 4^2 - 4 = 12$. Substituting for a_1, a_2, and a_3, we get $0 + 2 + 4 + a_4 = 12$. Hence, $a_4 = 6$.

27. a. 7, 20 **b.** 13, 150 **c.** $\frac{a - b}{2}, \frac{a + b}{2}$

Answers to Now Try This

1. In Figure 1, we have $1 + 100 = 101$. To obtain each successive pair from the previous one, we add 1 and subtract 1 and hence the sum does not change. Gauss's approach for the sum of squares does not work because the sums change; for example, $1^2 + 100^2 \neq 2^2 + 99^2$. **2.** First approach:
$25 + 26 + 27 + \ldots + 120 = (1 + 2 + 3 + \ldots + 25 + 26 + 27 + \ldots + 120) - (1 + 2 + 3 + \ldots + 24) =$
$\frac{(1 + 120) \cdot 120}{2} - \frac{(1 + 24) \cdot 24}{2} = 121 \cdot 60 - 25 \cdot 12 = 6960$
Second approach:
There are $120 - 24$ or 96 terms in the sum. Hence, using Gauss's approach, the sum equals $\frac{(25 + 120) \cdot 96}{2}$ or 6960. **3.** The first person played with 15 people; the second played with 14 because his game with the first person was already counted and so one. Thus, the total number of games played is $15 + 14 + 13 + \ldots + 1$, which using Gauss's approach is $\left(\frac{15 + 1}{2}\right) \cdot 15$ or 120. **4.** 23 floors; strategies vary. **5. a.** Answers

vary. For example, the next three terms could be △, △, ○. **b.** The pattern could be one circle, two triangles, one circle, two triangles, and so on.   **6. a.** Inductive reasoning   **b.** The next several numbers also work.   **c.** If $x = 11$, then $11^2 + 11 + 11$ is not prime because it is divisible by 11.   **7.** The following diagram shows the number of paths from A to every vertex and finally to B.

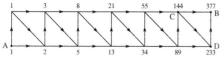

The pattern follows the Fibonacci sequence. Notice that to get to point B, we need to pass either through point C or through point D. To every path through C, there is only one way to get to point B without passing through D, that is, 144 possible paths. Thus, the number of paths to B is $144 + 233$ or 377. This reasoning applies to every vertex other than the first two vertices.

8. a. After 10 hours, there are $2 \cdot 3^{10} = 118{,}098$ bacteria, and after n hours, there are $2 \cdot 3^n$ bacteria.   **b.** After 10 hours, there are $2 + 10 \cdot 3 = 32$ bacteria, and after n hours, there are $2 + n \cdot 3$ bacteria. We can see that after only 10 hours geometric growth is much faster than arithmetic growth.   **9.** $10 \cdot 11$ or 110; $n(n + 1)$

Answer to the Preliminary Problem

Jill takes $1 + 2 + 3 + \ldots 10$, or 55 coins from the 10 boxes. If all the coins were genuine, the 55 coins would weigh $55 \cdot 2$ oz. or 110 oz. If the first box contained all the fake coins, the weight of all the coins would be $110 - 1$, or 109 oz. If the second box contained all the fake coins, the weight of all the coins would be $110 - 2$ or 108 oz. Thus, if all the 55 coins weigh 104 oz., Jill would write $104 = 110 - 6$ and she would know that the sixth box contains the fake coins. In general, if the coins weigh $110 - n$ oz., then the nth box contains the counterfeit coins.

Credits

Credits are listed in the order of appearance.

Text Credits

Excerpts from Standards for Mathematical Practice. Copyright by Common Core State Standards Initiative. Used by permission of Common Core State Standards Initiative.

Excerpt from Standards for Mathematical Practice. Copyright by Common Core State Standards Initiative. Used by permission of Common Core State Standards Initiative.

Excerpt from CCSS.Math.Practice.MP1 and MP3, Standards for Mathematical Practice. Copyright by Common Core State Standards Initiative. Used by permission of Common Core State Standards Initiative.

Excerpt from CCSS.Math.Practice.MP1 and MP.4, Standards for Mathematical Practice. Copyright by Common Core State Standards Initiative. Used by permission of Common Core State Standards Initiative. Randall Inners Charles, enVisionMATH, Grade 4 © 2012. Printed and Electronically reproduced by permission of Pearson Education, Inc., Upper Saddle River, New Jersey.

Randall Inners Charles, MATHEMATICS Common Core, Course 1, © 2013. Printed and Electronically reproduced by permission of Pearson Education, Inc., Upper Saddle River, New Jersey. Randall Inners Charles, enVisionMATH, Grade 4 © 2012. Printed and Electronically reproduced by permission of Pearson Education, Inc., Upper Saddle River, New Jersey.

MATHEMATICS Common Core, Course 1, © 2013. Printed and Electronically reproduced by permission of Pearson Education, Inc., Upper Saddle River, New Jersey.

Excerpt from Standards for Mathematical Practice. Copyright by Common Core State Standards Initiative. Used by permission of Common Core State Standards Initiative.

Image Credits

Sebastian Duda/Shutterstock

AP Images

Pearson Education

Pearson Education

Rational Numbers and Proportional Reasoning

1 The Set of Rational Numbers

2 Addition, Subtraction, and Estimation with Rational Numbers

3 Multiplication, Division, and Estimation with Rational Numbers

4 Proportional Reasoning

Preliminary Problem

A special rubber washer is made with two holes cut out as pictured. The area of the smaller of the two holes is $\frac{1}{7}$ of the whole piece of rubber while the area of the larger hole is $\frac{1}{4}$ of the whole. If the area of the original piece of rubber was $1\frac{3}{8}$ in^2, what is the area of the finished washer?

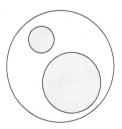

If needed, see Hint before the Chapter Summary.

From Chapter 6 of *A Problem Solving Approach to Mathematics*, Twelfth Edition. Rick Billstein, Shlomo Libeskind, Johnny W. Lott, and Barbara Boschmans. Copyright © 2016 by Pearson Education, Inc. All rights reserved.

Integers such as ⁻5 were invented to solve equations like $x + 5 = 0$. Similarly, a different type of number is needed to solve the equation $2x = 1$. We need notation for this new number. If multiplication is to work with this new type of number as with whole numbers, then $2x = x + x = 1$. In other words, the number $\frac{1}{2}$ (*one-half*) created to solve the equation must have the property that when added to itself, the result is 1. It is an element of the set of numbers of the form $\frac{a}{b}$, where $b \neq 0$ and a and b are integers. More generally, numbers of the form $\frac{a}{b}$ are solutions to equations of the form $bx = a$. This set Q of **rational numbers** is defined as follows:

$$Q = \left\{ \frac{a}{b} \,\middle|\, a \text{ and } b \text{ are integers and } b \neq 0 \right\}$$

Each member of Q is a *fraction*. In general, fractions are of the form $\frac{a}{b}$, where $b \neq 0$ but a and b are not necessarily integers. Each element $\frac{a}{b}$ of set Q has a as the **numerator** and b as the **denominator**.

The English words used for denominators of rational numbers are similar to words to tell "order," for example, the *fourth* person in a line, and the glass is three-fourths full. In contrast, $\frac{3}{4}$ is read "out of four parts, (take) three" in Chinese. The Chinese model enforces the idea of partitioning quantities into equal parts and choosing some number of these parts. The concept of sharing quantities and comparing sizes of shares provides entry points to introduce students to rational numbers.

 As early as grade 3 in the *Common Core Standards*, we find that students should "develop an understanding of fractions, beginning with unit fractions . . . view fractions as being built out of unit fractions . . . use fractions along with visual fraction models to represent parts of a whole." (p. 21) Additionally by grade 4, students should "understand a fraction as a number on the number line." (p. 24)

> **REMARK** A unit fraction has a numerator of 1.

1 The Set of Rational Numbers

1 Objectives

Students will be able to understand and explain

- Different representations for rational numbers.
- Equal fractions, equivalent fractions, and the simplest form of fractions.
- Ordering of rational numbers.
- Denseness property of rational numbers.

The rational number $\frac{a}{b}$ may also be represented as a/b or $a \div b$. The word *fraction* is derived from the Latin word *fractus*, meaning "broken." The word *numerator* comes from a Latin word meaning "numberer," and *denominator* comes from a Latin word meaning "namer." Frequently it is only in the upper grades of middle school that students begin to use integers for the parts of rational numbers, but prospective teachers should know and recognize that rational numbers are negative as well as positive and zero. Some uses of rational numbers that will be considered in this chapter are seen in Table 1.

Table 1	
Use	**Example**
Division problem or solution to a multiplication problem	The solution to $2x = 3$ is $\frac{3}{2}$.
Portion, or part, of a whole	Joe received $\frac{1}{2}$ of Mary's salary each month for alimony.
Ratio	The ratio of Republicans to Democrats on a Senate committee is three to five.
Probability	When you toss a fair coin, the probability of getting heads is $\frac{1}{2}$.

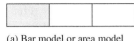

(a) Bar model or area model

0   1

(b) Number-line model

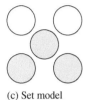

(c) Set model

Figure 1

Figure 1 illustrates the use of rational numbers as equal-sized parts of a whole in part (a), a distance on a number line in part (b), and a part of a given set in part (c). The simplest representation is from part (a) where 1 part of 3 equal-sized parts is shaded. The fractional representation for this part is $\frac{1}{3}$ where *the entire bar represents 1 unit and the shaded part is $\frac{1}{3}$ of the unit whole.* [Later the bar model of part (a) will be extended to an area model where the shape may be different than the rectangular bar. Additionally, the bar model is helpful when we consider proportional reasoning later in the chapter.]

An extension of the thinking in the bar model is seen in the remaining parts of Figure 1. For example, part (b) could represent two one-thirds of the unit length, or two-thirds of the unit segment. Part (c) could represent three one-fifths of the whole set, or three-fifths of the whole set.

Early student exposure to rational numbers as fractions usually takes the form of description rather than mathematical notation. They hear phrases such as "one-half of a pizza," "one-third of a cake," or "three-fourths of a pie." They encounter such questions as "If three identical fruit bars are distributed equally among four friends, how much does each receive?" The answer is that each receives $\frac{3}{4}$ of a bar.

When rational numbers are introduced as fractions that represent a part of a whole, we must pay attention to the whole from which a rational number is derived. For example, if we talk about $\frac{3}{4}$ of a pizza, then the amount of pizza depends on the size of the pizza, for example, 10" or 12", and the fractional part, $\frac{3}{4}$.

To understand the meaning of any fraction, $\frac{a}{b}$, where $a, b \in W$ and $b \neq 0$, using the parts-to-whole model, we must consider each of the following:

1. The *whole* being considered.
2. The number b of equal-size parts into which the whole has been divided.
3. The number a of parts of the whole that are selected.

A fraction $\frac{a}{b}$, where $0 \leq a < b$, is a **proper fraction**. A proper fraction is less than 1. For example, $\frac{4}{7}$ is a proper fraction, but $\frac{7}{4}, \frac{4}{4}$, and $\frac{9}{7}$ are not; $\frac{7}{4}$ is an **improper fraction**. In general $\frac{a}{b}$ is an improper fraction if $a \geq b > 0$. An improper fraction is greater than or equal to 1.

Egyptian Symbol for 1/3

The early Egyptian numeration system had symbols for fractions with numerators of 1 (unit fractions). Most fractions with other numerators were expressed as a sum of unit fractions, for example, $\frac{7}{12} = \frac{1}{3} + \frac{1}{4}$.

Fractions with denominator 60 or powers of 60 were seen in Babylon about 2000 BCE, where 12,35 meant $12 + \frac{35}{60}$. This usage was adopted by the Greek astronomer Ptolemy (approximately 125 CE), was used in Islamic and European countries, and is presently used in the measurements of angles.

The modern notation for fractions—a bar between numerator and denominator—is of Hindu origin. It came into general use in Europe in sixteenth-century books.

Other meanings of fractions can be considered using *whole-to-part* and *part-to-part* references. For example whole-to-part might give us an improper fraction and part-to-part allows us to write, for example, the ratio of the number of band students in the school to the number of non-band students in the school.

 The *Common Core Standards* state that grade 3 students should "express whole numbers as fractions, and recognize fractions that are equivalent to whole numbers." (p. 24)

Later students learn that every integer n can be represented as a rational number because $n = \dfrac{nk}{k}$, where k is any nonzero integer. In particular, $0 = \dfrac{0 \cdot k}{k} = \dfrac{0}{k}$.

Rational Numbers on a Number Line

 In the grade 3 *Common Core Standards*, we find the following standard:

Represent a fraction $\dfrac{a}{b}$ on a number line by marking off a lengths of $\dfrac{1}{b}$ from 0. Recognize that the resulting interval has size $\dfrac{a}{b}$ and that its endpoint locates the number $\dfrac{a}{b}$ on the number line. (p. 24)

Once the integers 0 and 1 are assigned to points on a line, the unit segment is defined and every other rational number is assigned to a specific point. For example, to represent $\dfrac{3}{4}$ on the number line, we divide the segment from 0 to 1 into 4 segments of equal length and mark the line accordingly. Then, starting from 0, we count 3 of these segments and stop at the mark corresponding to the right endpoint of the third segment to obtain the point assigned to the rational number $\dfrac{3}{4}$.

 The *Common Core Standards* for grade 3 talk about a lengths of $\dfrac{1}{b}$, where a and b are both positive (or a could be 0), but we also use integers as numerators or denominators of rational numbers, though negative integers are not used to talk about lengths. We think of the positive fractions described in the *Common Core Standards* as marked on a number line on the right side, and as with integers, we can consider the opposites of those fractions reflected over 0 to the left side of the number line as seen in Figure 2. We adopt two conventions for negative fractions, either $\dfrac{^-a}{b}$ or $-\dfrac{a}{b}$.

Figure 2 shows the points that correspond to $^-2, -\dfrac{5}{4} = \dfrac{^-5}{4}, ^-1, -\dfrac{3}{4} = \dfrac{^-3}{4}, 0, \dfrac{3}{4}, 1, \dfrac{5}{4}$, and 2.

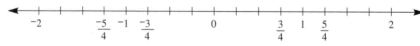

Figure 2

Example 1

Describe how to locate the following numbers on the number line of Figure 3: $\dfrac{1}{2}, -\dfrac{1}{2}, \dfrac{7}{4}$, and $-\dfrac{7}{4}$.

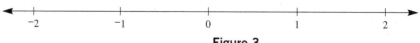

Figure 3

Solution To decide how to find the point on the number line representing $\frac{1}{2}$, we consider the unit length 1. We find the point that would be the rightmost endpoint of the segment starting at 0 and ending at the point marking the middle of the unit segment. This is seen in Figure 4.

To find the point on the number line representing $-\frac{1}{2}$, we find the mirror image of $\frac{1}{2}$ on the left side of the number line as seen in Figure 4 when it is reflected in 0.

To find the location of $-\frac{7}{4}$, we first find the image or $\frac{7}{4}$ on the right side of 0 by marking the unit length in four parts, duplicating the four parts to mark points between 1 and 2, and then counting 7 of those parts starting at 0. Once $\frac{7}{4}$ is found on the right side of 0, then its reflection image in 0 gives the point where $-\frac{7}{4} = \frac{^-7}{4}$ should be marked. This is seen in Figure 4.

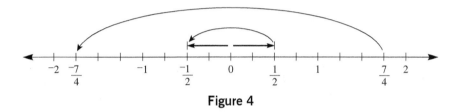

Figure 4

Equivalent or Equal Fractions

The grade 4 *Common Core Standards* state that students should be able to:

Explain why a fraction $\frac{a}{b}$ is equivalent to a fraction $\frac{na}{nb}$ by using visual fraction models with attention to how the number and the size of the parts differ even though the two fractions themselves are the same size. Use the principle to recognize and generate equivalent fractions. (p. 30)

Fractions may be introduced in the classroom through a concrete activity such as paperfolding. In Figure 5(a), 1 of 3 congruent parts, or $\frac{1}{3}$, is shaded. In this case, the whole is the rectangle. In Figure 5(b), each of the thirds has been folded in half so that now we have 6 sections, and 2 of 6 congruent parts, or $\frac{2}{6}$, are shaded. Thus, both $\frac{1}{3}$ and $\frac{2}{6}$ represent exactly the same shaded portion. Although the symbols $\frac{1}{3}$ and $\frac{2}{6}$ do not look alike, they represent the same rational number and are **equivalent fractions**, or **equal fractions**. *Equivalent fractions are numbers that represent the same point on a number line.* Because they represent equal amounts, we write $\frac{1}{3} = \frac{2}{6}$ and say that "$\frac{1}{3}$ equals $\frac{2}{6}$."

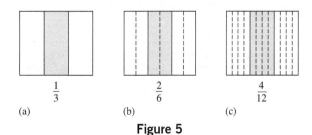

Figure 5

Figure 5(c) shows the rectangle with each of the original thirds folded into 4 equal parts with 4 of the 12 parts now shaded. Thus, $\frac{1}{3}$ is equal to $\frac{4}{12}$ because the same portion of the model is shaded. Similarly, we could illustrate that $\frac{1}{3}, \frac{2}{6}, \frac{3}{9}, \frac{4}{12}, \frac{5}{15}, \ldots$ are all equal.

Fraction strips can be used for generating equivalent fractions, as seen on the student page below. This technique makes use of the Fundamental Law of Fractions, which can be stated as follows: *The value of a fraction does not change if its numerator and denominator are multiplied by the same nonzero integer.* Under certain assumptions this Law of Fractions can be proved and is stated as a theorem.

Theorem 1: Fundamental Law of Fractions

If $\frac{a}{b}$ is a fraction and n a nonzero number, then $\frac{a}{b} = \frac{an}{bn}$.

School Book Page   Equivalent Fractions

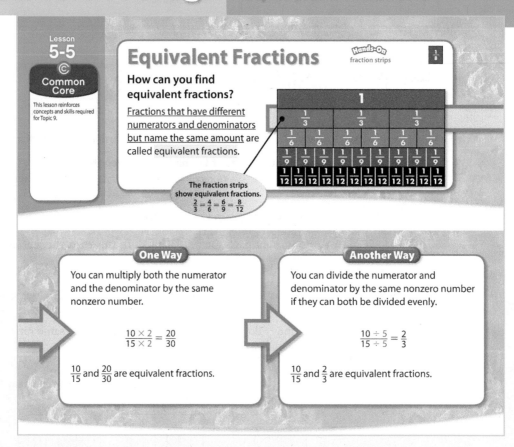

Source: pp. 132–133; From enVisionMATH Common Core (Grade 6). Copyright © 2012 Pearson Education, Inc., or its affiliates. Used by permission. All Rights Reserved.

From the Fundamental Law of Fractions, $\dfrac{7}{^-15} = \dfrac{^-7}{15}$ because $\dfrac{7}{^-15} = \dfrac{7(^-1)}{^-15(^-1)} = \dfrac{^-7}{15}$. Similarly, $\dfrac{a}{^-b} = \dfrac{^-a}{b}$. *The form* $\dfrac{^-a}{b}$, *where b is a positive number, is usually preferred.*

Simplifying Fractions

Theorem 1 implies that if d is a common factor of a and b, then $\dfrac{a}{b} = \dfrac{a \div d}{b \div d}$. Because d is a divisor of both a and b, we know that $a \div d = m$ is a nonzero integer. Also $b \div d = n$ is a nonzero integer. Thus, we have the following:

$$\frac{a}{b} = \frac{a \div d}{b \div d} = \frac{m}{n}$$

Hence, we have two equivalent forms of the same rational number. A numerical example is given next.

$$\frac{60}{210} = \frac{60 \div 10}{210 \div 10} = \frac{6}{21}$$

This process is referred to as **simplifying a fraction**. A slightly different look is seen below.

$$\frac{60}{210} = \frac{6 \cdot 10}{21 \cdot 10} = \frac{6}{21}$$

Also,

$$\frac{6}{21} = \frac{2 \cdot 3}{7 \cdot 3} = \frac{2}{7}.$$

We can simplify $\dfrac{60}{210}$ because the numerator and denominator have a common factor of 10. We can simplify $\dfrac{6}{21}$ because 6 and 21 have a common factor of 3. However, we cannot simplify $\dfrac{2}{7}$ because 2 and 7 have no positive common factor other than 1. We could also simplify $\dfrac{60}{210}$ in one step: $\dfrac{60}{210} = \dfrac{2 \cdot 30}{7 \cdot 30} = \dfrac{2}{7}$. Notice that $\dfrac{2}{7}$ is the **simplest form** of $\dfrac{60}{210}$ because both 60 and 210 have been divided by their greatest common divisor, 30.

Suppose we wanted to simplify the rational number $-\dfrac{60}{210}$ or its equivalent $\dfrac{^-60}{210}$. The problem could be addressed by simplifying $\dfrac{60}{210}$ as above and then taking the opposite of the result. This could be thought of as considering $-\dfrac{60}{210} = -\left|\dfrac{60}{210}\right| = -\dfrac{2}{7}$. Note that the same result could have been found using $-\dfrac{60}{210} = -\dfrac{|60|}{|210|} = -\dfrac{2}{7}$.

Definition of Simplest Form

A rational number $\dfrac{a}{b}$ is in **simplest form** or **lowest terms** if, and only if, GCD$(a, b) = 1$, that is, if a and b have no common factor greater than 1.

Scientific/fraction calculators can simplify fractions. For example, to simplify $\frac{6}{12}$, we enter $\boxed{6}\boxed{/}\boxed{1}\boxed{2}$ and press $\boxed{\text{SIMP}}\boxed{=}$, and $\frac{3}{6}$ appears on the screen. At this point, an indicator tells us that this is not in simplest form, so we press $\boxed{\text{SIMP}}\boxed{=}$ again to obtain $\frac{1}{2}$. At any time, we can view the factor that was removed by pressing the $\boxed{x\bigcirc y}$ key.

Example 2

Find a value for x such that $\frac{12}{42} = \frac{x}{210}$.

Solution   We use the mathematical practice of reasoning to see that because $210 \div 42 = 5$, we can use the Fundamental Law of Fractions to obtain $\frac{12}{42} = \frac{12 \cdot 5}{42 \cdot 5} = \frac{60}{210}$. Hence, $\frac{x}{210} = \frac{60}{210}$, and $x = 60$.

Alternative approach: $\frac{12}{42} = \frac{2 \cdot 6}{7 \cdot 6} = \frac{2}{7} = \frac{2 \cdot 30}{7 \cdot 30} = \frac{60}{210}$. Therefore $x = 60$.

Example 3

Write each of the following fractions in simplest form if they are not already.

a. $\dfrac{28ab^2}{42a^2b^2}$ b. $\dfrac{(a+b)^2}{3a+3b}$ c. $\dfrac{x^2+x}{x+1}$ d. $\dfrac{3+x^2}{3x^2}$

e. $\dfrac{3+3x^2}{3x^2}$ f. $\dfrac{a^2-b^2}{a-b}$ g. $\dfrac{a^2+b^2}{a+b}$

Solution

a. $\dfrac{28ab^2}{42a^2b^2} = \dfrac{2(14ab^2)}{3a(14ab^2)} = \dfrac{2}{3a}$

b. $\dfrac{(a+b)^2}{3a+3b} = \dfrac{(a+b)(a+b)}{3(a+b)} = \dfrac{a+b}{3}$

c. $\dfrac{x^2+x}{x+1} = \dfrac{x(x+1)}{x+1} = \dfrac{x(x+1)}{1(x+1)} = \dfrac{x}{1} = x$

d. $\dfrac{3+x^2}{3x^2}$ cannot be simplified because $3+x^2$ and $3x^2$ have no factors in common except 1.

e. $\dfrac{3+3x^2}{3x^2} = \dfrac{3(1+x^2)}{3x^2} = \dfrac{1+x^2}{x^2}$

f. The difference of squares formula: $a^2 - b^2 = (a-b)(a+b)$. Thus,
$$\frac{a^2-b^2}{a-b} = \frac{(a-b)(a+b)}{(a-b)1} = \frac{a+b}{1} = a+b.$$

g. The fraction is already in simplest form because a^2+b^2 does not have $(a+b)$ as a factor. Notice that $a^2 + b^2 \neq (a+b)^2$.

When an algebraic expression is written as a fraction, the denominator may not be 0. Thus, when the fraction is simplified, this restriction has to be maintained. For example, in part (c) of Example 3, $\dfrac{x^2 + x}{x + 1} = x$ if $x \neq {}^-1$, and in part (f) the result holds if $a - b \neq 0$, that is, if $a \neq b$.

Some students think of the Fundamental Law of Fractions as a *cancellation property* and "simplify" an expression like $\dfrac{6 + a^2}{3a}$ by thinking of it as $\dfrac{2 \cdot 3 + a \cdot a}{3a}$ and "canceling" equal numbers in the products to obtain $2 + a$ as the answer. Emphasizing the factor approach that neither 3 nor a is a factor of $6 + a^2$ may help to avoid such mistakes.

Equality of Fractions

We use three equivalent methods to show that two fractions, such as $\dfrac{12}{42}$ and $\dfrac{10}{35}$, are equal.

1. Simplify both fractions to simplest form.

$$\frac{12}{42} = \frac{2^2 \cdot 3}{2 \cdot 3 \cdot 7} = \frac{2}{7} \quad \text{and} \quad \frac{10}{35} = \frac{5 \cdot 2}{5 \cdot 7} = \frac{2}{7}$$

Thus,

$$\frac{12}{42} = \frac{10}{35}.$$

2. Rewrite both fractions with the same least common denominator. Since
   $\text{LCM}(42, 35) = 210$, then

$$\frac{12}{42} = \frac{60}{210} \quad \text{and} \quad \frac{10}{35} = \frac{60}{210}.$$

Thus,

$$\frac{12}{42} = \frac{10}{35}.$$

3. Rewrite both fractions with a common denominator (not necessarily the least). A common
   multiple of 42 and 35 may be found by finding the product $42 \cdot 35 = 1470$.

$$\frac{12}{42} = \frac{420}{1470} \quad \text{and} \quad \frac{10}{35} = \frac{420}{1470}$$

Hence,

$$\frac{12}{42} = \frac{10}{35}.$$

The third method suggests a general algorithm for determining whether two fractions $\dfrac{a}{b}$ and $\dfrac{c}{d}$ are equal. Rewrite both fractions with common denominator bd; that is,

$$\frac{a}{b} = \frac{ad}{bd} \quad \text{and} \quad \frac{c}{d} = \frac{bc}{bd}.$$

Because the denominators are the same, $\dfrac{ad}{bd} = \dfrac{bc}{bd}$ if, and only if, $ad = bc$. For example, $\dfrac{24}{36} = \dfrac{6}{9}$ because $24 \cdot 9 = 216 = 36 \cdot 6$. In general, the following theorem holds.

Theorem 2:   Equality of Fractions

Two fractions $\frac{a}{b}$ and $\frac{c}{d}$, with $b \neq 0$ and $d \neq 0$, are equal if, and only if, $ad = bc$.

Using a calculator, we determine whether two fractions are equal by using Theorem 2. Since both $\boxed{2}\,\boxed{\times}\,\boxed{2}\,\boxed{1}\,\boxed{9}\,\boxed{6}\,\boxed{=}$ and $\boxed{4}\,\boxed{\times}\,\boxed{1}\,\boxed{0}\,\boxed{9}\,\boxed{8}\,\boxed{=}$ yield a display of 4392, we see that $\frac{2}{4} = \frac{1098}{2196}$.

Ordering Rational Numbers

The grade 4 *Common Core Standards* state that a student should compare two fractions with different numerators and different denominators, e.g., by creating common denominators or numerators, or by comparing to a benchmark fraction such as $\frac{1}{2}$. Recognize that comparisons are valid only when two fractions refer to the same whole. (p. 30)

Example 4

Jim claims that $\frac{1}{3} > \frac{1}{2}$ because in Figure 6 the shaded portion for $\frac{1}{3}$ is larger than the shaded portion for $\frac{1}{2}$. How would you help him?

 Solution   Jim needs to understand as noted in the *Common Core Standards* that comparisons of two fractions are valid only when they refer to the same whole. In Figure 6, the circle is clearly larger than the square so the two wholes are not the same.

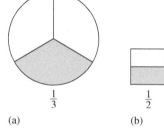

(a)   (b)

Figure 6

In order to compare two fractions referring to the same whole, it is easiest to compare fractions with like denominators. Children know that $\frac{7}{8} > \frac{5}{8}$ because if a pizza is divided into 8 parts of equal size, then 7 parts of the pizza is more than 5 parts. Similarly, $\frac{3}{7} < \frac{4}{7}$. Thus, given two fractions with common positive denominators, the one with the greater numerator is the greater fraction. To make ordering of rational numbers consistent with the ordering of whole numbers and integers we have the following definition.

Definition of Greater Than for Rational Numbers with Like Denominators

If a, b, and c are integers and $b > 0$, then $\frac{a}{b} > \frac{c}{b}$ if, and only if, $a > c$.

To compare fractions with unlike denominators, some students may incorrectly reason that $\frac{1}{8} > \frac{1}{7}$ because 8 is greater than 7. In another case, they might falsely believe that $\frac{6}{7}$ is equal to $\frac{7}{8}$ because in both fractions the difference between the numerator and the denominator is 1. Comparing positive fractions with unlike denominators may be aided by using fraction strips to compare the fractions visually. For example, consider the fractions $\frac{4}{5}$ and $\frac{11}{12}$ shown in Figure 7.

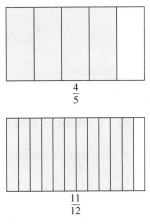

$$\frac{4}{5}$$

$$\frac{11}{12}$$

Figure 7

From Figure 7, students see that each fraction is one piece less than the same-size whole unit. However, they see that the missing piece for $\frac{11}{12}$ is smaller than the missing piece for $\frac{4}{5}$, so $\frac{11}{12}$ must be greater than $\frac{4}{5}$.

Comparing any fractions with unlike denominators can be accomplished by rewriting the fractions with the same positive common denominator. Using the common denominator bd, we can write the fractions $\frac{a}{b}$ and $\frac{c}{d}$ as $\frac{ad}{bd}$ and $\frac{bc}{bd}$. Because $b > 0$ and $d > 0$, then $bd > 0$; and we have the following:

$$\frac{a}{b} > \frac{c}{d} \text{ if, and only if, } \frac{ad}{bd} > \frac{bc}{bd}; \quad \text{and} \quad \frac{ad}{bd} > \frac{bc}{bd} \text{ if, and only if, } ad > bc.$$

Therefore, we have the following theorem.

Theorem 3

If $a, b, c,$ and d are integers with $b > 0$ and $d > 0$, then $\frac{a}{b} > \frac{c}{d}$ if, and only if, $ad > bc$.

Next consider two fractions with both numerators and denominators positive and with numerators that are the same. For example, consider $\frac{3}{4}$ and $\frac{3}{10}$. If the whole is the same for both fractions, this means that we have three $\frac{1}{4}$s and three $\frac{1}{10}$s. Because $\frac{1}{4}$ is greater than $\frac{1}{10}$, three of the larger parts is greater than three of the smaller parts. Thus, $\frac{3}{4} > \frac{3}{10}$.

Denseness of Rational Numbers

The set of rational numbers has a property unlike the set of whole numbers and the set of integers. Consider $\frac{1}{2}$ and $\frac{2}{3}$. To find a rational number between $\frac{1}{2}$ and $\frac{2}{3}$, we first rewrite the fractions with a common denominator, as $\frac{3}{6}$ and $\frac{4}{6}$. Because there is no whole number between the numerators 3 and 4, we next find two fractions equal, respectively, to $\frac{1}{2}$ and $\frac{2}{3}$ with greater denominators. For example, $\frac{1}{2} = \frac{6}{12}$ and $\frac{2}{3} = \frac{8}{12}$, and $\frac{7}{12}$ is between the two fractions $\frac{6}{12}$ and $\frac{8}{12}$. So $\frac{7}{12}$ is between $\frac{1}{2}$ and $\frac{2}{3}$. This property is generalized as follows and stated as a theorem.

> **Theorem 4:   Denseness Property for Rational Numbers**
>
> Given any two different rational numbers $\frac{a}{b}$ and $\frac{c}{d}$, there is another rational number between these two numbers.

▶ NOW TRY THIS 1

Explain why there are infinitely many rational numbers between any two rational numbers.

Example 5

 a. Find two fractions between $\frac{7}{18}$ and $\frac{1}{2}$.

 b. Show that the sequence $\frac{1}{2}, \frac{2}{3}, \frac{3}{4}, \frac{4}{5}, \ldots, \frac{n}{n+1} \ldots$, where $n \in N$, is an *increasing sequence*; that is, that each term starting from the second term is greater than the preceding term.

Solution

 a. Because $\frac{1}{2} = \frac{1 \cdot 9}{2 \cdot 9} = \frac{9}{18}$, we see that $\frac{8}{18}$, or $\frac{4}{9}$, is between $\frac{7}{18}$ and $\frac{9}{18}$. To find another fraction between the given fractions, we find two fractions equal to $\frac{7}{18}$ and $\frac{9}{18}$, respectively, but with greater denominators; for example, $\frac{7}{18} = \frac{14}{36}$ and $\frac{9}{18} = \frac{18}{36}$.

 We now see that $\frac{15}{36}, \frac{16}{36}$, and $\frac{17}{36}$ are all between $\frac{14}{36}$ and $\frac{18}{36}$ and thus between $\frac{7}{18}$ and $\frac{1}{2}$.

 b. Because the nth term of the sequence is $\frac{n}{n+1}$, the next term is $\frac{n+1}{(n+1)+1}$, or $\frac{n+1}{n+2}$. We need to show that for all positive integers n, $\frac{n+1}{n+2} > \frac{n}{n+1}$.

 The terms of the sequence are positive. The inequality will be true if, and only if, $(n+1)(n+1) > n(n+2)$. This inequality is equivalent to

$$n^2 + 2n + 1 > n^2 + 2n$$
$$2n + 1 > 2n$$
$$1 > 0, \text{ which is true.}$$

Therefore we have an increasing sequence.

Another way to find a number between any two rational numbers involves adding numerators and adding denominators. In Example 5(a), to find a number between $\frac{7}{18}$ and $\frac{1}{2}$ we could add the numerators and add the denominators to produce $\frac{7+1}{18+2} = \frac{8}{20}$. We see that $\frac{7}{18} < \frac{8}{20}$ because $140 < 144$. Also, $\frac{8}{20} < \frac{1}{2}$ because $16 < 20$. The general property is stated in the following theorem and explored in Now Try This 2.

Theorem 5

Let $\frac{a}{b}$ and $\frac{c}{d}$ be any rational numbers with positive denominators such that $\frac{a}{b} < \frac{c}{d}$. Then,

$$\frac{a}{b} < \frac{a+c}{b+d} < \frac{c}{d}.$$

▶ **NOW TRY THIS 2**

Prove Theorem 5. $\left(\textit{Hint: Prove that } \frac{a}{b} < \frac{a+c}{b+d} \text{ and } \frac{a+c}{b+d} < \frac{c}{d}. \right)$

The proof of Theorem 5 suggested in Now Try This 2 also proves Theorem 4.

Assessment 1A

1. Write a sentence that illustrates the use of $\frac{7}{8}$ in each of the following ways.
   a. As a division problem
   b. As part of a whole
   c. As a ratio

2. For each of the following, write a fraction to approximate the shaded portion as part of the whole.

   a.    **b.**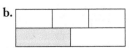

   c.   **d.**

3. If the entire rectangle is a whole, what fraction represents the shaded portion of the figure?

   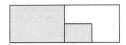

4. For each of the following four squares, write a fraction to describe the shaded portion. What property of fractions does the diagram illustrate?

   a.   **b.**   **c.**   **d.**

5. Based on your observations, could the shaded portions in the following figures represent the indicated fractions? If not, tell why.

   a.   **b.** 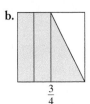   **c.**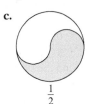

   $\frac{1}{4}$ $\frac{3}{4}$ $\frac{1}{2}$

6. In each case, subdivide the *whole* shown on the right to show the equivalent fraction.

a.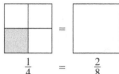
$$\frac{1}{4} = \frac{2}{8}$$

b.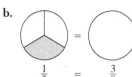
$$\frac{1}{3} = \frac{3}{9}$$

c.
$$\frac{1}{2} = \frac{3}{6}$$

7. Referring to the figure, represent each of the following quantities as a fraction.

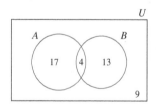

a. The dots in the interior of the circle as a part of all the dots
b. The dots in the interior of the rectangle as a part of all the dots
c. The dots in the intersection of the interiors of the rectangle and the circle as a part of all the dots
d. The dots outside the circular region but inside the rectangular region as part of all the dots

8. Use the Venn diagram pictured with A representing the people in an arts class and B representing the people in a botany class to express the fraction of elements in the indicated sets as a part of the universal set.

a. $A \cap B$ **b.** $A - B$
c. U **d.** $\overline{A \cap B}$

9. For each of the following fractions, write three equal fractions.

a. $\frac{2}{9}$ **b.** $\frac{^-2}{5}$

c. $\frac{0}{3}$ **d.** $\frac{a}{2}$

10. Find the simplest form for each of the following fractions.

a. $\frac{156}{93}$ **b.** $\frac{27}{45}$ **c.** $\frac{^-65}{91}$

11. For each of the following fractions, choose the expression in parentheses that equals or describes best the given fraction.

a. $\frac{0}{0}$ (1, undefined, 0)

b. $\frac{5}{0}$ (undefined, 5, 0)

c. $\frac{0}{5}$ (undefined, 5, 0)

d. $\frac{2 + a}{a}$ (2, 3, cannot be simplified)

e. $\frac{15 + x}{3x}$ $\left(\frac{5 + x}{x}, 5, \text{cannot be simplified}\right)$

12. Find the simplest form for each of the following fractions.
a. $\frac{a^2 - b^2}{3a + 3b}$ **b.** $\frac{14x^2 y}{63xy^2}$

13. Determine whether the following pairs are equal.
a. $\frac{3}{8}$ and $\frac{375}{1000}$ **b.** $\frac{18}{54}$ and $\frac{23}{69}$

14. Determine whether the following pairs are equal by changing both to have the same denominator.
a. $\frac{10}{16}$ and $\frac{12}{18}$ **b.** $\frac{^-21}{86}$ and $\frac{^-51}{215}$

15. Draw an area model to show that $\frac{3}{4} = \frac{6}{8}$.

16. If a fraction is equal to $\frac{3}{4}$ and the sum of the numerator and denominator is 84, what is the fraction?

17. Mr. Gomez filled his car's 16 gal gas tank. He took a trip and used $\frac{7}{8}$ of the gas.

a. Draw an arrow in the following figure to show what his gas gauge looked like after the trip:

b. How many gallons of gas were used?

18. Solve for x in each of the following.
a. $\frac{2}{3} = \frac{x}{16}$ **b.** $\frac{3}{4} = \frac{^-27}{x}$

19. For each of the following pairs of fractions, replace the comma with the correct symbol ($<, =, >$) to make a true statement:
a. $\frac{7}{8}, \frac{5}{6}$ **b.** $\frac{^-7}{8}, \frac{^-4}{5}$

20. Arrange each of the following in decreasing order.
a. $\frac{11}{22}, \frac{11}{16}, \frac{11}{13}$
b. $\frac{^-1}{5}, \frac{^-19}{36}, \frac{^-17}{30}$

21. For each of the following, find two rational numbers between the given fractions.
a. $\frac{3}{7}$ and $\frac{4}{7}$
b. $\frac{^-7}{9}$ and $\frac{^-8}{9}$

22. a. 6 oz is what part of a pound? A ton?
b. A dime is what fraction of a dollar?
c. 15 min is what fraction of an hour?
d. 8 hr is what fraction of a day?

23. Determine whether the following is true: If a, b, c are integers and $b < 0$, then $\dfrac{a}{b} > \dfrac{c}{b}$ if, and only if, $a > c$.

24. Based on your visual observation write a fraction to represent the shaded portion.

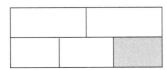

25. Fill in missing numbers for $x, y, z,$ and w to create a sequence with each term being greater than the preceding term.

a. $\dfrac{1}{3}, \dfrac{x}{4}, \dfrac{y}{5}, \dfrac{z}{6}$

b. $\dfrac{^-3}{x}, \dfrac{^-4}{y}, \dfrac{^-5}{z}, \dfrac{^-6}{w}$

26. Explain why in the Fundamental Law of Fractions (Theorem 1), n must be nonzero.

27. Prove that any integer n can be written as a fraction.

28. A typical English ruler is marked in sixteenths of an inch. Sketch a ruler marking $\dfrac{3}{8}$ in.

29. Ten light bulbs were in a chandelier. One-fifth of the bulbs were not shining. How many light bulbs were not shining?

30. At a party, there were 35 guests. Two-fifths of the guests were men. What fraction of the guests were women?

Assessment 1B

1. Write a sentence that illustrates the use of $\dfrac{7}{10}$ in each of the following ways:
  a. As a division problem
  b. As part of a whole
  c. As a ratio

2. For each of the following, write a fraction to approximate the shaded portion of the whole.

a.

b.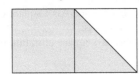

c.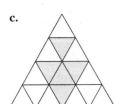

d.

3. If the entire rectangle is a whole, what fraction represents the shaded portion of the figure?

4. Complete each of the following figures so that it illustrates $\dfrac{3}{5}$.

a.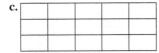

b.

c.

d.

e.

f.

5. Based on your observations, could the shaded portions in the following figures represent the indicated fractions? Tell why.

a. $\dfrac{1}{2}$

b. $\dfrac{1}{8}$

c. 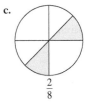 $\dfrac{2}{8}$

6. If each of the following models represents the given fraction, draw a model that represents the *whole*. Shade your answer.

a. 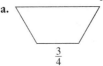 $\dfrac{3}{4}$

b. $\dfrac{4}{3}$

c. $\dfrac{1}{5}$

d. $\dfrac{1}{4}$

7. Referring to the figure, represent each of the following quantities as a fraction.

  a. The dots outside the circular region as a part of all the dots
  b. The dots outside the rectangular region as a part of all the dots
  c. The dots in the union of the rectangular and the circular regions as a part of all the dots
  d. The dots inside the circular region but outside the rectangular region as a part of all the dots.

8. Use the Venn diagram pictured with A representing the people in an algebra class and B representing the people in a biology class to express the fraction of elements in the indicated sets as a part of the universal set.

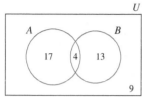

a. $A \cup B$ b. $A - \overline{B}$
c. $\varnothing$ d. $\overline{A \cup B}$

9. For each of the following, write three fractions equal to the given fractions.

a. $\dfrac{1}{3}$ b. $\dfrac{4}{5}$

c. $\dfrac{-3}{7}$ d. $\dfrac{a}{3}$

10. Find the simplest form for each of the following fractions.

a. $\dfrac{0}{68}$ b. $\dfrac{84^2}{91^2}$ c. $\dfrac{662}{703}$

11. For each of the following, choose the expression in parentheses that equals or describes best the given fraction.

a. $\dfrac{6 + x}{3x} \left(\dfrac{2 + x}{x}, 3, \text{cannot be simplified} \right)$

b. $\dfrac{2^6 + 2^5}{2^4 + 2^7} \left(1, \dfrac{2}{3}, \text{cannot be simplified} \right)$

c. $\dfrac{2^{100} + 2^{98}}{2^{100} - 2^{98}} \left(2^{196}, \dfrac{5}{3}, \text{too large to simplify} \right)$

12. Find the simplest form for each of the following fractions.

a. $\dfrac{a^2 + ab}{a + b}$ b. $\dfrac{a}{3a + ab}$

13. Determine whether the following pairs are equal.

a. $\dfrac{6}{16}$ and $\dfrac{3{,}750}{10{,}000}$ b. $\dfrac{17}{27}$ and $\dfrac{25}{45}$

14. Determine whether the following pairs are equal by changing both to the same denominator.

a. $\dfrac{3}{-12}$ and $\dfrac{-36}{144}$ b. $\dfrac{-21}{430}$ and $\dfrac{-51}{215}$

15. Draw an area model to show that $\dfrac{2}{3} = \dfrac{6}{9}$.

16. A board is needed that is exactly $\dfrac{11}{32}$ in. wide to fit a hole. Can a board that is $\dfrac{3}{8}$ in. be shaved down to fit the hole? If so, how much must be shaved from the board?

17. The following two parking meters are next to each other with the times left as shown. Which meter has more time left on it? How much more?

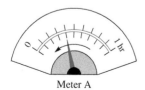
Meter A

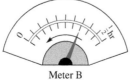
Meter B

18. Solve for x in each of the following.

a. $\dfrac{2}{3} = \dfrac{x}{18}$ b. $\dfrac{3}{x} = \dfrac{3x}{x^2}$

19. For each of the following pairs of fractions, replace the comma with the correct symbol $(<, =, >)$ to make a true statement.

a. $\dfrac{1}{-7}, \dfrac{1}{-8}$ b. $\dfrac{2}{5}, \dfrac{4}{10}$ c. $\dfrac{0}{7}, \dfrac{0}{17}$

20. For each of the following, find two rational numbers between the given fractions.

a. $\dfrac{5}{6}$ and $\dfrac{83}{100}$ b. $\dfrac{-1}{3}$ and $\dfrac{3}{4}$

21. a. 12 oz is what part of a pound?
    b. A nickel is what fraction of a dollar?
    c. 25 min is what fraction of an hour?
    d. 16 hr is what fraction of a 24-hr day?

22. Read each measurement as shown on the following ruler.

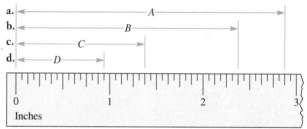

23. Fill in missing numbers for x, y, z, and w to create a sequence with each term being less than the preceding term.

a. $\dfrac{1}{3}, \dfrac{x}{4}, \dfrac{y}{5}, \dfrac{z}{6}$ b. $\dfrac{-3}{x}, \dfrac{-4}{y}, \dfrac{-5}{z}, \dfrac{-6}{w}$

24. Use the Fundamental Law of Fractions (Theorem 1) to show that 0 could be written in infinitely many ways.

25. Prove that a negative integer n can be written as a fraction with a positive denominator.

26. A typical metric ruler is marked in millimeters (mm) where

$1 \text{ mm} = \dfrac{1}{1000}$ m (where m is the designation of meter). How many millimeters would 5 meters be?

27. Ten light bulbs were in a chandelier. Three-fifth of the bulbs were shining. What fraction of the light bulbs were not shining?

28. At a party, there were 40 guests. One-fifth of the guests were men. What fraction of the guests were women?

29. Answer each of the following.
   a. If the area of the entire square is 1 square unit, find the area of each tangram piece.
   b. If the area of piece a is 1 square unit, find the area of each tangram piece.

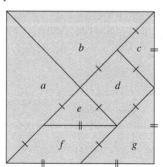

Mathematical Connections 1

Reasoning

1. Explain why 25 cents is one-fourth of a dollar, yet 15 minutes is one-fourth of an hour. Why should these one-fourths not be equal?

2. In each of two different fourth-grade classes, $\frac{1}{3}$ of the members are girls. Does each class have the same number of girls? Explain your answer.

3. Consider the set of all fractions equal to $\frac{1}{2}$. If you take any 10 of those fractions, add their numerators to obtain the numerator of a new fraction and add their denominators to obtain the denominator of a new fraction, how does the new fraction relate to $\frac{1}{2}$? Generalize what you found and explain.

4. Draw a Venn diagram showing the relationship among natural numbers, whole numbers, integers, and rational numbers. Use subset relations to explain your Venn diagram.

Open-Ended

5. Make three statements about yourself or your environment and use fractions in each. Explain why your statements are true. For example, your parents have three children, two of whom live at home; hence $\frac{2}{3}$ of their children live at home.

6. Consider the demographics of your class including gender and ethnicity. Write fractions to describe the demographics of the class.

7. Sketch four different windows having different numbers of window panes in each. Shade $\frac{3}{4}$ of the panes in each window.

Cooperative Learning

8. Assume that the shortest person in your group is 1 unit tall and do the following:
   a. Find rational numbers to approximately represent the heights of other members of the group.
   b. Make a number line and plot the rational number for each person ordered according to height.

9. Assume the tallest person in your group is 1 unit tall and do the following.
   a. Find rational numbers to approximately represent the heights of other members of the group.
   b. Make a number line and plot the rational number for each person ordered according to height.

Connecting Mathematics to the Classroom

10. A student asks if $\frac{0}{6}$ is in its simplest form. How do you respond?

11. A student writes $\frac{15}{53} < \frac{1}{3}$ because $3 \cdot 15 < 53 \cdot 1$. Another student writes $\frac{1\cancel{5}}{\cancel{5}3} = \frac{1}{3}$. Where is the fallacy?

12. A student claims that there are no numbers between $\frac{999}{1000}$ and 1 because they are so close together. What is your response?

13. A student argued that a pizza cut into 12 pieces was more than a pizza cut into 6 pieces. How would you respond?

14. Ann claims that she cannot show $\frac{3}{4}$ of the following faces because some are big and some are small. What do you tell her?

15. How would you respond to each of the following students?
    a. Iris claims that if we have two positive rational numbers, the one with the greater numerator is the greater.
    b. Shirley claims that if we have two positive rational numbers, the one with the greater denominator is the lesser.

16. Steve claims that the shaded circles below cannot represent $\frac{2}{3}$ since there are 10 circles shaded and $\frac{2}{3}$ is less than 1. How do you respond?

17. Carl says that $\frac{3}{8} > \frac{2}{3}$ because $3 > 2$ and $8 > 3$. How would you help Carl?

18. Mr. Jimenez and Ms. Cortez gave the same test. In Mr. Jimenez's class, 20 out of 25 students passed, and in Ms. Cortez's class, 24 of 30 passed. One of Ms. Cortez's students claimed that the classes did equally well. How could you explain the student's reasoning?

National Assessments

National Assessment of Educational Progress (NAEP) Questions

What fraction of the figure is shaded?

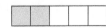

NAEP, Grade 4, 2007

In which of the following are the three fractions arranged from least to greatest?

A. $\frac{2}{7}, \frac{1}{2}, \frac{5}{9}$ B. $\frac{1}{2}, \frac{2}{7}, \frac{5}{9}$ C. $\frac{1}{2}, \frac{5}{9}, \frac{2}{7}$

D. $\frac{5}{9}, \frac{1}{2}, \frac{2}{7}$ E. $\frac{5}{9}, \frac{2}{7}, \frac{1}{2}$

NAEP, Grade 8, 2007

Kim, Les, Mario, and Nina each had a string 10 feet long.

    Kim cut hers into fifths.

    Les cut his into fourths.

    Mario cut his into sixths.

    Nina cut hers into thirds.

After the cuts were made, who had the longest pieces of string?

A. Kim

B. **Les**

C. Mario

D. **Nina**

NAEP, Grade 4, 2013

Which fraction has a value closest to $\frac{1}{2}$?

A. $\frac{5}{8}$

B. $\frac{1}{6}$

C. $\frac{2}{2}$

D. $\frac{1}{5}$

NAEP, Grade 4, 2011

2 Addition, Subtraction, and Estimation with Rational Numbers

2 Objectives

Students will be able to understand and explain

- Addition of rational numbers with like and unlike denominators.

- Rational numbers as mixed numbers.

- Subtraction of rational numbers with like and unlike denominators.

- Properties of addition and subtraction of rational numbers.

- Addition properties of equality.

- Estimation with rational numbers.

Addition and subtraction of rational numbers is very much like addition and subtraction of whole numbers and integers. We first demonstrate the addition of two rational numbers with like denominators, $\frac{2}{5} + \frac{1}{5}$, using an area model in Figure 8(a) and a number line model in Figure 8(b).

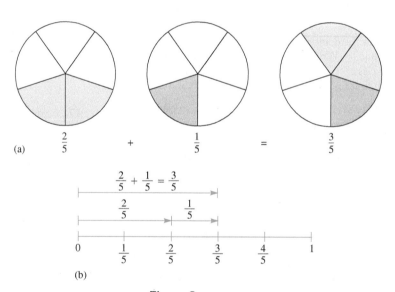

(a) $\frac{2}{5}$ $+$ $\frac{1}{5}$ $=$ $\frac{3}{5}$

(b)

Figure 8

Why does the area model in Figure 8(a) make sense? Suppose that someone gives us $\frac{2}{5}$ of a pie initially and then gives us another $\frac{1}{5}$ of the pie. In Figure 8(a), $\frac{2}{5}$ is represented by 2 pieces when the pie is cut into 5 equal-size pieces, and $\frac{1}{5}$ is represented by 1 piece of the 5 equal-size pieces. So you have $2 + 1 = 3$ pieces of the 5 equal-size pieces, or $\frac{3}{5}$ of the total (whole) pie. The number line model in Figure 8(b) works the same as the number line model for whole numbers.

Using a bar model, the addition $\frac{3}{5} + \frac{4}{5}$ is depicted in Figure 9.

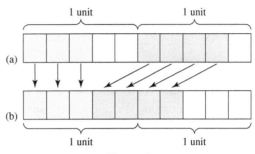

Figure 9

In Figure 9(a), we have $\frac{3}{5}$ and $\frac{4}{5}$ pictured as parts of two equal-sized wholes where each whole consists of five parts. In Figure 9(b), we have $\frac{3}{5} + \frac{4}{5}$ again pictured as parts of two equal-sized wholes, where each whole consists of five parts. We see that there is one whole and two parts of another whole shaded. Additionally, we see that there are seven of the one-fifth parts shaded. Thus, we could say that $\frac{3}{5} + \frac{4}{5} = \frac{7}{5}$. Also $\frac{3}{5} + \frac{4}{5} = 1 + \frac{2}{5}$, which could be written as $1\frac{2}{5}$. The latter representation is a *mixed number*, which is discussed later in the section.

The ideas illustrated in Figures 8 and 9 are summarized in the following definition.

Definition of Addition of Rational Numbers with Like Denominators

If $\frac{a}{b}$ and $\frac{c}{b}$ are rational numbers, then $\frac{a}{b} + \frac{c}{b} = \frac{a+c}{b}$.

CCSS In the grade 5 *Common Core Standards*, we find that students should be able to:

Add and subtract fractions with unlike denominators (including mixed numbers) by replacing given fractions with equivalent fractions in such a way as to produce an equivalent sum or difference of fractions with like denominators. (p. 36)

CCSS We use the four-step process and *Common Core Standards* practices to develop this concept.

Problem Solving Adding Rational Numbers Problem

Determine how to add the rational numbers $\frac{2}{3}$ and $\frac{1}{4}$.

Understanding the Problem We model $\frac{2}{3}$ and $\frac{1}{4}$ as parts of the same-sized whole, as seen in Figure 10, but we need a way to combine the two drawings to find the sum.

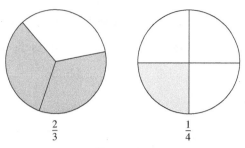

$$\frac{2}{3} \qquad\qquad \frac{1}{4}$$

Figure 10

Devising a Plan We use the strategy of *solving a related problem:* adding rational numbers with the same denominators. We can find the sum using reasoning to write each fraction with a common denominator and then complete the computation.

Carrying Out the Plan We know that $\frac{2}{3}$ has infinitely many representations, including $\frac{4}{6}, \frac{6}{9}, \frac{8}{12}$, and so on. Also $\frac{1}{4}$ has infinitely many representations, including $\frac{2}{8}, \frac{3}{12}, \frac{4}{16}$, and so on. We see that $\frac{8}{12}$ and $\frac{3}{12}$ have the same denominator. One is 8 parts of 12 equal parts, while the other is 3 parts of 12 equal parts. Consequently, the sum is $\frac{2}{3} + \frac{1}{4} = \frac{8}{12} + \frac{3}{12} = \frac{11}{12}$. Figure 11 illustrates the addition.

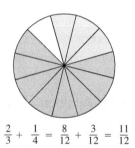

$$\frac{2}{3} + \frac{1}{4} = \frac{8}{12} + \frac{3}{12} = \frac{11}{12}$$

Figure 11

Looking Back To add two rational numbers with unlike denominators, we considered equal rational numbers with like denominators. A common denominator for $\frac{2}{3}$ and $\frac{1}{4}$ is 12. This is also the least common denominator, or the LCM, of 3 and 4. To add two fractions with unequal denominators such as $\frac{5}{12}$ and $\frac{7}{18}$, we could find equal fractions with $\text{LCM}(12, 18) = 36$ as the denominator. However, any common denominator will work as well, for example, 72 or even $12 \cdot 18$.

By considering the sum $\frac{2}{3} + \frac{1}{4} = \frac{2 \cdot 4}{3 \cdot 4} + \frac{1 \cdot 3}{4 \cdot 3} = \frac{8}{12} + \frac{3}{12} = \frac{8 + 3}{12} = \frac{11}{12}$, we can generalize to find the sum of two rational numbers with unlike denominators, as in the following.

Alternate Definition of Addition of Rational Numbers with Unlike Denominators

If $\frac{a}{b}$ and $\frac{c}{d}$ are rational numbers, then $\frac{a}{b} + \frac{c}{d} = \frac{ad + bc}{bd}$.

The definition of addition of rational numbers with unlike denominators can be applied to like denominators as seen below.

$$\frac{a}{b} + \frac{c}{b} = \frac{ab + cb}{b \cdot b} = \frac{(a + c)b}{b \cdot b} = \frac{a + c}{b}$$

Example 6

Find each of the following sums.

a. $\dfrac{2}{15} + \dfrac{4}{21}$ **b.** $\dfrac{2}{^-3} + \dfrac{1}{5}$ **c.** $\left(\dfrac{3}{4} + \dfrac{1}{5}\right) + \dfrac{1}{6}$ **d.** $\dfrac{3}{x} + \dfrac{4}{y}$ **e.** $\dfrac{2}{a^2 b} + \dfrac{3}{ab^2}$

Solution

a. $\text{LCM}(15, 21) = 3 \cdot 5 \cdot 7; \dfrac{2}{15} + \dfrac{4}{21} = \dfrac{2 \cdot 7}{15 \cdot 7} + \dfrac{4 \cdot 5}{21 \cdot 5} = \dfrac{14}{105} + \dfrac{20}{105} = \dfrac{34}{105}$

b. $\dfrac{2}{^-3} + \dfrac{1}{5} = \dfrac{(2)(5) + (^-3)(1)}{(^-3)(5)} = \dfrac{10 + {^-3}}{^-15} = \dfrac{7}{^-15} = \dfrac{7(^-1)}{^-15(^-1)} = \dfrac{^-7}{15}$

c. $\dfrac{3}{4} + \dfrac{1}{5} = \dfrac{3 \cdot 5 + 4 \cdot 1}{4 \cdot 5} = \dfrac{19}{20};$

$\left(\dfrac{3}{4} + \dfrac{1}{5}\right) + \dfrac{1}{6} = \dfrac{19}{20} + \dfrac{1}{6} = \dfrac{19 \cdot 6 + 20 \cdot 1}{20 \cdot 6} = \dfrac{134}{120} = \dfrac{67}{60}$

d. $\dfrac{3}{x} + \dfrac{4}{y} = \dfrac{3y}{xy} + \dfrac{4x}{xy} = \dfrac{3y + 4x}{xy}$

e. $\text{LCM}(a^2 b, ab^2) = a^2 b^2; \dfrac{2}{a^2 b} + \dfrac{3}{ab^2} = \dfrac{2b}{(a^2 b)b} + \dfrac{3a}{a(ab^2)} = \dfrac{2b + 3a}{a^2 b^2}$

Mixed Numbers

In everyday life, we often use **mixed numbers**, that is, numbers that are made up of an integer and a proper fraction. Figure 12 shows a nail that is $2\frac{3}{4}$ in. long. The mixed number $2\frac{3}{4}$ means $2 + \frac{3}{4}$. Students may infer that $2\frac{3}{4}$ means 2 times $\frac{3}{4}$, since xy means $x \cdot y$, but this is not correct. Also, the number $^-4\frac{3}{4}$ means $^-\left(4\frac{3}{4}\right) = {^-4} - \frac{3}{4}$, not $^-4 + \frac{3}{4}$.

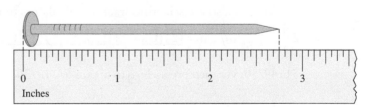

Figure 12

A mixed number is a rational number because it can always be written in the form $\dfrac{a}{b}$. For example,

$$2\frac{3}{4} = 2 + \frac{3}{4} = \frac{2}{1} + \frac{3}{4} = \frac{2 \cdot 4 + 1 \cdot 3}{1 \cdot 4} = \frac{8 + 3}{4} = \frac{11}{4}.$$

Example 7

Change each of the following mixed numbers to the form $\frac{a}{b}$, where a and b are integers:

a. $4\frac{1}{3}$ **b.** $^-3\frac{2}{5}$

Solution

a. $4\frac{1}{3} = 4 + \frac{1}{3} = \frac{4}{1} + \frac{1}{3} = \frac{4 \cdot 3 + 1 \cdot 1}{1 \cdot 3} = \frac{12 + 1}{3} = \frac{13}{3}$

b. $^-3\frac{2}{5} = {}^-\left(3 + \frac{2}{5}\right) = {}^-\left(\frac{3}{1} + \frac{2}{5}\right) = {}^-\left(\frac{3 \cdot 5 + 1 \cdot 2}{1 \cdot 5}\right) = {}^-\left(\frac{17}{5}\right) = \frac{^-17}{5}$

Example 8

Change $\frac{39}{5}$ to a mixed number.

Solution We divide 39 by 5 and use the division algorithm as follows:

$$\frac{39}{5} = \frac{7 \cdot 5 + 4}{5} = \frac{7 \cdot 5}{5} + \frac{4}{5} = 7 + \frac{4}{5} = 7\frac{4}{5}$$

In elementary schools, problems like Example 8 are usually computed using division, as follows:

$$
\begin{array}{r}
5 \\
5{\overline{\smash{\big)}\,29}} \\
\underline{25} \\
4
\end{array}
$$

Hence, $\frac{29}{5} = 5 + \frac{4}{5} = 5\frac{4}{5}$. The remainder of 4 in the division actually represents $\frac{4}{5}$ of a unit when put in context.

 Scientific/fraction calculators can change improper fractions to mixed numbers. For example, if we enter $\boxed{2}\,\boxed{9}\,\boxed{/}\,\boxed{5}$ and press $\boxed{Ab/c}$, then $5\sqcup4/5$ appears, which means $5\frac{4}{5}$.

We can also use scientific/fraction calculators to add mixed numbers. For example, to add $2\frac{4}{5} + 3\frac{5}{6}$, we enter $\boxed{2}\,\boxed{\text{Unit}}\,\boxed{4}\,\boxed{/}\,\boxed{5}\,\boxed{+}\,\boxed{3}\,\boxed{\text{Unit}}\,\boxed{5}\,\boxed{/}\,\boxed{6}\,\boxed{=}$, and the display reads $5\sqcup49/30$. We then press $\boxed{Ab/c}$ to obtain $6\sqcup19/30$, which means $6\frac{19}{30}$.

Adding Mixed Numbers

 Because mixed numbers are rational numbers, the method of adding rationals can be used to include mixed numbers. The student page shown on the next page shows a method for computing sums of mixed numbers that uses the commutative and associative properties discussed later in the next section.

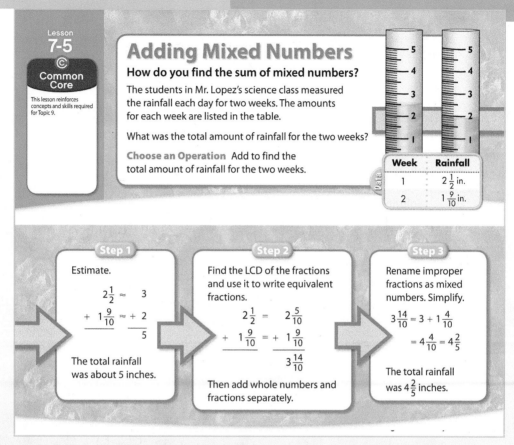

School Book Page — Equivalent Fractions

Lesson **7-5**

Common Core

This lesson reinforces concepts and skills required for Topic 9.

Adding Mixed Numbers

How do you find the sum of mixed numbers?

The students in Mr. Lopez's science class measured the rainfall each day for two weeks. The amounts for each week are listed in the table.

What was the total amount of rainfall for the two weeks?

Choose an Operation Add to find the total amount of rainfall for the two weeks.

Week	Rainfall
1	$2\frac{1}{2}$ in.
2	$1\frac{9}{10}$ in.

Step 1

Estimate.

$$2\frac{1}{2} \approx 3$$
$$+ \ 1\frac{9}{10} \approx + \ 2$$
$$\overline{\qquad\qquad 5}$$

The total rainfall was about 5 inches.

Step 2

Find the LCD of the fractions and use it to write equivalent fractions.

$$2\frac{1}{2} = 2\frac{5}{10}$$
$$+ \ 1\frac{9}{10} = + \ 1\frac{9}{10}$$
$$\overline{\qquad\qquad 3\frac{14}{10}}$$

Then add whole numbers and fractions separately.

Step 3

Rename improper fractions as mixed numbers. Simplify.

$$3\frac{14}{10} = 3 + 1\frac{4}{10}$$
$$= 4\frac{4}{10} = 4\frac{2}{5}$$

The total rainfall was $4\frac{2}{5}$ inches.

Source: pp. 172–173; From enVisionMATH Common Core (Grade 6). Copyright © 2013 Pearson Education, Inc., or its affiliates. Used by permission. All Rights Reserved.

Properties of Addition for Rational Numbers

Rational numbers have the following properties for addition: *closure, commutative, associative, additive identity,* and *additive inverse.* To emphasize the additive inverse property of rational numbers, we state it explicitly, as follows.

Theorem 6:   Additive Inverse Property of Rational Numbers

For any rational number $\frac{a}{b}$, there exists a unique rational number $-\frac{a}{b}$, the additive inverse of $\frac{a}{b}$, such that

$$\frac{a}{b} + \left(-\frac{a}{b}\right) = 0 = \left(-\frac{a}{b}\right) + \frac{a}{b}.$$

As mentioned earlier, another form of $-\dfrac{a}{b}$ can be found by considering the sum $\dfrac{a}{b} + \dfrac{{}^{-}a}{b}$. Because

$$\frac{a}{b} + \frac{{}^{-}a}{b} = \frac{a + {}^{-}a}{b} = \frac{0}{b} = 0,$$

it follows that $-\dfrac{a}{b}$ and $\dfrac{{}^{-}a}{b}$ are both additive inverses of $\dfrac{a}{b}$, so $-\dfrac{a}{b} = \dfrac{{}^{-}a}{b}$.

Example 9

Find the additive inverses for each of the following:

   a. $\dfrac{3}{5}$ **b.** $\dfrac{{}^{-}5}{11}$ **c.** $4\dfrac{1}{2}$

Solution

   a. $-\dfrac{3}{5}$ or $\dfrac{{}^{-}3}{5}$ **b.** $-\left(\dfrac{{}^{-}5}{11}\right) = \dfrac{{}^{-}({}^{-}5)}{11} = \dfrac{5}{11}$ **c.** ${}^{-}4\dfrac{1}{2}$, or $\dfrac{{}^{-}9}{2}$

Properties of the additive inverse for rational numbers are analogous to those of the additive inverse for integers, as shown in Table 2.

Table 2

Integers	Rational Numbers
1. ${}^{-}({}^{-}a) = a$	**1.** $-\left(\dfrac{{}^{-}a}{b}\right) = \dfrac{a}{b}$
2. ${}^{-}(a + b) = {}^{-}a + {}^{-}b$	**2.** $-\left(\dfrac{a}{b} + \dfrac{c}{d}\right) = \dfrac{{}^{-}a}{b} + \dfrac{{}^{-}c}{d}$

The set of rational numbers has the addition property of equality, which says that the same number can be added to both sides of an equation.

Theorem 7: Addition Property of Equality of Rational Numbers

If $\dfrac{a}{b}$ and $\dfrac{c}{d}$ are any rational numbers such that $\dfrac{a}{b} = \dfrac{c}{d}$ and $\dfrac{e}{f}$ is any rational number, then

$$\frac{a}{b} + \frac{e}{f} = \frac{c}{d} + \frac{e}{f}.$$

Subtraction of Rational Numbers

In elementary school, subtraction of rational numbers is usually introduced by using a take-away model. If we have $\dfrac{6}{7}$ of a pizza and $\dfrac{2}{7}$ of the original pizza is taken away, $\dfrac{4}{7}$ of the pizza remains; that is, $\dfrac{6}{7} - \dfrac{2}{7} = \dfrac{6 - 2}{7} = \dfrac{4}{7}$. In general, subtraction of rational numbers with like denominators is determined as follows:

$$\frac{a}{b} - \frac{c}{b} = \frac{a - c}{b}$$

As with integers, a number line can be used to model subtraction of nonnegative rational numbers. If a line is marked off in units of length $\frac{1}{b}$ and $a \geq c$, then $\frac{a}{b} - \frac{c}{b}$ is equal to $(a - c)$ units of length $\frac{1}{b}$, which implies that $\frac{a}{b} - \frac{c}{b} = \frac{a-c}{b}$.

When the denominators are not the same, we can perform the subtraction by finding a common denominator. For example,

$$\frac{3}{4} - \frac{2}{3} = \frac{3 \cdot 3}{4 \cdot 3} - \frac{2 \cdot 4}{3 \cdot 4} = \frac{9}{12} - \frac{8}{12} = \frac{9 - 8}{12} = \frac{1}{12}.$$

Subtraction of rational numbers, like subtraction of integers, can be defined in terms of addition as follows.

Definition of Subtraction of Rational Numbers in Terms of Addition

If $\frac{a}{b}$ and $\frac{c}{d}$ are any rational numbers, then $\frac{a}{b} - \frac{c}{d}$ is the unique rational number $\frac{e}{f}$ such that $\frac{a}{b} = \frac{c}{d} + \frac{e}{f}$.

As with integers, we can see that subtraction of rational numbers can be performed by adding the additive inverses as stated in the following theorem.

Theorem 8

If $\frac{a}{b}$ and $\frac{c}{d}$ are any rational numbers, then $\frac{a}{b} - \frac{c}{d} = \frac{a}{b} + \frac{^-c}{d}$.

Now, using Theorem 8, we obtain the following.

$$\frac{a}{b} - \frac{c}{d} = \frac{a}{b} + \frac{^-c}{d}$$
$$= \frac{ad + b(^-c)}{bd}$$
$$= \frac{ad + {}^-(bc)}{bd}$$
$$= \frac{ad - bc}{bd}$$

We proved the following theorem, which is sometimes given as a definition of subtraction.

Theorem 9

If $\frac{a}{b}$ and $\frac{c}{d}$ are any rational numbers, then $\frac{a}{b} - \frac{c}{d} = \frac{ad - bc}{bd}$.

Example 10

Find each difference.

a. $\dfrac{5}{8} - \dfrac{1}{4}$

b. $5\dfrac{1}{3} - 2\dfrac{3}{4}$

Solution

a. One approach is to find the LCM for the denominators. $\text{LCM}(8,4) = 8.$

$$\frac{5}{8} - \frac{1}{4} = \frac{5}{8} - \frac{2}{8} = \frac{3}{8}$$

An alternative approach follows.

$$\frac{5}{8} - \frac{1}{4} = \frac{5\cdot 4 - 8\cdot 1}{8\cdot 4} = \frac{20 - 8}{32} = \frac{12}{32} = \frac{3}{8}$$

b. Two methods of solution are given.

$$
\begin{array}{l}
5\dfrac{1}{3} = \;\;5\dfrac{4}{12} = 4 + 1\dfrac{4}{12} = \;\;4\dfrac{16}{12} \\[2mm]
-2\dfrac{3}{4} = -2\dfrac{9}{12} = -2\dfrac{9}{12} \;\;\;\;\;= -2\dfrac{9}{12} \\[2mm]
\hline
\phantom{-2\dfrac{3}{4} = -2\dfrac{9}{12} = -2\dfrac{9}{12} \;\;\;\;\;= \;} 2\dfrac{7}{12}
\end{array}
$$

$$
\begin{aligned}
5\dfrac{1}{3} - 2\dfrac{3}{4} &= \frac{16}{3} - \frac{11}{4} \\[2mm]
&= \frac{16\cdot 4 - 3\cdot 11}{3\cdot 4} \\[2mm]
&= \frac{64 - 33}{12} \\[2mm]
&= \frac{31}{12} = 2\frac{7}{12}
\end{aligned}
$$

The following examples show the use of fractions in algebra.

Example 11

Add or subtract, writing your answer in simplest form.

a. $\dfrac{x}{2} + \dfrac{x}{3}$

b. $\dfrac{2 - x}{6 - 3x} + \dfrac{4 - 2x}{3x - 6}$

c. $\dfrac{2}{a + b} - \dfrac{2}{a - b}$

d. $\dfrac{1}{x} - \dfrac{1}{2x^2}$

Solution

a. $\dfrac{x}{2} + \dfrac{x}{3} = \dfrac{3x}{3\cdot 2} + \dfrac{2x}{2\cdot 3}$

$\phantom{\dfrac{x}{2} + \dfrac{x}{3}} = \dfrac{3x + 2x}{6} = \dfrac{5x}{6}$

b. We first write each fraction in simplest form.

$$\frac{2 - x}{6 - 3x} = \frac{2 - x}{3(2 - x)} = \frac{1(2 - x)}{3(2 - x)} = \frac{1}{3}$$

$$\frac{4 - 2x}{3x - 6} = \frac{^-2(x - 2)}{3(x - 2)} = \frac{^-2}{3}$$

Thus, the sum is $\dfrac{1}{3} + \dfrac{^-2}{3} = \dfrac{^-1}{3}.$

c. We use Theorem 9.

$$\frac{2}{a+b} - \frac{2}{a-b} = \frac{2(a-b) - 2(a+b)}{(a+b)(a-b)}$$

$$= \frac{2a - 2b - 2a - 2b}{(a+b)(a-b)}$$

$$= \frac{^-4b}{(a+b)(a-b)} = \frac{^-4b}{a^2 - b^2}$$

d. $\dfrac{1}{x} - \dfrac{1}{2x^2} = \dfrac{2x \cdot 1}{2x \cdot x} - \dfrac{1}{2x^2}$

$$= \frac{2x}{2x^2} - \frac{1}{2x^2}$$

$$= \frac{2x - 1}{2x^2}$$

Estimation with Rational Numbers

Estimation helps us make practical decisions in our everyday lives. For example, suppose we need to double a recipe that calls for $\frac{3}{4}$ of a cup of flour. Will we need more or less than a cup of flour?

Many of the estimation and mental math techniques that we learned to use with whole numbers also work with rational numbers.

The grade 5 *Common Core Standards* calls for students to "use benchmark fraction and number sense of fractions to estimate mentally and assess the reasonableness of answers." (p. 36) Estimation plays an important role in judging the reasonableness of computations.

▶ **NOW TRY THIS 3**

A student added $\frac{3}{4} + \frac{1}{2}$ and obtained $\frac{4}{6}$. How would you use estimation to show that this answer could not be correct?

Sometimes to obtain an estimate it is desirable to round fractions to a ***convenient*** or ***benchmark*** fraction, such as $\frac{1}{2}, \frac{1}{3}, \frac{1}{4}, \frac{1}{5}, \frac{2}{3}, \frac{3}{4}$, or 1. For example, if a student had 59 correct answers out of 80 questions, the student answered $\frac{59}{80}$ of the questions correctly, which is approximately $\frac{60}{80}$, or $\frac{3}{4}$. We know $\frac{60}{80}$ is greater than $\frac{59}{80}$. The estimate $\frac{3}{4}$ for $\frac{59}{80}$ is a high estimate. In a similar way, we can estimate $\frac{31}{90}$ by $\frac{30}{90}$, or $\frac{1}{3}$. In this case, the estimate of $\frac{1}{3}$ is a low estimate of $\frac{31}{90}$. An example of benchmark estimation is seen on the student page shown on the next page.

School Book Page

Another Example How can you use benchmark fractions such as $\frac{1}{4}$, $\frac{1}{3}$, $\frac{1}{2}$, $\frac{2}{3}$, and $\frac{3}{4}$ to estimate?

Estimate $\frac{5}{8} - \frac{3}{16}$.

$\frac{5}{8}$ is close to $\frac{6}{8}$, and $\frac{6}{8} = \frac{3}{4}$.

$\frac{3}{16}$ is close to $\frac{4}{16}$, and $\frac{4}{16} = \frac{1}{4}$.

So, $\frac{5}{8} - \frac{3}{16}$ is close to $\frac{3}{4} - \frac{1}{4}$.

$\frac{3}{4} - \frac{1}{4} = \frac{2}{4}$ or $\frac{1}{2}$

So, $\frac{5}{8} - \frac{3}{16} \approx \frac{1}{2}$.

Source: p. 170; From enVisionMATH Common Core (Grade 6). Copyright © 2013 Pearson Education, Inc., or its affiliates. Used by permission. All Rights Reserved.

Example 12

A sixth-grade class is collecting cans to take to the recycling center. Becky's group brought the following amounts (in pounds). About how many pounds does her group have all together?

$$1\frac{1}{8}, \ 3\frac{4}{10}, \ 5\frac{7}{8}, \ \frac{6}{10}$$

Solution We can estimate the amount by using front-end estimation with the adjustment made by using 0 which is close to $\frac{1}{8}$, $\frac{1}{2}$ which is close to $\frac{4}{10}$ and $\frac{6}{10}$, and 1 which is close to $\frac{7}{8}$ as benchmark fractions. The front-end estimate is $1 + 3 + 5 = 9$. The adjustment is $0 + \frac{1}{2} + 1 + \frac{1}{2}$, or 2. An adjusted estimate would be $9 + 2 = 11$ lb.

Example 13

Estimate each of the following additions.

a. $\frac{27}{13} + \frac{10}{9}$ **b.** $3\frac{9}{10} + 2\frac{7}{8} + \frac{11}{12}$ **c.** $3\frac{7}{8} + 11\frac{1}{2} + 2\frac{2}{5} + 5\frac{1}{16}$

Solution

a. Because $\frac{27}{13}$ is slightly more than 2 and $\frac{10}{9}$ is slightly more than 1, an estimate might be 3. We know the estimate is low.

b. We first add the whole-number parts to obtain $3 + 2 = 5$. Because each of the fractions, $\frac{9}{10}$, $\frac{7}{8}$, and $\frac{11}{12}$, is close to but less than 1, their sum is close to but less than 3. The approximate answer is $5 + 3 = 8$. The estimate is high.

c. Using *grouping to nice numbers*, we group $\left(3\frac{7}{8} + 5\frac{1}{16}\right)$ and $\left(11\frac{1}{2} + 2\frac{2}{5}\right)$ to obtain approximately $9 + 14 = 23$. The estimate is high. (Why?)

Assessment 2A

1. Perform the following additions or subtractions.

   a. $\dfrac{1}{2} + \dfrac{2}{3}$

   b. $\dfrac{4}{12} - \dfrac{2}{3}$

   c. $\dfrac{5}{x} + \dfrac{^-3}{y}$

   d. $\dfrac{^-3}{2x^2y} + \dfrac{5}{2xy^2} + \dfrac{7}{x^2}$

   e. $\dfrac{5}{6} + 2\dfrac{1}{8}$

   f. $^-4\dfrac{1}{2} - 3\dfrac{1}{6}$

   g. $7\dfrac{1}{4} + 3\dfrac{5}{12} - 2\dfrac{1}{3}$

2. Change each of the following fractions to a mixed number.

   a. $\dfrac{56}{3}$

   b. $-\dfrac{293}{100}$

3. Change each of the following mixed numbers to a fraction in the form $\dfrac{a}{b}$, where a and b are integers and $b \neq 0$.

   a. $6\dfrac{3}{4}$

   b. $^-3\dfrac{5}{8}$

4. Approximate each of the following situations with a benchmark fraction. Tell whether your estimate is high or low.

   a. Giorgio had 15 base hits out of 46 times at bat.

   b. Ruth made 7 goals out of 41 shots.

   c. Laura answered 62 problems correctly out of 80.

   d. Jonathan made 9 baskets out of 19.

5. Use the information in the table to answer each of the following questions.

Team	Games Played	Games Won
Ducks	22	10
Beavers	19	10
Tigers	28	9
Bears	23	8
Lions	27	7
Wildcats	25	6
Badgers	21	5

   a. Which team won more than $\dfrac{1}{2}$ of its games and was closest to winning $\dfrac{1}{2}$ of its games?

   b. Which team won less than $\dfrac{1}{2}$ of its games and was closest to winning $\dfrac{1}{2}$ of its games?

   c. Which team won more than $\dfrac{1}{3}$ of its games and was closest to winning $\dfrac{1}{3}$ of its games?

6. Sort the following fraction cards into the ovals by estimating in which oval the fraction belongs.

   Sort these fraction cards.   About 0   About $\dfrac{1}{2}$ About 1

   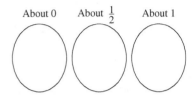

7. Approximate each of the following fractions by $0, \dfrac{1}{4}, \dfrac{1}{2}, \dfrac{3}{4},$ or 1. Tell whether your estimate is high or low.

   a. $\dfrac{19}{39}$

   b. $\dfrac{3}{197}$

   c. $\dfrac{150}{201}$

   d. $\dfrac{8}{9}$

8. Without actually finding the exact answer, state which of the numbers given in parentheses is the best approximation for the given sum.

   a. $\dfrac{6}{13} + \dfrac{7}{15} + \dfrac{11}{23} + \dfrac{17}{35} \left(1, 2, 3, 3\dfrac{1}{2}\right)$

   b. $\dfrac{30}{41} + \dfrac{1}{1000} + \dfrac{3}{2000} \left(\dfrac{3}{8}, \dfrac{3}{4}, 1, 2\right)$

9. Compute each of the following mentally.

   a. $1 - \dfrac{3}{4}$

   b. $3\dfrac{3}{8} + 2\dfrac{1}{4} - 5\dfrac{5}{8}$

10. The following ruler has regions marked M, A, T, H.

    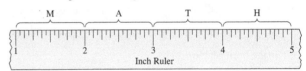

    Use estimation to determine into which region on the ruler each of the following measurements falls. For example, $\dfrac{12}{5}$ in. falls into region A.

    a. $\dfrac{20}{8}$ in.

    b. $\dfrac{36}{8}$ in.

    c. $\dfrac{60}{16}$ in.

    d. $\dfrac{18}{4}$ in.

11. Use *clustering* to estimate the following sum.

    $$3\dfrac{1}{3} + 3\dfrac{1}{5} + 2\dfrac{7}{8} + 2\dfrac{7}{9}$$

12. A class consists of $\dfrac{2}{5}$ freshmen, $\dfrac{1}{4}$ sophomores, and $\dfrac{1}{10}$ juniors; the rest are seniors. What fraction of the class is seniors?

13. A clerk sold three pieces of one type of ribbon to different customers. One piece was $\dfrac{1}{3}$ yd long, another was $2\dfrac{3}{4}$ yd long, and the third was $3\dfrac{1}{2}$ yd long. What was the total length of that type of ribbon sold?

14. Martine bought $8\frac{3}{4}$ yd of fabric. She wants to make a skirt using $1\frac{7}{8}$ yd, pants using $2\frac{3}{8}$ yd, and a vest using $1\frac{2}{3}$ yd. How much fabric will be left over?

15. Give an example illustrating each of the following properties of rational number addition.
    a. Closure   b. Commutative   c. Associative

16. Insert five fractions between the numbers 1 and 2 so that the seven numbers (including 1 and 2) constitute part of an arithmetic sequence.

17. a. Check that each of the following statements is true.
    i. $\frac{1}{3} = \frac{1}{4} + \frac{1}{3 \cdot 4}$
    ii. $\frac{1}{4} = \frac{1}{5} + \frac{1}{4 \cdot 5}$
    iii. $\frac{1}{5} = \frac{1}{6} + \frac{1}{5 \cdot 6}$

    b. Based on the examples in (a), write $\frac{1}{n}$ as a sum of two unit fractions; that is, as a sum of fractions with numerator 1.

18. Solve for x.
    a. $x + 2\frac{1}{2} = 3\frac{1}{3}$
    b. $x - 2\frac{2}{3} = \frac{5}{6}$

19. Al runs $\frac{5}{8}$ mi in 10 min. Bill runs $\frac{7}{8}$ mi in 10 min. If both runners continue to run at the same rate, how much farther can Bill run than Al in 20 min?

20. One recipe calls for $1\frac{3}{4}$ cups of milk and a second recipe calls for $1\frac{1}{2}$ cups of milk. If you only have 3 cups of milk, can you make both recipes? Why?

21. The table below shows census data from the state of Pennsylvania for 2011.

Population	2011
Total 8-yr. old	150,155
Boys	76,432
Girls	73,723
Total 9-yr. old	149,904
Boys	76,503
Girls	73,401
Total 10-yr. old	154,144
Boys	78,672
Girls	75,472

Data from 2011 Census taken from http://www.census.gov/schools/facts/pennsylvania.html

    a. About what part of the total population is 8- to 10-year-old boys?
    b. About what part of the total population is 8- to 10-year-old girls?
    c. If the population of the entire state of Pennsylvania in 2011 was 12,742,886, about what part of the population was boys of ages 8- to 10-year-olds?

22. According to the US Census Bureau, in October 2012, there were about 633,000 3- and 4-year-olds enrolled in schools. Additionally there were about 1,186,000 16- and 17-year-olds enrolled in schools. In the respective ages there were about 1,193,000 and 1,259,000 total. Which age group had the greater fraction in school?

23. There are 360° in a circle graph. If 40° of the graph represents rent and 5° of the graph represents savings, what fractional portion of the whole graph is represented by rent and savings?

24. The energy sources for the US in 2012 included $\frac{37}{100}$ coal, $\frac{3}{10}$ natural gas, $\frac{19}{100}$ nuclear, and $\frac{7}{100}$ hydropower. How much is unaccounted for in this list?

Assessment 2B

1. Perform the following additions or subtractions.
   a. $\frac{^-1}{2} + \frac{2}{3}$
   b. $\frac{5}{12} - \frac{2}{3}$
   c. $\frac{5}{4x} + \frac{^-3}{2y}$
   d. $\frac{^-3}{2x^2y^2} + \frac{5}{2xy^2} + \frac{7}{x^2y}$
   e. $\frac{5}{6} - 2\frac{1}{8}$
   f. $^-4\frac{1}{2} + 3\frac{1}{6}$
   g. $5\frac{1}{3} + 5\frac{5}{6} - 3\frac{1}{9}$

2. Change each of the following fractions to a mixed number.
   a. $\frac{14}{5}$ b. $-\frac{47}{8}$

3. Change each of the following mixed numbers to a fraction in the form $\frac{a}{b}$, where a and b are integers and $b \neq 0$.
   a. $7\frac{1}{2}$ b. $^-4\frac{2}{3}$

4. Place the numbers 2, 5, 6, and 8 in the following boxes to make the equation true.

$$\frac{\square}{\square} + \frac{\square}{\square} = \frac{23}{24}$$

5. Use the information in the table to answer each of the following questions.

Team	Games Played	Games Won
Ducks	22	10
Beavers	19	10
Tigers	28	9
Bears	23	8
Lions	27	7
Wildcats	25	6
Badgers	21	5

a. Which team won less than $\frac{1}{3}$ of its games and was closest to winning $\frac{1}{3}$ of its games?

b. Which team won more than $\frac{1}{4}$ of its games and was closest to winning of $\frac{1}{4}$ of its games?

c. Which teams won less than $\frac{1}{4}$ of their games?

6. Sort the following fraction cards into the ovals by estimating in which oval the fraction belongs.

Sort these fraction cards.

$\boxed{\frac{14}{16}}$ $\boxed{\frac{1}{100}}$ $\boxed{\frac{36}{70}}$ $\boxed{\frac{19}{36}}$ $\boxed{\frac{1}{30}}$ $\boxed{\frac{7}{800}}$

About 0   About $\frac{1}{2}$ About 1

7. Approximate each of the following fractions by $0, \frac{1}{4}, \frac{1}{2}, \frac{3}{4}$, or 1. Tell whether your estimate is high or low.

a. $\frac{113}{100}$

b. $\frac{3}{1978}$

c. $\frac{150}{198}$

d. $\frac{8}{9}$

8. Without actually finding the exact answer, state which of the numbers given in parentheses is the best approximation for the given sum.

a. $\frac{2}{13} + \frac{7}{15} + \frac{12}{23} + \frac{33}{35} \left(1, 2, 3, 3\frac{1}{2}\right)$

b. $\frac{30}{41} + \frac{220}{1000} + \frac{5}{2000} \left(\frac{3}{8}, \frac{3}{4}, 1, 2\right)$

9. Compute each of the following mentally.

a. $6 - \frac{7}{8}$

b. $2\frac{3}{5} + 4\frac{1}{10} + 3\frac{3}{10}$

10. The following ruler has regions marked M, A, T, H.

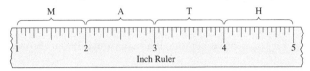

Use mental mathematics and estimation to determine into which region on the ruler each of the following measurements falls. For example, $\frac{12}{5}$ in. falls into region A.

a. $\frac{9}{8}$ in.

b. $\frac{18}{8}$ in.

c. $\frac{50}{16}$ in.

d. $\frac{17}{4}$ in.

11. A class consists of $\frac{1}{4}$ freshmen, $\frac{1}{5}$ sophomores, and $\frac{1}{10}$ juniors; the rest are seniors. What fraction of the class is seniors?

12. The Naturals Company sells its products in many countries. The following two circle graphs show the fractions of the company's earnings for 2012 and 2014. Based on this information, answer the following questions.

a. In 2012, how much greater was the fraction of sales for Japan than for Canada?

b. In 2014, how much less was the fraction of sales for England than for the United States?

c. How much greater was the fraction of total sales for the United States in 2014 than in 2012?

d. Is it true that the amount of sales in dollars in Australia was less in 2012 than in 2014? Why?

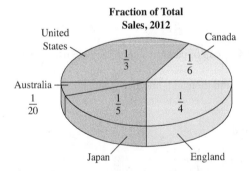

Fraction of Total Sales, 2012

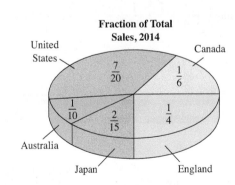

Fraction of Total Sales, 2014

13. A recipe requires $3\frac{1}{2}$ cups of milk. Ran put in $1\frac{3}{4}$ cups in a bowl. How much more milk does he need?

14. A $15\frac{3}{4}$ in. board is cut in a single cut from a $38\frac{1}{4}$ in. board. The saw cut takes $\frac{3}{8}$ in. How much of the $38\frac{1}{4}$ in. board is left after cutting?

15. Students from Rattlesnake School formed four teams to collect cans for recycling during the months of April and May. A record of their efforts follows.

Number of Pounds Collected

	Team 1	Team 2	Team 3	Team 4
April	$28\frac{3}{4}$	$32\frac{7}{8}$	$28\frac{1}{2}$	$35\frac{3}{16}$
May	$33\frac{1}{3}$	$28\frac{5}{12}$	$25\frac{3}{4}$	$41\frac{1}{2}$

   a. Which team collected the most for the 2-month period? How much did they collect?

   b. What was the difference between the total pounds collected in April and the total pounds collected in May?

16. Insert four fractions between the numbers 1 and 3 so that the six numbers (including 1 and 3) constitute part of an arithmetic sequence.

17. Solve for x in each of the following.

   a. $x - \frac{5}{6} = \frac{2}{3}$

   b. $x - \frac{7}{2^3 \cdot 3^2} = \frac{5}{2^2 \cdot 3^2}$

18. Joe has $\frac{3}{4}$ cup of paint in a container. He uses $\frac{1}{3}$ cup on a project and then adds another $\frac{1}{2}$ cup. How much paint does he have now?

19. a. Find $\frac{1}{2} + \frac{1}{4}$.

   b. Find $\frac{1}{2} + \frac{1}{4} + \frac{1}{8}$.

   c. Find $\frac{1}{2} + \frac{1}{4} + \frac{1}{8} + \frac{1}{16}$.

   d. If you continue in this pattern with powers of 2 in the denominator, will the sum ever become greater than 1? Why?

20. The table below shows census data from the state of Pennsylvania for 2011.

Population	2011
Total 8-yr. old	150,155
Boys	76,432
Girls	73,723
Total 9-yr. old	149,904
Boys	76,503
Girls	73,401
Total 10-yr. old	154,144
Boys	78,672
Girls	75,472

Data from 2011 Census taken from http://www.census.gov/schools/facts/pennsylvania.html

   a. About what fraction more of girls is there in the 8-year-olds are there than in the 10-year-olds?

   b. About what part of the total population of 8- to 9-year-olds are girls?

   c. If the population of the entire state of Pennsylvania in 2011 was 12,742,886, about what part of the population was girls of ages 8–10?

21. According to the US Census Bureau in October 2012, there were about 633,000 3- and 4-year olds enrolled in schools. Additionally there were about 1,186,000 16- and 17-year-olds enrolled in schools. In the respective ages there were about 1,193,000 and 1,259,000 total. Which of these age groups had the lesser fraction in school?

22. There are 360° in a circle graph. If 50° of the graph represents rent and 7° of the graph represents savings, what fractional portion of the whole graph is not represented by rent and savings?

23. The energy sources for the United States in 2012 included $\frac{37}{100}$ coal, $\frac{3}{10}$ natural gas, $\frac{19}{100}$ nuclear, and $\frac{7}{100}$ hydropower. What fraction more coal than natural gas is used?

Mathematical Connections 2

Reasoning

1. Suppose a large pizza is divided into 3 equal-size pieces and a small pizza is divided into 4 equal-size pieces and you get 1 piece from each pizza. Does $\frac{1}{3} + \frac{1}{4}$ represent the amount that you received? Explain why or why not.

2. a. When we add two fractions with unlike denominators and convert them to fractions with the same denominator, must we use the least common denominator? What are the advantages of using the least common denominator?

   b. When the least common denominator is used in adding or subtracting fractions, is the result always a fraction in simplest form?

3. Explain why we can do the following to convert $5\frac{3}{4}$ to a mixed number.

$$\frac{5 \cdot 4 + 3}{4} = \frac{23}{4}$$

4. Kara spent $\frac{1}{2}$ of her allowance on Saturday and $\frac{1}{3}$ of what she had left on Sunday. Can this situation be modeled as $\frac{1}{2} - \frac{1}{3}$? Explain why or why not.

5. Compute $3\frac{3}{4} + 5\frac{1}{3}$ in two different ways and leave your answer as a mixed number. Tell which way you prefer and why.

6. Explain whether each of the following properties holds for subtraction of rational numbers.
   a. Closure
   b. Commutative
   c. Associative
   d. Identity
   e. Inverse

Open-Ended

7. Write a story problem for $\frac{2}{3} - \frac{1}{4}$.

8. a. Write two fractions whose sum is 1. If one of the fractions is $\frac{a}{b}$, what is the other?
   b. Write three fractions whose sum is 1.
   c. Write two fractions whose difference is very close to 1 but not exactly 1.

9. a. With the exception of $\frac{2}{3}$, the Egyptians used only unit fractions (fractions that have numerators of 1). Every unit fraction can be expressed as the sum of two unit fractions in more than one way, for example, $\frac{1}{2} = \frac{1}{4} + \frac{1}{4}$ and $\frac{1}{2} = \frac{1}{3} + \frac{1}{6}$. Find at least two different unit fraction representations for each of the following.
   i. $\frac{1}{3}$
   ii. $\frac{1}{7}$
   b. Show that $\frac{1}{n} - \frac{1}{n+1} = \frac{1}{n(n+1)}$.
   c. Rewrite the equation in part (b) as a sum and then use the sum to answer part (a).
   d. Write $\frac{1}{17}$ as a sum of two different unit fractions.

Cooperative Learning

10. Interview 10 people and ask them if and when they add and subtract fractions in their lives. Combine their responses with those of the rest of the class to get a view of how "ordinary" people use computation of rational numbers in their daily lives.

Connecting Mathematics to the Classroom

11. Kendra showed that $\frac{1}{3} + \frac{3}{4} = \frac{4}{7}$ by using the following figure. How would you help her?

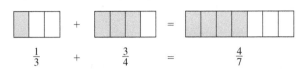

12. To show $2\frac{3}{4} = \frac{11}{4}$, the teacher drew the following picture. Ken said this shows a picture of $\frac{11}{12}$, not $\frac{11}{4}$. What is Ken thinking and how should the teacher respond?

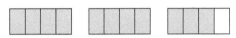

13. Jill claims that for positive fractions, $\frac{a}{b} + \frac{a}{c} = \frac{a}{b + c}$ because the fractions have a common numerator. How do you respond?

14. Explain the error pattern on Jon's test.
   a. $\frac{13}{35} = \frac{1}{5}, \quad \frac{27}{73} = \frac{2}{3}, \quad \frac{16}{64} = \frac{1}{4}$
   b. $\frac{4}{5} + \frac{2}{3} = \frac{6}{8}, \quad \frac{2}{5} + \frac{3}{4} = \frac{5}{9}, \quad \frac{7}{8} + \frac{1}{3} = \frac{8}{11}$
   c. $8\frac{3}{8} - 6\frac{1}{4} = 2\frac{2}{4}, \quad 5\frac{3}{8} - 2\frac{2}{3} = 3\frac{1}{5}, \quad 2\frac{2}{7} - 1\frac{1}{3} = 1\frac{1}{4}$

Review Problems

15. Simplify each rational number if possible.
   a. $\frac{14}{21}$
   b. $\frac{117}{153}$
   c. $\frac{5^2}{7^2}$
   d. $\frac{a^2 + a}{1 + a}$
   e. $\frac{a^2 + 1}{a + 1}$
   f. $\frac{a^2 - b^2}{a - b}$

16. Determine whether the fractions in each of the following pairs are equal.
   a. $\frac{a^2}{b}$ and $\frac{a^2 b}{b^2}$
   b. $\frac{377}{400}$ and $\frac{378}{401}$
   c. $\frac{0}{10}$ and $\frac{0}{-10}$
   d. $\frac{a}{b}$ and $\frac{a + 1}{b + 1}$, where $a \neq b$

17. There are 206 bones in the body. Can the fraction $\frac{27}{103}$ represent the number of bones in both hands as a part of the total number of bones in the body? Explain your answer.

18. Explain why there are infinitely many fractions equivalent to $\frac{3}{5}$.

19. Mary ate $\frac{3}{5}$ of the cookies and left the rest for Suzanne. What fraction of the cookies are left for Suzanne?

20. On a number line, explain why $\frac{^-1}{100}$ is greater than $\frac{^-1}{10}$.

National Assessments

National Assessment of Educational Progress (NAEP) Questions

$$\frac{1}{20}, \frac{4}{20}, \frac{7}{20}, \frac{10}{20}, \frac{13}{20}, \cdots$$

If the pattern shown continues, what is the first fraction in the pattern that will be greater than 1?

A. $\frac{20}{20}$ 　　　　　　　B. $\frac{21}{20}$

C. $\frac{22}{20}$ 　　　　　　　D. $\frac{25}{20}$

NAEP, Grade 4, 2013

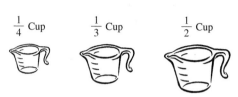

A recipe requires $1\frac{1}{3}$ cups of sugar. Which of the following ways describes how the measuring cups shown can be used to measure $1\frac{1}{3}$ cups of sugar accurately?

A. Use the $\frac{1}{2}$ cup three times.

B. Use the $\frac{1}{4}$ cup three times.

C. Use the $\frac{1}{2}$ cup twice and the $\frac{1}{3}$ cup once.

D. Use the $\frac{1}{3}$ cup twice and the $\frac{1}{2}$ cup once.

E. Use the $\frac{1}{4}$ cup once, the $\frac{1}{3}$ cup once, and the $\frac{1}{2}$ cup once.

NAEP, Grade 8, 2011

3 Multiplication, Division, and Estimation with Rational Numbers

3 Objectives

Students will be able to understand and explain

- Multiplication and division of rational numbers.

- Properties of multiplication and division of rational numbers.

- Estimation of multiplication and division with rational numbers.

- Extension of exponents to include negative integers.

Multiplication of Rational Numbers

To motivate the definition of multiplication of rational numbers, we use the interpretation of multiplication as repeated addition. Using repeated addition, we interpret $3\left(\frac{3}{4}\right)$ as follows:

$$3\left(\frac{3}{4}\right) = \frac{3}{4} + \frac{3}{4} + \frac{3}{4} = \frac{9}{4} = 2\frac{1}{4}$$

The area model in Figure 13 is another way to calculate this product.

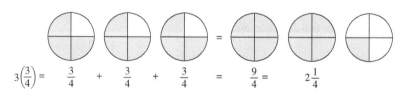

$$3\left(\frac{3}{4}\right) = \frac{3}{4} + \frac{3}{4} + \frac{3}{4} = \frac{9}{4} = 2\frac{1}{4}$$

Figure 13

We next consider $\left(\frac{3}{4}\right)3$. How should this product be interpreted? If the commutative property of multiplication of rational numbers is to hold, then $\left(\frac{3}{4}\right)3 = 3\left(\frac{3}{4}\right) = \frac{9}{4}$.

Next, we consider another interpretation of multiplication. What is $\frac{3}{4}$ of 3? In Figure 14(a) consider the 1-unit bar broken into fourths. Thus, there are four equal parts of the 1 unit, each of length $\frac{1}{4}$ unit. In Figure 14(b) suppose the length of the bar was 3 units. We want the same type of action to occur so it is divided into three-fourths using the same strategy. But analogously, each part would be 3 times the length of the bars in Figure 13(a). If this strategy is used then $\frac{3}{4}$ of 3 is seen as the shaded portion and $\frac{3}{4} \cdot 3 = \frac{9}{4}$ of 1 or simply $\frac{9}{4}$ is $\frac{3}{4}$ of 3.

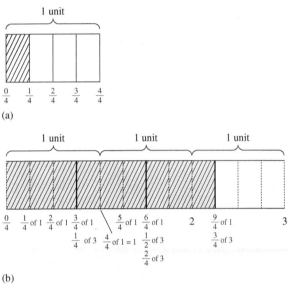

(a)

(b)

Figure 14

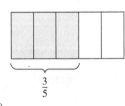

(a)

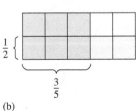

(b)

Figure 15

If forests once covered about $\frac{3}{5}$ of Earth's land and only about $\frac{1}{2}$ of these forests remain, what fraction of Earth is covered with forests today? We need to find $\frac{1}{2}$ of $\frac{3}{5}$, and can use an area model to find the answer.

Figure 15(a) shows a rectangle representing the *whole* separated into fifths, with $\frac{3}{5}$ shaded. To find $\frac{1}{2}$ of $\frac{3}{5}$, we divide the shaded portion of the rectangle in Figure 15(a) into two congruent parts and take one of those parts. The result would be the green portion of Figure 15(b). However, the green portion represents 3 parts out of 10, or $\frac{3}{10}$, of the whole. Thus,

$$\frac{1}{2} \text{ of } \frac{3}{5} = \frac{1}{2} \cdot \frac{3}{5} = \frac{3}{10} = \frac{1 \cdot 3}{2 \cdot 5}.$$

An area model like the one in Figure 14 is used on the student page shown on the next page.

School Book Page Multiplying Fractions

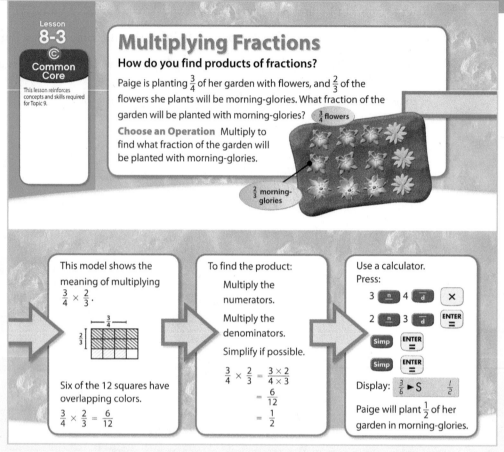

This discussion leads to the following definition of multiplication for rational numbers.

Definition of Multiplication of Rational Numbers

If $\frac{a}{b}$ and $\frac{c}{d}$ are any rational numbers, then $\frac{a}{b} \cdot \frac{c}{d} = \frac{ac}{bd}$.

Example 14

If $\frac{5}{6}$ of the population of a certain city are college graduates and $\frac{7}{11}$ of the city's college graduates are female, what fraction of the population of that city is female college graduates?

Solution The fraction should be $\frac{7}{11}$ of $\frac{5}{6}$, or $\frac{7}{11} \cdot \frac{5}{6} = \frac{7 \cdot 5}{11 \cdot 6} = \frac{35}{66}$.

The fraction of the population who are female college graduates is $\frac{35}{66}$.

Properties of Multiplication of Rational Numbers

Multiplication of rational numbers has properties analogous to the properties of multiplication of integers. These include the following properties for multiplication: closure, commutative, associative, and multiplicative identity. When we expand from the set of integers to the set of rationals, we pick up an additional property; that is, the multiplicative inverse property. For emphasis, we list the last two properties.

Theorem 10: Identity and Inverse Properties of Multiplication of Rational Numbers

Multiplicative Identity Property of Rational Numbers

The rational number 1 is the unique number such that for every rational number $\frac{a}{b}$,

$$1 \cdot \frac{a}{b} = \frac{a}{b} = \frac{a}{b} \cdot 1.$$

Multiplicative Inverse Property of Rational Numbers

For any nonzero rational number $\frac{a}{b}$, the multiplicative inverse (**reciprocal**) is the unique rational number $\frac{b}{a}$ such that

$$\frac{a}{b} \cdot \frac{b}{a} = 1 = \frac{b}{a} \cdot \frac{a}{b}.$$

Example 15

Find the multiplicative inverse, if possible, for each of the following rational numbers.

a. $\frac{2}{3}$ **b.** $\frac{^{-}2}{5}$ **c.** 4 **d.** 0 **e.** $6\frac{1}{2}$

Solution

a. $\frac{3}{2}$

b. $\frac{5}{^{-}2}$, or $\frac{^{-}5}{2}$

c. Because $4 = \frac{4}{1}$, the multiplicative inverse of 4 is $\frac{1}{4}$.

d. Even though $0 = \frac{0}{1}, \frac{1}{0}$ is undefined; there is no multiplicative inverse of 0.

e. Because $6\frac{1}{2} = \frac{13}{2}$, the multiplicative inverse of $6\frac{1}{2}$ is $\frac{2}{13}$.

Multiplication and addition are connected through the distributive property of multiplication over addition. Also, there are multiplication properties of equality and inequality for rational numbers and a multiplication property of zero similar to those for whole numbers and integers. These properties can be proved using the definition of operations on rational numbers and properties of integers. They are stated in the following theorem.

Theorem 11: Properties of Rational Number Operations

Distributive Properties of Multiplication Over Addition and Subtraction for Rational Numbers

Let $\frac{a}{b}, \frac{c}{d}$, and $\frac{e}{f}$ be any rational numbers. Then

$$\frac{a}{b}\left(\frac{c}{d} + \frac{e}{f}\right) = \frac{a}{b} \cdot \frac{c}{d} + \frac{a}{b} \cdot \frac{e}{f}; \text{ and } \frac{a}{b}\left(\frac{c}{d} - \frac{e}{f}\right) = \frac{a}{b} \cdot \frac{c}{d} - \frac{a}{b} \cdot \frac{e}{f}.$$

Multiplication Property of Equality for Rational Numbers

Let $\frac{a}{b}, \frac{c}{d}$, and $\frac{e}{f}$ be any rational numbers such that $\frac{a}{b} = \frac{c}{d}$; then $\frac{a}{b} \cdot \frac{e}{f} = \frac{c}{d} \cdot \frac{e}{f}$.

Multiplication Properties of Inequality for Rational Numbers

Let $\frac{a}{b}, \frac{c}{d}$, and $\frac{e}{f}$ be any rational numbers. Then

a. $\frac{a}{b} > \frac{c}{d}$ and $\frac{e}{f} > 0$, then $\frac{a}{b} \cdot \frac{e}{f} > \frac{c}{d} \cdot \frac{e}{f}$.

b. $\frac{a}{b} > \frac{c}{d}$ and $\frac{e}{f} < 0$, then $\frac{a}{b} \cdot \frac{e}{f} < \frac{c}{d} \cdot \frac{e}{f}$.

Multiplication Property of Zero for Rational Numbers

Let $\frac{a}{b}$ be any rational number; then $\frac{a}{b} \cdot 0 = 0 = 0 \cdot \frac{a}{b}$.

Example 16

A bicycle is on sale at $\frac{3}{4}$ of its original price. If the sale price is \$330, what was the original price?

Solution   Let x be the original price. Then $\frac{3}{4}$ of the original price is $\frac{3}{4}x$. Because the sale price is \$330, we have $\frac{3}{4}x = 330$. Solving for x gives

$$\frac{4}{3} \cdot \frac{3}{4}x = \frac{4}{3} \cdot 330$$
$$1 \cdot x = 440$$
$$x = 440.$$

Thus, the original price was \$440.

An alternative approach follows. Suppose the bar in Figure 16 represents the original price. We know that $\frac{3}{4}$ of the original price is the sale price \$330 as shown. We have 3 of the $\frac{1}{4}$ parts of the original price is \$330, and one part, $\frac{1}{4}$ of the original price, must be \$110. Thus, the original price is \$330 + \$110 = \$440.

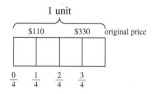

Figure 16

Multiplication with Mixed Numbers

In Figure 17, Johnny just figured out how to multiply mixed numbers while his colleagues seem to be struggling. How might we help them?

Figure 17

In Figure 17, Johnny may have decided one way to multiply $2\frac{1}{2} \cdot 2\frac{1}{2}$ is to change the mixed numbers to improper fractions and use the definition of multiplication as shown.

$$2\frac{1}{2} \cdot 2\frac{1}{2} = \frac{5}{2} \cdot \frac{5}{2} = \frac{25}{4}$$

We could then change $\frac{25}{4}$ to the mixed number $6\frac{1}{4}$.

Another way to multiply mixed numbers uses the distributive property of multiplication over addition, as seen below.

$$\begin{aligned}
2\frac{1}{2} \cdot 2\frac{1}{2} &= \left(2 + \frac{1}{2}\right)\left(2 + \frac{1}{2}\right) \\
&= \left(2 + \frac{1}{2}\right)2 + \left(2 + \frac{1}{2}\right)\frac{1}{2} \\
&= 2 \cdot 2 + \frac{1}{2} \cdot 2 + 2 \cdot \frac{1}{2} + \frac{1}{2} \cdot \frac{1}{2} \\
&= 4 + 1 + 1 + \frac{1}{4} \\
&= 6 + \frac{1}{4} \\
&= 6\frac{1}{4}
\end{aligned}$$

Multiplication of fractions enables us to obtain equivalent fractions, to perform addition and subtraction of fractions, as well as to solve equations in a different way, as shown in the following example.

Example 17

Use the definition of multiplication of fractions and its properties to justify the following.

   a. The Fundamental Law of Fractions: $\dfrac{a}{b} = \dfrac{an}{bn}$ if $b \neq 0, n \neq 0$.

   b. Addition of fractions using a common denominator.

Solution

   a. $\dfrac{a}{b} = \dfrac{a}{b} \cdot 1 = \dfrac{a}{b} \cdot \dfrac{n}{n} = \dfrac{an}{bn}$

   b. $\dfrac{a}{b} + \dfrac{c}{d} = \dfrac{a}{b} \cdot \dfrac{d}{d} + \dfrac{c}{d} \cdot \dfrac{b}{b}$

   $= \dfrac{ad}{bd} + \dfrac{bc}{bd}$

   $= \dfrac{ad + bc}{bd}$

Division of Rational Numbers

 In the grade 6 *Common Core Standards,* we find the following concerning division of rational numbers:

Apply and extend previous understandings of multiplication and division to divide fractions by fractions.

   1. Interpret and compute quotients of fractions and solve word problems involving division of fractions by fractions, e.g., by using visual fraction models and equations to represent the problem. (p. 42)

We apply and extend division of whole numbers by recalling that $6 \div 3$ means "How many 3s are there in 6?" We found that $6 \div 3 = 2$ because $3 \cdot 2 = 6$ and, in general, when $a, b, c \in W$, $a \div b = c$ if, and only if, c is the unique whole number such that $bc = a$. Consider $3 \div \left(\dfrac{1}{2}\right)$, which is equivalent to finding how many halves there are in 3. We see from the area model in Figure 18 that there are 6 half pieces in the 3 whole pieces. We record this as $3 \div \left(\dfrac{1}{2}\right) = 6$. This is true because $\left(\dfrac{1}{2}\right)6 = 3$.

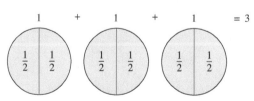

Figure 18

Another way to show that $3 \div \left(\dfrac{1}{2}\right) = 6$ is on a ruler. In Figure 19 we see that there are six $\dfrac{1}{2}$s in 3.

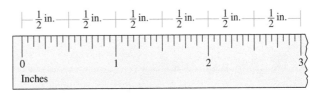

Figure 19

With whole numbers, one way to think about division is in terms of *repeated subtraction*. We found that $6 \div 2 = 3$ because 2 could be subtracted from 6 three times; that is, $6 - 3 \cdot 2 = 0$. Similarly, with $3 \div \frac{1}{2}$, we want to know how many halves can be subtracted from 3. Because $3 - 6\left(\frac{1}{2}\right) = 0$, we know that $3 \div \frac{1}{2} = 6$.

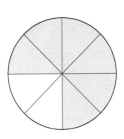

Figure 20

Next, consider $\frac{3}{4} \div \frac{1}{8}$. This means "How many $\frac{1}{8}$s are in $\frac{3}{4}$?" Figure 20 shows that there are six $\frac{1}{8}$s in the shaded portion, which represents $\frac{3}{4}$ of the whole. Therefore, $\frac{3}{4} \div \frac{1}{8} = 6$. This is true because $\left(\frac{1}{8}\right)6 = \frac{3}{4}$.

The measurement, or number-line, model may be used to understand division of fractions. For example, consider $\frac{7}{8} \div \frac{3}{4}$. First we draw a number line divided into eighths, as shown in Figure 21. Next we want to know how many $\frac{3}{4}$s there are in $\frac{7}{8}$. The bar of length $\frac{3}{4}$ is made up of 6 equal-size pieces of length $\frac{1}{8}$. We see that there is at least one length of $\frac{3}{4}$ in $\frac{7}{8}$. If we put another bar of length $\frac{3}{4}$ on the number line, we see there is 1 more of the 6 equal-length segments needed to make $\frac{7}{8}$. Therefore, the answer is $1\frac{1}{6}$, or $\frac{7}{6}$.

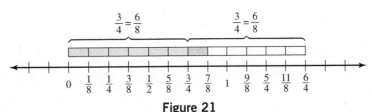

Figure 21

Additionally we know that $\frac{3}{4} \cdot \frac{7}{6} = \frac{21}{24} = \frac{7}{8}$, so the answer is correct.

In the previous examples, we saw a relationship between division and multiplication of rational numbers. We can define division for rational numbers formally in terms of multiplication in the same way that we defined division for whole numbers.

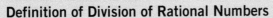

Definition of Division of Rational Numbers

Let $\frac{a}{b}, \frac{c}{d}$, and $\frac{e}{f}$ be rational numbers such that $\frac{c}{d} \neq 0$. Then $\frac{a}{b} \div \frac{c}{d} = \frac{e}{f}$ if, and only if, $\frac{e}{f}$ is the unique rational number such that $\frac{c}{d} \cdot \frac{e}{f} = \frac{a}{b}$.

In the above definition of division, $\frac{c}{d} \neq 0$ because division by 0 is not defined.

▶ **NOW TRY THIS 4**

Students often confuse finding half of a number with dividing by one-half. Notice that

$$a \div 2 = \frac{a}{2} = \frac{1}{2}a, \text{ but } a \div \frac{1}{2} = x \text{ if, and only if, } \frac{1}{2}x = a \text{ which implies } 2\left(\frac{1}{2}x\right) = 2a \text{ and } x = 2a.$$

Write a real-life story that will help students see the difference between finding half of a number and division by $\frac{1}{2}$.

The partial student page below illustrates a method for dividing called "invert and multiply."

Algorithm for Division of Rational Numbers

Does the *invert-and-multiply* method make sense based on what we know about rational numbers? Consider what such a division might mean. For example, using the definition of division of rational numbers,

$$\frac{2}{3} \div \frac{5}{7} = x \quad \text{if, and only if,} \quad \frac{2}{3} = \frac{5}{7}x.$$

To solve for x, we multiply both sides of the equation by $\frac{7}{5}$, the reciprocal of $\frac{5}{7}$. Thus,

$$\frac{7}{5} \cdot \frac{2}{3} = \frac{7}{5}\left(\frac{5}{7}x\right) = \left(\frac{7}{5} \cdot \frac{5}{7}\right)x = 1 \cdot x = x.$$

Therefore, $\frac{2}{3} \div \frac{5}{7} = \frac{2}{3} \cdot \frac{7}{5}$. This illustrates the "invert-and-multiply" method, or the "use the reciprocal and multiply" method.

School Book Page

To divide by a fraction, multiply by the reciprocal of the fraction. You can remember this by thinking "invert and multiply."

KEY CONCEPTS **Dividing Fractions**

Arithmetic	**Algebra**
$\frac{3}{5} \div \frac{1}{3} = \frac{3}{5} \cdot \frac{3}{1}$	$\frac{a}{b} \div \frac{c}{d} = \frac{a}{b} \cdot \frac{d}{c}$, where b, c, and d are not 0.

A traditional justification of this rule follows. The algorithm for division of fractions is usually justified in the middle grades by using the Fundamental Law of Fractions, $\frac{a}{b} = \frac{ac}{bc}$, where a, b, and c are fractions, or equivalently, the identity property of multiplication. For example,

$$\frac{2}{3} \div \frac{5}{7} = \frac{\frac{2}{3}}{\frac{5}{7}} = \frac{\frac{2}{3}}{\frac{5}{7}} \cdot 1 = \frac{\frac{2}{3}}{\frac{5}{7}} \cdot \frac{\frac{7}{5}}{\frac{7}{5}} = \frac{\frac{2}{3} \cdot \frac{7}{5}}{1} = \frac{2}{3} \cdot \frac{7}{5}.$$

Theorem 12: Algorithm for Division of Fractions

If $\frac{a}{b}$ and $\frac{c}{d}$ are any rational numbers with $\frac{c}{d} \neq 0$, then

$$\frac{a}{b} \div \frac{c}{d} = \frac{a}{b} \cdot \frac{d}{c}.$$

Alternative Algorithm for Division of Rational Numbers

An alternative algorithm for division of fractions can be found by first dividing fractions that have equal denominators. For example, $\frac{9}{10} \div \frac{3}{10} = \frac{9}{10} \cdot \frac{10}{3} = \frac{9}{3}$ and $\frac{15}{23} \div \frac{5}{23} = \frac{15}{23} \cdot \frac{23}{5} = \frac{15}{5}$. These examples suggest that when two fractions with the same denominator are divided, the result can be obtained by dividing the numerator of the first fraction by the numerator of the second; that is, $\frac{a}{b} \div \frac{c}{b} = \frac{a}{c}$. To divide fractions with different denominators, we rename the fractions so that the denominators are equal. Thus,

$$\frac{a}{b} \div \frac{c}{d} = \frac{ad}{bd} \div \frac{bc}{bd} = \frac{ad}{bd} \cdot \frac{bd}{bc} = \frac{ad}{bc}.$$

▶ NOW TRY THIS 5

Show that $\frac{a}{b} \div \frac{c}{d}$ and $\frac{a \div c}{b \div d}$ are equal.

The next three examples illustrate the use of division of rational numbers.

Example 18

A radio station provides 36 min for public service announcements for every 24 hr of broadcasting.

 a. What part of the 24-hr broadcasting day is allotted to public service announcements?

 b. How many $\frac{3}{4}$-min public service announcements can be broadcast in the 36 min?

Solution

 a. There are 60 min in an hour and $60 \cdot 24$ min in the broadcasting day. Thus, $36 \div (60 \cdot 24)$, or $\frac{1}{40}$, of the day is allotted for the announcements.

 b. $36 \div \left(\frac{3}{4}\right) = 36\left(\frac{4}{3}\right) = 48$ announcements are broadcast.

Example 19

We have $35\frac{1}{2}$ yd of material available to make towels. Each towel requires $\frac{3}{8}$ yd of material.

  a. How many towels can be made?
  b. How much material will remain?

Solution

  a. We need to find the integer part of the answer to $35\frac{1}{2} \div \frac{3}{8}$.

$$35\frac{1}{2} \div \frac{3}{8} = \frac{71}{2} \cdot \frac{8}{3} = \frac{284}{3} = 94\frac{2}{3}$$

  Thus, we can make 94 towels.

  b. Because the division in part (a) was by $\frac{3}{8}$, the amount of material remaining is $\frac{2}{3}$ of $\frac{3}{8}$, or

$$\frac{2}{3} \cdot \frac{3}{8} = \frac{1}{4} \text{ yd.}$$

Example 20

A bookstore has a shelf that is $37\frac{1}{2}$ in. long. Each book that is to be placed on the shelf is $1\frac{1}{4}$ in. thick. How many books can be placed on the shelf?

Solution   We need to find how many $1\frac{1}{4}$s there are in $37\frac{1}{2}$.

$$\frac{37\frac{1}{2}}{1\frac{1}{4}} = \frac{75}{2} \div \frac{5}{4}$$

$$= \frac{75}{2} \cdot \frac{4}{5}$$

$$= \frac{300}{10}$$

$$= 30$$

Note that we could compute $\frac{75}{2} \cdot \frac{4}{5}$ by first eliminating common factors; that is, $\frac{75}{2} \cdot \frac{4}{5} = \frac{15 \cdot 2}{1 \cdot 1} = \frac{30}{1} = 30$.

  Therefore, 30 books can be placed on the shelf.

Mental Math and Estimation with Rational Numbers

Mental math strategies developed with whole numbers can also be used with rational numbers.

Example 21

Use rational number properties to mentally compute the following products.

a. $(12 \cdot 25)\frac{1}{4}$ **b.** $\left(5\frac{1}{6}\right)12$ **c.** $\frac{4}{5}(20)$

Solution   Each computation shown is a possible approach.

a. $(12 \cdot 25)\frac{1}{4} = 25\left(12 \cdot \frac{1}{4}\right) = 25 \cdot 3 = 75$

b. $\left(5\frac{1}{6}\right)12 = \left(5 + \frac{1}{6}\right)12 = 5 \cdot 12 + \frac{1}{6} \cdot 12 = 60 + 2 = 62$

c. $\frac{4}{5}(20) = 4\left(\frac{1}{5} \cdot 20\right) = 4 \cdot 4 = 16$

Similarly, estimation strategies developed with whole number can be used with rational numbers.

Example 22

Estimate each of the following.

a. $3\frac{1}{4} \cdot 7\frac{8}{9}$ **b.** $24\frac{5}{7} \div 4\frac{1}{8}$

Solution

a. Using rounding, the product will be close to $3 \cdot 8 = 24$. If we use the range strategy, we can say the product must be between $3 \cdot 7 = 21$ and $4 \cdot 8 = 32$.

b. We can use compatible numbers and think of the estimate as $24 \div 4 = 6$ or $25 \div 5 = 5$.

Extending the Notion of Exponents

Recall that a^m was defined for any whole number a and any natural number m as the product of m a's. We define a^m for any rational number a in a similar way as follows.

> **Definition of a to the mth Power**
>
> $a^m = \underbrace{a \cdot a \cdot a \cdot \ldots \cdot a}_{m \text{ factors}}$, where a is any rational number and m is any natural number.

From the definition, $a^3 \cdot a^2 = (a \cdot a \cdot a)(a \cdot a) = a^{3+2} = a^5$. In a similar way, it follows that

Statement 1: If a is a rational number and m and n are any natural numbers, $a^m \cdot a^n = a^{m+n}$.
If Statement 1 is to be true for all whole numbers m and n, then because $a^1 \cdot a^0 = a^{1+0} = a^1$, we must have $a^0 = 1$. Hence, it is useful to give meaning to a^0 when $a \neq 0$ as follows.

Statement 2: For any nonzero rational number a, $a^0 = 1$.
If $a^m \cdot a^n = a^{m+n}$ is extended to all integer powers of a, then how should a^{-3} be defined? If Statement 1 is to be true for all integers m and n, then $a^{-3} \cdot a^3 = a^{-3+3} = a^0 = 1$. Therefore, $a^{-3} = \frac{1}{a^3}$. This is true in general and we have the following.

Statement 3: Definition: For any nonzero rational number a and any natural number n, $a^{-n} = \frac{1}{a^n}$.

In elementary grades the definition of a^{-n} is typically motivated by looking at patterns. Notice that as the following exponents decrease by 1, the numbers on the right are divided by 10. Thus, the pattern might be continued, as shown.

$$10^3 = 10 \cdot 10 \cdot 10$$
$$10^2 = 10 \cdot 10$$
$$10^1 = 10$$
$$10^0 = 1$$
$$10^{-1} = \frac{1}{10} = \frac{1}{10^1}$$
$$10^{-2} = \frac{1}{10} \cdot \frac{1}{10} = \frac{1}{10^2}$$
$$10^{-3} = \frac{1}{10^2} \cdot \frac{1}{10} = \frac{1}{10^3}$$

If the pattern is extended in this way, then we would predict that $10^{-n} = \dfrac{1}{10^n}$. Notice that this is inductive reasoning and hence is not a mathematical justification.

Consider whether the property $a^m \cdot a^n = a^{m+n}$ can be extended to include all powers of a, where the exponents are integers. For example, is it true that $2^4 \cdot 2^{-3} = 2^{4+^-3} = 2^1$? The definitions of 2^{-3} and the properties of nonnegative exponents ensure this is true, as shown next.

$$2^4 \cdot 2^{-3} = 2^4 \cdot \frac{1}{2^3} = \frac{2^4}{2^3} = \frac{2^1 \cdot 2^3}{2^3} = 2^1$$

Similarly, $2^{-4} \cdot 2^{-3} = 2^{-4+^-3} = 2^{-7}$ is true because

$$2^{-4} \cdot 2^{-3} = \frac{1}{2^4} \cdot \frac{1}{2^3} = \frac{1 \cdot 1}{2^4 \cdot 2^3} = \frac{1}{2^{4+3}} = \frac{1}{2^7} = 2^{-7}.$$

In general, with integer exponents, the following theorem holds.

Theorem 13

For any nonzero rational number a and any integers m and n, $a^m \cdot a^n = a^{m+n}$.

If $a = 0$ and either m or n is negative, then $a^m \cdot a^n$ is undefined.

Other properties of exponents can be developed by using the properties of rational numbers. For example,

$$\frac{2^5}{2^3} = \frac{2^3 \cdot 2^2}{2^3} = 2^2 = 2^{5-3} \quad \text{and} \quad \frac{2^5}{2^8} = \frac{2^5}{2^5 \cdot 2^3} = \frac{1}{2^3} = 2^{-3} = 2^{5-8}.$$

With integer exponents, the following theorem holds.

Theorem 14

For any nonzero rational number a and any integers m and n, $\dfrac{a^m}{a^n} = a^{m-n}$.

At times, we may encounter an expression like $(2^4)^3$. This expression can be written as a single power of 2 as follows:

$$(2^4)^3 = 2^4 \cdot 2^4 \cdot 2^4 = 2^{4+4+4} = 2^{3 \cdot 4} = 2^{12}$$

In general, if a is any rational number and m and n are positive integers, then

$$(a^m)^n = \underbrace{a^m \cdot a^m \cdot \ldots \cdot a^m}_{n \text{ factors}} = \overbrace{a^{m+m+ \ldots +m}}^{n \text{ terms}} = a^{nm} = a^{mn}.$$

Does this theorem hold for negative-integer exponents? For example, does $(2^3)^{-4} = 2^{(3)(-4)} = 2^{-12}$? The answer is yes because $(2^3)^{-4} = \dfrac{1}{(2^3)^4} = \dfrac{1}{2^{12}} = 2^{-12}$. Also, $(2^{-3})^4 = \left(\dfrac{1}{2^3}\right)^4 = \dfrac{1}{2^3} \cdot \dfrac{1}{2^3} \cdot \dfrac{1}{2^3} \cdot \dfrac{1}{2^3} = \dfrac{1^4}{(2^3)^4} = \dfrac{1}{2^{12}} = 2^{-12}$.

Theorem 15

For any nonzero rational number a and any integers m and n,

$$(a^m)^n = a^{mn}.$$

Using the definitions and theorems developed, we derive additional properties. For example:

$$\left(\frac{2}{3}\right)^4 = \frac{2}{3} \cdot \frac{2}{3} \cdot \frac{2}{3} \cdot \frac{2}{3} = \frac{2 \cdot 2 \cdot 2 \cdot 2}{3 \cdot 3 \cdot 3 \cdot 3} = \frac{2^4}{3^4}$$

This property is generalized as follows.

Theorem 16

For any nonzero rational number $\dfrac{a}{b}$ and any integer m,

$$\left(\frac{a}{b}\right)^m = \frac{a^m}{b^m}.$$

From the definition of negative exponents, the preceding theorem, and division of fractions, we have

$$\left(\frac{a}{b}\right)^{-m} = \frac{1}{\left(\dfrac{a}{b}\right)^m} = \frac{1}{\dfrac{a^m}{b^m}} = \frac{b^m}{a^m} = \left(\frac{b}{a}\right)^m.$$

Theorem 17

For any nonzero rational number $\dfrac{a}{b}$ and any integer m, $\left(\dfrac{a}{b}\right)^{-m} = \left(\dfrac{b}{a}\right)^m.$

A property similar to the one in Theorem 16 holds for multiplication. For example,

$$(2 \cdot 3)^{-3} = \frac{1}{(2 \cdot 3)^3} = \frac{1}{2^3 \cdot 3^3} = \left(\frac{1}{2^3}\right) \cdot \left(\frac{1}{3^3}\right) = 2^{-3} \cdot 3^{-3}.$$

Theorem 18 considers the distributive property of exponentiation over multiplication.

Theorem 18

For any nonzero rational numbers a and b and any integer m,

$$(a \cdot b)^m = a^m \cdot b^m.$$

Theorem 18 is also true when a or $b = 0$ and $m > 0$.

The properties of exponents are summarized below.

Theorem 19:   Properties of Exponents

For any nonzero rational numbers a and b and integers m and n, the following are true.

a. $a^0 = 1$

b. $a^{-m} = \dfrac{1}{a^m}$

c. $a^m \cdot a^n = a^{m+n}$

d. $\dfrac{a^m}{a^n} = a^{m-n}$

e. $(a^m)^n = a^{mn}$

f. $\left(\dfrac{a}{b}\right)^m = \dfrac{a^m}{b^m}$

g. $\left(\dfrac{a}{b}\right)^{-m} = \left(\dfrac{b}{a}\right)^m$

h. $(ab)^m = a^m b^m$

Notice that property (h) is for multiplication. Analogous properties do not hold for addition and subtraction. For example, in general, $(a + b)^{-1} \neq a^{-1} + b^{-1}$. To see why, a numerical example is sufficient, but it is instructive to write each side with positive exponents:

$$(a + b)^{-1} = \frac{1}{a + b}$$

$$a^{-1} + b^{-1} = \frac{1}{a} + \frac{1}{b}$$

We know from addition of fractions, $\dfrac{1}{a + b} \neq \dfrac{1}{a} + \dfrac{1}{b}$. Therefore, $(a + b)^{-1} \neq a^{-1} + b^{-1}$.

Example 23

In each of the following statements, show each equality or inequality is true in general for nonzero rational numbers x, a, and b.

a. $(^-x)^{-2} \neq {}^-x^{-2}$
b. $(^-x)^{-3} = {}^-x^{-3}$
c. $ab^{-1} \neq (ab)^{-1}$ unless $a = 1$ or $a = {}^-1$
d. $(a^{-2} b^{-2})^{-1} = a^2 b^2$
e. $(a^{-2} + b^{-2})^{-1} \neq a^2 + b^2$

Solution

a. $\left({}^{-}x\right)^{-2} = \dfrac{1}{\left({}^{-}x\right)^2} = \dfrac{1}{x^2}$

$\qquad {}^{-}x^{-2} = -(x^{-2}) = {}^{-}\left(\dfrac{1}{x^2}\right) = \dfrac{{}^{-}1}{x^2}$.

Hence, $\left({}^{-}x\right)^{-2} \neq {}^{-}x^{-2}$.

b. $\left({}^{-}x\right)^{-3} = \dfrac{1}{\left({}^{-}x\right)^3} = \dfrac{1}{{}^{-}x^3} = {}^{-}\left(\dfrac{1}{x^3}\right)$

$\qquad {}^{-}x^{-3} = {}^{-}(x^{-3}) = {}^{-}\left(\dfrac{1}{x^3}\right)$

Hence, $\left({}^{-}x\right)^{-3} = {}^{-}x^{-3}$.

c. $ab^{-1} = a(b^{-1}) = a \cdot \dfrac{1}{b} = \dfrac{a}{b}$, but $(ab)^{-1} = \dfrac{1}{ab}$. Hence, $ab^{-1} \neq (ab)^{-1}$.

d. $(a^{-2}b^{2})^{-1} = (a^{-2})^{-1}(b^{2})^{-1}$

$\qquad\qquad = a^{({}^{-}2)({}^{-}1)}b^{(2)({}^{-}1)}$

$\qquad\qquad = a^2 b^{-2}$

e. $(a^{-2} + b^{-2})^{-1} = \left(\dfrac{1}{a^2} + \dfrac{1}{b^2}\right)^{-1} = \left(\dfrac{a^2 + b^2}{a^2 b^2}\right)^{-1} = \dfrac{a^2 b^2}{a^2 + b^2} \neq a^2 + b^2$

Observe that all the properties of exponents refer to powers with either the same base or the same exponent. To evaluate expressions using exponents where different bases and powers are used, perform all the computations or rewrite the expressions in either the same base or the same exponent, if possible. For example, $\dfrac{27^4}{81^3}$ can be rewritten $\dfrac{27^4}{81^3} = \dfrac{(3^3)^4}{(3^4)^3} = \dfrac{3^{12}}{3^{12}} = 1$.

Example 24

Perform the following computations and express your answers without negative exponents.

a. $16^2 \cdot 8^{-3}$

b. $20^2 \div 2^4$

c. $(10^{-1} + 5 \cdot 10^{-2} + 3 \cdot 10^{-3})10^3$

d. $(x^3 y^{-2})^{-4}$

Solution

a. $16^2 \cdot 8^{-3} = (2^4)^2 \cdot (2^3)^{-3} = 2^8 \cdot 2^{-9} = 2^{8+{}^{-}9} = 2^{-1} = \dfrac{1}{2}$

b. $\dfrac{20^2}{2^4} = \dfrac{(2^2 \cdot 5)^2}{2^4} = \dfrac{2^4 \cdot 5^2}{2^4} = 5^2 \text{ or } 25$

c. $(10^{-1} + 5 \cdot 10^{-2} + 3 \cdot 10^{-3})10^3 = 10^{-1} \cdot 10^3 + 5 \cdot 10^{-2} \cdot 10^3 + 3 \cdot 10^{-3} \cdot 10^3$

$\qquad\qquad\qquad\qquad\qquad\qquad = 10^{{}^{-}1+3} + 5 \cdot 10^{{}^{-}2+3} + 3 \cdot 10^{{}^{-}3+3}$

$\qquad\qquad\qquad\qquad\qquad\qquad = 10^2 + 5 \cdot 10^1 + 3 \cdot 10^0$

$\qquad\qquad\qquad\qquad\qquad\qquad = 153$

d. $(x^3 y^{-2})^{-4} = (x^3)^{-4} \cdot (y^{-2})^{-4} = x^{3({}^{-}4)} \cdot y^{({}^{-}2)({}^{-}4)} = x^{-12}y^8 = \left(\dfrac{1}{x^{12}}\right)y^8 = \dfrac{y^8}{x^{12}}$, if $x, y \neq 0$

Assessment 3A

1. In the following figures, a unit rectangle is used to illustrate the product of two fractions. Name the fractions and their products.

   a.   **b.**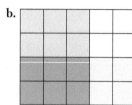

2. Use a rectangular region to illustrate each of the following products.

   a. $\dfrac{1}{3} \cdot \dfrac{3}{4}$

   b. $\dfrac{2}{3} \cdot \dfrac{1}{5}$

3. Find each of the following products. Write your answers in simplest form.

   a. $\dfrac{49}{65} \cdot \dfrac{26}{98}$ **b.** $\dfrac{a}{b} \cdot \dfrac{b^2}{a^2}$ **c.** $\dfrac{xy}{z} \cdot \dfrac{z^2 a}{x^3 y^2}$

4. Use the distributive property of multiplication over addition to find each product.

   a. $4\dfrac{1}{2} \cdot 2\dfrac{1}{3}$

   b. $3\dfrac{1}{3} \cdot 2\dfrac{1}{2}$

5. Find the multiplicative inverse of each of the following.

   a. $\dfrac{^{-}1}{3}$ **b.** $3\dfrac{1}{3}$

   c. $\dfrac{x}{y}$, if $x \neq 0$ **d.** $^{-}7$

6. Solve for x.

   a. $\dfrac{2}{3}x = \dfrac{7}{6}$

   b. $\dfrac{3}{4} \div x = \dfrac{1}{2}$

   c. $\dfrac{5}{6} + \dfrac{2}{3}x = \dfrac{3}{4}$

   d. $\dfrac{2x}{3} - \dfrac{1}{4} = \dfrac{x}{6} + \dfrac{1}{2}$

7. Show that the following properties do not hold for the division of rational numbers.
   a. Commutative
   b. Associative

8. Compute the following mentally. Find the exact answers.

   a. $3\dfrac{1}{4} \cdot 8$

   b. $7\dfrac{1}{4} \cdot 4$

   c. $9\dfrac{1}{5} \cdot 10$

   d. $8 \cdot 2\dfrac{1}{4}$

9. Choose from among the numbers in parentheses the number that best approximates each of the following.

   a. $3\dfrac{11}{12} \cdot 5\dfrac{3}{100}$ $(8, 20, 15, 16)$

   b. $2\dfrac{1}{10} \cdot 7\dfrac{7}{8}$ $(16, 14, 4, 3)$

   c. $\dfrac{1}{101} \div \dfrac{1}{103}$ $\left(0, 1, \dfrac{1}{2}, \dfrac{1}{4}\right)$

10. Without actually doing the computations, choose the phrase in parentheses that correctly describes each.

    a. $\dfrac{13}{14} \cdot \dfrac{17}{19}$ (greater than 1, less than 1)

    b. $3\dfrac{2}{7} \div 5\dfrac{1}{9}$ (greater than 1, less than 1)

    c. $4\dfrac{1}{3} \div 2\dfrac{3}{100}$ (greater than 2, less than 2)

11. A sewing project requires $6\dfrac{1}{8}$ yd of material that sells for $4 per yard and $3\dfrac{1}{4}$ yd of material that sells for $3 per yard.

    Choose the best estimate for the cost of the project:
    a. Between $30 and $40
    b. Between $20 and $34
    c. Between $36 and $40
    d. Between $33 and $40

12. Five-eighths of the students at Salem State College live in dormitories. If 6000 students at the college live in dormitories, how many students are there in the college?

13. Alberto owns $\dfrac{5}{9}$ of the stock in the N.W. Tofu Company. His sister Renatta owns half as much stock as Alberto. What part of the stock is owned by neither Alberto nor Renatta?

14. A suit is on sale for $180.00. What was the original price of the suit if the discount was $\dfrac{1}{4}$ of the original price?

15. John took all his money out of his savings account. He spent $50.00 on a radio and $\dfrac{3}{5}$ of what remained on presents. Half of what was left he put in his checking account, and the remaining $35.00 he donated to charity. How much money did John originally have in his savings account?

16. Al gives $\frac{1}{2}$ of his marbles to Bev. Bev gives $\frac{1}{2}$ of these to Carl. Carl gives $\frac{1}{2}$ of these to Dani. If Dani was given four marbles, how many did Al have originally?

17. Write each of the following in simplest form using positive exponents in the final answer.

    a. $3^{-7} \cdot 3^{-6}$ **b.** $3^7 \cdot 3^6$

    c. $5^{15} \div 5^4$ **d.** $5^{15} \div 5^{-4}$

    e. $(^-5)^{-2}$ **f.** $\dfrac{a^2}{a^{-3}}$

18. Write each of the following in simplest form using positive exponents in the final answer.

    a. $\left(\dfrac{1}{2}\right)^3 \cdot \left(\dfrac{1}{2}\right)^7$

    b. $\left(\dfrac{1}{2}\right)^9 \div \left(\dfrac{1}{2}\right)^6$

    c. $\left(\dfrac{2}{3}\right)^5 \cdot \left(\dfrac{4}{9}\right)^2$

    d. $\left(\dfrac{3}{5}\right)^7 \div \left(\dfrac{3}{5}\right)^7$

19. If a and b are rational numbers, with $a \neq 0$ and $b \neq 0$, and if m and n are integers, which of the following statements are always true? Justify your answers.

    a. $a^m \cdot b^n = (ab)^{m+n}$ **b.** $a^m \cdot b^n = (ab)^{mn}$

    c. $a^m \cdot b^m = (ab)^{2m}$ **d.** $(ab)^0 = 1$

    e. $(a + b)^m = a^m + b^m$

    f. $(a + b)^{-m} = \dfrac{1}{a^m} + \dfrac{1}{b^m}$

20. Solve for the integer n in each of the following.

    a. $2^n = 32$ **b.** $n^2 = 36$

    c. $2^n \cdot 2^7 = 2^5$ **d.** $2^n \cdot 2^7 = 8$

21. Solve each of the following inequalities for x, where x is an integer.

    a. $3^x \leq 9$ **b.** $25^x < 125$

    c. $3^{2x} > 27$ **d.** $4^x > 1$

22. Determine which fraction in each of the following pairs is greater.

    a. $\left(\dfrac{1}{2}\right)^3$ or $\left(\dfrac{1}{2}\right)^4$

    b. $\left(\dfrac{3}{4}\right)^{10}$ or $\left(\dfrac{3}{4}\right)^8$

    c. $\left(\dfrac{4}{3}\right)^{10}$ or $\left(\dfrac{4}{3}\right)^8$

    d. $\left(\dfrac{3}{4}\right)^{10}$ or $\left(\dfrac{4}{5}\right)^{10}$

    e. 32^{50} or 4^{100}

    f. $(^-27)^{-15}$ or $(^-3)^{-75}$

23. Show that the arithmetic mean of two rational numbers is between the two numbers; that is, prove if $\dfrac{a}{b} < \dfrac{c}{d}$, then
$$\dfrac{a}{b} < \dfrac{1}{2}\left(\dfrac{a}{b} + \dfrac{c}{d}\right) < \dfrac{c}{d}.$$

24. In the Corcoran School of Design in 2014, $\frac{17}{25}$ of the students were male.

    a. What fraction were female?

    b. Does this imply 17 students are male?

25. The reported tax revenue in dollars for Washington DC in 2011 is shown below.

Corporate Income	\$36,802,396
Personal Income	32,020,924
Social Security & Other Taxes	620,501
Hotel Tax	212,565,755
Property Taxes	183,005,144
Excise & Fees	21,723,515
Sales Tax	187,656,061
Restaurant	119,487,765
Retail	58,122,531
Airport	7,155,614
Car Rental	2,890,151
Total	**674,394,296**

    a. Approximately what is the fractional part of the total tax is the difference in restaurant sales tax and retail sales tax?

    b. If the sales tax were abolished, approximately what fraction of the total tax package would be lost?

26. According to the Washington DC City Government, the following lists the number of homicides in the city since 2004.

2013	2012	2011	2010	2009	2008	2007	2006	2005	2004
104	88	108	132	144	186	181	169	196	198

    a. What year showed the greatest fractional increase from the previous year?

    b. What year showed the greatest fractional decrease from the previous year?

27. If $\dfrac{1}{33}$ of all deer in the United States are in Mississippi and $\dfrac{2}{7}$ of the deer are in Montana, what total fractional part of the deer population is in those two states?

28. If $\dfrac{1}{4}$ of an estate is to be distributed equally to 8 cousins, what fractional part of the entire estate does each cousin receive?

Assessment 3B

1. In the following figure a unit rectangle is used to illustrate the product of two fractions. Name the fractions and their products.

   a. 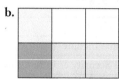 b.

2. Use a rectangular region to illustrate each of the following products.

   a. $\dfrac{2}{5} \cdot \dfrac{1}{3}$

   b. $\dfrac{2}{3} \cdot \dfrac{2}{3}$

3. Find each of the following products of rational numbers. Write your answers in simplest form.

   a. $2\dfrac{1}{3} \cdot 3\dfrac{3}{4}$

   b. $\dfrac{22}{7} \cdot 4\dfrac{2}{3}$

   c. $\dfrac{^-5}{2} \cdot 2\dfrac{1}{2}$

   d. $2\dfrac{3}{4} \cdot 2\dfrac{1}{3}$

   e. $\dfrac{a^2}{b^3} \cdot \dfrac{b^2}{a^3}$

   f. $\dfrac{x^3 y^2}{z} \cdot \dfrac{z}{x^2 y}$

4. Use the distributive property to find each product of rational numbers.

   a. $2\dfrac{1}{3} \cdot 4\dfrac{3}{5}$

   b. $\left(\dfrac{x}{y} + 1\right)\left(\dfrac{y}{x} - 1\right)$

   c. $248\dfrac{2}{5} \cdot 100\dfrac{1}{8}$

5. Find the multiplicative inverse of each of the following.

   a. $\dfrac{6}{7}$

   b. 8

   c. $4\dfrac{1}{5}$

   d. $^-1\dfrac{1}{2}$

6. Solve for x.

   a. $\dfrac{2}{3}x = \dfrac{11}{6}$

   b. $\dfrac{3}{4} \div x = \dfrac{1}{3}$

   c. $\dfrac{5}{6} - \dfrac{2}{3}x = \dfrac{3}{4}$

   d. $\dfrac{2x}{3} + \dfrac{1}{4} = \dfrac{x}{6} - \dfrac{1}{2}$

7. Find a fraction such that if you add the denominator to the numerator and place the sum over the original denominator, the new fraction has triple the value of the original fraction.

8. Compute the following mentally; find the exact answers.

   a. $3\dfrac{1}{2} \cdot 8$

   b. $7\dfrac{3}{4} \cdot 4$

   c. $9\dfrac{1}{5} \cdot 6$

   d. $8 \cdot 2\dfrac{1}{3}$

   e. $3 \div \dfrac{1}{2}$

   f. $3\dfrac{1}{2} \div \dfrac{1}{2}$

   g. $3 \div \dfrac{1}{3}$

   h. $4\dfrac{1}{2} \div 2$

9. Choose from among the numbers in parentheses the number that best approximates each of the following.

   a. $20\dfrac{2}{3} \div 9\dfrac{7}{8} \left(2, 180, \dfrac{1}{2}, 10\right)$

   b. $3\dfrac{1}{20} \cdot 7\dfrac{77}{100} \left(21, 24, \dfrac{1}{20}, 32\right)$

   c. $\dfrac{1}{10^3} \div \dfrac{1}{1001} \left(\dfrac{1}{10^3}, 1, 1001, 0\right)$

10. Without actually doing the computations, choose the phrase in parentheses that correctly describes each.

    a. $4\dfrac{1}{3} \div 2\dfrac{13}{100}$ (greater than 2, less than 2)

    b. $16 \div 4\dfrac{3}{18}$ (greater than 4, less than 4)

    c. $16 \div 3\dfrac{8}{9}$ (greater than 4, less than 4)

11. When you multiply a certain number by 3 and then subtract $\dfrac{7}{18}$, you get the same result as when you multiply the number by 2 and add $\dfrac{5}{12}$. What is the number?

12. Di Paloma University had a faculty reduction and lost $\dfrac{1}{5}$ of its faculty. If 320 faculty members were left after the reduction, how many members were there originally?

13. A person has $29\dfrac{1}{2}$ yd of material available to make doll outfits. Each outfit requires $\dfrac{3}{4}$ yd of material.

    a. How many outfits can be made?

    b. How much material will be left over?

14. Every employee's salary at the Sunrise Software Company increases each year by $\dfrac{1}{10}$ of that person's salary the previous year.

    a. If Martha's present annual salary is $100,000, what will her salary be in 2 yr?

    b. If Aaron's present salary is $99,000, what was his salary 1 yr ago?

    c. If Juanita's present salary is $363,000, what was her salary 2 yr ago?

15. Jasmine is reading a book. She has finished $\dfrac{3}{4}$ of the book and has 82 pages left to read. How many pages has she read?

16. Peter, Paul, and Mary start at the same time walking around a circular track in the same direction. Peter takes $\dfrac{1}{2}$ hr to walk around the track. Paul takes $\dfrac{5}{12}$ hr, and Mary takes $\dfrac{1}{3}$ hr.

    a. How many minutes does it take each person to walk around the track?

    b. How many times will each person go around the track before all three meet again at the starting line?

17. Write each of the following rational numbers in simplest form using positive exponents in the final answer.

    a. $\left(\dfrac{1}{3}\right)^{-1}$ b. $\dfrac{a^{-3}}{a}$ c. $\dfrac{(a^{-4})^3}{a^{-4}}$

    d. $\dfrac{a}{a^{-1}}$ e. $\dfrac{a^{-3}}{a^{-2}}$

18. Write each of the following in simplest form using positive exponents in the final answer.

    a. $\left(\dfrac{1}{2}\right)^{10} \div \left(\dfrac{1}{2}\right)^{2}$

    b. $\left(\dfrac{2}{3}\right)^{5}\left(\dfrac{4}{9}\right)^{-2}$

    c. $\left(\dfrac{3}{5}\right)^{7} \div \left(\dfrac{5}{3}\right)^{4}$

    d. $\left[\left(\dfrac{5}{6}\right)^{7}\right]^{3}$

19. If a and b are rational numbers, with $a \neq 0$ and $b \neq 0$, and if m and n are integers, which of the following statements are always true? Justify your answers.

    a. $\dfrac{a^m}{b^n} = \left(\dfrac{a}{b}\right)^{m-n}$

    b. $(ab)^{-m} = \dfrac{1}{a^m} \cdot \dfrac{1}{b^m}$

    c. $\left(\dfrac{2}{a^{-1}+b^{-1}}\right)^{-1} = \dfrac{1}{2} \cdot \dfrac{1}{a+b}$

    d. $2(a^{-1}+b^{-1})^{-1} = \dfrac{2ab}{a+b}$

    e. $a^{mn} = a^m \cdot a^n$

    f. $\left(\dfrac{a}{b}\right)^{-1} = \dfrac{b}{a}$

20. Solve, if possible, for n where n is an integer in each of the following.

    a. $2^n = {}^{-}32$ b. $n^3 = \dfrac{{}^{-}1}{27}$

    c. $2^n \cdot 2^7 = 1024$ d. $2^n \cdot 2^7 = 64$

    e. $(2+n)^2 = 2^2 + n^2$ f. $3^n = 27^5$

21. Solve each of the following inequalities for x, where x is an integer.

    a. $3^x \geq 81$ b. $4^x \geq 8$

    c. $3^{2x} \leq 27$ d. $2^x < 1$

22. Determine which fraction in each of the following pairs is greater.

    a. $\left(\dfrac{4}{3}\right)^{10}$ or $\left(\dfrac{4}{3}\right)^{8}$

    b. $\left(\dfrac{3}{4}\right)^{10}$ or $\left(\dfrac{4}{5}\right)^{10}$

    c. $\left(\dfrac{4}{3}\right)^{10}$ or $\left(\dfrac{5}{4}\right)^{10}$

    d. $\left(\dfrac{3}{4}\right)^{100}$ or $\left(\dfrac{3}{4} \cdot \dfrac{9}{10}\right)^{100}$

23. In the following, determine which number is greater.

    a. 32^{100} or 4^{200}

    b. $({}^{-}27)^{-15}$ or $({}^{-}3)^{-50}$

24. Brandy bought a horse for $270 and immediately started paying for his keep. She sold the horse for $540. Considering the cost of his keep she found that she had lost an amount equal to half of what she paid for the horse plus one-fourth of the cost of his keep. How much did Brandy lose on the horse?

25. In 2014 in the Corcoran School of Design, $\dfrac{8}{25}$ of the students were female. What fraction was male?

26. The reported tax revenue in dollars for Washington DC in 2011 is shown below.

Corporate Income	$36,802,396
Personal Income	32,020,924
Social Security & Other Taxes	620,501
Hotel Tax	212,565,755
Property Taxes	183,005,144
Excise & Fees	21,723,515
Sales Tax	187,656,061
Restaurant	119,487,765
Retail	58,122,531
Airport	7,155,614
Car Rental	2,890,151
Total	**674,394,296**

   a. Approximately what is the fractional part of the total tax is the difference in hotel tax and property tax?

   b. If the sales tax was increased $\dfrac{1}{11}$, approximately what fraction of the total tax package would be gained?

27. According to the Washington DC City Government, the following lists the number of homicides in the city since 2004.

2013	2012	2011	2010	2009	2008	2007	2006	2005	2004
104	88	108	132	144	186	181	169	196	198

   a. What is the fractional decrease in homicides from 2005 to 2012?

   b. What is the fractional increase in homicides from 2012 to 2013?

28. If $\dfrac{1}{33}$ of all deer in the United States are in Mississippi, and $\dfrac{2}{7}$ of the deer are in Montana, what fractional part of the deer population is not in those two states?

29. If $\dfrac{1}{4}$ of an estate consists of $\dfrac{2}{5}$ stocks and $\dfrac{3}{5}$ bonds, what part of the estate is each of the stocks and bonds?

Mathematical Connections 3

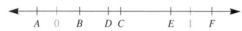

Reasoning

1. Suppose you divide a natural number n by a positive rational number less than 1. Will the answer always be less than n, sometimes less than n, or never less than n? Why?
2. If the fractions represented by points C and D on the following number line are multiplied, what point best represents the product? Explain why.

```
◄──┼──┼──┼──┼─┼──┼──┼──┼──►
   A  0  B  D C    E  1  F
```

3. If the product of two numbers is 1 and one of the numbers is greater than 1, what do you know about the other number? Explain your answer.

Open-Ended

4. Write a story or model for $1\frac{3}{4} \div \frac{1}{2}$.
5. Complete a survey of your class asking questions such as their favorite color, favorite type of shoe, and favorite math concept. Use fractions to summarize your information and find any differences in male and female preference.
6. Consider the demographics of students in each undergraduate class (freshman, sophomore, junior, and senior) at your university. Describe the fractional differences in males and females in each class.

Cooperative Learning

7. Choose a brick building on your campus. Measure the height of one brick and the thickness of mortar between bricks. Estimate the height of the building and then calculate the height of the building. Were rational numbers used in your computations?
8. Have each student in your group choose a state or city and find the demographics on taxes as in Exercise 26 in Assessment 3B. Compare fractions representing sales taxes for each chosen location. Which has the highest? Lowest?
9. In each group of a class, describe your group using fractions in the explanation. Use at least three sets of fractions in your description. Pass the descriptions to the teacher who will then distribute the descriptions to a different group. The goal is to describe your group well enough that others can identify the groups.

Connecting Mathematics to the Classroom

10. Bente says to do the problem $12\frac{1}{4} \div 3\frac{3}{4}$ you just find $12 \div 3 = 4$ and $\frac{1}{4} \div \frac{3}{4} = \frac{1}{3}$ to get $4\frac{1}{3}$. How do you respond?
11. Amy says that dividing a number by $\frac{1}{2}$ is the same as taking half of a number. How do you respond?
12. Dani says that if we have $\frac{3}{4} \cdot \frac{2}{5}$, we could just multiply $\frac{3}{5} \cdot \frac{2}{4} = \frac{3}{5} \cdot \frac{1}{2} = \frac{3}{10}$. Is she correct? Explain why.

13. Noah says that dividing a number by 2 is the same as multiplying it by $\frac{1}{2}$. He wants to know if he is right, and if so, why. How do you respond?
14. Jim is not sure when to use multiplication by a fraction and when to use division. He has the following list of problems. How would you help him solve these problems in a way that would enable him to solve similar problems on his own?
    a. $\frac{3}{4}$ of a package of sugar fills $\frac{1}{2}$ c. How many cups of sugar are in a full package of sugar?
    b. How many packages of sugar are needed to fill 2 c?
    c. If $\frac{1}{3}$ c sugar is required to make two loaves of challah, how many cups of sugar are needed for three loaves?
    d. If $\frac{3}{4}$ c sugar is required for 1 gal of punch, how many gallons can be made with 2 c of sugar?
    e. If you have $22\frac{3}{8}$ in. of ribbon, and need $1\frac{1}{4}$ in. to decorate one doll, how many dolls can be decorated, and how much ribbon will be left over?
15. A student claims that division always makes things smaller so $5 \div \left(\frac{1}{2}\right)$ cannot be 10 because 10 is greater than the number 5 she started with. How do you respond?
16. A student simplified the fraction $\frac{m+n}{p+n}$ to $\frac{m}{p}$. How would you help this student?
17. Jillian says she learned that 17 divided by 5 can be written as $17 \div 5 = 3 \text{ R2}$, but she thinks that writing $17 \div 5 = \frac{17}{5} = 3\frac{2}{5}$ is much better. How do you respond?

Review Problems

18. Perform each of the following computations. Leave your answers in simplest form or as mixed numbers.
    a. $\frac{^-3}{16} + \frac{7}{4}$
    b. $\frac{1}{6} + \frac{^-4}{9} + \frac{5}{3}$
    c. $\frac{^-5}{2^3 \cdot 3^2} - \frac{^-5}{2 \cdot 3^3}$
    d. $3\frac{4}{5} + 4\frac{5}{6}$
    e. $5\frac{1}{6} - 3\frac{5}{8}$
    f. $^-4\frac{1}{3} - 5\frac{5}{12}$
19. Each student at Sussex Elementary School takes one foreign language. Two-thirds of the students take Spanish, $\frac{1}{9}$ take French, $\frac{1}{18}$ take German, and the rest take some other foreign language. If there are 720 students in the school, how many do not take Spanish, French, or German?
20. Find each sum or difference; simplify if possible.
    a. $\frac{3x}{xy^2} + \frac{y}{x^2}$
    b. $\frac{a}{xy^2} - \frac{b}{xyz}$
    c. $\frac{a^2}{a^2 - b^2} - \frac{a-b}{a+b}$

21. Determine which of the following is always correct.

a. $\dfrac{ab + c}{b} = a + c$

b. $\dfrac{a + b}{a + c} = \dfrac{b}{c}$

c. $\dfrac{ab + ac}{ac} = \dfrac{b + c}{c}$

National Assessments

National Assessment of Educational Progress (NAEP) Questions

Both figures below show the same scale. The marks on the scale have no labels except the zero point.

The weight of the cheese is $\dfrac{1}{2}$ pound. What is the total weight of the two apples?

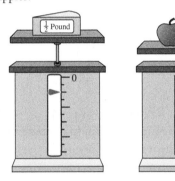

NAEP, Grade 8, 2007

Jim has $\dfrac{3}{4}$ of a yard of string which he wishes to divide into pieces each $\dfrac{1}{8}$ of a yard long. How many pieces will he have?

A. 3
B. 4
C. 6
D. 8

NAEP, Grade 8, 2003

Nick has a whole pizza.

Nick says he will eat $\dfrac{1}{2}$ of the pizza.

He says he will give $\dfrac{3}{8}$ of the pizza to Sam and $\dfrac{3}{8}$ of the pizza to Joe.

Can Nick do what he says?

◯ Yes　◯ No

NAEP, Grade 4, 2013

4 Proportional Reasoning

4 Objectives

Students will be able to understand and explain

- Ratios and their relation to rational numbers.
- Proportions and their properties.
- Constant of proportionality.
- Scaling.

Proportional reasoning is an extremely important concept taught in grades K–8. Proportionality has connections to most, if not all, of the other foundational middle-school topics and can provide a context to study these topics.

For grade 7, the *Common Core Standards* state that students should "analyze proportional relationships and use them to solve real-world and mathematical problems." Additionally we find that students should "decide whether two quantities are in a proportional relationship," "identify the constant of proportionality (unit rate) in tables, graphs, equations, diagrams and verbal descriptions," represent proportional relationships in equations," and "use proportional relationships to solve multistep ratio and percent problems." (p. 48)

Ratios are encountered in everyday life. For example, there may be a 2-to-3 ratio of Democrats to Republicans on a certain legislative committee, a friend may be given a speeding ticket for driving 69 miles per hour, or eggs may cost $2.40 a dozen. Each of these illustrates a **ratio**.

Definition of Ratio

A **ratio**, denoted as $\dfrac{a}{b}$, a/b, or $a{:}b$, where a and b are rational numbers, is a comparison of two quantities.

A ratio of 1:3 for boys to girls in a class means that the number of boys is $\frac{1}{3}$ that of girls; that is, there is 1 boy for every 3 girls. We could also say that the ratio of girls to boys is 3:1, or that there are 3 times as many girls as boys. Ratios can represent **part-to-whole** or **whole-to-part** comparisons. For example, if the ratio of boys to girls in a class is 1:3, then the ratio of boys (part) to children (whole) is 1:4. If there are b boys and g girls, then $\frac{b}{g} = \frac{1}{3}$ and $g = 3b$. Also, the ratio of boys to the entire class is $\frac{b}{b + g} = \frac{b}{b + 3b} = \frac{b}{4b} = \frac{1}{4}$. We could also say that the ratio of all children (whole) to boys (part) is 4:1. Some ratios give **part-to-part** comparisons, such as the ratio of the number of boys to girls or the number of students to one teacher. For example, a school might say that the average ratio of students to teachers cannot exceed 24:1.

The ratio of 1:3 for boys to girls in a class does not tell us how many boys and how many girls there are in the class. It only tells us the relative size of the groups. There could be 2 boys and 6 girls, or 3 boys and 9 girls, or 4 boys and 12 girls, or some other numbers that give a ratio equal to $\frac{1}{3}$.

Example 25

There were 7 males and 12 females in the Dew Drop Inn on Monday evening. In the game room next door were 14 males and 24 females.

a. Express the number of males to females at the inn as a ratio (part-to-part).
b. Express the number of males to females at the game room as a ratio (part-to-part).
c. Express the number of males in the game room to the number of people in the game room as a ratio (part-to-whole).

Solution

a. The ratio is $\frac{7}{12}$.

b. The ratio is $\frac{14}{24} = \frac{7}{12}$.

c. The ratio is $\frac{14}{38} = \frac{7}{19}$.

Proportions

In a study, children were shown a picture of a carton of orange juice and were told that the orange juice was made from orange concentrate and water. Then they were shown two glasses—a large glass and a small glass—and they were told that both glasses were filled with orange juice from the carton. They were then asked if the orange juice from each of the two glasses would taste equally "orangey" or if one would taste more "orangey." About half of the students said they were not equally orangey. Of those about half the students said the larger glass would be more "orangey" and about half said the smaller glass would be more "orangey." These students may have been thinking of only one quantity—the water alone or the orange concentrate alone.

Suppose Recipe A for an orange drink calls for 2 cans of orange concentrate for every 3 cans of water. We could say that the ratio of cans of orange concentrate to cans of water is 2:3.

We represent this pictorially in Figure 22(a), where O represents a can of orange concentrate and W represents a can of water. In Figure 22(b) and (c), we continue the process of adding 2 cans of orange concentrate for every 3 cans of water.

Recipe A

O O   O O   O O   O O   O O   O O
W W W   W W W W W W   W W W W W W W W W
(a)   (b)   (c)

Figure 22

From Figure 22 we could develop and continue the **ratio table**, as shown in Table 3.

Table 3						
Cans of Orange Concentrate	2	4	6	8	10	12
Cans of Water	3	6	9	?	?	?

In Table 3, the ratios $\frac{2}{3}$ and $\frac{4}{6}$ are equal. The equation $\frac{2}{3} = \frac{4}{6}$ is a proportion. In general, we have the following definition.

Definition of a Proportion

A **proportion** is a statement that two given ratios are equal.

If Recipe B calls for 4 cans of orange concentrate for every 8 cans of water, then the ratio of cans of orange concentrate to cans of water for this recipe is 4:8. We picture this in Figure 23(a).

Recipe B

O O O O   O O O O
W W W W   W W W W
W W W W   W W W W
(a)   (b)

Figure 23

Which of the two recipes produces a drink that tastes more "orangey"? In Figure 22(a), we see that in Recipe A there are 2 cans of orange concentrate for every 3 cans of water. In Figure 23(a), we see that in Recipe B there are 4 cans of orange concentrate for every 8 cans of water.

To compare the two recipes, we need either the same number of cans of orange concentrate or the same number of cans of water. Either is possible. Figure 22(b) shows that for Recipe A there are 4 cans of orange concentrate for every 6 cans of water. In Recipe B, for 4 cans of orange concentrate there are 8 cans of water. Recipe B calls for more water per 4 cans of orange concentrate, so it is less "orangey." An alternative is to observe that in Figure 23(b), Recipe B shows that there are 2 cans of orange concentrate for every 4 cans of water. We compare this with Figure 22(a), showing 2 cans of orange concentrate for every 3 cans of water, and reach the same conclusion.

From our work in Section 1, we know that $\frac{2}{3} = \frac{4}{6}$ because $2 \cdot 6 = 3 \cdot 4$. Hence $\frac{2}{3} = \frac{4}{6}$ is a proportion. Also $\frac{2}{3} \neq \frac{4}{8}$ because $2 \cdot 8 \neq 3 \cdot 4$; this is not a proportion. In general, we have the following theorem that follows from Theorem 2 developed in Section 1.

Theorem 20

If a, b, c, and d are rational numbers and $b \neq 0$ and $d \neq 0$, then

$$\frac{a}{b} = \frac{c}{d} \text{ is a proportion if, and only if, } ad = bc.$$

The proportion $\frac{a}{b} = \frac{c}{d}$ may be read as "a is to b as c is to d."

Students in the lower grades typically experience problems that are *additive*. Consider the problem below.

Allie and Bente type at the same speed. Allie started typing first. When Allie had typed 8 pages, Bente had typed 4 pages. When Bente has typed 10 pages, how many has Allie typed?

This is an example of an *additive* relationship. Students should reason that since the two people type at the same speed, when Bente has typed an additional 6 pages, Allie should have also typed an additional 6 pages, so she should have typed $8 + 6$, or 14, pages.

Next consider the following problem:

Carl can type 8 pages for every 4 pages that Dan can type. If Dan has typed 12 pages, how many pages has Carl typed?

If students try an *additive* approach, they will conclude that since Dan has typed 8 more pages than in the original relationship, then Carl should have typed an additional 8 pages for a total of 16 pages. However, the correct reasoning is that since Carl types twice as fast as Dan he will type twice as many pages as Dan. Therefore, when Dan has typed 12 pages, Carl has typed 24 pages. The relationship between the ratios is *multiplicative*. Another way to solve this problem is to set up the proportion $\frac{8}{4} = \frac{x}{12}$, where x is the number of pages that Carl will type, and solve for x. Because $\frac{8}{4} = \frac{8 \cdot 3}{4 \cdot 3} = \frac{24}{12}$, then $x = 24$ pages.

In the problem above, one term in the proportion is missing:

$$\frac{8}{4} = \frac{x}{12}$$

One way to solve the equation is to multiply both sides by 12, as follows:

$$\frac{8}{4} \cdot 12 = \frac{x}{12} \cdot 12$$

$$8 \cdot 3 = x$$

$$24 = x$$

Another method of solution uses Theorem 20. This is often called the *cross-multiplication method*. The equation $\frac{8}{4} = \frac{x}{12}$ is a proportion if, and only if,

$$8 \cdot 12 = 4x$$
$$96 = 4x$$
$$24 = x.$$

Example 26

If there are 3 cars for every 8 students at a high school, how many cars are there for 1200 students?

Solution We use the strategy of *setting up a table*, as shown in Table 4.

Table 4

Number of cars	3	x
Number of students	8	1200

The ratio of cars to students is always the same:

$$\begin{array}{l} \text{Cars} \quad \rightarrow \\ \text{Students} \rightarrow \end{array} \frac{3}{8} = \frac{x}{1200}$$
$$3 \cdot 1200 = 8x$$
$$3600 = 8x$$
$$450 = x$$

Thus, there are 450 cars.

Next consider two car rental companies where the rates for 1–4 days are given in Table 5.

Table 5

(a) Ace Car Rental		(b) Better Car Rental	
Days	Cost	Days	Cost
1	$20	1	$20
2	$40	2	$35
3	$60	3	$48
4	$80	4	$52

The first two days for Ace Car Rental rates can be used to write a proportion because $\frac{1 \, day}{\$20} = \frac{2 \, days}{\$40}$. In a proportion, the units of measure must be in the same relative positions. In this case, the numbers of days are in the numerators and the costs are in the denominators.

For the Better Car Rental we see that $\frac{1 \, day}{\$20} \neq \frac{2 \, days}{\$35}$, so a proportion is not formed.

Consider Table 6, which is a ratio table built from the values for Ace Car Rental.

Table 6				
Days (*d*)	1	2	3	4
Cost (*c*)	20	40	60	80

The ratios $\frac{d}{c}$ are all equal, that is, $\frac{1}{20} = \frac{2}{40} = \frac{3}{60} = \frac{4}{80}$. Thus, each pair of ratios forms a proportion. In this case, $\frac{d}{c} = \frac{1}{20}$ for all values of *c* and *d*. This is expressed by saying that *d is proportional to c* or *d varies proportionally to c* or *d varies directly with c*. In this case, $d = \frac{1}{20}c$ for every *c* and *d*. The number $\frac{1}{20}$ is the **constant of proportionality**. We can say that *gas used by a car is proportional to the miles traveled* or *lottery profits vary directly with the number of tickets sold.*

Definition of Constant of Proportionality

If the variables *x* and *y* are related by the equality $y = kx \left(\text{or } k = \frac{y}{x} \right)$, then **y is proportional to x** and **k** is the **constant of proportionality** between **y** and **x**.

A central idea in proportional reasoning is that a relationship between two quantities is such that the ratio of one quantity to the other remains unchanged as the numerical values of both quantities change.

It is important to remember that in the ratio $a{:}b$ or $\frac{a}{b}$, *a* and *b* do not have to be whole numbers. For example, if in Eugene, Oregon, $\frac{7}{10}$ of the population exercise regularly, then $\frac{3}{10}$ of the population do not exercise regularly, and the ratio of those who do to those who do not is $\frac{7}{10}{:}\frac{3}{10}$. This ratio can be written 7:3.

It is important to pay special attention to units of measure when working with proportions. For example, if a turtle travels 5 in. every 10 sec, how many feet does it travel in 50 sec? If units of measure are ignored, we might set up the following proportion:

$$\frac{5}{10} = \frac{x}{50}$$

In this proportion the units of measure are not listed. A more informative proportion that often prevents errors is the following:

$$\frac{5 \text{ in.}}{10 \text{ sec}} = \frac{x \text{ in.}}{50 \text{ sec}}$$

This implies that $x = 25$. Consequently, since 12 in. = 1 ft, the turtle travels $\frac{25}{12}$ ft, or $2\frac{1}{12}$ ft, or 2 ft 1 in. in 50 sec.

Another approach for solving proportions uses the **scaling strategy**. Suppose we are asked whether it is better to buy 12 tickets for $15.00 or 20 tickets for $23.00. One way to approach the problem is to find the cost of a common number of tickets from each scenario.

Because LCM(12, 20) = 60, we could choose to find the cost of 60 tickets under each plan.

In the first plan, since 12 tickets cost $15.00, then 60 tickets cost $75.00.

In the second plan, since 20 tickets cost $23.00, then 60 tickets cost $69.00.

Therefore, the second plan is a better buy.

The **unit-rate strategy** for solving this problem involves finding the cost of one ticket under each plan and then comparing unit costs.

In the first plan, since 12 tickets cost $15.00, then 1 ticket costs $1.25.

In the second plan, since 20 tickets cost $23.00, then 1 ticket costs $1.15.

 CCSS The grade 6 *Common Core Standards* state the following:

Solve unit rate problems including those involving unit pricing and constant speed. For example, if it took 7 hours to mow 4 lawns, then at that rate how many lawns could be mowed in 35 hours? (p. 42)

 NOW TRY THIS 6

Work the problem posed in the grade 6 *Common Core Standards*.

Example 27

Kai, Paulus, and Judy made $2520 for painting a house. Kai worked 30 hr, Paulus worked 50 hr, and Judy worked 60 hr. They divided the money in proportion to the number of hours worked. If they all earn the same rate of pay, how much did each earn?

Solution Let x be the unit rate or the rate of pay per hour. Then $30x$ denotes the amount of money that Kai received; Paulus received $50x$ and Judy received $60x$. Because the total amount of money received is $30x + 50x + 60x$, we have

$$30x + 50x + 60x = 2520$$
$$140x = 2520$$
$$x = 18 \,(\text{dollars per hour}).$$

Hence,

$$\text{Kai received } 30x = 30 \cdot 18, \text{ or } \$540.$$
$$\text{Paulus received } 50x = 50 \cdot 18, \text{ or } \$900.$$
$$\text{Judy received } 60x = 60 \cdot 18, \text{ or } \$1080.$$

Dividing each of the amounts by 18 shows that the proportion is as required.

Consider the proportion $\dfrac{15}{30} = \dfrac{3}{6}$. Because the ratios in the proportion are equal and because equal nonzero fractions have equal reciprocals, it follows that $\dfrac{30}{15} = \dfrac{6}{3}$. Also notice that the proportions are true because each results in $15 \cdot 6 = 30 \cdot 3$. In general, we have the following theorem.

Theorem 21

For any rational numbers $\dfrac{a}{b}$ and $\dfrac{c}{d}$, with $a \neq 0$ and $c \neq 0$, $\dfrac{a}{b} = \dfrac{c}{d}$ if, and only if, $\dfrac{b}{a} = \dfrac{d}{c}$.

Consider $\dfrac{15}{30} = \dfrac{3}{6}$ again. Notice that $\dfrac{15}{3} = \dfrac{30}{6}$; that is, the ratio of the numerators is equal to the ratio of the corresponding denominators. In general, we have the following theorem.

Theorem 22

For any rational numbers $\dfrac{a}{b}$ and $\dfrac{c}{d}$, with $c \neq 0$, $\dfrac{a}{b} = \dfrac{c}{d}$ if, and only if, $\dfrac{a}{c} = \dfrac{b}{d}$.

Scale Drawings

Ratios and proportions are used in scale drawings. For example, if the scale is 1:300, then the length of 1 cm in such a drawing represents 300 cm, or 3 m in true size. The **scale** is the ratio of the size of the drawing to the size of the object. The following example shows the use of scale drawings.

Example 28

The floor plan of the main floor of a house in Figure 24 is drawn in the scale of 1:300. Find the dimensions in meters of the living room.

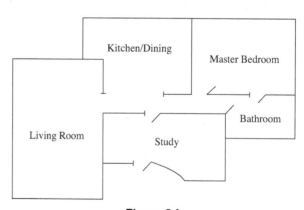

Figure 24

Solution   If the dimensions of the living room are approximately 3 cm by 2 cm. Because the scale is 1:300, 1 cm in the drawing represents 300 cm, or 3 m in true size. Hence, 3 cm represents $3 \cdot 3 = 9$ m, and 2 cm represents $2 \cdot 3 = 6$ m. Hence, the dimensions of the living room are approximately 9 m by 6 m.

Example 29

The ratio of men to women at a party was 5:2 before 14 more women appeared. At that point, the ratio was 4:3. How many men and how many women were at the party?

Solution We find the solution using a *bar method*. In Figure 25 each unit of men and women contain the same number of people giving the ratio 5:2.

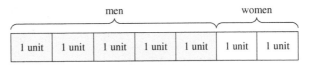

Figure 25

When 14 women joined the group, we have the situation in Figure 26(a). Additionally the ratio is now 4:3, and the number of people in each original unit has changed. The number of men has not changed so 5 of the original units equal 4 of the new ones.

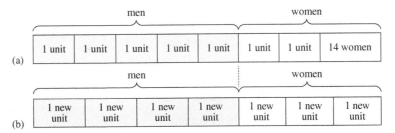

Figure 26

Thus, we have the following equations.

For the men: 5 original units = 4 new units.

For the women: 2 original units + 14 = 3 new units.

Adding the two together we get

7 original units + 14 = 7 new units, or

1 original unit + 2 = 1 new unit.

Equivalently, 4 original units + 8 = 4 new units.

Substituting we have, 4 old units + 8 = 5 old units, or 8 = 1 original unit.

In the Figure 25, there are 5 units of men at 8 men per unit = 40 men, and 2 units of women at 8 women per unit for 16 women. Thus, there were 56 people at the party originally. When 14 more women joined, there were 70 total.

Assessment 4A

1. Answer the following regarding the English alphabet.
   a. Determine the ratio of vowels to consonants.
   b. What is the ratio of consonants to vowels?
   c. What is the ratio of consonants to letters?
   d. Write a word that has a ratio of 2:3 of vowels to consonants.

2. Solve for x in each of the following proportions.
   a. $\dfrac{12}{x} = \dfrac{18}{45}$
   b. $\dfrac{x}{7} = \dfrac{^{-}10}{21}$
   c. $\dfrac{5}{7} = \dfrac{3x}{98}$
   d. $3\dfrac{1}{2}$ is to 5 as x is to 15.

3. **a.** If the ratio of boys to girls in a class is 2:3, what is the ratio of boys to all the students in the class? Why?

   b. If the ratio of boys to girls in a class is $m:n$, what is the ratio of boys to all the students in the class?

   c. If $\frac{3}{5}$ of the class are girls, what is the ratio of girls to boys?

4. There are approximately 2 lb of muscle for every 5 lb of body weight. For a 90-lb person, approximately how much of the weight is muscle?

5. Which is a better buy—4 grapefruits for 80¢ or 12 grapefruits for $2?

6. On a map, $\frac{1}{3}$ in. represents 5 mi. If New York and Aluossim are 18 in. apart on the map, what is the actual distance between them?

7. David reads 40 pages of a book in 50 min. How many pages should he be able to read in 80 min if he reads at a constant rate?

8. Two numbers are in the ratio 3:4. Find the numbers if
   a. their sum is 98.
   b. their product is 768.

9. Gary, Bill, and Carmella invested in a corporation in the ratio of 2:3:5, respectively. If they divide the profit of $82,000 proportionally to their investment, approximately how much will each receive?

10. Sheila and Dora worked $3\frac{1}{2}$ hr and $4\frac{1}{2}$ hr, respectively, on a programming project. They were paid $176 for the project. How much did each earn if they are both paid at the same rate?

11. Vonna scored 75 goals in her soccer kicking practice. If her success-to-failure rate is 5:4, how many times did she attempt a goal?

12. Express each of the following ratios in the form $\frac{a}{b}$, where a and b are natural numbers.

   a. $\frac{1}{6}:1$ **b.** $\frac{1}{3}:\frac{1}{3}$ **c.** $\frac{1}{6}:\frac{2}{7}$

13. Use Theorems 21 and 22 to write three other proportions that follow from the following proportion.

   $$\frac{12¢}{36\,oz} = \frac{16¢}{48\,oz}$$

14. The *rise* and *span* for a house roof are identified as shown on the drawing. The *pitch* of a roof is the ratio of the rise to the half-span.

   a. If the rise is 10 ft and the span is 28 ft, what is the pitch?

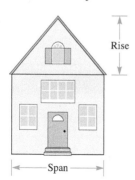

   b. If the span is 16 ft and the pitch is $\frac{3}{4}$, what is the rise?

15. Gear ratios are used in industry. A gear ratio is the comparison of the number of teeth on two gears. When two gears are meshed, the revolutions per minute (rpm) are inversely proportional to the number of teeth; that is,

   $$\frac{rpm\ of\ large\ gear}{rpm\ of\ small\ gear} = \frac{Number\ of\ teeth\ on\ small\ gear}{Number\ of\ teeth\ on\ large\ gear}.$$

   a. The rpm ratio of the large gear to the small gear is 4:6. If the small gear has 18 teeth, how many teeth does the large gear have?

   b. The large gear revolves at 200 rpm and has 60 teeth. How many teeth are there on the small gear, which has an rpm of 600?

16. A Boeing 747 jet is approximately 230 ft long and has a wingspan of 195 ft. If a scale model of the plane is about 40 cm long, approximately what is the model's wingspan?

17. A recipe calls for 1 tsp of mustard seeds, 3 c of tomato sauce, $1\frac{1}{2}$ c of chopped scallions, and $3\frac{1}{4}$ c of beans. If one ingredient is altered as specified, how must the other ingredients be changed to keep the proportions the same?
   a. 2 c of tomato sauce
   b. 1 c of chopped scallions
   c. $1\frac{3}{4}$ c of beans

18. The electrical resistance of a wire, measured in ohms (Ω), is proportional to the length of the wire. If the electrical resistance of a 5-ft wire is 4 Ω, what is the resistance of 20 ft of the same wire?

19. In a photograph of a father and his daughter, the daughter's height is 2 cm and the father's height is 6 cm. If the father is actually 183 cm tall, how tall is the daughter?

20. The amount of gold in jewelry and other products is measured in karats (K), where 24K represents pure gold. The mark 14K on a chain indicates that the ratio between the mass of the gold in the chain and the mass of the chain is 14:24. If a gold ring is marked 18K and it weighs 4 oz, what is the value of the gold in the ring if pure gold is valued at $1800 per oz?

21. If Amber is paid $8 per hour for typing, the table shows how much she earns.

Hours (*h*)	1	2	3	4	5
Wages (*w*)	$8	$16	$24	$32	$40

   a. How much would Amber make for a 40-hr work week?
   b. What is the constant of proportionality?

22. **a.** In Room A there are 1 man and 2 women; in Room B there are 2 men and 4 women; and in Room C there are 5 men and 10 women. If all the people in Rooms B and C go to Room A, what will be the ratio of men to women in Room A?

   b. Prove the following generalization of the proportions used in part (a).

   $$If\ \frac{a}{b} = \frac{c}{d} = \frac{e}{f},\ then\ \frac{a}{b} = \frac{c}{d} = \frac{e}{f} = \frac{a+c+e}{b+d+f}.$$

23. Use the bar method of Example 29 to solve the following exercise. One-half of the length of stick A is $\frac{2}{3}$ of the length of stick B. Stick B is 18 cm shorter than stick A. What is the length of both sticks?

24. A car travels about 26 miles on 1 gallon of gas while a truck travels about 250 miles on 14 gallons of gas. Which gets the better gas mileage?

25. Susan bikes 20 miles in 2 hours while Nick bikes 32 miles in 3 hours. Who travels faster?

26. There are 40 students in a classroom, and the desired ratio of students to computers is 3:1. How many computers are needed for the classroom to achieve the desired ratio?

27. The ratio of oblong tables to round tables at a conference is 5:1. The total number of tables at the conference is 102. How many of each type are there?

28. A recipe uses $1\frac{1}{2}$ c flour to make 2 dozen cookies. Is 4 c flour enough to make 6 dozen cookies with this recipe? Explain your answer.

Assessment 4B

1. Answer the following regarding the letters in the word *Mississippi*.
 a. Determine the ratio of vowels to consonants.
 b. What is the ratio of consonants to vowels?
 c. What is the ratio of consonants to letters?

2. Solve for x in each of the following proportions.
 a. $\dfrac{5}{x} = \dfrac{30}{42}$
 b. $\dfrac{x}{8} = \dfrac{^-12}{32}$
 c. $\dfrac{7}{8} = \dfrac{3x}{48}$
 d. $3\frac{1}{2}$ is to 8 as x is to 24

3. There are 5 adult drivers to each teenage driver in Aluossim. If there are 12,345 adult drivers in Aluossim, how many teenage drivers are there?

4. A candle is 30 in. long. After burning for 12 min, the candle is 25 in. long. If it continues to burn at the same rate, how long will it take for the whole candle to burn?

5. A rectangular yard has a width-to-length ratio of 5:9. If the distance around the yard is 2800 ft, what are the dimensions of the yard?

6. A grasshopper can jump 20 times its length. If jumping ability in humans (height) were proportional to a grasshopper's (length), how far could a 6-ft-tall person jump?

7. Jim found out that after working for 9 months he had earned 6 days of vacation time. How many days per year does he earn at this rate?

8. At Rattlesnake School the teacher–student ratio is 1:30. If the school has 1200 students, how many additional teachers must be hired to change the ratio to 1:20?

9. At a particular time, the ratio of the height of an object that is perpendicular to the ground to the length of its shadow is the same for all objects. If a 30-ft tree casts a shadow of 12 ft, how tall is a tree that casts a shadow of 14 ft?

10. The following table shows several possible widths W and corresponding lengths L of a rectangle whose area is 10 ft^2.

Width (*W*) (Feet)	Length (*L*) (Feet)	Area (Square Feet)
$\frac{1}{2}$	20	$\frac{1}{2} \cdot 20 = 10$
1	10	$1 \cdot 10 = 10$
2	5	$2 \cdot 5 = 10$
$2\frac{1}{2}$	4	$2\frac{1}{2} \cdot 4 = 10$
4	$2\frac{1}{2}$	$4 \cdot 2\frac{1}{2} = 10$
5	2	$5 \cdot 2 = 10$
10	1	$10 \cdot 1 = 10$
20	$\frac{1}{2}$	$20 \cdot \frac{1}{2} = 10$

L

Area = 10 ft^2 *W*

 a. Use the values in the table and some additional values to graph the length L on the vertical axis versus the width W on the horizontal axis.
 b. What is the algebraic relationship between L and W?

11. Find three sets of x- and y-values for the following proportions.

$$\frac{4 \text{ tickets}}{\$20} = \frac{x \text{ tickets}}{\$y}$$

12. If rent is \$850 for each 2 weeks, how much is the rent for 7 weeks?

13. Leonardo da Vinci in his drawing *Vitruvian Man* showed that the man's armspan was equal to the man's height. Some other ratios are listed below.

$$\frac{\text{Length of hand}}{\text{Length of foot}} = \frac{7}{9}$$

$$\frac{\text{Distance from elbow to end of hand}}{\text{Distance from shoulder to elbow}} = \frac{8}{5}$$

$$\frac{\text{Length of hand}}{\text{Length of big toe}} = \frac{14}{3}$$

Using the ratios above, answer the following questions.
 a. If the length of a big toe is 6 cm, how long should the hand be?
 b. If a hand is 21 cm, how long is the foot?

14. On a city map, a rectangular park has a length of 4 in. If the actual length and width of the park are 300 ft and 200 ft, respectively, how wide is the park on the map?

15. Jim's car will travel 240 mi on 15 gal of gas. How far can he expect to go on 3 gal of gas?

16. Some model railroads use an O scale in replicas of actual trains. The O scale uses the ratio 1 in./48 in. How many feet long is the actual locomotive if an O scale replica is 18 in. long?

17. a. On an American flag, what is the ratio of stars to stripes?
 b. What is the ratio of stripes to stars?

18. On an American flag, the ratio of the length of the flag to its width must be 19:10.
 a. If a flag is to be $9\frac{1}{2}$ ft long, how wide should it be?
 b. The flag that was placed on the Moon measured 5 ft by 3 ft. Does this ratio form a proportion with the official length-to-width ratio? Why?

19. If $\dfrac{x}{y} = \dfrac{a}{b}$, $a \neq 0$, $x \neq 0$, is true, what other proportions do you know are true?

105

20. If a certain recipe takes $1\frac{1}{2}$ c flour and 4 c milk, how much milk should be used if the cook only has 1 c flour?

21. To estimate the number of fish in a lake, scientists use a tagging and recapturing technique. A number of fish are captured, tagged, and then released back into the lake. After a while, some fish are captured and the number of tagged fish is counted.

    Let T be the total number of fish captured, tagged, and released into the lake, n the number of fish in a recaptured sample, and t the number of fish found tagged in that sample. Finally, let x be the number of fish in the lake. The assumption is that the ratio between tagged fish and the total number of fish in any sample is approximately the same, and hence scientists assume $\frac{t}{n} = \frac{T}{x}$. Suppose 173 fish were captured, tagged, and released. Then 68 fish were recaptured and among them 21 were found to be tagged. Estimate the number of fish in the lake.

22. A car travels about 36 miles on 1 gallon of gas while a truck travels about 200 miles on 14 gallons of gas. Which gets the better gas mileage?

23. Susan bikes 18 miles in 2 hours while Nick bikes 30 miles in 3 hours. Who travels faster?

24. There are 32 students in a classroom, and the desired ratio of students to computers is 3:1. How many computers are needed for the classroom to achieve the desired ratio?

25. The ratio of oblong tables to round tables at a conference is 6:1. The total number of tables at the conference is 112. How many of each type are there?

26. A recipe uses $1\frac{1}{2}$ c flour to make 3 dozen cookies. Is 4 c flour enough to make 6 dozen cookies with this recipe? Explain your answer.

27. Jennifer weighs 160 lb on Earth and 416 lb on Jupiter. Find Amy's weight on Jupiter if she weights 120 lb on Earth.

Mathematical Connections 4

Reasoning

1. Iris has found some dinosaur bones and a fossil footprint. The length of the footprint is 40 cm, the length of the thigh bone is 100 cm, and the length of the body is 700 cm.
   a. Iris found a new track that she believes was made by the same species of dinosaur. If the footprint was 30 cm long and if the same ratio of foot length to body length holds, how long is the dinosaur?
   b. In the same area, Iris also found a 50-cm thigh bone. Do you think this thigh bone belonged to the same dinosaur that made the 30-cm footprint that Iris found? Why or why not?

2. Suppose a 10-in. circular pizza costs $4.00. To find the price, x, of a 14-in. circular pizza, is it correct to set up the proportion $\frac{x}{4} = \frac{14}{10}$? Why or why not?

3. Prove that if $\frac{a}{b} = \frac{c}{d}$ and $a \neq {}^{-}b$, then the following are true.
   a. $\frac{a + b}{b} = \frac{c + d}{d} \left(Hint: \frac{a}{b} + 1 = \frac{c}{d} + 1 \right)$
   b. $\frac{a}{a + b} = \frac{c}{c + d}$ c. $\frac{a - b}{a + b} = \frac{c - d}{c + d}$
   d. $\frac{d}{c - d} = \frac{b}{a - b}$.

4. Nell said she can tell just by looking at the ratios $15:7$ and $15:8$ that these do not form a proportion. Is she correct? Why?

5. Sol had photographs that were 4 in. by 6 in., 5 in. by 7 in., and 8 in. by 10 in. Do the dimensions vary proportionately? Explain why.

6. Can $\frac{a}{b}$ and $\frac{a + b}{b}$ ever form a proportion? Why?

7. In a condo complex, $\frac{2}{3}$ of the men were married to $\frac{3}{4}$ of the women. What is the ratio of married people to the total adult population of the condo complex? Explain how you can obtain this ratio without knowing the actual number of men or women.

Open-Ended

8. List three real-world situations that involve ratio and proportion.

9. Find the ratio of Democrats to Republicans in the U.S. House of Representatives and the U.S. Senate. Determine how many each party would need to hold a majority and how many would be needed to stop a filibuster under the existing rules.

10. Most fertilizers used for gardening and crops are listed with a ratio of 1:2:1. Research the meaning of this ratio and find an acceptable mixture for flowers and foliage. If a fertilizer package showed a ratio of 10:20:10, what would be the meaning of this?

11. Research the golden ratio that the Greeks may have used in the design of the Parthenon. Write a report on this ratio and include a drawing of a golden rectangle.

Cooperative Learning

12. In *Gulliver's Travels* by Jonathan Swift we find the following:

    The seamstresses took my measure as I lay on the ground, one standing at my neck and another at mid-leg, with a strong cord extended, that each held by the end, while the third measured the length of the cord with a rule of an inch long. Then they measured my right thumb and desired no more; for by a mathematical computation, that twice around the thumb is once around the wrist, and so on to the neck and the waist; and with the help of my old shirt, which I displayed on the ground before them for a pattern, they fitted me exactly.

    a. Explore the measurements of those in your group to see if you believe the ratios mentioned for Gulliver.
    b. Suppose the distance around a person's thumb is 9 cm. What is the distance around the person's neck?

c. What ratio could be used to compare a person's height to armspan?

d. Do you think there is a ratio between foot length and height? If so, what might it be?

e. Estimate other body ratios and then see how close you are to actual measurements.

Connecting Mathematics to the Classroom

13. Mary is working with measurements and writes the following proportion.

$$\frac{12 \text{ in.}}{1 \text{ ft}} = \frac{5 \text{ ft}}{60 \text{ in.}}$$

How would you help her?

14. Nora said she can use division to decide whether two ratios form a proportion; for example, $32:8$ and $40:10$ form a proportion because $32 \div 8 = 4$ and $40 \div 10 = 4$. Is she correct? Why?

15. Al is 5 ft tall and has a shadow that is 18 in. long. At the same time, a tree has a shadow that is 15 ft long. Al sets up and solves the proportion as follows:

$$\frac{5 \text{ ft}}{15 \text{ ft}} = \frac{18 \text{ in.}}{x}, \quad \text{so } x = 54 \text{ in.}$$

How would you help him?

16. Mandy read that the arm of the Statue of Liberty is 42 ft long. She would like to know how long the Statue of Liberty's nose is. How would you advise her to proceed?

17. One student in the class says that her sister is in a school using the Singapore math materials and much of the work with fractions is done with bars. The student continues, saying, "I don't understand how bars can help me understand it with an exercise like that found in exercise 13 above." Can you help her?

Review Problems

18. If the numerator of a rational number is 6 times the denominator and the numerator is also 5 more than the denominator, what are the numerator and denominator?

19. Explain whether $\frac{3}{4}$ is a proper fraction or an improper fraction and why.

20. Explain why any integer is a rational number.

21. A student says that $\frac{20}{30}$ can be simplified by crossing out the 0s and that in general, this procedure works for simplifying fractions. Explain whether or not the statement is true using the rational number $\frac{25}{35}$.

22. In an old Sam Loyd puzzle, a watch is described as having stopped when the minute and hour hands formed a straight line and the second hand was not on 12. At what time can this happen?

23. If $\frac{2}{3}$ of a class was absent due to illness and $\frac{4}{5}$ of the school was absent due to illness, is the fractional portion of the absent class equivalent to the fractional portion of the school absenteeism?

24. Prove that $\frac{99}{98}$ is less than $\frac{97}{96}$.

25. a. Amal can finish a job in $\frac{1}{2}$ of a day working by herself. Her son Sharif can finish the same job in $\frac{1}{4}$ of a day working alone. How long will it take to finish the job if they work together?

    b. If Amal can finish a job in a hours and Sharif in b hours, then how long will it take to finish the job if they work together?

National Assessments

National Assessment of Educational Progress (NAEP) Questions

Sarah has a part-time job at Better Burgers restaurant and is paid $5.50 for each hour she works. She has made the chart below to reflect her earnings but needs your help to complete it.

A. Fill in the missing entries in the chart.

Hours Worked	Money Earned (in dollars)
1	$5.50
4	
	$38.50
$7\frac{3}{4}$	$42.63

B. If Sarah works h hours, then in terms of h, how much will she earn?

NAEP, Grade 8, 2007

The length of a photograph is 5 inches and its width is 3 inches. The photograph is enlarged proportionally. The length of the enlarged photograph is 10 inches. What is the width of the enlarged photograph?

A. 6 inches

B. 7 inches

C. 9 inches

D. 15 inches

E. $16\frac{2}{3}$ inches

NAEP, Grade 8, 2013

Hint for Solving the Preliminary Problem

Find the fraction of the whole washer that the two holes represent and then find the portion not represented by the holes. This should aid in finding the area of the washer.

Chapter Summary

KEY CONCEPTS	DEFINITIONS, DESCRIPTIONS, AND THEOREMS
Section 1	
Rational number	A number in the form $\frac{a}{b}$, or a/b, where a and b are integers and $b \neq 0$.
	In the rational number $\frac{a}{b}$, a is the *numerator* and b is the *denominator*.
Uses of rational numbers	• Division problem • Portion, or part, of a whole • Ratio • Probability
Types of fractions	*Proper fraction*—any fraction $\frac{a}{b}$, where $0 \leq a < b$; a proper fraction is always less than 1. *Improper fraction*—any fraction $\frac{a}{b}$, where $a \geq b > 0$; an improper fraction is always greater than or equal to 1. *Equivalent, or equal, fractions*—numbers that represent the same point on a number line.
Fundamental Law of Fractions	*Theorem:* If $\frac{a}{b}$ is a fraction and n is a nonzero rational number, then $\frac{a}{b} = \frac{an}{bn}$.
Simplest form	A rational number $\frac{a}{b}$ is in *simplest form*, or *lowest terms* if, and only if, $\text{GCD}(a, b) = 1$; that is, if a and b have no common factor greater than 1.
Equality of fractions	Two fractions $\frac{a}{b}$ and $\frac{c}{d}$, where $b \neq 0$ and $d \neq 0$, are *equal* (or *equivalent*) if, and only if, $ad = bc$.
Ordering of rational numbers	*Like denominators*—If a, b, and c are any integers and $b > 0$, then $\frac{a}{b} > \frac{c}{b}$ if, and only if, $a > c$. *Unlike denominators*—If $a, b, c,$ and d are any integers such that $b > 0$ and $d > 0$, then $\frac{a}{b} > \frac{c}{d}$ if, and only if $ad > bc$.
Denseness property for rational numbers	Given any two different rational numbers $\frac{a}{b}$ and $\frac{c}{d}$, there is another rational numbers between these two numbers. *Theorem:* Let $\frac{a}{b}$ and $\frac{c}{d}$ be any rational numbers with positive denominators, where $\frac{a}{b} < \frac{c}{d}$. Then $\frac{a}{b} < \frac{a+c}{b+d} < \frac{c}{d}$.
Section 2	
Addition of rational numbers	*Like denominators*—If $\frac{a}{b}$ and $\frac{c}{b}$ are rational numbers, then $\frac{a}{b} + \frac{c}{b} = \frac{a+c}{b}$. *Unlike denominators*—If $\frac{a}{b}$ and $\frac{c}{d}$ are rational numbers, then $\frac{a}{b} + \frac{c}{d} = \frac{ad+bc}{bd}$.

Section 2

Addition properties for rational numbers

- *Additive inverse*—for any rational number $\frac{a}{b}$, there exists a unique rational number $-\frac{a}{b}$ such that $\frac{a}{b} + \left(-\frac{a}{b}\right) = 0 = \left(-\frac{a}{b}\right) + \frac{a}{b}$.

- *Property of equality*—if $\frac{a}{b}$ and $\frac{c}{d}$ are any rational numbers such that $\frac{a}{b} = \frac{c}{d}$ and $\frac{e}{f}$ is any rational number, then $\frac{a}{b} + \frac{e}{f} = \frac{c}{d} + \frac{e}{f}$.

Subtraction of rational numbers

If $\frac{a}{b}$ and $\frac{c}{d}$ are any rational numbers, then $\frac{a}{b} - \frac{c}{d}$ is the unique rational number $\frac{e}{f}$ such that $\frac{a}{b} = \frac{c}{d} + \frac{e}{f}$.

If $\frac{a}{b}$ and $\frac{c}{d}$ are any rational numbers, then $\frac{a}{b} - \frac{c}{d} = \frac{a}{b} + \frac{^-c}{d}$.

If $\frac{a}{b}$ and $\frac{c}{d}$ are any rational numbers, then $\frac{a}{b} - \frac{c}{d} = \frac{ad - bc}{bd}$.

Estimation with rational numbers

Round fractions to *convenient*, or *benchmark* numbers, such as $\frac{1}{2}, \frac{1}{3}, \frac{1}{4}, \frac{1}{5}, \frac{2}{3}, \frac{3}{4}$, or 1.

Section 3

Multiplication of rational numbers

If $\frac{a}{b}$ and $\frac{c}{d}$ are any rational numbers, then $\frac{a}{b} \cdot \frac{c}{d} = \frac{ac}{bd}$.

Multiplication properties for rational numbers

- *Multiplicative identity*—the rational number 1 is the unique number such that for every rational number $\frac{a}{b}$, $1 \cdot \frac{a}{b} = \frac{a}{b} = \frac{a}{b} \cdot 1$.

- *Multiplicative inverse*—for any nonzero rational number $\frac{a}{b}$, the multiplicative inverse (reciprocal) is the unique rational number $\frac{b}{a}$ such that $\frac{a}{b} \cdot \frac{b}{a} = 1 = \frac{b}{a} \cdot \frac{a}{b}$.

- *Property of 0*—let $\frac{a}{b}$ be any rational number. Then $\frac{a}{b} \cdot 0 = 0 = 0 \cdot \frac{a}{b}$.

- *Property of equality*—let $\frac{a}{b}, \frac{c}{d}$, and $\frac{e}{f}$ be any rational numbers such that $\frac{a}{b} = \frac{c}{d}$. Then $\frac{a}{b} \cdot \frac{e}{f} = \frac{c}{d} \cdot \frac{e}{f}$.

- *Properties of inequality*—let $\frac{a}{b}, \frac{c}{d}$, and $\frac{e}{f}$ be any rational numbers:

  If $\frac{a}{b} > \frac{c}{d}$ and $\frac{e}{f} > 0$, then $\frac{a}{b} \cdot \frac{e}{f} > \frac{c}{d} \cdot \frac{e}{f}$.

  If $\frac{a}{b} > \frac{c}{d}$ and $\frac{e}{f} < 0$, then $\frac{a}{b} \cdot \frac{e}{f} < \frac{c}{d} \cdot \frac{e}{f}$.

Distributive property of multiplication over addition or subtraction

Let $\frac{a}{b}, \frac{c}{d}$, and $\frac{e}{f}$ be any rational numbers. Then

$$\frac{a}{b}\left(\frac{c}{d} + \frac{e}{f}\right) = \frac{a}{b} \cdot \frac{c}{d} + \frac{a}{b} \cdot \frac{e}{f} \quad \text{and} \quad \frac{a}{b}\left(\frac{c}{d} - \frac{e}{f}\right) = \frac{a}{b} \cdot \frac{c}{d} - \frac{a}{b} \cdot \frac{e}{f}.$$

Division of rational numbers

If $\frac{a}{b}$ and $\frac{c}{d}$ are any rational numbers, with $\frac{c}{d} \neq 0$, then $\frac{a}{b} \div \frac{c}{d} = \frac{e}{f}$ if, and only if, $\frac{e}{f}$ is the unique rational number such that $\frac{c}{d} \cdot \frac{e}{f} = \frac{a}{b}$.

Algorithm for Division of Fractions

If $\frac{a}{b}$ and $\frac{c}{d}$ are any rational numbers, with $\frac{c}{d} \neq 0$, then $\frac{a}{b} \div \frac{c}{d} = \frac{a}{b} \cdot \frac{d}{c}$.

Section 3

| a^m | If a is any rational number and m is any natural number, then $$a^m = \underbrace{a \cdot a \cdot a \cdot \ldots \cdot a.}_{m \text{ factors}}$$ |

| a^{-n} | For any nonzero rational number a and any natural number n, $a^{-n} = \dfrac{1}{a^n}$. |

| **Exponents of rational numbers theorems** | *Theorem:* For any nonzero rational number a and any integers m and n, $$a^m \cdot a^n = a^{m+n}.$$ *Theorem:* For any nonzero rational number a and any integers m and n, $$\frac{a^m}{a^n} = a^{m-n}.$$ *Theorem:* For any nonzero rational number a and any integers m and n, $$(a^m)^n = a^{mn}.$$ *Theorem:* For any nonzero rational number $\frac{a}{b}$ and any integer m, $\left(\dfrac{a}{b}\right)^m = \dfrac{a^m}{b^m}.$ *Theorem:* For any nonzero rational number $\frac{a}{b}$ and any integer m, $$\left(\frac{a}{b}\right)^{-m} = \left(\frac{b}{a}\right)^{m}.$$ *Theorem:* For any nonzero rational numbers a and b and any integer m, $$(a \cdot b)^m = a^m \cdot b^m.$$ |

Section 4

| **Ratio** | A comparison of two quantities a and b, where a and b are rational numbers, denoted as $\dfrac{a}{b}$, a/b, or $a\!:\!b$ and read as "*a to b*". |

| **Proportion** | A statement that two given ratios are equal. *Theorem:* If a, b, c, and d are rational numbers and $b \neq 0$ and $d \neq 0$, then $\dfrac{a}{b} = \dfrac{c}{d}$ if, and only if, $ad = bc$. |

| **Constant of Proportionality** | If the variables x and y are related by the equality $y = kx$, or $k = \dfrac{y}{x}$, then y is *proportional to* x and k is the *constant of proportionality* between y and x. |

| **Proportionality theorems** | *Theorem:* For any rational numbers $\frac{a}{b}$ and $\frac{c}{d}$, with $a \neq 0$ and $c \neq 0$, $\dfrac{a}{b} = \dfrac{c}{d}$ if, and only if, $\dfrac{b}{a} = \dfrac{d}{c}$. *Theorem:* For any rational numbers $\frac{a}{b}$ and $\frac{c}{d}$, with $c \neq 0$, $\dfrac{a}{b} = \dfrac{c}{d}$ if, and only if, $$\frac{a}{c} = \frac{b}{d}.$$ |

Chapter Review

1. For each of the following, draw a diagram illustrating the fraction.

   a. $\dfrac{3}{4}$ b. $\dfrac{2}{3}$ c. $\dfrac{3}{4} \cdot \dfrac{2}{3}$

2. Write three rational numbers equal to $\dfrac{5}{6}$.

3. Write each of the following rational numbers in simplest form.

   a. $\dfrac{24}{28}$ b. $\dfrac{ax^2}{bx}$ c. $\dfrac{0}{17}$

   d. $\dfrac{45}{81}$ e. $\dfrac{b^2 + bx}{b + x}$ f. $\dfrac{16}{216}$

   g. $\dfrac{x + a}{x - a}$ h. $\dfrac{xa}{x + a}$

4. In each of the following pairs, replace the comma with $>$, $<$, or $=$ to make a true statement.

a. $\dfrac{6}{10}, \dfrac{120}{200}$

b. $\dfrac{^-3}{4}, \dfrac{^-5}{6}$

c. $\left(\dfrac{4}{5}\right)^{10}, \left(\dfrac{4}{5}\right)^{20}$

d. $\left(1 + \dfrac{1}{3}\right)^2, \left(1 + \dfrac{1}{3}\right)^3$

5. Find the additive and multiplicative inverses for each of the following.

a. 3

b. $3\dfrac{1}{7}$

c. $\dfrac{5}{6}$

d. $-\dfrac{3}{4}$

6. Order the following numbers from least to greatest.

$$^-1\dfrac{7}{8}, 0, ^-2\dfrac{1}{3}, \dfrac{69}{140}, \dfrac{71}{140}, \left(\dfrac{71}{140}\right)^{300}, \dfrac{1}{2}, \left(\dfrac{74}{73}\right)^{300}$$

7. Can $\dfrac{4}{5} \cdot \dfrac{7}{8} \cdot \dfrac{5}{14}$ be written as $\dfrac{4}{8} \cdot \dfrac{7}{14} \cdot \dfrac{5}{5}$ to obtain the same answer? Why or why not?

8. Use mental math to compute the following. Explain your method.

a. $\dfrac{1}{3} \cdot (8 \cdot 9)$

b. $36 \cdot 1\dfrac{5}{6}$

9. John has $54\dfrac{1}{4}$ yd of material.

a. If he needs to cut the cloth into pieces that are $3\dfrac{1}{12}$ yd long, how many pieces can he cut?

b. How much material will be left over?

10. Without actually performing the given operations, choose the most appropriate estimate (among the numbers in parentheses) for the following expressions.

a. $\dfrac{30\dfrac{3}{8}}{4\dfrac{1}{9}} \cdot \dfrac{8\dfrac{1}{3}}{3\dfrac{8}{9}}$ $(15, 20, 8)$

b. $\left(\dfrac{3}{800} + \dfrac{4}{5000} + \dfrac{15}{6}\right)6$ $(15, 0, 132)$

c. $\dfrac{1}{407} \div \dfrac{1}{1609}$ $\left(\dfrac{1}{4}, 4, 0\right)$

11. Write a story problem that models $4\dfrac{5}{8} \div \dfrac{1}{2}$. Solve the problem by drawing appropriate diagrams.

12. Find two rational numbers between $\dfrac{3}{4}$ and $\dfrac{4}{5}$.

13. Suppose the $\boxed{\div}$ button on your calculator is broken, but the $\boxed{1/x}$ button works. Explain how you could compute $504792/23$.

14. Jim is starting a diet. When he arrived home, he ate $\dfrac{1}{3}$ of the half of a pizza that was left from the previous night. The whole pizza contains approximately 2000 calories. How many calories did Jim consume?

15. If a person got heads on a flip of a fair coin one-half the time and obtained 376 heads, how many times was the coin flipped?

16. If a person obtained 240 heads when flipping a coin 1000 times, what fraction of the time did the person obtain heads? Put the answer in simplest form.

17. If the University of New Mexico won $\dfrac{3}{4}$ of its women's basketball games and $\dfrac{5}{8}$ of its men's basketball games, explain whether it is reasonable to say that the university won $\dfrac{3}{4} + \dfrac{5}{8}$ of its basketball games.

18. The carvings of the faces at Mount Rushmore in South Dakota measure 60 ft from chin to forehead. If the distance from chin to forehead is typically 9 in., and the distance between the pupils of the eyes is typically $2\dfrac{1}{2}$ in., what is the approximate distance between the pupils on the carving of George Washington's head?

19. A student argues that the following fraction is not a rational number because it is not the quotient of two integers:

$$\dfrac{\dfrac{2}{3}}{\dfrac{3}{4}}$$

How would you respond?

20. Molly wants to fertilize 12 acres of park land. If it takes $9\dfrac{1}{3}$ bags for each acre, how many bags does she need?

21. If $\dfrac{2}{3}$ of all students in the academy are female and $\dfrac{2}{5}$ of those are blondes, what fraction describes the number of blond females in the academy?

22. Explain which is greater: $\dfrac{^-11}{9}$ or $\dfrac{^-12}{10}$.

23. Solve for x in each of the following.

a. $7^x = 343$

b. $2^{-3x} = \dfrac{1}{512}$

c. $2x - \dfrac{5}{3} = \dfrac{5}{6}$

d. $x + 2\dfrac{1}{2} = 5\dfrac{2}{3}$

e. $\dfrac{20 + x}{x} = \dfrac{4}{5}$

f. $2x + 4 = 3x - \dfrac{1}{3}$

24. Write each of the following in simplest form. Leave all answers with positive exponents.

a. $\dfrac{\left(x^3 a^{-1}\right)^{-2}}{x a^{-1}}$

b. $\left(\dfrac{x^2 y^{-2}}{x^{-3} y^2}\right)^{-2}$

25. Find each sum or difference.

a. $\dfrac{3a}{xy^2} + \dfrac{b}{x^2 y^2}$

b. $\dfrac{5}{xy^2} - \dfrac{2}{3x}$

c. $\dfrac{a}{x^3 y^2 z} - \dfrac{b}{xyz}$

d. $\dfrac{7}{2^3 3^2} + \dfrac{5}{2^2 3^3}$

26. Mike drew the following picture to find out how many pieces of ribbon $\frac{1}{2}$ yd long could be cut from a strip of ribbon $1\frac{3}{4}$ yd long.

From the picture he concluded that $1\frac{3}{4} \div \frac{1}{2}$ is 3 pieces with $\frac{1}{4}$ yd left over, so the answer is $3\frac{1}{4}$ pieces. He checked this using the algorithm $\frac{7}{4} \cdot \frac{2}{1} = \frac{14}{4} = 3\frac{1}{2}$ and is confused why he has two different answers. How would you help him?

27. Tom tossed a coin 30 times and got 17 heads.
   a. What is the ratio of heads to coin tosses?
   b. What is the ratio of heads to tails?
   c. What is the ratio of tails to heads?

28. Which bottle of juice is a better buy (cost per fluid ounce): 48 fl oz for $3 or 64 fl oz for $4?

29. Eighteen-karat gold contains 18 parts (grams) gold and 6 parts (grams) other metals. Amy's new ring contains 12 parts gold and 3 parts other metals. Is the ring 18-karat gold? Why?

30. A recipe for fruit salad serves 4 people. It calls for 3 oranges and 16 grapes. How many oranges and grapes do you need to serve 11 people?

31. If the scale on a drawing of a house is 1 cm to $2\frac{1}{2}$ m, what is the length of the house if it measures 3 cm on the scale drawing?

32. In water (H_2O), the ratio of the weight of oxygen to the weight of hydrogen is approximately 8:1. How many ounces of hydrogen are in 1 lb of water?

33. A manufacturer produces the same kind of computer chip in two plants. In the first plant, the ratio of defective chips to good chips is 15:100 and in the second plant, that ratio is 12:100. A buyer of a large number of chips is aware that some come from the first plant and some from the second. However, she is not aware of how many come from each. The buyer would like to know the ratio of defective chips to good chips in any given order. Can she determine that ratio? If so, explain how. If not, explain why not.

34. Suppose the ratio of the lengths of the sides in two squares is $1:r$. What is the ratio of their areas? ($A = s^2$)

35. The Grizzlies won 18 games and lost 7.
   a. What is the ratio of games won to games lost?
   b. What is the ratio of games won to games played?

36. Express each of the following as a ratio $\frac{a}{b}$ where a and b are whole numbers.
   a. $\frac{1}{5} : 1$ **b.** $\frac{2}{5} : \frac{3}{4}$

37. The ratio of boys to girls in Mr. Good's class is 3 to 5, the ratio of boys to girls in Ms. Garcia's is the same, and you know that there are 15 girls in Ms. Garcia's class. How many boys are in Ms. Garcia's class?

38. If the ratio of the number of states of the United States using the *Common Core Standards* to those not using it is 9:10, how many states are not using these *Standards*?

39. From about 1978 to 1985, there was a trend towards conservatism among university professors with about $\frac{1}{20}$ of professors identifying themselves as strongly left-wing, about a third identifying themselves as liberals, about $\frac{1}{4}$ identifying themselves as moderates, $\frac{1}{4}$ as conservative, and $\frac{1}{20}$ as strongly conservative. What fraction identified themselves with none of the labels?

40. Since 1985, the fraction of liberal professors has grown steadily, with research finding somewhere between 7 to 9 liberals for each professor of another political persuasion. What statement with ratios could you make about professors of other political persuasions?

41. In an equilateral triangle, all sides have the same length and the perimeter is the sum of those lengths. What is the ratio of the perimeters of two equilateral (all sides of equal length) triangles whose sides each have lengths 6 cm and 10 cm respectively?

42. If a cup of coffee with 1 oz of cream is compared to another cup with $\frac{9}{10}$ oz cream, which has more cream?

43. In a package of tulip bulbs, the seller guarantees that at least $\frac{45}{99}$ of the bulbs will bloom. If you planted a package of 121 bulbs, at least how many would be expected not to bloom?

44. A woman's will decreed that her cats be shared among her three daughters as follows: $\frac{1}{2}$ of the cats to the eldest daughter, $\frac{1}{3}$ of the cats to the middle daughter, and $\frac{1}{9}$ of the cats to the youngest daughter. Since the woman had 17 cats, the daughters decided that they could not carry out their mother's wishes. The judge who held the will agreed to lend the daughters a cat so that they could share the cats as their mother wished. Now, $\frac{1}{2}$ of 18 is 9; $\frac{1}{3}$ of 18 is 6; and $\frac{1}{9}$ of 18 is 2. Since $9 + 6 + 2 = 17$, the daughters were able to divide the 17 cats and return the borrowed cat. They obviously did not need the extra cat to carry out their mother's bequest, but they could not divide 17 into halves, thirds, and ninths. Has the woman's will really been followed?

45. Prince Juan was allowed to take a number of bags of gold as he went into exile. However, a guard at the first bridge he crossed demanded half the bags of gold plus one more bag. Juan met this demand and proceeded to the next bridge. Guards at the second, third, and fourth bridges made identical demands, all of which the prince met. When Juan finally crossed all the bridges, a single bag of gold was left. With how many bags did Juan start?

Answers to Problems

Answers to odd-numbered Mathematical Connections problems are available at www.pearsonhighered.com/mathstatsresources <http://www.pearsonhighered.com/mathstatsresources>.

Assessment 1A

1. Answers vary. **a.** The solution to $8x = 7$ is $\frac{7}{8}$. **b.** Jane ate $\frac{7}{8}$ of the pizza. **c.** The ratio of boys to girls is 7 to 8. **2. a.** $\frac{1}{6}$ **b.** $\frac{1}{4}$ **c.** $\frac{2}{6} = \frac{1}{3}$ **d.** $\frac{7}{12}$ **3.** $\frac{5}{8}$ **4. a.** $\frac{2}{3}$ **b.** $\frac{4}{6} = \frac{2}{3}$ **c.** $\frac{6}{9} = \frac{2}{3}$ **d.** $\frac{\cdot 8}{12} = \frac{2}{3}$. The diagrams illustrate the Fundamental Law of Fractions. **5. a.** No, the parts do not have equal areas. The shaded part could be $\frac{1}{4}$ of the circle, but we can't tell from the figure. **b.** Yes **c.** Yes **6.** Answers vary. **a.** **b.** $\frac{2}{8}$ $\frac{3}{9}$

c. $\frac{3}{6}$ **7. a.** $\frac{9}{24} = \frac{3}{8}$ **b.** $\frac{12}{24} = \frac{1}{2}$ **c.** $\frac{4}{24} = \frac{1}{6}$ **d.** $\frac{8}{24} = \frac{1}{3}$

8. a. $\frac{4}{43}$ **b.** $\frac{17}{43}$ **c.** 1 **d.** $\frac{39}{43}$ **9.** Answers vary. **a.** $\frac{4}{18}, \frac{6}{27}, \frac{8}{36}$ **b.** $\frac{-4}{10}, \frac{2}{-5}, \frac{-10}{25}$ **c.** $\frac{0}{1}, \frac{0}{2}, \frac{0}{4}$ **d.** $\frac{2a}{4}, \frac{3a}{6}, \frac{4a}{8}$ **10. a.** $\frac{52}{31}$ **b.** $\frac{3}{5}$

c. $\frac{-5}{7}$ **11. a.** Undefined **b.** Undefined **c.** 0 **d.** Cannot be simplified **e.** Cannot be simplified **12. a.** $\frac{a-b}{3}$ **b.** $\frac{2x}{9y}$

13. a. Equal **b.** Equal **14. a.** Not equal **b.** Not equal

15. Answers vary. **16.** $\frac{36}{48}$

17. a. **b.** 14 gallons **18. a.** $\frac{32}{3}$ **b.** $^-36$

19. a. > **b.** < **20. a.** $\frac{11}{13}, \frac{11}{16}, \frac{11}{22}$

b. $\frac{-1}{5}, \frac{-19}{36}, \frac{-17}{30}$ **21.** Answers vary. **a.** $\frac{10}{21}, \frac{11}{21}$ **b.** $\frac{-22}{27}, \frac{-23}{27}$

22. a. $\frac{6}{16} = \frac{3}{8}; \frac{6}{32,000} = \frac{3}{16,000}$ **b.** $\frac{10}{100} = \frac{1}{10}$ **c.** $\frac{15}{60} = \frac{1}{4}$

d. $\frac{8}{24} = \frac{1}{3}$ **23.** False **24.** $\frac{1}{6}$ **25.** Answers vary. **a.** 2, 3, 4 **b.** 3, 5, 7, 9 **26.** n cannot be 0; otherwise there would $\frac{0}{0}$ in the theorem. **27.** $n = \frac{n}{1}$ for all integers n, so every integer can be written as a fraction. **28.** Drawing is only a representation, not to scale. $\frac{1}{8}\ \frac{2}{8}\ \frac{3}{8}\ \frac{4}{8}\ \frac{5}{8}\ \frac{6}{8}\ \frac{7}{8}\ 1$ **29.** 2 **30.** $\frac{3}{5}$

Assessment 2A

1. a. $\frac{7}{6} = 1\frac{1}{6}$ **b.** $\frac{-4}{12} = \frac{-1}{3}$ **c.** $\frac{5y - 3x}{xy}$

d. $\frac{-3y + 5x + 14y^2}{2x^2y^2}$ **e.** $\frac{71}{24} = 2\frac{23}{24}$ **f.** $\frac{-23}{3} = -7\frac{2}{3}$

g. $8\frac{4}{12} = 8\frac{1}{3}$ **2. a.** $18\frac{2}{3}$ **b.** $^-2\frac{93}{100}$ **3.** Answers vary.

a. $\frac{27}{4}$ **b.** $\frac{-29}{8}$ **4.** Answers vary. **a.** $\frac{1}{3}$, high **b.** $\frac{1}{6}$, low

c. $\frac{3}{4}$, low **d.** $\frac{1}{2}$, high **5. a.** Beavers **b.** Ducks **c.** Bears

6.

About 0	About $\frac{1}{2}$	About 1
$\frac{1}{10}$ $\frac{1}{100}$	$\frac{4}{7}$ $\frac{8}{12}$ $\frac{2}{5}$ $\frac{9}{18}$	$\frac{7}{8}$ $\frac{13}{10}$

7. a. $\frac{1}{2}$, high **b.** 0, low **c.** $\frac{3}{4}$, high **d.** 1, high **8. a.** 2 **b.** $\frac{3}{4}$

9. a. $\frac{1}{4}$ **b.** 0 **10. a.** A **b.** H **c.** T **d.** H

11. Answers vary. Approximately $4 \cdot 3 = 12$ **12.** $\frac{1}{4}$ **13.** $6\frac{7}{12}$ yd

14. $2\frac{5}{6}$ yd **15.** Answers vary. **a.** $\frac{1}{2} + \frac{3}{4} \in Q$

b. $\frac{1}{2} + \frac{3}{4} = \frac{3}{4} + \frac{1}{2}$ **c.** $\left(\frac{1}{2} + \frac{1}{3}\right) + \frac{1}{4} = \frac{1}{2} + \left(\frac{1}{3} + \frac{1}{4}\right)$

16. $1, \frac{7}{6}, \frac{8}{6}, \frac{9}{6}, \frac{10}{6}, \frac{11}{6}, 2$

17. a. i. $\frac{1}{4} + \frac{1}{3 \cdot 4} = \frac{1}{4} + \frac{1}{12} = \frac{16}{48} = \frac{1}{3}$

ii. $\frac{1}{5} + \frac{1}{4 \cdot 5} = \frac{1}{5} + \frac{1}{20} = \frac{25}{100} = \frac{1}{4}$

iii. $\frac{1}{6} + \frac{1}{5 \cdot 6} = \frac{1}{6} + \frac{1}{30} = \frac{36}{180} = \frac{1}{5}$

b. $\frac{1}{n} = \frac{1}{n+1} + \frac{1}{n(n+1)}$ **18. a.** $\frac{5}{6}$ **b.** $\frac{21}{6} = 3\frac{1}{2} = \frac{7}{2}$

19. $\frac{1}{2}$ mi **20.** No, you need $\frac{1}{4}$ cup more milk.

21. Answers vary. **a.** About $\frac{23}{45}$ **b.** About $\frac{22}{45}$ **c.** About $\frac{2}{127}$

22. The 16- and 17-year-olds **23.** $\frac{1}{8}$ **24.** $\frac{7}{100}$

Assessment 3A

1. Answers vary. **a.** $\frac{1}{4} \cdot \frac{1}{3} = \frac{1}{12}$ **b.** $\frac{2}{4} \cdot \frac{3}{5} = \frac{6}{20}$

2. Answers vary. **a.** **b.**

3. a. $\frac{1}{5}$ **b.** $\frac{b}{a}$ **c.** $\frac{za}{x^2y}$ **4. a.** $10\frac{1}{2}$ **b.** $8\frac{1}{3}$ **5. a.** $^-3$ **b.** $\frac{3}{10}$

c. $\frac{y}{x}$ **d.** $\frac{-1}{7}$ **6. a.** $\frac{21}{12} = \frac{7}{4}$ **b.** $\frac{6}{4} = \frac{3}{2}$ **c.** $\frac{-1}{8}$ **d.** $\frac{3}{2}$

7. Answers vary. For example, **a.** $6 \div 2 \neq 2 \div 6$
b. $(8 \div 4) \div 2 \neq 8 \div (4 \div 2)$ **8. a.** 26 **b.** 29 **c.** 92 **d.** 18
9. a. 20 **b.** 16 **c.** 1 **10. a.** Less than 1 **b.** Less than 1

c. Greater than 2 **11.** d **12.** 9600 students **13.** $\dfrac{1}{6}$

14. $240 **15.** $225 **16.** 32 marbles **17. a.** $\dfrac{1}{3^{13}}$ **b.** 3^{13}

c. 5^{11} **d.** 5^{19} **e.** $\dfrac{1}{5^2}$ **f.** a^5 **18. a.** $\left(\dfrac{1}{2}\right)^{10} = \dfrac{1}{2^{10}}$ **b.** $\left(\dfrac{1}{2}\right)^{3}$

c. $\left(\dfrac{2}{3}\right)^{9}$ **d.** 1 **19. a., b., c., e.,** and **f.** are false; counterexamples

vary. **d.** True; $ab \neq 0$; use Theorem 19a. **20. a.** 5
b. 6 or $^-6$ **c.** $^-2$ **d.** $^-4$ **21. a.** $x \leq 2$ **b.** $x < 2$ **c.** $x \geq 2$
d. $x \geq 1$ **22. a.** $\left(\dfrac{1}{2}\right)^{3}$ **b.** $\left(\dfrac{3}{4}\right)^{8}$ **c.** $\left(\dfrac{4}{3}\right)^{10}$ **d.** $\left(\dfrac{4}{5}\right)^{10}$

e. 32^{50} **f.** $(^-3)^{-75}$ **23.** Answers vary.
$2\left(\dfrac{a}{b}\right) = \dfrac{a}{b} + \dfrac{a}{b} < \dfrac{a}{b} + \dfrac{c}{d}$ because $\dfrac{a}{b} < \dfrac{c}{d}$. Thus,
$2\left(\dfrac{a}{b}\right) < \dfrac{a}{b} + \dfrac{c}{d}, \dfrac{a}{b} < \dfrac{1}{2}\left(\dfrac{a}{b} + \dfrac{c}{d}\right)$. Also, $\dfrac{1}{2}\left(\dfrac{a}{b} + \dfrac{a}{b}\right) <$
$\dfrac{1}{2}\left(\dfrac{a}{b} + \dfrac{c}{d}\right) < \dfrac{1}{2}\left(\dfrac{c}{d} + \dfrac{c}{d}\right) = \dfrac{1}{2}\left(\dfrac{2c}{d}\right) = \dfrac{c}{d}$. Thus,
$\dfrac{a}{b} < \dfrac{1}{2}\left(\dfrac{a}{b} + \dfrac{c}{d}\right) < \dfrac{c}{d}$. **24. a.** $\dfrac{8}{25}$ **b.** No; this only describes
the fraction of students, not the total number of either males or
females. **25.** Answers vary. **a.** About $\dfrac{1}{11}$ **b.** About $\dfrac{1}{6}$

26. a. 2012 to 2013 **b.** 2008 to 2009 **27.** $\dfrac{73}{231}$ **28.** $\dfrac{1}{32}$

Assessment 4A

1. a. 5:21 **b.** 21:5 **c.** 21:26 **d.** Answers vary. For example,
minor. **2. a.** 30 **b.** $^-3\dfrac{1}{3}$ **c.** $23\dfrac{1}{3}$ **d.** $10\dfrac{1}{2}$
3. a. 2:5. Because the ratio is 2:3, there are $2x$ boys and $3x$ girls;
hence, the ratio of boys to all students is $\dfrac{2x}{2x + 3x} = \dfrac{2}{5}$.
b. $m:(m + n)$ **c.** 3:2 **4.** 36 lb **5.** 12 grapefruits for $2
6. 270 mi **7.** 64 pages **8. a.** 42, 56 **b.** 24 and 32, or $^-24$ and $^-32$
9. $16,400; $24,000; $41,000 **10.** $77 and $99

11. 135 **12. a.** $\dfrac{1}{6}$ **b.** $\dfrac{1}{1}$ **c.** $\dfrac{7}{12}$

13. Answers vary. $\dfrac{36\,\text{oz}}{12¢} = \dfrac{48\,\text{oz}}{16¢}, \dfrac{12¢}{16¢} = \dfrac{36\,\text{oz}}{48\,\text{oz}}, \dfrac{16¢}{12¢} = \dfrac{48\,\text{oz}}{36\,\text{oz}}$

14. a. $\dfrac{5}{7}$ **b.** 6 ft **15. a.** 27 **b.** 20 **16.** Approximately 34 cm

17. a. $\dfrac{2}{3}$ tsp mustard seeds, 1 c scallions, $2\dfrac{1}{6}$ c beans

b. $\dfrac{2}{3}$ tsp mustard seeds, 2 c tomato sauce, $2\dfrac{1}{6}$ c beans

c. $\dfrac{7}{13}$ tsp mustard seeds, $1\dfrac{8}{13}$ c tomato sauce, $\dfrac{21}{26}$ c scallions
18. 16 ohms **19.** 61 cm **20.** The ratio between the mass of
the gold in the ring and the mass of the ring is $\dfrac{18}{24}$.
If x is the number of ounces of pure gold in the ring which weighs
4 oz, we have $\dfrac{18}{24} = \dfrac{x}{4}$. Hence, $x = \dfrac{(18 \cdot 4)}{24}$, or 3 oz.
Consequently, the price of the gold in the ring is

$3 \cdot $1800 or $5400. **21. a.** $320 **b.** 8 **22. a.** 1:2
b. Let $\dfrac{a}{b} = \dfrac{c}{d} = \dfrac{e}{f} = r$. Then, $a = br$, $c = dr$, $e = fr$.
So, $a + c + e = br + dr + fr$
$$a + c + e = r(b + d + f)$$
$$\dfrac{a + c + e}{b + d + f} = r.$$

23. As seen in the drawing, $\dfrac{1}{2}$ of stick A is $\dfrac{2}{3}$ of stick B, and stick B
is 18 cm shorter than stick A.

We have the following: Stick B is $3 \cdot 18$ unit sections while stick A
is $4 \cdot 18$ unit sections. Thus, the lengths of the sticks are A, 72
cm, and B, 54 cm. **24.** The car **25.** Nick **26.** 14 computers **27.** 17 round ones and 85 oblong ones **28.** No, 6 dozen
cookies would take $4\dfrac{1}{2}$ c flour.

Chapter Review

1. Answers vary. **a.**   **b.** **c.**

2. Answers vary; for example, $\dfrac{10}{12}, \dfrac{15}{18}, \dfrac{20}{24}$. **3. a.** $\dfrac{6}{7}$

b. $\dfrac{ax}{b}$ **c.** $\dfrac{0}{1} = 0$ **d.** $\dfrac{5}{9}$ **e.** b **f.** $\dfrac{2}{27}$ **g.** Cannot be simplified

h. Cannot be simplified **4. a.** $=$ **b.** $>$ **c.** $>$ **d.** $<$
5. a. $^-3, \dfrac{1}{3}$ **b.** $^-3\dfrac{1}{7}, \dfrac{7}{22}$ **c.** $\dfrac{^-5}{6}, \dfrac{6}{5}$ **d.** $\dfrac{3}{4}, \dfrac{^-4}{3}$

6. $^-2\dfrac{1}{3}, ^-1\dfrac{7}{8}, 0, \left(\dfrac{71}{140}\right)^{300}, \dfrac{69}{140}, \dfrac{1}{2}, \dfrac{71}{140}, \left(\dfrac{74}{73}\right)^{300}$

7. Yes. By the definition of multiplication and the commutative
and associative laws of multiplication, we can do the following:

$$\dfrac{4}{5} \cdot \dfrac{7}{8} \cdot \dfrac{5}{14} = \dfrac{4 \cdot 7 \cdot 5}{5 \cdot 8 \cdot 14}$$
$$= \dfrac{4 \cdot 7 \cdot 5}{8 \cdot 14 \cdot 5}$$
$$= \dfrac{4}{8} \cdot \dfrac{7}{14} \cdot \dfrac{5}{5}$$

8. Answers vary. **a.** 24, because $\dfrac{1}{3}(8 \cdot 9)$ is equal to
$\left(\dfrac{1}{3} \cdot 9\right) \cdot 8 = 3 \cdot 8 = 24$. **b.** 66, because $36 \cdot 1\dfrac{5}{6}$ is equal to
$36 \cdot \dfrac{11}{6} = 6 \cdot 11 = 66$. **9. a.** 17 pieces **b.** $1\dfrac{5}{6}$ yd

10. a. 15 **b.** 15 **c.** 4 **11.** Answers vary.

12. Answers vary. For example, $\dfrac{76}{100}$ and $\dfrac{78}{100}$.

13. $\boxed{5}\,\boxed{0}\,\boxed{4}\,\boxed{7}\,\boxed{9}\,\boxed{2}\,\boxed{\times}\,\boxed{2}\,\boxed{3}\,\boxed{1/x}\,\boxed{=}$

14. Approximately 333 calories **15.** 752 times **16.** $\dfrac{240}{1000} = \dfrac{6}{25}$

17. It is not reasonable to say that the university won $\frac{3}{4} + \frac{5}{8}$, or $\frac{11}{8}$, of its basketball games. The correct fraction cannot be determined without additional information but it is between $\frac{5}{8}$ and $\frac{3}{4}$. **18.** $16\frac{2}{3}$ ft **19.** You should show him that the given fraction could be written as an integer over an integer. In this case, the result is $\frac{8}{9}$. **20.** 112 bags **21.** $\frac{4}{15}$ **22.** $\frac{^-12}{10}$ is greater than $\frac{^-11}{9}$ because $^-12 \cdot 9 > ^-11 \cdot 10$. Alternatively, $\frac{^-12}{10} - \frac{^-11}{9} = \frac{^-108}{90} - \frac{^-110}{90} = \frac{2}{90}$, which is positive; therefore $\frac{^-12}{10} > \frac{^-11}{9}$. **23. a.** 3 **b.** 3 **c.** $\frac{5}{4}$ or $1\frac{1}{4}$ **d.** $\frac{19}{6}$ or $3\frac{1}{6}$ **e.** $^-100$ **f.** $\frac{13}{3}$ or $4\frac{1}{3}$ **24. a.** $\frac{a^3}{x^7}$ **b.** $\frac{y^8}{x^{10}}$ **25. a.** $\frac{3ax + b}{x^2 y^2}$ **b.** $\frac{15 - 2y^2}{3xy^2}$ **c.** $\frac{a - bx^2 y}{x^3 y^2 z}$ **d.** $\frac{31}{216}$ **26.** Answers vary.

For example, the problem is to find how many $\frac{1}{2}$-yd pieces of ribbon there are in $1\frac{3}{4}$ yd. There are 3 pieces of length $\frac{1}{2}$ yd with $\frac{1}{4}$ yd left over. This $\frac{1}{4}$ yd is $\frac{1}{2}$ of a $\frac{1}{2}$-yd piece. Therefore, there are 3 pieces of $\frac{1}{2}$-yd ribbon and 1 piece that is $\frac{1}{2}$ of the $\frac{1}{2}$-yd piece or $3\frac{1}{2}$ of the $\frac{1}{2}$-yd pieces. Thus, "3 pieces and $\frac{1}{4}$ yd left" and "$3\frac{1}{2}$ pieces" are correct answers. **27. a.** 17:30 **b.** 17:13 **c.** 13:17

28. Neither; same price **29.** No, $\frac{18}{6} \neq \frac{12}{3}$ **30.** $8\frac{1}{4}$ oranges and 44 grapes **31.** $7\frac{1}{2}$ m **32.** The ratio of hydrogen to the total is 1:9. Therefore, $\frac{1}{9} = \frac{x}{16}$ implies $x = 1\frac{7}{9}$ oz. **33.** No, the ratio depends on how many chips came from each plant. **34.** $1:r^2$

35. a. 18:7 **b.** 18:25 **36. a.** 1:5 **b.** 8:15 **37.** 9 **38.** 5 states **39.** $\frac{1}{15}$ **40.** The ratio of professors of other political persuasions to liberals is 1:7 to 1:9. **41.** The ratio of perimeters is 3:5. **42.** The cup that has 1 oz cream **43.** 66 **44.** No, the will is impossible because the fractions of cats to be shared do not add to 1. If the woman had x cats then the number of cats her will directs to be distributed is $\frac{1}{2}x + \frac{1}{3}x + \frac{1}{9}x = \frac{17}{18}x$, but the sum should be $1x$, or $\left(\frac{18}{18}\right)x$. **45.** 46 bags.

Answers to Now Try This

1. Consider two rational numbers $\frac{a}{b}$ and $\frac{c}{d}$, where $\frac{a}{b} < \frac{c}{d}$. By the denseness property of rational numbers we can find a rational number x_1 between the two fractions. Since $\frac{a}{b} < x_1$, there is a rational number x_2 between $\frac{a}{b}$ and x_1. We next can find a rational number x_3 between $\frac{a}{b}$ and x_2 and so on. This process can be repeated indefinitely, and hence we obtain infinitely many rational numbers $x_1, x_2, x_3, \ldots$ between $\frac{a}{b}$ and $\frac{c}{d}$. **2.** Because $\frac{a}{b} < \frac{c}{d}$ with $b > 0$ and $d > 0$, Theorem 3 implies $ad < bc$. Adding ab to each side of the inequality, we now have $ab + ad < ab + bc$. Thus, by factoring $a(b + d) < b(a + c)$. **3.** $\frac{3}{4}$ is greater than $\frac{1}{2}, \frac{1}{2} + \frac{1}{2} = 1$, so $\frac{3}{4} + \frac{1}{2} > 1$. $\frac{4}{6}$ is less than 1, so it cannot be the correct answer for $\frac{3}{4} + \frac{1}{2}$. **4.** Answers vary. For example, consider the following. If Caleb has $10.00, how many chocolate bars can he buy if **a.** the price of one bar is $2.00? **b.** the price of one bar is $\$\frac{1}{2}$? For (a) the answer is $10 \div 2$ or 5. For (b) the answer is $10 \div \frac{1}{2}$, which is the same as finding the number of $\frac{1}{2}$s in 10. Since there are two halves in 1, in 10 there are 20. Hence Caleb can buy 20 bars.

5. $\dfrac{a \div c}{b \div d} = \dfrac{\frac{a}{c}}{\frac{b}{d}} = \dfrac{\frac{a}{c} \cdot \frac{d}{b}}{\frac{b}{d} \cdot \frac{d}{b}} = \dfrac{\frac{a}{c} \cdot \frac{d}{b}}{1} = \dfrac{ad}{bc} = \dfrac{a}{b} \div \dfrac{c}{d}$

6. 20 lawns

Answer to Preliminary Problem

The area of the holes is $\frac{1}{4} + \frac{1}{7} = \frac{11}{28}$ of the whole washer. Thus the area of the rubber in the finished product is $1 - \frac{11}{28} = \frac{17}{28}$ of the whole washer. If the area of the original piece of rubber is $1\frac{3}{8}$, then the area of the finished washer is $\left(\frac{17}{28}\right)\left(1\frac{3}{8}\right) = \left(\frac{17}{28}\right)\left(\frac{11}{8}\right) = \frac{187}{224}$ in.^{2} or about $\frac{5}{6}$ in.^{2}

Credits

Credits are listed in the order of appearance.

Text Credits

Excerpt from Grade 3, Standards for Mathematical Practice. Copyright by Common Core State Standards Initiative. Used by permission of Common Core State Standards Initiative. Excerpt from Grade 3, Number and Operations—Fractions, Standards for Mathematical Practice. Copyright by Common Core State Standards Initiative. Used by permission of Common Core State Standards Initiative.

Excerpts from Grade 3, Number and Operations—Fractions, Standards for Mathematical Practice. Copyright by Common Core State Standards Initiative. Used by permission of Common Core State Standards Initiative.

Excerpt from Grade 4, Number and Operations—Fractions, Standards for Mathematical Practice. Copyright by Common Core State Standards Initiative. Used by permission of Common Core State Standards Initiative.

Randall Inners Charles, enVisionMATH, Grade 6 Common Core, © 2012. Printed and Electronically reproduced by permission of Pearson Education, Inc., Upper Saddle River, New Jersey.

Excerpt from Grade 4, Number and Operations—Fractions, Standards for Mathematical Practice. Copyright by Common Core State Standards Initiative. Used by permission of Common Core State Standards Initiative.

Excerpt from Grade 5, Number and Operations—Fractions, Standards for Mathematical Practice. Copyright by Common Core State Standards Initiative. Used by permission of Common Core State Standards Initiative.

enVisionMATH, Grade 6 Common Core, © 2012. Printed and Electronically reproduced by permission of Pearson Education, Inc., Upper Saddle River, New Jersey.

Excerpt from Grade 5, Number and Operations—Fractions, Standards for Mathematical Practice. Copyright by Common Core State Standards Initiative. Used by permission of Common Core State Standards Initiative.

Randall Inners Charles, enVisionMATH, Grade 6 Common Core, © 2012. Printed and Electronically reproduced by permission of Pearson Education, Inc., Upper Saddle River, New Jersey.

Randall Inners Charles, enVisionMATH, Grade 6 Common Core, © 2013. Printed and Electronically reproduced by permission of Pearson Education, Inc., Upper Saddle River, New Jersey.

Excerpt from Grade 6, The Number System, Standards for Mathematical Practice. Copyright by Common Core State Standards Initiative. Used by permission of Common Core State Standards Initiative.

MATHEMATICS Common Core, Course 1, © 2013. Printed and Electronically reproduced by permission of Pearson Education, Inc., Upper Saddle River, New Jersey.

Excerpt from Grade 7, Ratios and Proportional Relationships, Standards for Mathematical Practice. Copyright by Common Core State Standards Initiative. Used by permission of Common Core State Standards Initiative.

Excerpt from Grade 6, Ratios and Proportional Relationships, Standards for Mathematical Practice. Copyright by Common Core State Standards Initiative. Used by permission of Common Core State Standards Initiative.

Excerpt from Gulliver's Travels by Jonathan Swift. Published by Plain Label Books, © 2011.

Image Credits

Gary Fiedtkou/GLT Products

Pearson Education

Real Numbers and Algebraic Thinking

Preliminary Problem

A sheet of paper of the international standard size (used in most countries other than the United States and Canada) has the ratio of length (the longer side) to width (the shorter side) such that when cut or folded widthwise, the halves have the same length to width ratio.

a. What is that ratio?

b. what will the ratio of length to width of a larger sheet of paper be if two such standard sheets are joined along their length?

If needed, see Hint before the Chapter Summary.

The development of numbers was inspired by such commercial uses as negative numbers to indicate debts and to think about fractions as parts of a whole. The development of real numbers was comparable. The Pythagoreans knew a right triangle with two sides of length 1 had to have a new type of number to describe the length of the third side. Ancient Greeks struggled with finding a number to describe the ratio of the circumference of a circle to its diameter. These examples involve irrational numbers, but the formal definition of a real number came long after such numbers began to be used.

The grade 8 *Common Core Standards* recognize that students need to know that "there are numbers that are not rational, and [how to] approximate them by rational numbers." (p. 54)

In this chapter, we explore real numbers and examine aspects of algebra including the analysis and solution of linear equations, pairs of simultaneous linear equations, and other algebraic notions including functions, and the coordinate system.

 These topics are reflected in the grade 8 *Common Core Standards* in the following:

- **Work with radicals and integer exponents**
- **Analyze and solve linear equations and pairs of simultaneous linear equations. (p. 53)**

1 Real Numbers

Every rational number can be represented either as a terminating decimal or as a repeating decimal. But the ancient Greeks discovered numbers that are not rational, that is, numbers with a decimal representation that neither terminates nor repeats. To find such decimals, consider their characteristics.

1. There must be an infinite number of nonzero digits to the right of the decimal point.
2. There cannot be a repeating block of digits (a *repetend*).

One way to construct a nonterminating, nonrepeating decimal is to devise a pattern of infinite digits so that there is no repetend. For example, consider the number $0.1010010001\ldots$. If the pattern continues, the next groups of digits are four 0's followed by 1, five 0's followed by 1, and so on. Because this decimal is nonterminating and nonrepeating, it cannot represent a rational number. Numbers that are not rational numbers are **irrational numbers**, and there are infinitely many of them. In the mid-eighteenth century, it was proved that the ratio of the circumference of a circle to its diameter, symbolized by $\boldsymbol{\pi}$ **(pi)**, is an irrational number. The numbers $\dfrac{22}{7}$, 3.14, or 3.14159 are rational number approximations of π. The value of π has been computed to over 5 trillion decimal places and the digits appear to be random.

(Historical Note)

Although the Pythagoreans seem to have known about some irrational numbers, it was not until 1872 that German mathematician Richard Dedekind introduced a method of constructing irrational numbers from sets of rational numbers by showing that an irrational number could be thought of as a cut in a number line that separates the set of rational numbers into two disjoint non-empty subsets, one of which has no least element and the other of which has no greatest element, with all elements of one set less than the elements of the other set.

The set of **real numbers** is the union of the set of rational and irrational numbers. Every real number can be represented as a decimal and corresponds to a point on a number line.

> ### Definition of Real Numbers
> A **real number** is any number that can be represented by a decimal.

Square Roots

Irrational numbers occur in the study of area. For example, to find the area of a square as in Figure 1(a), we could use the formula $A = s^2$, where A is the area and s is the length of a side of the square. If a side of a square is 3 cm long as in Figure 1(b), then the area of the square is 9 cm^2 (square centimeters).

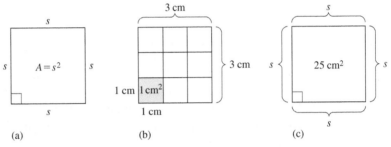

Figure 1

Conversely, given the area, we can use the formula to find the length s of a side of a square. If the area of a square is 25 cm^2 as in Figure 1(c), then $s^2 = 25$ and hence $s = 5$ or $s = {}^-5$.

Each of these solutions is a **square root** of 25. However, because lengths are always non-negative, 5 is the only possible solution to the equation. The non-negative solution of $s^2 = 25$ (namely, 5) is the **principal square root** of 25 and is denoted $\sqrt{25}$. Similarly, the principal square root of 2 is denoted $\sqrt{2}$. Also $\sqrt{16} \neq {}^-4$ because $^-4$ is not the principal square root of 16.

> ### Definition of the Square Root and Principal Square Root
> 1. A **square root** of non-negative number a is a number x, such that $x^2 = a$.
> 2. If a is any non-negative number, the **principal square root** of a (denoted $\sqrt{a}$) is the non-negative number x such that $x^2 = a$.

> **REMARK** The phrase "the square root of a" is commonly used to mean the principal square root of a.

Example 1

Find the following:

a. The square roots of 144

b. $\sqrt{144}$

c. $\sqrt{\dfrac{4}{9}}$

d. The solutions of $x^2 = 5$.

Solution

a. The square roots of 144 are 12 and $^-12$.

b. $\sqrt{144} = 12$

c. $\sqrt{\dfrac{4}{9}} = \dfrac{2}{3}$

d. $\sqrt{5}$ or $^-\sqrt{5}$

Other Roots

We have seen that the non-negative solution to $s^2 = 25$ is denoted $\sqrt{25}$. Similarly, the non-negative solution to $s^4 = 25$ is denoted $\sqrt[4]{25}$. In general, if n is even, the positive solution to $x^n = 25$ is $\sqrt[n]{25}$ and is the principal **nth root** of 25. The number n is the **index**. In the expression $\sqrt{25}$, the index 2 is understood and not written. In general, *the non-negative solution to $x^n = b$, where b is non-negative, is $\sqrt[n]{b}$.* Thus if b is non-negative, $\sqrt[n]{b}$ is a non-negative number, which raised to the nth power results in b. Hence:

$$\left(\sqrt[n]{b}\right)^n = b$$

If b is negative and n is even, $\sqrt[n]{b}$ is not a real number. For example, $\sqrt[4]{^-16}$. If $\sqrt[4]{^-16} = x$, then $x^4 = {}^-16$. Because any nonzero real number raised to the fourth power is positive, there is no real-number solution to $x^4 = {}^-16$ and therefore $\sqrt[4]{^-16}$ is not a real number. Similarly, if we are restricted to real numbers, it is not possible to find *any* even root of a negative number. However, the value $^-2$ is the only real number solution to the equation $x^3 = {}^-8$. We write, $\sqrt[3]{^-8} = {}^-2$. Because there is only one real number solution to $x^3 = {}^-8$, $\sqrt[3]{^-8}$ is the cube root of $^-8$, and there is no meaning to "principle cube root of $^-8$." *In general, the odd root of a negative number is a negative number.*

Because $\sqrt{a}$, if it exists, is non-negative by definition, $\sqrt{(^-3)^2} = \sqrt{9} = 3$. In general,

$$\sqrt{a^2} = |a|.$$

Similarly, $\sqrt[4]{a^4} = |a|$ and $\sqrt[6]{a^6} = |a|$, but $\sqrt[3]{a^3} = a$ for all a. (Why?) Notice that when n is even and $b > 0$, the equation $x^n = b$ has two real-number solutions, $\sqrt[n]{b}$ and $^-\sqrt[n]{b}$. If n is odd, the equation has only one real-number solution, $\sqrt[n]{b}$, for any real number b.

Historical Note

Evaluating square roots may have been known by Vedic Hindu scholars before 600 BCE. Sanskrit texts contain incredibly accurate approximations for some square roots. The discovery of irrational numbers by members of the Pythagorean Society was kept secret. Legend has it that a society member was drowned because the secret was relayed to persons outside the society. In 1525, Christoff Rudolff, a German mathematician, became the first to use the symbol $\sqrt{}$ for a radical or a root. ●

Irrationality of Square Roots and Other Roots

Some square roots are rational numbers. Others, like $\sqrt{2}$, are irrational numbers. To see this, we note that $1^2 = 1$ and $2^2 = 4$ and that there is no whole number s such that $s^2 = 2$. Is there a rational number $\frac{a}{b}$ such that $\left(\frac{a}{b}\right)^2 = 2$? To decide, we use the strategy of *indirect reasoning*. If we assume there is such a rational number $\frac{a}{b}$, then the following must be true:

$$\left(\frac{a}{b}\right)^2 = 2$$

$$\frac{a^2}{b^2} = 2$$

$$a^2 = 2b^2$$

If $a^2 = 2b^2$, then by the Fundamental Theorem of Arithmetic, the prime factorizations of a^2 and $2b^2$ must be the same. In particular, the prime 2 appears the same number of times in the prime factorization of a^2 as it does in the factorization of $2b^2$. Because $b^2 = bb$, no matter how many times 2 appears in the prime factorization of b, it appears twice as many times in bb.

Also, a^2 has an even number of 2s for the same reason b^2 does. In $2b^2$, another factor of 2 is introduced, resulting in an odd number of 2s in the prime factorization of $2b^2$. Because $a^2 = 2b^2$, we have 2 appearing both an odd number of times and an even number of times on different sides of the equality, and thus there is a contradiction.

This contradiction could have been caused only by the assumption that $\sqrt{2}$ is a rational number. Consequently, $\sqrt{2}$ cannot be rational and therefore, $\sqrt{2}$ must be an irrational number. We can use a similar argument to show that $\sqrt{3}$ is irrational or $\sqrt{n}$ is irrational, where n is a whole number greater than 1 but not the square of a whole number.

Example 2

Show that if $\frac{a}{b}$ and $\frac{c}{d}$ are rational numbers (a, b, c, and d integers), then $\frac{a}{b} + \frac{c}{d}\sqrt{2}$ is an irrational number.

Solution   We use *indirect reasoning*. Suppose the expression is a rational number; then $\frac{a}{b} + \frac{c}{d}\sqrt{2} = \frac{e}{f}$, where e and f are integers. We can obtain a contradiction by expressing $\sqrt{2}$ in terms of the integers a, b, c, d, e, and f, which will show that $\sqrt{2}$ is rational. This would be a contradiction to the fact that $\sqrt{2}$ is an irrational number. It would follow then that the assumption that $\frac{a}{b} + \frac{c}{d}\sqrt{2}$ is a rational number is wrong and consequently that it is an irrational number. We proceed according to this plan.

$$\frac{a}{b} + \frac{c}{d}\sqrt{2} = \frac{e}{f} \quad \text{implies}$$

$$\frac{c}{d}\sqrt{2} = \frac{e}{f} - \frac{a}{b} = \frac{eb - af}{bf}$$

We multiply both sides of the above equation by $\frac{d}{c}$ to isolate $\sqrt{2}$.

$$\frac{d}{c} \cdot \frac{c}{d}\sqrt{2} = \frac{d}{c} \cdot \frac{eb - af}{bf}$$

$$\sqrt{2} = \frac{deb - daf}{cbf}$$

Because all the letters are integers, it follows that $\sqrt{2}$ is a rational number, a contradiction. Consequently, $\frac{a}{b} + \frac{c}{d}\sqrt{2}$ is an irrational number.

Many irrational numbers can be interpreted geometrically. For example, we find a point on a number line to represent $\sqrt{2}$ by using the **Pythagorean Theorem**. That is, *if a and b are the lengths of the shorter sides (legs) of a right triangle and c is the length of the longer side (hypotenuse), then $a^2 + b^2 = c^2$*, as shown in Figure 2.

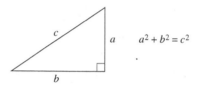

Figure 2

Figure 3 shows a segment 1 unit long constructed perpendicular to a number line at point P. Thus two sides of the triangle shown are each 1 unit long. If $a = b = 1$, then $c^2 = 2$ and $c = \sqrt{2}$. To find a point on the number line that corresponds to $\sqrt{2}$, we need to find a point Q on the number line such that the distance from 0 to Q is $\sqrt{2}$. Because $\sqrt{2}$ is the length of the hypotenuse, the point Q can be found by marking an arc with center 0 and radius c. The intersection of the positive number line with the arc is point Q.

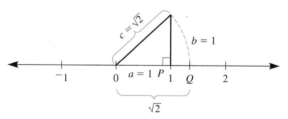

Figure 3

Similarly, other principal square roots can be constructed, as shown in Figure 4 and placed on a number line using the method of Figure 3. Also, their opposites can then be constructed, as shown in Figure 4.

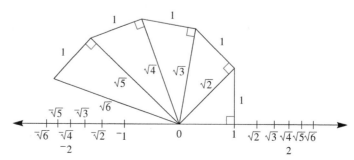

Figure 4

Estimating a Square Root

From Figure 4, we see that $\sqrt{2}$ must have a value between 1 and 2; that is, $1 < \sqrt{2} < 2$. To obtain a closer approximation of $\sqrt{2}$, we attempt to "squeeze" $\sqrt{2}$ between two numbers that are between 1 and 2. Because $(1.4)^2 = 1.96$ and $(1.5)^2 = 2.25$, it follows that $1.4 < \sqrt{2} < 1.5$. Because a^2 can be interpreted as the area of a square with side of length a, this discussion can be pictured geometrically, as in Figure 5.

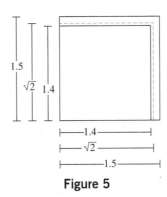

Figure 5

For a more accurate approximation for $\sqrt{2}$, we continue this squeezing process. We see that $(1.4)^2 = 1.96$, is closer to 2 than is $(1.5)^2 = 2.25$, so we choose numbers closer to 1.4 to find the next approximation. We find the following:

$$(1.42)^2 = 2.0164$$
$$(1.41)^2 = 1.9981$$

Thus, $1.41 < \sqrt{2} < 1.42$. We continue this process until we obtain the desired approximation. If a calculator has a square-root key, we can obtain an approximation directly. In fact, $\sqrt{2}$ is approximately 1.41421356.

▶ NOW TRY THIS 1

One algorithm for calculating square roots is sometimes attributed to Archimedes though the Babylonians had a similar method. The method is also referred to as Newton's method. The algorithm finds closer and closer estimates to the square root. To find the square root of a positive number, n, we first make a positive number guess, *Guess*1. Now compute as follows:

Step 1. Divide n by *Guess*1.
Step 2. Now add *Guess*1 to the quotient obtained in step 1.
Step 3. Divide the sum in step 2 by 2. The quotient becomes *Guess*2.
Step 4. Repeat steps 1–3 using *Guess*2 to obtain a successive guess.
Step 5. The process may be repeated until the desired accuracy is achieved.

  a. Use the method described to find the square root of 13 to three decimal places.
  b. Write the steps for the algorithm in a recursive formula.

The System of Real Numbers, Operations, and Their Properties

Real numbers can be represented as, terminating, repeating, or nonterminating and nonrepeating decimals.

    Every integer is a rational number as well as a real number. Every rational number is a real number, but not every real number is rational, as has been shown with $\sqrt{2}$. The relationships among sets of numbers are summarized in the diagram in Figure 6.

Real Numbers: $R = \{x \mid x \text{ can be written as a decimal}\}$

Irrational Numbers:

Rationals: $Q = \left\{ x \mid x = \dfrac{a}{b}, \text{ where } a, b \in I \text{ and } b \neq 0 \right\}$

$S = \{x \mid x \text{ is a non-repeating and non terminating decimal}\}$

Integers: $I = \{\ldots, {}^-3, {}^-2, {}^-1, 0, 1, 2, 3, \ldots\}$

Whole Numbers: $W = \{0, 1, 2, 3, 4, \ldots\}$

Natural Numbers: $N = \{1, 2, 3, 4, 5, \ldots\}$

Figure 6

The set of fractions can be extended to be of the form $\dfrac{a}{b}$, where a and b are real numbers with $b \neq 0$, such as $\dfrac{\sqrt{3}}{5}$.

Addition, subtraction, multiplication, and division are defined on the set of real numbers in such a way that all the properties of these operations on rationals still hold. The properties are summarized next.

Theorem 1:	**Properties of Operations on Real Numbers**
Closure properties	For real numbers a and b, $a + b$ and ab are unique real numbers.
Commutative properties	For real numbers a and b, $a + b = b + a$ and $ab = ba$.
Associative properties	For real numbers a, b, and c, $a + (b + c) = (a + b) + c$ and $a(bc) = (ab)c$.
Identity properties	The number 0 is the unique additive identity because for any real number a, $a + 0 = a = 0 + a$.
	The number 1 is the unique multiplicative identity because for any real number a, $a \cdot 1 = a = 1 \cdot a$.
Inverse properties	For every real number a, ${}^-a$ is its unique additive inverse; that is, $a + {}^-a = 0 = {}^-a + a$.
	For every nonzero real number a, $\dfrac{1}{a}$ (or a^{-1}) is its unique multiplicative inverse; that is, $a\left(\dfrac{1}{a}\right) = 1 = \left(\dfrac{1}{a}\right)a$.
Distributive property of multiplication over addition and subtraction	For real numbers a, b, and c, $a(b + c) = ab + ac$; $a(b - c) = ab - ac$.
Multiplication property of zero	For all real numbers a, $a \cdot 0 = 0 = 0 \cdot a$.
Density property for real numbers	For real numbers a and b with $a < b$, there exists a real number c such that $a < c < b$.
Inverse properties	For every real number a, ${}^-a$ is it unique additive inverse; that is $a + {}^-a = 0 = {}^-a + a$.
	For every nonzero real number a, $\dfrac{1}{a}$ (or a^{-1}) is its unique multiplicative inverse, that is, $a\left(\dfrac{1}{a}\right) = 1 = \left(\dfrac{1}{a}\right)a$.

By the denseness property, we can always find a real number between any two other real numbers. This leads to infinitely many real numbers.

In 1874 Georg Cantor showed that the set of all real numbers cannot be put in a one-to-one correspondence with the set of natural numbers and showed that there are infinities of many different sizes.

Order of Operations

The set of real numbers follows the same order of operations given earlier; that is, when addition, subtraction, multiplication, division, and exponentiation appear without parentheses, exponentiation is done first in order from right to left, then multiplications and divisions in the order of their appearance from left to right, and then additions and subtractions in the order of their appearance from left to right. Arithmetic operations that appear inside parentheses must be done first.

Radicals and Rational Exponents

Scientific calculators have a $\boxed{y^x}$ key with which we find the values of expressions like $4^{1/2}$ and $3.41^{2/3}$. What does $4^{1/2}$ mean? By extending the properties of exponents previously developed for integer exponents,

$$4^{1/2} \cdot 4^{1/2} = 4^{(1/2+1/2)} = 4^1$$
$$(4^{1/2})^2 = 4^1 = 4$$

and consequently, $4^{1/2}$ must be a square root of 4. To obtain a unique value, it is defined to be the principal square root, that is:

$$4^{1/2} = \sqrt{4}$$

In general, if x is a nonnegative real number, then $x^{1/2} = \sqrt{x}$. Similarly, $(x^{1/3})^3 = x^{(1/3)3} = x^1$ and $x^{1/3} = \sqrt[3]{x}$. This discussion leads to the following definitions.

> **Definition of Real Number Raised to Rational Exponent**
>
> If x is a real number, n is a positive integer and m is an integer then:
>
> **1.** $x^{1/n} = \sqrt[n]{x}$, when $\sqrt[n]{x}$ is meaningful.
> **2.** $x^{m/n} = \sqrt[n]{x^m}$, if $GCD(m, n) = 1$ and $\sqrt[n]{x^m}$ is meaningful.

From part (1) it follows that $(x^m)^{1/n} = \sqrt[n]{x^m}$ if $\sqrt[n]{x^m}$ is meaningful. If n is odd then $\sqrt[n]{x^n} = x$ for all real x, but if n is even then $\sqrt[n]{x^n} = |x|$. For example $\sqrt[4]{(^-2)^4} = \sqrt[4]{16} = 2$.

More about Properties of Exponents

It can be shown that the properties of integer exponents also hold for rational exponents. These properties are equivalent to the corresponding properties of radicals *if the expressions involving radicals are meaningful.*

Let r and s be any rational numbers, x and y be any real numbers, and n a positive integer. If all the expressions are meaningful then,

a. $x^{-r} = \dfrac{1}{x^r}.$

b. $(xy)^r = x^r y^r$ which implies $(xy)^{1/n} = x^{1/n} y^{1/n}$ and $\sqrt[n]{xy} = \sqrt[n]{x}\sqrt[n]{y}.$

c. $\left(\dfrac{x}{y}\right)^r = \dfrac{x^r}{y^r}$ which implies $\left(\dfrac{x}{y}\right)^{1/n} = \dfrac{x^{1/n}}{y^{1/n}}$ and $\sqrt[n]{\dfrac{x}{y}} = \dfrac{\sqrt[n]{x}}{\sqrt[n]{y}}.$

d. $(x^r)^s = x^{rs}$ which implies $(x^{1/n})^p = x^{p/n}$ and hence $(\sqrt[n]{x})^p = \sqrt[n]{x^p}$, where p is an integer.

The preceding properties can be used to write equivalent and simplified expressions for many roots. For example, $\sqrt{96} = \sqrt{16 \cdot 6} = \sqrt{16}\sqrt{6} = 4\sqrt{6}$. Similarly, $\sqrt[3]{54} = \sqrt[3]{27 \cdot 2} = \sqrt[3]{27}\sqrt[3]{2} = 3\sqrt[3]{2}.$

Example 3

Simplify each of the following if possible.

a. $16^{1/4}$ **b.** $16^{5/4}$ **c.** $(^-8)^{1/3}$

d. $125^{-4/3}$ **e.** $(^-16)^{1/4}$

Solution

a. $16^{1/4} = (2^4)^{1/4} = 2^1 = 2$. Also $16^{1/4} = \sqrt[4]{16} = 2$

b. $16^{5/4} = 16^{(1/4)5} = (16^{1/4})^5 = 2^5 = 32$

c. $(^-8)^{1/3} = ((^-2)^3)^{1/3} = (^-2)^1 = ^-2$ or $(^-8)^{1/3} = \sqrt[3]{^-8} = ^-2$

d. $125^{-4/3} = (5^3)^{-4/3} = 5^{-4} = \dfrac{1}{5^4} = \dfrac{1}{625}$

e. Because every real number raised to the fourth power is positive, $\sqrt[4]{^-16}$ is not a real number. Consequently, $(^-16)^{1/4}$ is not a real number. A simplification is not possible.

▶ **NOW TRY THIS 2**

Compute $\sqrt[8]{10}$ on a calculator using the following sequence of keys:

$$\boxed{10}\ \boxed{\checkmark}\ \boxed{\checkmark}\ \boxed{\checkmark}$$

a. Explain why this approach works.
b. For what values of n can $\sqrt[n]{10}$ be computed using only the $\boxed{\checkmark}$ key? Why?

▶ **NOW TRY THIS 3**

The properties of integer exponents were extended to rational exponents and can be extended to real number exponents. Consider a base with a decimal exponent such as $8^{0.3}$ and $8^{0.101001\ldots}$. Write an explanation for a possible meaning of these decimal exponents.

Assessment 1A

1. Write an irrational number whose digits are 2s and 3s.
2. Use the Pythagorean Theorem to find the value for x.

a. b. c.

3. Arrange the following real numbers in order from greatest to least.

$$0.9, \quad 0.\overline{9}, \quad 0.\overline{98}, \quad 0.9\overline{88}, \quad 0.9\overline{98}, \quad 0.\overline{898}, \quad \sqrt{0.98}$$

4. Determine which of the following represent irrational numbers.
   a. $\sqrt{51}$ b. $\sqrt{64}$ c. $\sqrt{324}$
   d. $\sqrt{325}$ e. $2 + 3\sqrt{2}$ f. $\sqrt{2} \div 5$
5. If possible, find each of the following without using a calculator.
   a. The principal square root of 225
   b. $\sqrt{169}$
   c. $^-\sqrt{81}$
   d. $\sqrt{625}$
   e. $\sqrt{\dfrac{1}{4}}$
   f. $\sqrt{0.0001}$
6. Find the approximate square root of each of the following, rounded to hundredths, using the squeezing method.
   a. 7   b. 0.0120
7. Classify each of the following statements as true or false. If false, give a counterexample.
   a. The sum of any rational number and any irrational number is a rational number.
   b. The sum of any two irrational numbers is an irrational number.
   c. The product of any two irrational numbers is an irrational number.
   d. The difference of two irrational numbers could be a rational number.
8. Find three irrational numbers between each of the following pairs of rational numbers.
   a. 1 and 3
   b. $0.\overline{54}$ and $0.\overline{55}$
   c. $\dfrac{1}{2}$ and $\dfrac{1}{3}$
9. Based on your answers in exercise 8, argue that there are infinitely many irrational numbers.
10. If R is the set of real numbers, Q is the set of rational numbers, I is the set of integers, W is the set of whole numbers, and S is the set of irrational numbers, find each of the following:
    a. $Q \cup S$ b. $Q \cap S$ c. $Q \cap R$
    d. $S \cap W$ e. $W \cup R$ f. $Q \cup R$

11. The letters in the following table correspond to the sets listed in exercise 10. Complete the table by placing checkmarks in the appropriate columns. (N is the set of natural numbers.)

	N	I	Q	S	R
a. 6.7					
b. 5					
c. $\sqrt{2}$					
d. $^-5$					
e. $3\dfrac{1}{7}$					

12. The letters in following table correspond to the sets listed in exercise 10. Put a checkmark under each set of numbers for which a solution to the problem exists. (N is the set of natural numbers.)

	N	I	Q	S	R
a. $x^2 + 1 = 5$					
b. $2x - 1 = 32$					
c. $x^2 = 3$					
d. $\sqrt{x} = ^-1$					
e. $\dfrac{3}{4}x = 0.\overline{4}$					

13. Determine for what real number values of x, if any, each of the following statements is true.
    a. $\sqrt{x} = 8$ b. $\sqrt{x} = ^-8$
    c. $\sqrt{^-x} = 8$ d. $\sqrt{^-x} = ^-8$
    e. $\sqrt{x} > 0$ f. $\sqrt{x} < 0$
14. Write each of the following roots in the form $a\sqrt{b}$, where a and b are integers and b has the least value possible.
    a. $\sqrt{180}$ b. $\sqrt{363}$ c. $\sqrt{252}$
15. Write each of the following in the simplest form or as $a\sqrt[n]{b}$, where a and b are integers, $b > 0$, and b has the least value possible.
    a. $\sqrt[3]{54}$ b. $\sqrt[5]{96}$
    c. $\sqrt[3]{250}$ d. $\sqrt[5]{243}$
16. If each of the following is a part of a geometric sequence, find the missing terms.
    a. 5, ____, ____, 10
    b. 2, ____, ____, ____, 1
    c. ____, 5, ____, 3
    d. ____, $^-2$, ____, $^-3$

17. The expression $2^{10} \cdot 16^t$ approximates the number of bacteria after t hr.

    a. What is the initial number of bacteria, that is, the number when $t = 0$?

    b. After $\dfrac{1}{4}$ hr, how many bacteria are there?

    c. After $\dfrac{1}{2}$ hr, how many bacteria are there?

18. Evaluate each of the following without using a calculator.

    a. $(0.008)^{\frac{2}{3}}$ **b.** $(6.25)^{\frac{3}{2}}$

    c. $\left(\dfrac{25}{81}\right)^{-\frac{3}{2}}$ **d.** $(0.0000128)^{\frac{3}{7}}$

    e. $(^-27)^{-\frac{4}{3}}$ **f.** $^-(27)^{-\frac{4}{3}}$

19. In each of the following, find all real numbers x that satisfy the given equation. If none satisfy the equation, then state the answer as "None."

    a. $3^x = 243$ **b.** $9^{-x} = 27$

    c. $\left(\dfrac{9}{4}\right)^{3x} = \dfrac{32}{243}$ **d.** $\sqrt{^-x} = 3\sqrt{2}$

    e. $x^{-\frac{3}{4}} = 2$ **f.** $(x - 1)^2 = 2$

20. Write an equation in x not involving radical signs or fractional exponents with the following as a solution.

    a. $\sqrt[5]{20}$ **b.** $\sqrt[3]{^-2}$

    c. $\sqrt[3]{10} - 1$ **d.** $\dfrac{\sqrt{2}}{\sqrt{3}}$

21. Use the "guess and check" strategy to approximate $\sqrt[3]{103}$ to the nearest whole number.

22. Determine which of the following are irrational.

    a. $\dfrac{\sqrt{500}}{\sqrt{20}}$

    b. $8^{\frac{1}{3}} + 8^{-\frac{1}{3}}$

    c. $\dfrac{2}{\sqrt{2}} - \sqrt{2}$

    d. $\sqrt{1000}$

Assessment 1B

1. Write an irrational number whose digits are 4s and 5s.

2. Use the Pythagorean Theorem to find x.

  a. 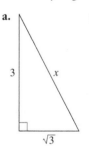   **b.** 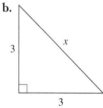   **c.**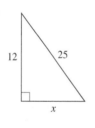

3. Arrange the following real numbers in order from greatest to least.

$$0.8, 0.\overline{8}, 0.\overline{89}, 0.8\overline{89}, \sqrt{0.7744}$$

4. Determine which of the following represent irrational numbers.

    a. $\sqrt{78}$ **b.** $\sqrt{81}$ **c.** $\sqrt[3]{343}$

    d. $3 + \sqrt{81}$ **e.** $2 \div \sqrt{2}$

5. If possible, find each of the following without using a calculator.

    a. The principle square root of 256

    b. $\sqrt{324}$

    c. $\sqrt[4]{^-1}$

    d. All x such that $x^2 = 1024$

6. Find the approximate principal square root for each of the following, rounded to hundredths, using the squeezing method.

    a. 20.3   **b.** 1.64

7. Classify each of the following statements as true or false. If false, give a counterexample.

    a. The sum of any two rational numbers is a rational number.

    b. The difference of any two irrational numbers is an irrational number.

    c. The product of any rational number and any irrational number is an irrational number.

8. Find three irrational numbers between each of the following pairs of numbers.

    a. 3 and 4

    b. $0.\overline{55}$ and $0.\overline{56}$

    c. 0.01 and 0.011

9. Describe infinitely many irrational numbers between 1 and 2 in terms of $\sqrt{2}$.

10. If R is the set of real numbers, Q is the set of rational numbers, I is the set of integers, W is the set of whole numbers, N is the set of natural numbers, and S is the set of irrational numbers, simplify or answer the following.

    a. $Q \cap I$ **b.** $S - Q$ **c.** $R \cup S$

    d. Which of the sets could be a universal set for the rest of the sets?

    e. If the universal set is R, how would you describe $\overline{S}$?

11. The letters in the table correspond to the sets listed in exercise 10. Complete the following table by placing checkmarks in the appropriate columns.

	N	I	Q	S	R
a. $\sqrt{3}$					
b. $4\dfrac{1}{2}$					
c. $^-3\dfrac{1}{7}$					

12. The letters in the following table correspond to the sets listed in exercise 10. Put a checkmark under each set of numbers for which a solution to the problem exists.

	N	I	Q	S	R
a. $x^2 + 2 = 4$					
b. $1 - 2x = 32$					
c. $x^3 = 4$					
d. $\sqrt{x} = {}^-2$					
e. $0.\overline{7}x = 5$					

13. Determine for what real values of x, if any, each of the following statements is true.
    a. $\sqrt{x} = 5$
    b. $\sqrt{x} = {}^-7$
    c. $\sqrt{{}^-x} = 5$
    d. ${}^-\sqrt{x} = 7$
    e. ${}^-\sqrt{x} = {}^-5$

14. Write each of the following square roots in the form $a\sqrt{b}$, where a and b are integers and b has the least value possible.
    a. $\sqrt{360}$
    b. $\sqrt{40}$
    c. $\sqrt{240}$

15. Write each of the following in the simplest form or as $a\sqrt[n]{b}$, where a and b are integers and $b > 0$ and b is as small as possible.
    a. $\sqrt[3]{{}^-102}$
    b. $\sqrt[6]{64}$
    c. $\sqrt[3]{64}$

16. If each of the following is a part of a geometric sequence, find the missing terms.
    a. $4, \underline{\quad}, \underline{\quad}, 8$
    b. $1, \underline{\quad}, \underline{\quad}, 2$
    c. $\underline{\quad}, \underline{\quad}, 2, \sqrt{2}$
    d. $\underline{\quad}, 1, \underline{\quad}, 2$

17. In the expression 8^t, let t represents time in hours.
    a. What is the value of the expression when $t = 0$?
    b. After $\frac{1}{3}$ hour what is the value of the expression?

18. Evaluate each of the following without using a calculator.
    a. $(0.008)^{-\frac{2}{3}}$
    b. $(0.04)^{\frac{3}{2}}$
    c. $\left(\frac{{}^-8}{27}\right)^{-\frac{2}{3}}$
    d. $(0.00000256)^{\frac{3}{8}}$
    e. $({}^-32)^{-\frac{4}{5}}$
    f. ${}^-(32)^{-\frac{4}{5}}$

19. In each of the following, find all real numbers x that satisfy the given equation. If none satisfy the equation, then state the answer as "None."
    a. $3^x = {}^-243$
    b. $81^{-x} = 27$
    c. $\left(\frac{4}{9}\right)^{-3x} = \frac{32}{243}$
    d. $\sqrt[3]{x} = 2\sqrt[3]{3}$
    e. $x^{-\frac{2}{5}} = 2$
    f. $(x + 1)^2 = 2$

20. Write an equation in x not involving radical signs or fractional exponents with the following as a solution.
    a. $\sqrt[3]{5}$
    b. $\sqrt[5]{2}$
    c. $\sqrt{2} - 1$
    d. $\frac{\sqrt{2}}{\sqrt[3]{2}}$

21. Use the "guess and check" strategy to approximate $\sqrt[3]{2001}$ to the nearest whole number.

22. Determine which of the following irrational.
    a. $\frac{\sqrt{320}}{\sqrt{20}}$
    b. $2\sqrt{50} - 8\sqrt{5}$
    c. $\frac{\sqrt{2}}{2} - \sqrt{2}$
    d. $\sqrt{10^9}$

Mathematical Connections 1

Reasoning

1. Use the fact that each prime in the prime factorization of a^3 (a is a whole number) appears a number of times that is a multiple of 3 to prove that $\sqrt[3]{2}$ is irrational.

2. Find the value of $\sqrt{3}$ on a calculator. Explain why this cannot be the exact value of $\sqrt{3}$.

3. Is it true that $\sqrt{a + b} = \sqrt{a} + \sqrt{b}$ for all a and b? If not, find all the values of a and b for which it is true. Explain.

4. The number $\frac{22}{7}$ can be written as an infinite repeating decimal. Could $\pi = \frac{22}{7}$? Why or why not?

5. a. Use the fact that if a prime p appears in the prime factorization of a perfect square then it must appear an even number of times, to prove that for all primes p, $\sqrt{p}$ is irrational.
   b. Prove that $\sqrt{\frac{7}{2}}$ is irrational.

6. Without using a calculator, order the following. Explain your reasoning.
$$(4/25)^{-1/3}, (25/4)^{1/3}, (4/25)^{-1/4}$$

7. a. To prove that $\frac{2}{\sqrt{3}} < \frac{3}{\sqrt{5}}$ a student wrote the following:
$$\frac{3}{\sqrt{5}} - \frac{2}{\sqrt{3}} = \frac{3\sqrt{3} - 2\sqrt{5}}{\sqrt{15}} = \frac{\sqrt{9} \cdot \sqrt{3} - \sqrt{4} \cdot \sqrt{5}}{\sqrt{15}}$$
$$= \frac{\sqrt{27} - \sqrt{20}}{\sqrt{15}} > 0$$

Explain why this proves that $\frac{2}{\sqrt{3}} < \frac{3}{\sqrt{5}}$.

   b. Prove that $\frac{5}{\sqrt{6}} < \frac{6}{\sqrt{7}}$, using the approach in part(a).

Open-Ended

8. The sequence $1, 1.01, 1.001, 1.0001, \ldots$ is an infinite sequence of rational numbers (each term has one more zero between the ones than the preceding term).
   a. Describe several other infinite sequences of rational numbers.
   b. Describe an infinite sequence of irrational numbers.

9. a. Define three irrational numbers between $\frac{1}{2}$ and $\frac{3}{4}$, each of which has the form $\frac{a}{b}\sqrt{2}$ where a and b are integers.

b. Describe an infinite sequence of irrational numbers between $\frac{1}{2}$ and $\frac{3}{4}$.

Cooperative Learning

10. Let each member of a group choose a number between 0 and 1 on a calculator and check what happens when the $\boxed{x^2}$ key is pressed in succession until it is clear that there is no reason to go on.

a. Compare your answers and write a conjecture based on what you observe.

b. Use other keys on the calculator in a similar way. Describe the process and state a corresponding conjecture.

c. Why do you get the result you do in parts (a) and (b)?

11. A calculator displays the following: $(3.7)^{2.4} = 23.103838$. In your group, discuss the meaning of the expression $(3.7)^{2.4}$ in view of what you know about exponents. Compare your findings with those of other groups.

Connecting Mathematics to the Classroom

12. Jim asked, if $\sqrt{2}$ can be written as $\frac{\sqrt{2}}{1}$, why is it not rational? How would you answer him?

13. A student claims that $(\sqrt{a} + \sqrt{b})^2 = a + b$ because $(\sqrt{a})^2 = a$ and $(\sqrt{b})^2 = b$. How would you help the student?

14. A student wants to know how to write $\sqrt{\sqrt{\sqrt{\sqrt{2}}}}$ with a single radical sign. How would you help the student?

15. A student says that she saw online that the solution of $x^2 = 2$ was written as $x = \pm\sqrt{2}$. She claims that if this is true then $\sqrt{2}$ has two values: one positive and one negative. How would you respond?

16. A student noticed that $\sqrt[3]{5} < \sqrt{5}$ and wants to know if whenever $a > 0$, $\sqrt[3]{a} < \sqrt{a}$. How do you respond?

17. Jose says that the equation $\sqrt{-x} = 3$ has no solution, since the square root of a negative number does not exist. How would you help him?

18. A student wants to know what is wrong with the following "proof" that $^-1 = 1$. How do you respond?

$$\sqrt{a}\sqrt{b} = \sqrt{ab}$$
$$\text{Let } a = b = {}^-1.$$
$$\sqrt{{}^-1}\sqrt{{}^-1} = \sqrt{({}^-1)({}^-1)} = \sqrt{1} = 1$$
$$\text{But also } \sqrt{{}^-1}\sqrt{{}^-1} = {}^-1.$$
$$\text{Thus, } {}^-1 = 1.$$

---

2 Variables

2 Objectives

Students will be able to understand and explain

- Variables to translate word phrases into algebraic expressions.

- Solving equations and word problems.

- The formulas for the nth term of arithmetic and geometric sequences.

Algebraic thinking is important in mathematics at all levels—from the early grades on. In this section, we focus not only on patterns but on other features of algebraic thinking as well, including solving equations, word problems.

Today, the importance of integrating algebraic thinking and problem solving at all levels begins with kindergarten.

CCSS In grade 4, *Common Core Standards* emphasizes using algebraic equations and says that students should:

Multiply or divide to solve word problems involving multiplicative comparison, for instance by using drawings and equations with a symbol for the unknown number to represent the problem, distinguishing multiplicative comparison from additive comparison. Solve multistep word problems posed with whole numbers and having whole-number answers using the four operations, including problems in which remainders must be interpreted. Represent these problems using equations with a letter standing for the unknown quantity. Assess the reasonableness of answers using mental computation and estimation strategies including rounding. (p. 29)

Grade 6 *Common Core Standards* suggests that students:

use variables to represent numbers and write expressions when solving a real-world or mathematical problem. . . . (p. 44)

al-Khowarizmi

Fibonacci

The word *algebra* comes from the book *Hidab al-jabr wa'l muqabalah*, written by Mohammed ibn Musa al-Khowarizmi (ca. 825 CE). In his book he synthesized Hindu work on the notions of algebra and used the words *jabr* and *muqubalah* to designate two basic operations in solving equations: *jabr* meant to transpose subtracted terms to the other side of the equation; *muqubalah* meant to cancel like terms on opposite sides of the equation.

Another contributor to the development of algebra was Diophantus (ca. 200–284 CE) whose *Arithmetica* is the most prominent work on algebra in Greek mathematics. About 900 years later, Leonardo di Pisa (Fibonacci) (ca. 1170–1250) introduced algebra to Europe.

A fourth contributor to algebra was François Viète (1540–1603), known as "the father of modern algebra," who introduced the first systematic algebraic notation in his book *In Artem Analyticam Isagoge*.

Algebra is a branch of mathematics in which symbols, usually letters, represent numbers or members of a given set. Elementary algebra is used to generalize arithmetic. For example, the fact that $7 + (3 + 5) = (7 + 3) + 5$, or that $9 + (3 + 8) = (9 + 3) + 8$, are special cases of $a + (b + c) = (a + b) + c$, where a, b, and c are numbers from a given set; whole numbers, integers, rational numbers, or real numbers. Similarly, $2 + 3 = 3 + 2$ and $2 \cdot 3 = 3 \cdot 2$ are special cases of $a + b = b + a$ and $a \cdot b = b \cdot a$ for all whole numbers a and b.

A major concept of algebraic thinking is that of **variable**. In basic arithmetic we have fixed numbers, or **constants**, as in $4 + 3 = 7$, but in algebra we have values that vary—hence the term *variable*.

- A variable may stand for a missing element or unknown, as in $x + 2 = 5$.
- A variable can represent more than one thing. For example, in a group of children, we could say that their heights vary with their ages. If h represents height and a represents age, then both h and a can have different values for different children in the group. Here a variable represents a changing quantity.
- A variable can be used in generalizations of patterns.
- A variable can be an element of a set, or a set itself. For example, in the definition of the intersection of two sets $A \cap B = \{x \mid x \in A \text{ and } x \in B\}$, x is any element that belongs to both sets.

To apply algebra in solving problems, we frequently need to translate given information into a mathematical expression involving variables designated by letters or words. In all such examples, we may name the variables as we choose.

In the student page shown on the next page, simple word statements are translated into **algebraic expressions**.

Mary Everest Boole

Mary Everest Boole (1832–1916), born in England and raised in France, was a self-taught mathematician and is most well-known for her works on mathematics and science education. In *Philosophy and Fun of Algebra* (London: C. W. Daniel, LTD, 1909), a book for children, she writes:

But when we come to the end of our arithmetic we do not content ourselves with guesses; we proceed to algebra—that is to say, to dealing logically with the fact of our own ignorance. . . .

Instead of guessing whether we are to call it nine, or seven, or a hundred and twenty, or a thousand and fifty, let us agree to call it x, and let us always remember that x stands for the Unknown. . . . This method of solving problems by honest confession of one's ignorance is called Algebra.

School Book Page

Using Variables to Write Expressions

Step-UP
Lesson

2

Common Core

5.OA.2 Write simple expressions that record calculations with numbers, and interpret numerical expressions without evaluating them.

Using Variables to Write Expressions

How can you write an algebraic expression?

Donnie bought CDs for $10 each. How can you represent the total cost of the CDs?

A variable is <u>a quantity that can change or vary and is often represented with a letter</u>. Variables help you translate word phrases into algebraic expressions.

$10 each

CDs cost $10 each. The operation is multiplication.

Number of CDs	Total Cost
1	$10 × 1
2	$10 × 2
3	$10 × 3
4	$10 × 4

Use the variable n to represent the number of CDs and write an algebraic expression.

$$\$10 \times n$$

An algebraic expression is <u>a mathematical phrase that has at least one variable and one operation</u>. The total cost of the CDs is represented by

$$10 \times n$$
or $10n$.

The operation is multiplication. The variable is n.

Other Examples

The table shows algebraic expressions for given situations.

Word Phrase	Operation	Algebraic Expression
5 dollars more than cost c	addition	$c + 5$
eleven pencils decreased by a number n	subtraction	$11 - n$
six times a distance d	multiplication	$6 \times d$ or $6d$
b bananas divided by seven	division	$b \div 7$ or $\frac{b}{7}$
four less than two times an amount x	multiplication and subtraction	$2x - 4$

Example 4

In each of the following descriptions, translate the given information into a symbolic expression involving variables.

a. The cost of renting a car for any number of days if the charge per day is $40
b. The distance a car traveled at a constant speed of 65 mph for any number of hours
c. One weekend, a store sold twice as many CDs as full-size DVDs and 25 fewer mini DVDs than CDs. If the store sold d full-size DVDs, how many mini DVDs and CDs did it sell?
d. French fries have about 12 calories apiece. A hamburger has about 600 calories. Akiva is on a diet of 2000 calories per day. If he ate f french fries and one hamburger, how many more calories can he consume that day?

Solution

a. If d is the number of days, the cost of renting the car for d days at $40 per day is $40d$ dollars.
b. If h is the number of hours traveled at 65 mph, the total distance traveled in h hours is $65h$ miles.
c. Because d full-size DVDs were sold, twice as many CDs as full-size DVDs implies $2d$ CDs. Thus, 25 fewer mini DVDs than CDs implies $2d - 25$ mini DVDs.
d. First, find how many calories Akiva consumed eating f french fries and one hamburger. Then, to find how many more calories he can consume, subtract this expression from 2000.

$$1 \text{ french fry} \rightarrow 12 \text{ calories}$$

$$f \text{ french fries} \rightarrow 12f \text{ calories}$$

Therefore, the number of calories in f french fries and one hamburger is $600 + 12f$.

The number of calories left for the day is $2000 - (600 + 12f)$, or $2000 - 600 - 12f$, or $1400 - 12f$.

Example 5

A teacher asked her class to do the following:

Take any real number and add 15 to it. Now multiply that sum by 4. Next subtract 8 and divide the difference by 4. Now subtract 12 from the quotient and tell me the answer. I will tell you the original number.

Analyze the instructions to see whether the teacher can determine the original number.

Solution Translate the information into an algebraic expression as seen in Table 1.

Table 1

Instructions	Discussion	Symbols/Algebraic Expressions
Take any real number.	Since any number is used, we need a variable to represent the number. Let n be that variable.	n
Add 15 to it.	We are told to add 15 to "it." "It" refers to the variable n.	$n + 15$
Multiply that sum by 4.	We are told to multiply "that sum" by 4. "That sum" is $n + 15$.	$4(n + 15)$
Subtract 8.	We are told to subtract 8 from the product.	$4(n + 15) - 8$
Divide the difference by 4.	The difference is $4(n + 15) - 8$. Divide it by 4.	$\dfrac{4(n + 15) - 8}{4}$
Subtract 12 from the quotient and tell me the answer.	We are told to subtract 12 from the quotient.	$\dfrac{4(n + 15) - 8}{4} - 12$

Translating what the teacher asked the class to do results in the algebraic expression $\frac{4(n + 15) - 8}{4} - 12$. We are to determine whether the teacher can take a given student answer and produce the original number. We use the strategy of *working backward* to help with this determination. Suppose a student gives the teacher an answer of r. Think about how r was obtained and reverse the steps in Table 1. Just before obtaining "r," the student had subtracted 12. To reverse that operation, add 12 to obtain $r + 12$. Prior to that, the student had divided by 4. To reverse that, multiply by 4 to obtain $4r + 48$. To get that result, the student had subtracted 8, so now add 8 to obtain $4r + 56$. Just prior to that, the student had multiplied by 4, so now divide $4r + 56$ by 4 to obtain $r + 14$. The first operation had been to add 15, so now subtract 15 from $r + 14$ to get $r - 1$. Thus, the teacher knows when the student tells the final result of r, it is 1 more than the number with which the student started, or the number with which the student started n is the result minus 1.

This analysis can also be shown in a different way as follows:

$$\frac{4(n + 15) - 8}{4} - 12 = \frac{4(n + 15 - 2)}{4} - 12$$
$$= (n + 13) - 12$$
$$= n + 1$$

Therefore $n + 1 = r$ and $n = r - 1$.

▶ NOW TRY THIS 4

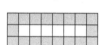

Noah has some white square tiles and some blue square tiles. They are all the same size. He first makes a row of white tiles and then surrounds the white tiles with a single layer of blue tiles, as shown in Figure 7.

How many blue tiles does he need:

Figure 7

a. to surround a row of 100 white tiles?
b. to surround a row of n white tiles?

Generalizations for Arithmetic Sequences

We saw examples of arithmetic sequences, and we were able to determine their nth terms. We now generalize this work and find the nth term of any arithmetic sequence.

An arithmetic sequence is determined by its first term and the difference. Suppose the first term of an arithmetic sequence is a_1, and the difference is d. The strategy of *making a table* can be used to find the general term for the sequence $a_1, a_1 + d, a_1 + 2d, a_1 + 3d, \ldots$, as shown in Table 2.

Table 2	
Number of Term	**Term**
1	a_1
2	$a_2 = a_1 + d = a_1 + (2 - 1)d$
3	$a_3 = a_1 + 2d = a_1 + (3 - 1)d$
4	$a_4 = a_1 + 3d = a_1 + (4 - 1)d$
5	$a_5 = a_1 + 4d = a_1 + (5 - 1)d$
$\vdots$	$\vdots$
n	$a_n = a_1 + (n - 1)d$

Observe that the number of ds in the given terms is 1 less than the number of the term. This pattern continues since we add d to get the next term. Thus, the *nth term of any arithmetic sequence with first term a_1 and difference d is given by $a_n = a_1 + (n - 1)d$, where n is a natural number.*

For example, in the arithmetic sequence $5, 9, 13, 17, 21, 25, \ldots$, the first term a_1 is 5, and the difference d is 4. Thus, the nth term is given by $a_n = 5 + (n - 1)4$. Simplifying, we obtain $a_n = 5 + (n - 1)4 = 5 + 4n - 4 = 4n + 1$.

Example 6

In an arithmetic sequence with the second term 11 and the fifth term 23, find the 100th term.

Solution We know that in the arithmetic sequence $a_2 = 11, a_5 = 23$, and we need to find a_{100}. To find the 100th term, we use the formula developed in Table 2: $a_{100} = a_1 + (100 - 1)d = a_1 + 99d$. Thus to find a_{100}, we need to know a_1 and d. This becomes our *subgoal*. We have $a_2 = 11$ and $a_5 = 23$. Hence, $11 = a_2 = a_1 + d$ and $23 = a_5 = a_1 + (5 - 1)d = a_1 + 4d$. Thus,

$$a_1 + d = 11 \quad \text{and}$$
$$a_1 + 4d = 23.$$

Because we know that $11 = a_1 + d$, we write

$$a_1 + 4d = (a_1 + d) + 3d = 23$$
$$11 + 3d = 23$$
$$3d = 12$$
$$d = 4.$$

To find the first term, we have $11 = a_1 + d$, so

$$11 = a_1 + 4, \text{or } a_1 = 7.$$

To find the 100th term, we know that $a_{100} = a_1 + (100 - 1)d$, or that $a_{100} = 7 + (100 - 1)4 = 403$.

Generalizations for Geometric Sequences

It is possible to find the nth term, a_n, of any geometric sequence when given the first term and the ratio. For example, in the geometric sequence $3, 12, 48, 192, \ldots$, the first term is 3, and the ratio is 4. To generalize geometric sequences, let the first term be a_1 and the ratio be r, so that the third term is $a_1 r^2$, and the fourth term is $a_1 r^3$ as seen in Table 3.

Table 3	
Number of Term	**Term**
1	a_1
2	$a_1 r$
3	$a_1 rr = a_1 r^2$
4	$a_1 r^2 r = a_1 r^3$
5	$a_1 r^3 r = a_1 r^4$
$\vdots$	$\vdots$
n	$a_1 r^{n-1}$

The power of r in each term is 1 less than the number of the term. This pattern continues since we multiply by r to get the next term. Thus, *the nth term a_n, of a geometric sequence, is $a_n = a_1 r^{n-1}$.* In the geometric sequence $3, 12, 48, 192, \ldots$, the first term is 3, and the ratio is 4, so the nth term is $a_n = 3 \cdot 4^{n-1}$.

Example 7

a. Find the nth term of the geometric sequence $2, 3, \dfrac{9}{2}, \dfrac{27}{4}, \ldots$

b. If a geometric sequence has first term 3 and ratio $\sqrt{2}$, find its 10th term.

Solution

a. By dividing any term from the 2nd on by its previous term, we can find the ratio r of the geometric sequence. For this sequence, $r = \dfrac{3}{2}$. Thus, the nth term is

$$a_n = a_1 r^{n-1} = 2\left(\frac{3}{2}\right)^{n-1}.$$

b. The 10th term is computed as follows:

$$a_{10} = 3(\sqrt{2})^{10-1} = 3(\sqrt{2})^9 = 3(2^{9/2}) = 3(2^{8/2})(2^{1/2}) = 3 \cdot 2^4 \cdot 2^{1/2} = 48\sqrt{2}$$

▶ **NOW TRY THIS 5**

a. Two bacteria are in a dish. The number of bacteria triples every hour. Following this pattern, find the number of bacteria in the dish after 10 hours and after n hours.

b. Suppose that instead of increasing geometrically as in part (a), the number of bacteria increases arithmetically by 3 bacteria each hour. Compare the geometric and arithmetic sequences after 10 hours and after n hours. Comment on the growth of a geometric sequence versus an arithmetic sequence.

The Fibonacci Sequence

Both arithmetic and geometric sequences may be defined *recursively*. A sequence is defined recursively when one or more initial terms are given, and each subsequent term is defined in terms of the preceeding term or terms. In a geometric sequence a_1 is given and $a_n = a_{n-1} r$, for $n = 2, 3, \ldots$. In an arithmetic sequence, a_1 is given and $a_n = a_{n-1} + d$, for $n = 2, 3, \ldots$. Similarly the Fibonacci sequence (see Section 1-2) is defined recursively. Fibonacci sequence has F_1 as the first term, F_2 as the second term, and in general, F_n as the nth term. The two terms before the nth, F_n, are F_{n-1} and F_{n-2}. With this notation, the rule for generating the Fibonacci sequence can be written as follows:

$$F_n = F_{n-1} + F_{n-2}, \text{ for } n = 3, 4, \ldots$$

This rule cannot be applied to the first two Fibonacci terms. Because $F_1 = 1$ and $F_2 = 1$, then $F_3 = 1 + 1$, or 2. The beginning terms, or seeds, $F_1 = 1$ and $F_2 = 1$ and the equation $F_n = F_{n-1} + F_{n-2}$ for $n \geq 3$ is a recursive definition because the rule for the sequence defines each term after the first two using previous terms in the same sequence.

More Algebraic Thinking

Algebraic thinking can occur in different ways. One example that uses pictures is seen in Example 8.

Example 8

At a local farmer's market, three purchases were made for the prices shown in Figure 8. What is the cost of each object?

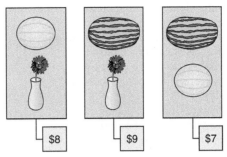

Figure 8

Solution Approaches to this problem may vary. For example, if the objects in the first two purchases are put together, the total cost would be $8 + $9, or $17. That cost would be for two vases with flowers and one each of the cantaloupe and watermelon, as in Figure 9.

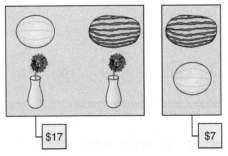

Figure 9

Now if the cantaloupe and watermelon are taken away from that total, then according to the cost of those two objects from the tag on the right, the cost should be reduced to $10 for two vases with flowers. That means each of the two vases costs $5. This in turn tells us that the cantaloupe costs $8 − $5, or $3, and the watermelon costs $9 − $5, or $4.

Assessment 2A

1. Translate the following phrases into algebraic expressions:
   a. The 4th term of an arithmetic sequence whose first term is 10 and whose difference is d
   b. 15 less than twice a number
   c. 15 times the square of a number
   d. The difference between the square of a number and twice the number
2. a. Translate the following instructions into an algebraic expression: Take any number, add $\sqrt{3}$ to it, multiply the sum by 7, subtract 14, and divide the difference by 7. Finally, subtract the original number.
   b. Simplify your answer in part (a).

3. In the tile pattern sequence of figures shown, each figure starting from the second has two more blue squares than the preceding one. The pattern represents an arithmetic sequence.

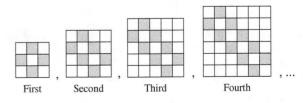

First , Second , Third , Fourth , ...

Answer the following questions.

a. How many blue tiles are there in the nth figure if this arithmetic sequence continues?

b. If the pattern of large square tiles with shaded blue ones continues, how many white tiles are there in the nth figure?

4. In the following descriptions, write an expression in terms of the given variable that represents the indicated quantity.

a. The cost of having a plumber spend h hours at your house if the plumber charges $50 for coming to the house and $60 per hour for labor

b. The amount of money in cents in a jar containing d dimes and some nickels and quarters if there are 3 times as many nickels as dimes and 3 times as many quarters as nickels

c. The sum of three consecutive integers if the least integer is x

d. The amount of bacteria after n min if the initial amount of bacteria is q and the amount of bacteria doubles every minute (*Hint:* The answer should contain q as well as n.)

e. The temperature after t hr if the initial temperature is 40°F and each hour it drops by 3°F

f. Pawel's total earnings after 3 yr if the first year his salary was s dollars, the second year it was $5000.00 higher, and the third year it was twice as much as the second year

g. The sum of three consecutive odd natural numbers if the least is x

h. The sum of three consecutive natural numbers if the middle is m

5. In a college, there are P professors and S students. There are 45 times as many students as professors. Write an algebraic equation that shows this relationship.

6. Suppose a class has g girls and b boys, and there are 5 more girls than boys. Write an algebraic equation that shows this relationship.

7. Ryan is building matchstick sequences as shown. How many matchsticks will he use for the nth figure if the pattern of adding one new square horizontally and one vertically continues?

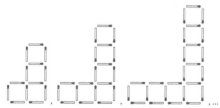

8. Write an algebraic equation relating the variables described in each of the following situations:

a. The pay, P, for t hr if you are paid $8 an hour

b. The pay, P, for t hr if you are paid $15 for the first hour and $10 for each additional hour

9. For a particular event, a student pays $5 per ticket and a nonstudent pays $13 per ticket. If x students and 100 nonstudents buy tickets, find the total revenue from the sale of the tickets in terms of x.

10. Suppose a will decreed that three siblings will each receive a cash inheritance according to the following: The eldest receives 3 times as much as the youngest, and twice as much as the middle sibling. Answer the following.

a. If the youngest sibling receives $$x$, how much do the other two receive in terms of x?

b. If the middle sibling receives $$y$, how much do the other two receive in terms of y?

c. If the oldest sibling receives $$z$, how much do the other two receive in terms of z?

11. In each of the following arithmetic sequences, find (i) the 100th term; (ii) the nth term.

a. $0, ^-3, ^-6, \ldots$

b. $1 - \sqrt{2}, 1 + \sqrt{2}, \ldots$

c. $\sqrt{3} + 0.5, \sqrt{3} + 2.5, \sqrt{3} + 4.5, \ldots$

12. In each of the following geometric sequences, find an expression for (i) the 17th term; (ii) for the nth term.

a. $2, 2\sqrt{3}, 6, \ldots$

b. $2, ^-2\sqrt{2}, \ldots$

c. $^-\sqrt{5}, 5, \ldots$

13. Find the first term and the difference in an arithmetic sequence, if the 100th term is $\sqrt{2}$ and the 200th term is $\sqrt{3}$.

14. Find the first term in a geometric sequence, if the 11th term is $^-128$ and the ratio is $^-\sqrt{2}$.

15. A ball is dropped from a height of 10 ft and bounces 80% of its previous height on each bounce. How high off the ground is the ball at the top of the 5th bounce?

16. Jake bought contact lenses and was told to wear them only 2 hours the first day and to increase the length of time by 20 minutes each day. On what day will Jake be able to wear the contacts for 12 hours?

17. In a Fibonacci-like sequence, the first term is $\sqrt{2}$, the second is $\sqrt{3}$, and each subsequent term is the sum of two previous terms. Find the following.

a. The first 10 terms in simplest form without computing $\sqrt{2}$ or $\sqrt{3}$.

b. If the terms in the Fibonacci sequence are $F_1, F_2, F_3, \ldots$, and the terms in the Fibonacci-like sequence in this question are $L_1, L_2, L_3, \ldots$, answer the following.

　i. Verify that $L_7 = F_5\sqrt{2} + F_6\sqrt{3}$.

　ii. Write $L_8, L_9,$ and L_{10} using the terms of the Fibonacci sequence, $\sqrt{2}$, and $\sqrt{3}$.

　iii. Use your answers in the previous part to conjecture an expression for L_n in terms of $\sqrt{2}$, $\sqrt{3}$, and Fibonacci terms.

Assessment 2B

1. Translate the following phrases into algebraic expressions.

a. 10 more than a number

b. 10 less than a number

c. half a number

d. The sum of a number and 10

e. The difference between the cube of a number and the square of the number

2. a. Translate the following instructions into an algebraic expression: Take any number, add 25 to it, multiply the sum by 4, subtract 60, and divide the difference by 4. Finally, add 5.

b. Simplify your answer in part (a).

3. Discover a possible tile pattern in the following sequence and answer the following.

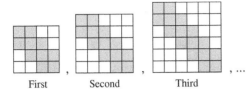

First, Second, Third, ...

   a. How many shaded tiles are there in the nth figure of your pattern if the arithmetic sequence of shaded tiles continues?
   b. How many white tiles are there in the nth figure of your pattern?

4. In the following descriptions, write an expression in terms of the given variables that represents the indicated quantity:
   a. The cost of having a plumber spend h hours at your house if the plumber charges $30 for coming to the house and $$x$ per hour for labor
   b. The amount of money in cents in a jar containing some nickels and d dimes and some quarters if there are 4 times as many nickels as dimes and 3 times as many quarters as nickels
   c. The sum of three consecutive integers if the greatest integer is x
   d. The amount of bacteria after n min if the initial amount of bacteria is q and the amount of bacteria triples every 20 sec. (The answer should contain q as well as n.)
   e. The temperature t hr ago if the present temperature is 40°F and each hour it drops by 3°F
   f. Pawel's total earnings after 3 yr if the first year his salary was s dollars, the second year it was $5000 higher, and the third year it was twice as much as the first year
   g. The sum of three consecutive even whole numbers if the greatest is x

5. If a school has w women and m men and you know that there are 100 more men than women, write an algebraic equation relating w and m.

6. Suppose there are c chairs and t tables in a classroom and there are 15 more chairs than tables. Write an algebraic equation relating c and t.

7. Ryan is building triangle sequences so that one triangle is added to the right each time, as shown. How many matchsticks will he use for the nth figure and for the figure one before the nth?

△, △▽, △▽△, ...

8. Write an algebraic equation relating the variables described in each of the following situations:
   a. The pay, P, for t hours if you are paid $$d$ an hour
   b. The pay, P, for t hours if you are paid $25 for the first hour and $$k$ for each additional hour
   c. The total pay, P, for a visit and t hours of gardening if you are paid $30 for the visit and $10 for each hour of gardening

   d. The total cost, C, of membership in a health club that charges a $300 initiation fee and $4 for each of n days attended
   e. The cost, C, of renting a midsized car for 1 day of driving m mi if the rent is $30 per day plus 35¢ per mile

9. For a particular event, students pay $$d$ per ticket and non-students pay twice as much. If x students and 100 nonstudents buy tickets, find the total revenue from the sale of the tickets in terms of x and d.

10. Matt has twice as many stickers as David. If David has d stickers, and Matt gives David 10 stickers, how many stickers does each have in terms of d?

11. In each of the following arithmetic sequences, find (i) the 100th term; (ii) the nth term.
   a. $0, {}^{-}5, {}^{-}10, \ldots$
   b. $1 + \sqrt{2}, 1 - \sqrt{2}, \ldots$
   c. $x + \sqrt{3}, 2x + 3\sqrt{3}, \ldots$

12. In each of the following geometric sequences, find an expression for (i) the 20th term; (ii) for the nth term.
   a. $\sqrt{\dfrac{3}{2}}, \sqrt{3}, \ldots$
   b. $\sqrt{2}, 2, 2\sqrt{2} \ldots$
   c. $^{-}\sqrt{3}, 3, \ldots$
   d. $3, {}^{-}3\sqrt{3}, \ldots$

13. In a geometric sequence, find the first term and the ratio if the 10th term is 25 and the 20th term is 100.

14. **a.** Find the difference in the arithmetic sequence whose nth term is $3n + 5$.
   b. Find the ratio of a geometric sequence whose nth term is $3^{\frac{3}{2}n}$.

15. A ball is dropped from a height of 20 meters and bounces 90% of its previous height on each bounce. How high off the ground is the ball at the top of the 4th bounce?

16. Consider the following arithmetic sequences. Determine the first time when a term of the first sequence is greater than the corresponding term of the second.

   $0.01, 0.11, 0.21, \ldots$
   $100, 100.01, 100.02, \ldots$

17. Find the following.
   a. The first seven terms of the Fibonacci-type sequence with seeds 1, 2
   b. The sum of the first three terms of the sequence in part (a)
   c. The sum of the first four terms of the sequence in part (a)
   d. The sum of the first five terms of the sequence in part (a)
   e. The sum of the first six terms of the sequence in part (a)
   f. The sum of the first seven terms of the sequence in part (a)
   g. A pattern for the sums in parts (b)–(f).
   h. A rule for the pattern found in part (g) using the notation for Fibonacci terms.

Mathematical Connections 2

Reasoning

1. Students were asked to write an algebraic expression for the sum of five consecutive natural numbers. One student wrote $x + (x + 1) + (x + 2) + (x + 3) + (x + 4) = 5x + 10$. Another wrote $(x - 2) + (x - 1) + x + (x + 1) + (x + 2) = 5x$.
   a. Explain who is correct and why.
   b. Does either approach prove that the sum of five consecutive integers equals 5 times the middle integer?
   c. Does the statement in part (b) generalize to the sum of five consecutive terms in every arithmetic sequence? Justify your answer.

2. a. Choose seven consecutive terms in any arithmetic sequence and check that the arithmetic average (the sum of the seven terms divided by 7) equals the middle term.
   b. Prove that the result in part (a) is true for every arithmetic sequence.

3. A teacher instructed her class as follows:

   Take any number, multiply it by 4, add 16, and divide the result by 2. Subtract 7 from the quotient and tell me your answer. I will tell you the original number.

   Explain how the teacher was able to tell each student's original number.

Open-Ended

4. A teacher instructed her class to take any number and perform a series of computations using that number. The teacher was able to tell each student's original number by subtracting 1 from the student's answer. Create similar instructions for students so that the teacher needs to do only the following to obtain the student's original number.
   a. Add 1 to the answer.
   b. Multiply the answer by 2.
   c. Multiply the answer by 1.

5. Give an example of a geometric sequence whose first 3 terms are very close to 1 but whose terms are eventually very close to 0. Use a calculator to check that your sequence has the desired property.

Cooperative Learning

6. Examine several elementary school textbooks for grades 1 through 5 and report on which algebraic concepts involving variables are introduced at each grade level.

Connecting Mathematics to the Classroom

7. A student writes $a(bc) = (ab)(ac)$. How do you respond?
8. A student wonders if sets can ever be considered as variables. What do you tell her?
9. A student thinks that if A and B are sets, then the statements $A \cup B = B \cup A$ and $A \cap B = B \cap A$ are set properties in a way similar to the statements $a + b = b + a$ and $ab = ba$ are arithmetic properties of numbers. How do you respond?
10. A student wants to know how can she prove that a sequence whose nth term is $5n + 4$ is arithmetic and a sequence whose nth term is $5 \cdot 3^{\frac{n}{2}}$ is geometric. How do you respond?

Review Problems

11. Find two rational numbers and two irrational numbers between 1.41 and $\sqrt{2}$.
12. Determine which of the following are rational and which are irrational numbers.
   a. $\sqrt[3]{728}$
   b. $\dfrac{2}{\sqrt{2}}$
   c. $\sqrt[3]{2^9 \cdot 3^{12}}$
   d. $\sqrt[3]{2} \cdot \sqrt[3]{4}$
   e. $(\sqrt{3} - \sqrt{2})(\sqrt{3} + \sqrt{2})$
   f. $(\sqrt{3} - \sqrt{2})^2$
13. Compute the following, if possible. If a number is not a real number, write "not real."
   a. $\left(\dfrac{^{-}8}{27}\right)^{-\frac{2}{3}}$
   b. $\left(\dfrac{^{-}9}{4}\right)^{\frac{3}{2}}$
   c. $^{-}\left(\dfrac{9}{4}\right)^{\frac{3}{2}}$
14. Find all real number values for x, if possible. If there is no real solution, write "None."
   a. $\sqrt{^{-}x} = 5$
   b. $\sqrt{x^2} = ^{-}x$
   c. $(^{-}x)^{\frac{1}{2}} = 125$
15. Find all integers n such that $n < \sqrt[3]{50} < n + 1$.

National Assessments

National Assessment of Educational Progress (NAEP) Questions

A yellow box holds 72 pencils.

$\boxed{Y}$ is the same as $\boxed{72}$.

Two red boxes hold as many pencils as 1 yellow box.

$\boxed{R}\ \boxed{R}$ is the same as $\boxed{Y}$.

Three blue boxes hold as many pencils as 1 red box.

$\boxed{B}\ \boxed{B}\ \boxed{B}$ is the same as $\boxed{R}$.

How many pencils does 1 blue box hold?

Answer: _____

Show or explain how you got your answer.
NAEP, Grade 4, 2013

$2 + n$	5
$3 + n$	6
$4 + n$	7
$5 + n$	8

What number does n represent in the table?
A. 2
B. 3
C. 4
D. 5
NAEP, Grade 4, 2009

A. If c and d are different prime numbers less than 10 and the sum $c + d$ is a *composite* number greater than 10, what is one possible pair of values for c and d?

$c =$ _____ $d =$ _____

B. If j and k are different prime numbers less than 10 and the sum $j + k$ is a *prime* number less than 10, what is one possible pair of values for j and k?

$j =$ _____ $k =$ _____

C. If s and t are different prime numbers greater than 10, explain why the sum $s + t$ cannot be a prime number.

NAEP, Grade 8, 2013

3 Equations

3 Objectives

Students will be able to understand and explain

- Properties of equality and equations.

- Solutions of equations using properties of equations.

- Solutions of word problems.

With variables w and c, we consider equations such as $w + c = \sqrt{7}$. The equal sign indicates that the values on both sides of the equation are the same even though they do not look the same.

To solve equations, we need several properties of equality. Many of these can be discovered by using a balance scale. For example, consider two objects a and b of the same weight on the balances, as in Figure 10(a). If the balance is level, then $a = b$. When we add an equal amount of weight, c, to both sides, the balance is still level, as in Figure 10(b).

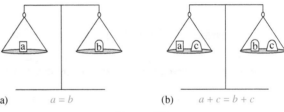

(a)　　$a = b$　　　　(b)　　$a + c = b + c$

Figure 10

This demonstrates that *if $a = b$, then $a + c = b + c$*, which is *the addition property of equality*.

Similarly, if the scale is balanced with amounts a and b, as in Figure 11(a), and we put additional a's on one side and an equal number of b's on the other side, the scale remains level, as in Figure 11(b).

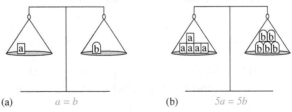

(a)　　$a = b$　　　　(b)　　$5a = 5b$

Figure 11

Figure 11 suggests that *if c is any natural number and $a = b$, then $ac = bc$*. This property can be extended to all real numbers c. The extension is the *multiplication property of equality*. These properties are summarized in the next theorem.

Theorem 2:　The Addition and Multiplication Properties of Equality

a. For any real numbers a, b, and c, if $a = b$, then $a + c = b + c$.

b. For any real numbers a, b, and c, if $a = b$, then $ac = bc$.

Because $a - c = a + (^-c)$ and if $c \neq 0$ then $\dfrac{a}{c} = a \cdot \dfrac{1}{c}$, Theorem 2 implies the subtraction and division properties of equality.

Equality is not affected if we substitute a number for its equal. This property is referred to as the **substitution property**. Examples of substitution follow:

a. If $a + b = c + d$ and $d = 5$, then $a + b = c + 5$.
b. If $a + b = c + d$, $b = e$, and $d = f$, then $a + e = c + f$.

Using the substitution property, we can see that equations can be added or subtracted as stated in the following theorem.

> **Theorem 3:   Addition and Subtraction Property of Equations**
>
> If a, b, c, d are real numbers, $a = b$ and $c = d$, then $a + c = b + d$ and $a - c = b - d$.

Theorem 2 implies that we may add the same real number to both sides of an equation or multiply both sides of the equation by the same real number without affecting the equality. If $a + c = b + c$ and $ac = bc$, the cancellation properties of equality can be developed by adding ^-c to both sides of the first equation and multiplying both sides by $\dfrac{1}{c}$, where $c \neq 0$, in the second equation.

> **Theorem 4:   Cancellation Properties of Equality**
>
> **a.** For any real numbers a, b, and c, if $a + c = b + c$, then $a = b$.
> **b.** For any real numbers a, b, and c, with $c \neq 0$, if $ac = bc$, then $a = b$.

If $ab = 0$, then at least one factor, a or b, must be 0. Thus, we have the following: *For any real numbers a and b, if ab = 0, then a = 0 or b = 0.*

An algebraic use of the italized statement is seen when we find a solution to an equation like $(x - 3)(x - 5) = 0$. We know that $x - 3 = 0$ or $x - 5 = 0$. Hence $x = 3$ or $x = 5$. The above theorems and properties for real numbers also hold for algebraic expressions.

When using the commutative property of multiplication, each of the distributive properties can be written in the equivalent forms:

$$ab + ac = a(b + c)$$
$$ab - ac = a(b - c)$$

When the distributive properties are written in the above equivalent forms, we refer to them as *factoring* and say that a has been "factored out."

Solving Equations with One Variable

Finding solutions to equations is a major part of algebra. Use of tangible objects can increase students' engagement and comprehension when they work with equations. A balance-scale model fosters understanding of the basic concepts used in solving equations and inequalities.

For example, consider Figure 12. If we release the pan on the left, what happens? Upon release, the scale tilts down on the right side and we have an *inequality*, $2 \cdot 3 < 3 + (2 \cdot 2)$.

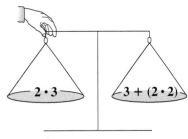

Figure 12

Next consider Figure 13. If we release the pan, then the sides will balance and we have the *equality* $2 \cdot 3 = (1 + 1) + 4$.

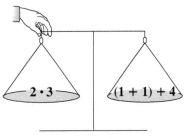

Figure 13

A balance scale can also be used to reinforce the idea of a replacement set for a variable. Name some solutions in Figure 14 that keep the scale balanced. For example, $3(5/2)$ balances $2(15/4)$, $3\sqrt{16}$ balances $2 \cdot 6 = 12$, and so on.

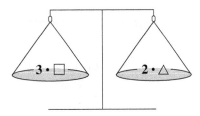

Figure 14

Other types of balance scale problems may help students with algebra. Work through Now Try This 6 before proceeding.

▶ NOW TRY THIS 6

What are the values of □ and △ in parts (a) and (b) below?

a.

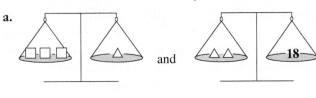
and

b.

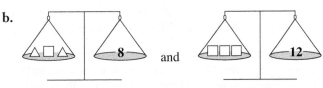
and

To solve equations, we may think of the properties of equality used on a balance pan. Consider $3x - 14 = 1$. Put the equal expressions on the opposite pans of the balance scale. Because the expressions are equal, the pans should be level, as in Figure 15.

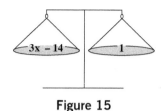

Figure 15

To solve for x, we use the properties of equality to manipulate the expressions on the scale so that after each step, the scale remains level and, at the final step, only an x remains on one side of the scale. The number on the other side of the scale represents the solution to the original equation. To find x in the equation of Figure 15, consider the scales pictured in successive steps in Figure 16, where each successive scale represents an equation that is equivalent to the original equation; that is, each has the same solution as the original. The last scale shows $x = 5$. To check that 5 is the correct solution, we substitute 5 for x in the original equation. Because $3 \cdot 5 - 14 = 1$ is a true statement, 5 is the solution to the original equation.

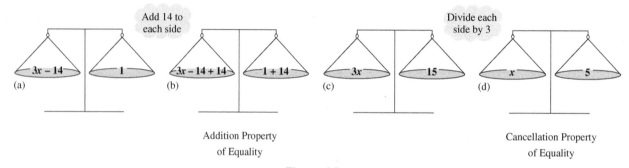

Figure 16

 Concrete objects are used in solving equations on the student page shown on the next page.

Historical Note

Mary Fairfax Somerville

Born in Scotland, Mary Fairfax Somerville (1780–1872) when she was 13 saw mysterious symbols in a women's fashion magazine. After persuading her brother's tutor to purchase some literature for her on the subject, she began her study of algebra. As a young mother and widow, she obtained books providing her with a background in mathematics. Throughout her life, Somerville distinguished herself as a skilled scientific writer. When she was 89 she published *Molecular and Microscopic Science*. In her autobiography Somerville wrote of how she "was sometimes annoyed when in the midst of a difficult problem" a visitor would enter. Shortly before her death she wrote:

> I am now in my ninety-second year, . . . , I am extremely deaf, and my memory of ordinary events, and especially of the names of people, is failing, but not for mathematical and scientific subjects. I am still able to read books on the higher algebra for four or five hours in the morning and even to solve the problems. Sometimes I find them difficult, but my old obstinacy remains, for if I do not succeed today, I attack them again tomorrow.

School Book Page — Modeling Equations

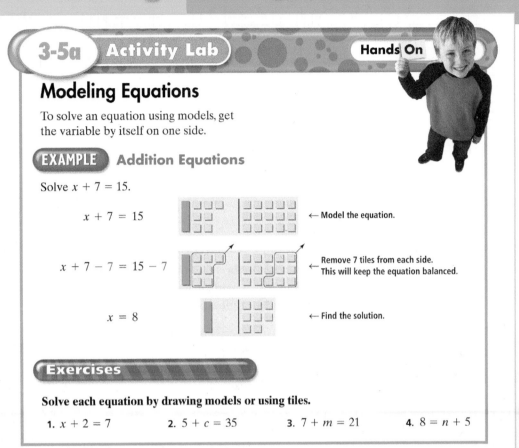

3-5a **Activity Lab** **Hands On**

Modeling Equations

To solve an equation using models, get the variable by itself on one side.

EXAMPLE **Addition Equations**

Solve $x + 7 = 15$.

$$x + 7 = 15 \qquad \leftarrow \text{Model the equation.}$$

$$x + 7 - 7 = 15 - 7 \qquad \leftarrow \begin{array}{l}\text{Remove 7 tiles from each side.} \\ \text{This will keep the equation balanced.}\end{array}$$

$$x = 8 \qquad \leftarrow \text{Find the solution.}$$

Exercises

Solve each equation by drawing models or using tiles.

1. $x + 2 = 7$ **2.** $5 + c = 35$ **3.** $7 + m = 21$ **4.** $8 = n + 5$

Example 9

Solve each of the following equations for x.

a. $x + \sqrt[3]{4} = 20$

b. $3x = x + \sqrt{10}$

c. $\dfrac{4}{3}x = 33x - \dfrac{1}{3}$

d. $4(x + 3) + 5(x + 3) = 99$

Solution

a.
$$x + \sqrt[3]{4} = 20$$
$$\left(x + \sqrt[3]{4}\right) - \sqrt[3]{4} = 20 - \sqrt[3]{4}$$
$$x = 20 - \sqrt[3]{4}$$

b.
$$3x = x + \sqrt{10}$$
$$3x - x = (x + \sqrt{10}) - x$$
$$(3 - 1)x = (\sqrt{10} + x) - x$$
$$2x = \sqrt{10}$$
$$x = \frac{\sqrt{10}}{2}$$

c.

$$\frac{4}{3}x = 33x - \frac{1}{3}$$

$$3 \cdot \frac{4}{3}x = 3\left(33x - \frac{1}{3}\right)$$

$$4x = 99x - 1$$

$$4x + 1 = 99x - 1 + 1$$

$$4x + 1 = 99x$$

$$^{-}4x + (4x + 1) = \,^{-}4x + 99x$$

$$1 = (^{-}4 + 99)x$$

$$1 = 95x$$

$$\frac{1}{95} = x$$

d.

$$4(x + 3) + 5(x + 3) = 99$$

$$(4 + 5)(x + 3) = 99 \,(\text{Why?})$$

$$9(x + 3) = 99$$

$$x + 3 = 11$$

$$x = 8$$

Application Problems

Figure 17 demonstrates a method for solving application problems with a third-grade example: formulate the problem with a mathematical model, solve that mathematical model, and interpret the solution in terms of the original problem.

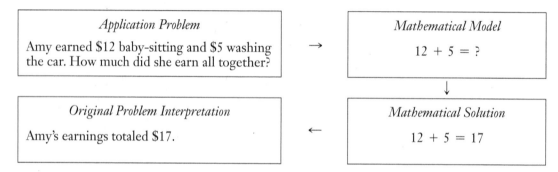

Figure 17

We apply the four-step problem-solving process to solving word problems with algebraic thinking. In Understanding the Problem, we identify what is given and what is to be found. In Devising a Plan, we assign letters to the unknown quantities and try to translate the information in the problem into a model involving equations. In Carrying Out the Plan, we solve the equations or inequalities. In Looking Back, we interpret and check the solution in terms of the original problem.

Problem Solving Overdue Books

Bruno has five books overdue at the library. The fine for overdue books is 10¢ a day per book. He remembers that he checked out an astronomy book a week before he checked out four novels. If his total fine was $8.70, how long was each book overdue?

Understanding the Problem Bruno has five books overdue. The astronomy book was checked out seven days before the four novels. The fine per day for each book is 10¢, and the total fine was $8.70. We need to find out how many days each book is overdue.

Devising a Plan Let d be the number of days that each of the four novels is overdue. The astronomy book was due seven days before the novels so it is $(d + 7)$ days overdue. To *write an equation* using d, we express the total fine in two ways. The total fine is $8.70. This fine in cents equals the fine for the four novels, plus the fine for the astronomy book.

$$\text{Fine for each of the novels} = \underbrace{\text{Fine per day}}_{10} \underbrace{\text{times}}_{\cdot} \underbrace{\text{number of overdue days}}_{d}$$

$$\text{Fine for the four novels} = \underbrace{\text{1 day's fine for novels}}_{4 \cdot 10} \underbrace{\text{times}}_{\cdot} \underbrace{\text{number of overdue days}}_{d}$$

$$= (4 \cdot 10)d$$

$$= 40d$$

$$\text{Fine for the astronomy book} = \underbrace{\text{Fine per day}}_{10} \underbrace{\text{times}}_{\cdot} \underbrace{\text{number of overdue days}}_{(d + 7)}$$

$$= 10(d + 7)$$

Because each of the expressions is in cents, we write the total fine of $8.70 as 870¢ to produce the following:

$$\text{Fine for the four novels} + \text{Fine for the astronomy book} = \text{Total fine}$$
$$40d \qquad + \qquad 10(d + 7) \qquad = 870$$

Carrying Out the Plan Solve the equation for d.

$$40d + 10(d + 7) = 870$$
$$40d + 10d + 70 = 870$$
$$50d + 70 = 870$$
$$50d = 800$$
$$d = 16$$

Thus, each of the four novels was 16 days overdue, and the astronomy book was overdue $d + 7 = 23$ days.

Looking Back To check the answer, follow the original information. Each of the four novels was 16 days overdue, and the astronomy book was 23 days overdue. Because the fine was 10¢ per day per book, the fine for each of the novels was $16 \cdot 10$¢, or 160¢. Hence, the fine for all four novels was $4 \cdot 160$¢, or 640¢. The fine for the astronomy book was $23 \cdot 10$¢, or 230¢. Consequently, the total fine was 640¢ + 230¢, or 870¢, which agrees with the given information of $8.70 as the total fine.

Problem Solving **Newspaper Delivery**

In a small town, 3 children deliver all the newspapers. Abby delivers 3 times as many papers as Bob, and Connie delivers 13 more than Abby. If the 3 children deliver a total of 496 papers, how many papers does each deliver?

Understanding the Problem The problem asks for the number of papers each child delivers. We are given information comparing the number of papers that each child delivers as well as the total number of papers delivered in the town.

Devising a Plan Let a, b, and c be the number of papers delivered by Abby, Bob, and Connie, respectively. We translate the given information into *algebraic equations* as follows:

Abby delivers 3 times as many papers as Bob: $a = 3b$

Connie delivers 13 more papers than Abby: $c = a + 13$

Total delivery is 496: $a + b + c = 496$

To reduce the number of variables, substitute $3b$ for a in the second and third equations:

$c = a + 13$ becomes $c = 3b + 13$

$a + b + c = 496$ becomes $3b + b + c = 496$

Next, make an equation in one variable, b, by substituting $3b + 13$ for c in the equation $3b + b + c = 496$; solve for b; and then find a and c.

Carrying Out the Plan

$$3b + b + 3b + 13 = 496$$
$$7b + 13 = 496$$
$$7b = 483$$
$$b = 69$$

Thus, $a = 3b = 3 \cdot 69 = 207$. Also, $c = a + 13 = 207 + 13 = 220$. So, Abby delivers 207 papers, Bob delivers 69 papers, and Connie delivers 220 papers.

Looking Back To check the answers, follow the original information, using $a = 207$, $b = 69$, and $c = 220$. The information in the first sentence, "Abby delivers 3 times as many papers as Bob," checks, since $207 = 3 \cdot 69$. The second sentence, "Connie delivers 13 more papers than Abby," is true because $220 = 207 + 13$. The information on the total delivery checks, since $207 + 69 + 220 = 496$.

▶ **NOW TRY THIS 7**

Solve the *Newspaper Delivery* problem above by introducing only one unknown for the number of newspapers Bob delivered.

Assessment 3A

1. Consider the balances:

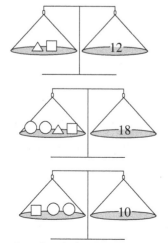

What is the value of each shape?

2. Solve each of the following if x is a real number. If a real number solution does not exist, write "No solution."
   a. $x + \sqrt{3} = 2\sqrt{3} - x$
   b. $\frac{3}{2}x - 3 = x + \sqrt{2}$
   c. $5(2x + \sqrt{2}) + 7(2x + \sqrt{2}) = 12$
   d. $3(\sqrt{x} - 3) = 5(\sqrt{x} - 3)$
   e. $(\sqrt{x} - 5)^2 = 9$

3. Ryan is building matchstick square sequences so that one square is added to the right each time a new figure is formed, as shown. He used 67 matchsticks to form the last figure in his sequence. How many squares are in this last figure?

4. For a particular event, 812 tickets were sold for a total of $1912. If students paid $2 per ticket and non-students paid $3 per ticket, how many student tickets were sold?

5. An estate of $486,000 is left to three siblings. The eldest receives 3 times as much as the youngest. The middle sibling receives $14,000 more than the youngest. How much did each receive?

6. A 10 ft board is to be cut into three pieces, two equal-length ones and the third 3 in. shorter than each of the other two. If the cutting does not result in any length being lost, how long are the pieces?

7. A box contains 67 coins, only dimes and nickels. The amount of money in the box is $4.20. How many dimes and how many nickels are in the box?

8. Miriam is 10 years older than Ricardo. Two years ago, Miriam was 3 times as old as Ricardo is now. How old are they now?

9. In a college, 20 times as many undergraduate students as graduate students are enrolled. If the total student enrollment at the college is 21,000, how many graduate students are there?

10. A farmer has 1200 yd of fencing to enclose a rectangular pasture for her goats. Since one side of the pasture borders

a river, that side does not need to be fenced. Side *b* must be twice as long as side *a*. Find the dimensions of the rectangular pasture.

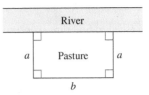

11. The sum of three consecutive terms in the arithmetic sequence 1, 4, 7, 10, . . . is 903; find these three terms.

12. The perimeter of a rectangle (the sum of the lengths of the 4 sides) is 100 feet and the shorter side is $\frac{1}{3}$ of the length of the longer side. Find the length of the diagonal. (Use the Pythagorean Theorem.)

Assessment 3B

1. Consider the following balances:

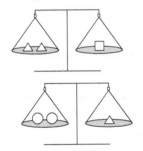

   a. Which shape weighs the most? Tell why.
   b. Which shape weighs the least? Tell why.

2. Solve each of the following if *x* is a real number and if a real number solution does not exist, write "no real solution."
   a. $x - \sqrt{2} = 3\sqrt{2} - x$
   b. $-\frac{3}{2}x - 2 = x - \sqrt{2}$
   c. $5(2x - \sqrt{3}) - 7(2x - \sqrt{3}) = 2$
   d. $2(x^2 - 3) = x^2 - 3$
   e. $(\sqrt{x} - 5)^2 = 9$

3. Ryan is building matchstick square sequences, as shown. He used 599 matchsticks to form the last two figures in his sequence. How many matchsticks did he use in each of the last two figures?

4. At the Out-Rage Benefit Concert, 723 tickets were sold for $3/student and $5/non-student. The benefit raised $2815. How many non-student tickets were sold?

5. An estate of $2,000,000 is left to four siblings. The eldest is to receive 3 times as much as the youngest. The other two siblings are each to receive $16,000 more than the youngest. How much will each receive?

6. Ten years from now Alex's age will be 3 times her present age. Find Alex's age now.

7. Matt has twice as many stickers as David. How many stickers must Matt give David so that they will each have 120 stickers? Check that your answer is correct.

8. Miriam is four years older than Ricardo. Ten years ago Miriam was 3 times as old as Ricardo was then.
   a. How old are they now?
   b. Determine whether your answer is correct by checking that it satisfies the conditions of the problem.

9. In a college there are 13 times as many students as professors. If together the students and professors number 28,000, how many students are there in the college?

10. A farmer has 800 yd of fencing to enclose a rectangular pasture. One side of the pasture borders a river and does not need to be fenced. If side *a* must be twice as long as side *b* parallel to the river, what are the dimensions of the rectangular pasture? (see drawing in exercise 10 Assessment 3A)

11. The sum of the first two terms of a geometric sequence is 100 times the first term. What is the common ratio?

12. In a rectangle, one side is $\frac{1}{3}$ of the length of the other side and the length of a diagonal is 9 feet, how long are the sides of the rectangle?

Mathematical Connections 3

Reasoning

1. Students were asked to find three consecutive whole numbers whose sum is 393. One student wrote the equation $x + (x + 1) + (x + 2) = 393$. Another wrote $(x - 1) + x + (x + 1) = 393$. Explain whether either approach works to find the answer to the question.
2. Explain how to solve the equation $3x + 5 = 5x - 3$ using a balance scale.
3. Rails lengthen in hot weather. Clips anchor the welded rails to concrete or steel sleepers. Without these clips a one mile length of track might expand 2 ft. and buckle in an arc as shown. Use AC as an approximation of half of the bow to estimate the height h of the buckle.

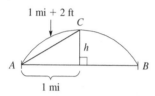

4. **a.** A pipe can fill a pool in 12 hours. Another pipe can fill the pool in 18 hours. How long will it take for the two pipes to fill the pool if they operate simultaneously?
   b. Answer the question in part (a) if the first pipe can fill the pool in a hours and the second in b hours. Write your answer in as simple a form as possible in terms of a and b.

Open-Ended

5. Create an equation with x on both sides of the equation for each of the following.
   a. Every real number is a solution.
   b. No real number is a solution.
   c. 0 is a solution.
6. Create an equation not involving radicals or fractional exponents for each of the following.
   a. $\sqrt{3}$ and $^-\sqrt{3}$ are the solutions
   b. $\sqrt[3]{2}$ is the only solution

Cooperative Learning

7. Examine several elementary school textbooks for grades 1 through 5 and report how algebraic concepts involving equations are introduced in each grade level.
8. Each person in your group is to search the Internet for two word problems that seem interesting and somewhat challenging, and bring them back to the group. Next, the group is to discuss the problems and choose which one is most interesting. Each person then is to create a clear, well-written solution. The group should discuss the different solutions and choose the best one. Discuss what makes the chosen solution good.

Connecting Mathematics to the Classroom

9. A student claims that the equation $3x = 5x$ has no solution because $3 \neq 5$. How do you respond?
10. A student claims that because in the following problem we need to find three unknown quantities, he must set up equations with three unknowns. How do you respond?

    Abby delivers twice as many papers as Jillian, and Brandy delivers 50 more papers than Abby. How many papers does each deliver if the total number of papers delivered is 550?
11. A student was told that in order to check a solution to a word problem like the one in exercise 10, it is not enough to check that the solution found satisfies the equation set up, but rather that it is necessary to check the answer against the original problem. She would like to know why. How do you respond?
12. On a test, a student was asked to solve the equation $4x + 5 = 3(x + 15)$. He proceeded as follows:

    $$4x + 5 = 3x + 45 = x + 5 = 45 = x = 40$$

    Hence, $x = 40$. He checked that $x = 40$ satisfies the original equation; however, he did not get full credit for the problem and wants to know why. How do you respond?

Review Problems

13. If the number of sophomores, juniors, and seniors combined is denoted by x and it is 3 times the number of freshmen, denoted by y, write an algebraic equation that shows the relationship.
14. Write the sum of five consecutive even numbers if the middle one is $2n$. Simplify your answer.
15. If Julie has twice as many CDs as Jack and Tyto has 3 times as many as Julie, write an algebraic expression for the number of CDs each has in terms of one variable.
16. Write an algebraic equation relating the variables described in each of the following.
    a. The total pay P for 3 hours if you are paid \$30 for the first hour and \$$d$ more than the preceding hour for each hour thereafter.
    b. Jimmy's total pay P after 4 years if the first year his salary was d dollars and then each year thereafter his salary is twice as much as in the preceding year
17. **a.** Show that the sum of every three consecutive terms in every arithmetic sequence equals 3 times the middle term.
    b. State and justify a statement similar to the one in part(a) for a product of every three consecutive terms in every geometric sequence.
18. If the first term of a geometric sequence is $\sqrt{5}$ and the ratio is 0.5, find the 6th term of the sequence.
19. In a geometric sequence, the first term is 12 and the 4th term is $\sqrt{5}$. Find the ratio.

National Assessments

National Assessment of Educational Progress (NAEP) Questions

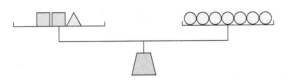

The objects on the scale above make it balance exactly. According to this scale, if △ balances ◯◯◯, then ▢ balances which of the following?

NAEP, Grade 8, 2013

While she was on vacation, Tara sent 14 friends either a letter or a postcard. She spent $3.84 on postage. If it costs $0.20 to mail a postcard and $0.33 to mail a letter, how many letters did Tara send? Show what you did to get your answer.

NAEP, Grade 8, 2013

4 Functions

4 Objectives

Students will be able to understand and explain

- The concept of a function including domain and range.

- Different representations of functions.

- Derivation of the formulas for the sum of *n* terms of arithmetic and geometric sequences.

- The concept of a relation.

CCSS The concept of a function is central to all of mathematics and particularly to algebra, as elaborated in the following excerpt from grade 8 *Common Core Standards*. We find that students should:

- **Define, evaluate, and compare functions.**
- **Use functions to model relationships between quantities. (p. 53)**

Functions can model many real-world phenomena. In this section, we explore different ways to represent functions—as *rules, machines, equations, arrow diagrams, tables, ordered pairs, and graphs*. It is important that students see a variety of ways of representing functions.

Functions as Rules Between Two Sets

The following problem is an example of a game called "guess my rule," and often used to introduce the concept of a function.

> When Tom said 2, Noah said 5. When Dick said 4, Noah said 7. When Mary said 10, Noah said 13. When Liz said 6, what did Noah say? What is Noah's rule?

The answer to the first question may be 9, and the rule could be "Take the original number and add 3"; that is, for any number *n*, Noah's answer is $n + 3$.

Example 10

Guess the teacher's rule for the following responses:

a.

Student	Teacher
1	3
0	0
4	12
10	30

b.

Student	Teacher
2	5
3	7
5	11
10	21

c.

Student	Teacher
2	0
4	0
7	1
21	1

Solution

a. The teacher's rule could be "Multiply the given number n by 3"; that is, for any number n the teacher's answer is $3n$.

b. The teacher's rule could be "Double the original number n and add 1;" that is, for any number n the teacher's answer is $2n + 1$.

c. The teacher's rule could be "If the number n is even, answer 0; if the number is odd, answer 1." Another possible rule is "If the number is less than 5, answer 0; if greater than or equal to 5, answer 1."

Note that in Example 10, the rule connects the set describing what the student says to the set describing the teacher's responses.

Functions as Machines

Another way to prepare students for the concept of a function is by using a "function machine." Functions are commonly given letter names, in particular f or g. The following partial student page shows an example of a function machine. What goes into the machine is referred to as *input* and what comes out as *output*. On the student page below, if the input to the function, f, is 3, the output is 12. For any input element x, the output could be denoted as $f(x)$, read "f of x." For the function in the example on the student page, one possibility is to write it as $f(x) = 4x$, where x is a real number.

School Book Page Why Learn This?

Why Learn This?

Pretend you have a machine. You can put any number, or input, into the machine. The machine performs an operation on the number and provides a result, or output. A **function** is a rule that assigns exactly one output value to each input value.

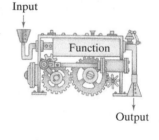

Input

Function

Output

Suppose you tell the machine to multiply by 4. A function table, such as the one at the right, shows the input and output values.

Input	Output
3	12
−7	−28

Historical Note

Leonhard Euler

The Babylonians of Mesopotamia (ca. 2000 BCE) developed a precursor to a function. To them, a function was a table or a correspondence.

In his book *Geometry* (1637), René Descartes (1596–1650) used functions to describe many mathematical relationships. Almost 50 years after the publication of Descartes's book, Gottfried Wilhelm Leibniz (1646–1716) introduced the term *function*. Function was further formalized by Leonhard Euler (pronounced "oiler," 1707–1783), who introduced the notation $y = f(x)$. In the early twenty-first century, on most graphing calculators, Y1, Y2, Y3, . . . serve as function notations where Y1 acts like $f(x)$ if the function rule is written in terms of x.

Example 11

Consider the function machine in Figure 18. For the function named f, what happens when the numbers 0, 1, 3, 4, and 6 are input?

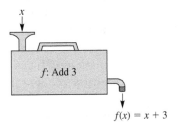

Figure 18

Solution   For the given values of x, the corresponding values $f(x)$ are described in Table 4.

Table 4

x	f(x)
0	3
1	4
3	6
4	7
6	9

Functions as Equations

The equation $f(x) = x + 3$ describes the function in Example 11. The output values can be obtained by substituting the values 0, 1, 3, 4, and 6 for x in $f(x) = x + 3$, as shown:

$$f(0) = 0 + 3 = 3$$
$$f(1) = 1 + 3 = 4$$
$$f(3) = 3 + 3 = 6$$
$$f(4) = 4 + 3 = 7$$
$$f(6) = 6 + 3 = 9$$

   In many applications, both the inputs and the outputs of a function machine are numbers. However, inputs and outputs can be any objects. For example, consider a particular candy machine that accepts only 25¢, 50¢, and 75¢ and outputs one of three types of candy with costs of 25¢, 50¢, and 75¢, respectively. A function machine associates *exactly one output with each input*. If we enter some element x as input and obtain $f(x)$ as output, then every time we enter the same x as input, we obtain the same $f(x)$ as output. The idea of a function machine associating exactly one output with each input according to some rule leads to a definition of a function as a relation between two sets as seen below.

> **Definition of Function**
>
> A **function** from set A to set B is a correspondence from A to B in which each element of A is paired with one, and only one, element of B.

From the definition it follows that f is a function from set A to set B if for every $x \in A$, x is paired with a single element in B, denoted by $f(x)$ the image of x. Later in this section we will see that functions are sets of ordered pairs.

The set, A, of all allowable inputs in the definition of a function is the **domain** of the function. Normally, *if no domain is given to describe a function, then the domain is assumed to contain all elements for which the rule is meaningful.* Set B, the **codomain**, is any set that includes all the possible outputs. The set of all actual outputs is the **range** of the function. Set B includes the range and could be the range itself. The distinction is made for convenience sake, since sometimes the range is not easy to find. Students frequently have trouble with the language of functions (for example, *image, domain, range*, and *one-to-one*), which subsequently impacts their ability to work with graphical representations of functions.

A typical calculator contains many functions. For example, the $\boxed{\pi}$ button always displays an approximation for π, such as 3.1415927; the $\boxed{+/-}$ button either displays a negative sign in front of a number or removes an existing negative sign; and the $\boxed{x^2}$ and $\boxed{\sqrt{}}$ buttons square numbers and take the principal square root of numbers, respectively.

Not all input-output machines are function machines. Consider the machine in Figure 19. For any *natural-number* input x, the machine outputs a number that is less than x. If, for example, the number 10 is input, the machine may output 9, since 9 is less than 10. If 10 is input again, the machine may output 3, since 3 is less than 10. Such a machine is not a function machine because the same input may have different outputs; it is an example of a *relation*.

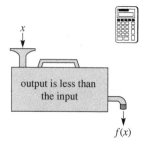

Figure 19

Example 12

A bicycle manufacturer incurs a daily fixed cost of $1400 for overhead expenses and a cost of $500 per bike manufactured.

a. Find the total cost $C(x)$ of manufacturing x bikes in a day.
b. If the manufacturer sells each bike for $700 and the profit (or loss) in producing and selling x bikes in a day is $P(x)$, find $P(x)$ in terms of x.
c. Find the break-even point, that is, the number of bikes x produced and sold that will result in neither a profit nor a loss.

Solution

a. Since the cost of producing each bike is $500, the cost of producing x bikes is $500x$ dollars. Because of the fixed cost of $1400 per day, the total cost, $C(x)$ in dollars, of producing x bikes in a given day is $C(x) = 500x + 1400$.
b. $P(x) = $ Income from selling x bikes $-$ total cost of manufacturing x bikes

$$P(x) = 700x - (500x + 1400)$$
$$= 200x - 1400$$

c. We need the number of bikes x to be produced so that $P(x) = 0$; that is, we need to solve $200x - 1400 = 0$.

$$200x - 1400 = 0$$
$$200x = 1400$$
$$x = \frac{1400}{200} = 7$$

Thus, the manufacturer needs to produce and sell 7 bikes to break even.

Functions as Arrow Diagrams

Arrow diagrams can be used to examine whether a correspondence represents a function. This representation is normally used when sets A and B are finite sets with few elements. Example 13 shows how arrow diagrams can be used to examine both functions and nonfunctions.

Example 13

Which, if any, of the parts of Figure 20 exhibit a function from A to B? If a correspondence is a function from A to B, find the range of the function.

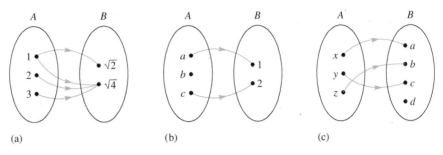

(a)   (b)   (c)

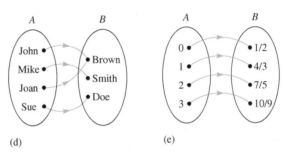

(d)   (e)

Figure 20

Solution

a. Figure 20(a) does not define a function from A to B, because the element 1 is paired with both $\sqrt{2}$ and $\sqrt{4}$.

b. Figure 20(b) does not define a function from A to B, since the element b is not paired with any element of B. (It is a function from a subset of A to B.)

c. Figure 20(c) does define a function from A to B, since there is one, and only one, arrow leaving each element of A. The fact that d, an element of B, is not paired with any element in the domain does not violate the definition. The range is $\{a, b, c\}$ and does not include d because d is not an output of this function, as no element of A is paired with d.

d. Figure 20(d) illustrates a function from A to B, since there is one, and only one, arrow leaving each element in A. It does not matter that an element of set B, Brown, has two arrows pointing to it. The range is {Brown, Smith, Doe}.

e. Figure 20(e) illustrates a function from A to B whose range is $\left\{ \dfrac{1}{2}, \dfrac{4}{3}, \dfrac{7}{5}, \dfrac{10}{9} \right\}$.

Figure 20(e) also illustrates a **one-to-one correspondence between A and B**. In fact, *any one-to-one correspondence between A and B defines a function from A to B as well as a function from B to A.*

▶ **NOW TRY THIS 8**

Determine which of the following are functions from the set of natural numbers to $\{0, 1\}$.

a. For every natural-number input, the output is 0.

b. For every natural-number input, the output is 0 if the input is an even number, and the output is 1 if the input is an odd number.

Functions as Tables and Ordered Pairs

One way to describe a function is with a table. Consider the information in Table 5 relating the amounts spent on advertising and the resulting sales in a given month for a small business. The information is given in thousands of dollars. We could define a function between the set of amounts of dollars, A, spent in Advertising and the set of amounts of dollars in Sales, S, or we could simply define the function as follows. If $A = \{0, 1, 2, 3, 4\}$ and $S = \{1, 3, 5, 7, 9\}$, the table describes a function from A to S, where A represents thousands of dollars in advertising and S represents thousands of dollars in sales. For example, $(2, 5)$ means \$2000 was spent on advertising resulting in \$5000 in sales.

Table 5

Amount of Advertising (in \$1000s)	Amount of Sales (in \$1000s)
0	1
1	3
2	5
3	7
4	9

The function could be given using *ordered pairs* as $\{(0, 1), (1, 3),\ (2, 5), (3, 7),$ and $(4, 9)\}$. The first component in each ordered pair is the *input* and the second is the *output*.

Example 14

Which of the following sets of ordered pairs represent functions? If a set represents a function, give its domain and range. If it does not, explain why.

a. $\{(1, 2), (1, 3), (2, 3), (3, 4)\}$

b. $\left\{\left(1, \frac{1}{2}\right), \left(2, \frac{1}{3}\right), \left(3, \frac{1}{4}\right), \left(4, \frac{1}{5}\right)\right\}$

c. $\{(1, 0), (2, 0), (3, 0), (4, 4)\}$

d. $\{(a, b) \mid a \in N \text{ and } b = 2a\}$

Solution

a. This is not a function because the input 1 has two different outputs.

b. This is a function with domain $\{1, 2, 3, 4\}$. Because the range is the set of outputs corresponding to these inputs set of outputs, the range is $\left\{\frac{1}{2}, \frac{1}{3}, \frac{1}{4}, \frac{1}{5}\right\}$.

c. This is a function with domain $\{1, 2, 3, 4\}$ and range $\{0, 4\}$. The output 0 appears more than once, but this does not contradict the definition of a function in that each input corresponds to only one output.

d. This is a function with domain N and range, the set of all even natural numbers.

Functions as Graphs

A sequence can be viewed as a function whose domain, is the set of natural numbers. For example in Figure 21(a), we see a partial *graph* of the arithmetic sequence: $3, 5, 7, 9, 11, \ldots,$ $2n + 1, \ldots$. The graph of this sequence is depicted on the grid with points given as $(1, 3), (2, 5), (3, 7), (4, 9),$ and $(5, 11)$. Each ordered pair (a, b) is paired with a point on the grid. The horizontal axis in this case is used for the inputs (the numbers of the terms) and the vertical scale depicts the outputs (the terms of the sequence).

In general, to plot an ordered pair (a, b), we move to the point a (the **abscissa**) on the horizontal scale, and then move (up or down) to the point b (the **ordinate**) along the vertical line that goes through a.

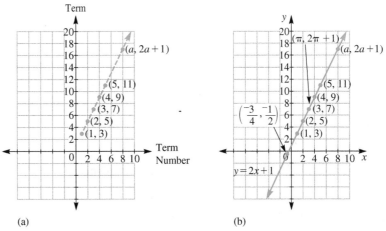

Figure 21

For example, to mark the point corresponding to $(1, 3)$, we start at 1 on the horizontal scale and move up 3 units on the vertical grid line through 1. Marking the point that corresponds to an ordered pair is referred to as **graphing** the ordered pair. The set of all points corresponding to all ordered pairs is the **graph** of the function or relation. In the graph of 21(a) the points are connected by a dashed ray to emphasize that they lie on a straight line, but not every point on the ray belongs to the graph.

Using all real numbers in the domain of the function, $y = 2x + 1$ is depicted in Figure 21(b) and the graph is drawn as a solid line because for every real number a, there is a corresponding real number $2a + 1$ resulting in the ordered pair $(a, 2a + 1)$, which lies on that line. For example, $(\pi, 2\pi + 1)$ and $(^{-}3/4, ^{-}1/2)$ are points on the line. The domain and range in this case are each the set of real numbers. Additionally, the horizontal scale in this case is the *x*-**axis**; the vertical scale is the *y*-**axis**.

Example 15

Explain why a telephone company would not set rates for telephone calls as depicted on the graph in Figure 22.

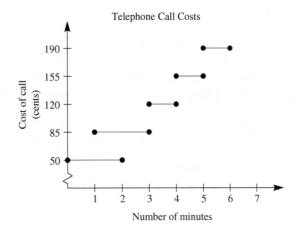

Figure 22

Solution The graph does not depict a function. For example, a customer could be charged either $0.50 or $0.85 for a 2-min call; hence, not every input has a unique output.

Sequences as Functions

As mentioned earlier, arithmetic, geometric, and other sequences can be thought of as functions whose inputs are natural numbers and whose outputs are the terms of the particular sequences. For example, an arithmetic sequence 2, 4, 6, 8, ..., whose nth term a_n is $2n$ can be described as a function from the set N (natural numbers) to the set E (even natural numbers) using the rule $f(n) = 2n$, where n is a natural number representing the number of the term and $f(n)$ stands for the value of the nth term, a_n. Thus, $f(n) = a_n$.

Example 16

If $f(n)$ denotes the nth term of a sequence, find $f(n)$ in terms of n for each of the following:

a. An arithmetic sequence whose first term is 3 and whose difference is 3.
b. A geometric sequence whose first term is 3 and whose ratio is 3.

Solution

a. $a_n = a_1 + (n - 1)d = 3 + (n - 1)3 = 3 + n \cdot 3 - 3 = 3n$. Thus, $f(n) = 3n$, where n is a natural number.
b. $a_n = a_1 r^{n-1} = 3 \cdot 3^{n-1} = 3^n$. Hence, $f(n) = 3^n$, where n is a natural number.

Sums of Sequences as Functions

Gauss's Problem to find the sum of $1 + 2 + 3 + \ldots + 100$ is an example of finding the sum of an arithmetic sequence with 100 terms. Recall that one way to find this sum was to write it twice as follows:

$$S = \quad 1 + \quad 2 + \quad 3 + \ldots + 100$$
$$S = 100 + 99 + 98 + \ldots + \quad 1$$

Adding equals to equals:

$$S + S = (1 + 100) + (2 + 99) + (3 + 98) + \ldots + (100 + 1)$$
$$2S = 100 \cdot 101$$
$$S = \frac{100 \cdot 101}{2} = 5050$$

The same process can be used to find the sum of the first n terms of any arithmetic sequence. $a_1 + (a_1 + d) + (a_1 + 2d) + (a_1 + 3d) + \ldots + (a_1 + (n - 1)d)$. We observe that the sum could also be written backwards as $a_n + (a_n - d) + (a_n - 2d) + (a_n - 3d) + \ldots + (a_n - (n - 1)d)$. (Why?) Using $S(n)$ as a function notation to represent the sum of n terms, we have.

$$S(n) = a_1 + (a_1 + d) + (a_1 + 2d) + \ldots + (a_1 + (n - 1)d)$$
$$S(n) = a_n + (a_n - d) + (a_n - 2d) + \ldots + (a_n - (n - 1)d)$$

Adding as before:

$$S(n) + S(n) = (a_1 + a_n) + (a_1 + a_n) + (a_1 + a_n) + \ldots + (a_1 + a_n)$$

Thus, $2S(n) = n(a_1 + a_n)$ and therefore

$$S(n) = \left(\frac{n}{2}\right)(a_1 + a_n) = \left(\frac{a_1 + a_n}{2}\right)n.$$

This proves Theorem 5.

Theorem 5

The sum S_n of the first n terms of an arithmetic sequence with first term a_1 and nth term a_n is given by
$$S(n) = \left(\frac{a_1 + a_n}{2}\right)n = \frac{(a_1 + a_n)n}{2}.$$

Because $a_n = a_1 + (n - 1)d$, we may substitute for a_n to obtain an equivalent expression for the sum:

$$S(n) = \left(\frac{a_1 + a_1 + (n - 1)d}{2}\right)n = \left(\frac{2a_1 + (n - 1)d}{2}\right)n = a_1 n + \frac{n(n - 1)}{2}d$$

The sum can be thought of as a function of n where n is the number of terms of the sequence. In this case the domain is the set of natural numbers and the output for input n is the sum of the first n terms of the sequence. There is no need to memorize the above two formulas for $S(n)$. Knowing Theorem 5 and the expression $a_n = a_1 + (n - 1)d$ is sufficient.

Example 17

Find the sum of the first 100 terms of the following arithmetic sequence: $3, 7, 11, 15, 19, \ldots$.

Solution   In this arithmetic sequence $a_1 = 3$ and $d = 7 - 3 = 4$.

From Theorem 5, we have $S(100) = \left(\frac{a_1 + a_{100}}{2}\right)100 = \left(\frac{3 + a_{100}}{2}\right)100$. Thus, our *subgoal* is to compute a_{100}. We have $a_{100} = 3 + (100 - 1)4 = 399$. Thus, $S(100) = \left(\frac{3 + 399}{2}\right)100 = 20{,}100$.

Similarly, we can find the sum of the first n terms of a geometric sequence. Consider the geometric sequence $a_1, a_1r, a_1r^2, a_1r^3, \ldots, a_1r^{(n-1)}$. Let
$$S(n) = a_1 + a_1r + a_1r^2 + \ldots + a_1r^{n-1}.$$

Because the terms are very similar, suppose we multiply both sides of the equation by r obtaining $rS_n = a_1r + a_1rr + a_1r^2r + \ldots + a_1r^{n-1}r = a_1r + a_1r^2 + a_1r^3 + \ldots + a_1r^n$. Then:

$$S(n) = a_1 + a_1r + a_1r^2 + \ldots + a_1r^{n-1}$$
$$rS(n) = \qquad a_1r + a_1r^2 + a_1r^3 + \ldots + a_1r^n$$

Subtracting, we obtain:

$$S(n) - rS(n) = a_1 - a_1r^n$$
$$S(n)(1 - r) = a_1(1 - r^n)$$
$$S(n) = a_1\frac{1 - r^n}{1 - r}$$

Note that in the above formula, $r \neq 1$ because division by 0 is not defined.
This proves Theorem 6.

Theorem 6

The sum of the first n terms of a geometric sequence whose first term is a_1, and whose ratio is $r \neq 1$ is
$$S(n) = a_1\frac{1 - r^n}{1 - r}.$$

If the sum of n terms of a geometric sequence is multiplied by $(^-1)/(^-1)$, it can be written as $S(n) = a_1\left(\dfrac{r^n - 1}{r - 1}\right)$. As with the arithmetic sequence sum, the sum of the first n terms of a geometric sequence is a function of n, the number of terms. It is common to write the sum of n terms of a sequence as S_n, we used $S(n)$ to emphasize that the sum is a function of n.

Example 18

Find the sum of the first 10 terms of the geometric sequence: $3, -\dfrac{3}{2}, \dfrac{3}{4}, -\dfrac{3}{8}, \ldots$

Solution The geometric sequence has first term 3 and ratio $\dfrac{-\dfrac{3}{2}}{3} = -\dfrac{1}{2}$. Thus, the sum of the first

10 terms is $S(10) = 3\left(\dfrac{1 - \left(-\dfrac{1}{2}\right)^{10}}{1 - \left(-\dfrac{1}{2}\right)}\right) = 3\left(\dfrac{1 - \left(\dfrac{1}{2}\right)^{10}}{\dfrac{3}{2}}\right) = 2\left(1 - \left(\dfrac{1}{2}\right)^{10}\right) = \dfrac{1023}{512} \doteq 1.998.$

Problem Solving **Computer Chips Problem**

Employees working at the same rate produce an order for computer chips. If all were to start at the same time they would complete the job in 3 hours. However, the employees did not start at the same time; each (starting from the second) came to work a fixed number of hours after the first employee so that the one who arrived first worked 11 times longer than the one who arrived last. If they all stayed working until the job was done, how many hours did the first employee work?

Understanding the Problem We know that the first employee worked the most, 11 times more than the last. We designate the number of hours that the last employee worked by b. Then the first worked $11b$ hours. Each employee thereafter worked a certain number of hours, d less than the proceeding one. Thus, the number of hours that each employee worked is an arithmetic sequence. We subtract a fixed number to see how much the next employee worked; that is add ^-d. We also know that if all employees were to start the job at the same time, they would have completed it in 24 hours.

Devising a Plan Suppose there were n employees. We write expressions for the total number of working hours in terms of the unknowns introduced. On the one hand, the total number of working hours is $3n$. (Each of the n employees would work 3 hours until the job was finished.) On the other hand, the total working hours is the sum of the hours that each employee worked. Because the hours that each employee worked form an arithmetic sequence, we know that the sum is $\dfrac{(b + 11b)n}{2}$. We now write an equation and solve it for b.

Carrying Out the Plan Equating the total number of working hours to complete the job we get:

$$3n = \frac{(b + 11b)n}{2}$$

$$3n = \frac{12bn}{2}$$

$$3n = 6bn$$

We divide both sides of the equation by n:

$$3 = 6b$$

$$\frac{1}{2} = b$$

Thus, $11b = 11 \cdot \frac{1}{2} = 5\frac{1}{2}$ and therefore the first employee worked $5\frac{1}{2}$ hours.

Looking Back We notice that the answer to the problem is the same regardless of the number of employees. We also did not have to know d, the number of hours that an employee, starting from the second one, worked less than the preceding one. However, d can be found if n is known. Show that $d = \dfrac{5}{n-1}$.

Composition of Functions

Consider the function machines in Figure 23. If 2 is entered in the top machine, then $f(2) = 2 + 4 = 6$. The number 6 is then entered in the second machine and $g(6) = 2 \cdot 6 = 12$. The functions in Figure 23 illustrate the **composition of two functions**. In the composition of two functions, the range of the first function must be a subset of the domain of the second function.

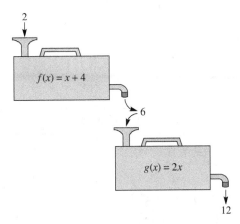

Figure 23

If the first function f is followed by a second function g, as in Figure 23, we symbolize the composition of the functions as $g \circ f$. If we input 3 in the function machines of Figure 23, then the output is symbolized by $(g \circ f)(3)$. Because f acts first on 3, to compute $(g \circ f)(3)$ we find $f(3) = 3 + 4 = 7$ and then $g(7) = 2 \cdot 7 = 14$. Hence, $(g \circ f)(3) = 14$. Observe that $(g \circ f)(3) = g(f(3))$, which is read as "g of f of 3." Also $(g \circ f)(x) = g(f(x)) = 2f(x) = 2(x + 4)$ and hence $g(f(3)) = 2(3 + 4) = 14$.

Example 19

If $f(x) = 2x + 3$ and $g(x) = x - 3$, find the following outputs:

  a. $(f \circ g)(3)$ **b.** $(g \circ f)(3)$ **c.** $(f \circ g)(x)$ **d.** $(g \circ f)(x)$

Solution
  a. $(f \circ g)(3) = f(g(3)) = f(3 - 3) = f(0) = 2 \cdot 0 + 3 = 3$
  b. $(g \circ f)(3) = g(f(3)) = g(2 \cdot 3 + 3) = g(9) = 9 - 3 = 6$
  c. $(f \circ g)(x) = f(g(x)) = 2g(x) + 3 = 2(x - 3) + 3 = 2x - 6 + 3 = 2x - 3$
  d. $(g \circ f)(x) = g(f(x)) = f(x) - 3 = (2x + 3) - 3 = 2x$

Example 19 shows that composition of functions is not commutative, since $(f \circ g)(3) \neq (g \circ f)(3)$.

Calculator or Computer Representation of a Function

A function can be represented in a variety of ways: pictures of sets with arrows, function machines, tables, equations, or graphs. Depending on the situation, one representation may be more useful than another. For example, if the domain of a function has many elements, a table is not a convenient representation. Graphing calculators or computer graphing applications can be used to display a graph of most functions given by equations with specified domains.

A sketch of the function $f(x) = 2x + 1$ is shown in Figure 24 using a graphing calculator downloaded on a computer. Note that on this graphing calculator $f(x)$ is depicted as y_1, and the domain was automatically chosen.

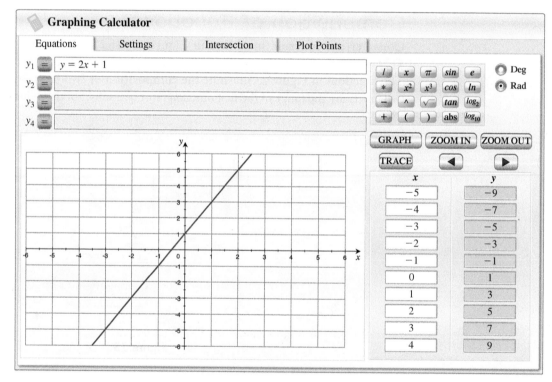

Figure 24

Because $f(x) = 2x + 1$ in Figure 24 and x is the only variable; we say that f is a function of *single variable*. However, we can also have functions of two or more variables. For example, the function that assigns to each ordered pair (x, y) the number $x + y$ is written $f(x, y) = x + y$, and is a function of two variables. If a particle moves at a speed V miles per hour for t hours, the distance S that it travels is Vt. If we let V as well as t vary, then $S(V, t) = Vt$ is a function of two variables. The function $f(x, y, z) = (x + y)z$ is an example of a function of three variables.

Relations

A function from set A to set B is a form of a *relation from set A to set B*. In a relation from A to B, there is a correspondence between elements of A and elements of B, but we do not require that each element of A be paired with one, and only one, element of B. Consequently, any set of ordered pairs is a relation. With appropriate set definitions, examples of relations include the following:

"is a daughter of"   "is the same color as"
"is less than"   "is greater than or equal to"

Consider the relation "is a sister of". Figure 25 illustrates this relation among children on a playground, with letters *A* through *J* representing the children. An arrow from *I* to *J* indicates that *I* "is a sister of" *J*. The arrows from *F* to *G* and from *G* to *F* indicate that *F* is a sister of *G* and *G* is a sister of *F*. This implies that *F* and *G* are girls. On the other hand, the absence of an arrow from *J* to *I* implies that *J* is not a sister of *I*. Thus, *I* is a girl and *J* is a boy.

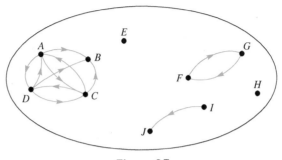

Figure 25

▶ NOW TRY THIS 9

All sister relationships are indicated in Figure 25.

a. Which children are boys and which are girls?
b. For which children is there not enough information to determine gender?

Another way to depict the arrow relation "*A* is a sister of *B*" is as an ordered pair (A, B). Using this notation, the relation "is a sister of" can be described for the children on the playground in Figure 26 as the set

$$\{(A, B), (A, C), (A, D), (C, A), (C, B), (C, D), (D, A), (D, B), (D, C), (F, G), (G, F), (I, J)\}.$$

This set is a subset of the Cartesian product $\{A, B, C, D, E, F, G, H, I, J\} \times \{A, B, C, D, E, F, G, H, I, J\}$.

This observation motivates the following definition of a relation.

Definition of a Relation from Set *A* to Set *B*

Given any two sets *A* and *B*, a **relation** from *A* to *B* is a subset of $A \times B$; that is, *R* is a relation from set *A* to set *B* if, and only if, $R \subseteq A \times B$.

In the definition, if $A = B$, we say that the **relation is on** *A*. Using the concept of a relation a function from set *A* to set *B* can be defined as a relation from set *A* to set *B* such that:

- for each $a \in A$, there exist some element $b \in B$ such that (a, b) is in the relation and,
- two different ordered pairs in the relation cannot have the same first component.

Properties of Relations

Figure 26 represents a set of children in a small group. The children have drawn all possible arrows representing the relation "has the same first letter in his or her name as." Three properties of relations are illustrated in Figure 26.

Definition of the Reflexive Property

A relation *R* on a set *X* is **reflexive** if, and only if, for every element $a \in X$, *a* is related to *a*; that is, for every $a \in X$, $(a, a) \in R$.

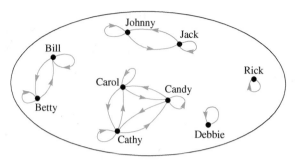

Figure 26

In the diagram, there is a loop at every point. For example, Rick has the same first initial as himself, namely R. A relation such as "is taller than" is not reflexive because people cannot be taller than themselves.

Definition of the Symmetric Property

A relation R on a set X is **symmetric** if, and only if, for all elements a and b in X, whenever a is related to b, then b also is related to a; that is, if $(a, b) \in R$, then $(b, a) \in R$.

In terms of the diagram, every pair of points that has an arrow headed in one direction also has a return arrow. For example, if Bill has the same first initial as Betty, then Betty has the same first initial as Bill. A relation such as "is a brother of" is not symmetric since Dick can be a brother of Jane, but Jane cannot be a brother of Dick.

Definition of the Transitive Property

A relation R on a set X is **transitive** if, and only if, for all elements a, b, and c of X, whenever a is related to b and b is related to c, then a is related to c. That is, if $(a, b) \in R$ and $(b, c) \in R$, then $(a, c) \in R$.

In the definitions for the symmetric and transitive properties, a, b, and c are variables and do not have to be different.

The relation in Figure 26 is transitive. For example, if Carol has the same first initial as Candy, and Candy has the same first initial as Cathy, then Carol has the same first initial as Cathy. A relation such as "is the father of" is not transitive since, if Tom Jones is the father of Tom Jones, Jr. and Tom Jones, Jr. is the father of Joe Jones, then Tom Jones is not the father of Joe Jones. He is, instead, the grandfather of Joe Jones.

The relation "is the same color as" is reflexive, symmetric, and transitive. In general, relations that satisfy all three properties are **equivalence relations**.

Definition of the Equivalence Relation

An **equivalence relation** is any relation R that satisfies the reflexive, symmetric, and transitive properties.

The most natural equivalence relation encountered in elementary school is "is equal to" on the set of all numbers. The relation on W (the set of whole numbers) defined by "have the same remainder upon division by m ($m \geq 2$)" is an equivalence relation. (Why?) For example if $m = 3$, W is partitioned into three disjoint subsets by this relation, all the elements of W that have remainder 0 when divided by 3, remainder 1 when divided by 3, and those that have remainder 2 when divided by 3.

Equivalence relations are useful in mathematics because of the property that an equivalence relation on a set S partitions the set into disjoint subsets whose union is S. We will see other examples of equivalence relations, such as congruence and similarity in geometry.

Assessment 4A

1. The following sets of ordered pairs are functions. Give a rule that could describe each function.
   a. $\{(^-1, 2), (0, 0), (1, ^-2), (2\frac{1}{2}, ^-2\frac{3}{2})\}$
   b. $\{(^-6, 0), (0, 6), (5, 11), (\sqrt{3}, \sqrt{3} + 6)\}$
   c. $\{(^-1, 1), (1, 1), (2, 4), (\sqrt{3}, 3)\}$

2. Which of the following are functions from the set $\{1, 2, 3\}$ to the set $\{a, b, c, d\}$? If the set of ordered pairs is not a function, explain why not.
   a. $\{(1, a), (2, b), (3, c), (1, d)\}$
   b. $\{(1, a), (2, b), (3, a)\}$
   c. $\{(1, a), (2, a), (3, a)\}$
   d. $\{(1, a), (2, b), (3, b)\}$

3. a. Draw an arrow diagram of a function with domain $\{1, 2, 3, 4, 5\}$ and range $\{a, b\}$.
   b. How many possible functions are there for part (a)?

4. Suppose $f(x) = 2x + 1$ and the domain is $\{0, 1, \sqrt{2}, \sqrt{3}, 4\}$. Describe the function in the following ways.
   a. Draw an arrow diagram involving two sets.
   b. Use ordered pairs.
   c. Make a table.
   d. Draw a graph to depict the function.

5. Determine which of the following are functions from the set of real numbers, R, or a subset of R, to R. If your answer is that it is not a function, explain why not.
   a. $f(x) = 2$ for all $x \in R$
   b. $f(x) = \sqrt{x}$
   c. $\{(x, y) \mid x = y^2, x \geq 0\}$
   d. $\{(x, y) \mid x = y^3\}$

6. a. Make an arrow diagram for each of the following.
      i. Rule: "when doubled is"

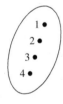
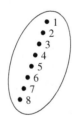

      ii. Rule: "is greater than"

   b. Which, if any, of the parts in (a) exhibits a function from A to B? If it is a function, tell why and find the range of the function.

7. The dosage of a certain drug is related to the weight of a child as follows: 50 mg of the drug and an additional 15 mg for each 2 lb or fraction of 2 lb of body weight above 30 lb. Sketch the graph of the dosage as a function of the weight of a child for children who weigh between 20 and 40 lb.

8. For each of the following, guess what might be Latifah's rule. In each case, if n is your input and $L(n)$ is Latifah's answer, express $L(n)$ in terms of n.

   a.
You	Latifah
3	8
4	11
5	14
10	29

   b.
You	Latifah
0	1
3	10
5	26
8	65

9. Quick-Talk advertises monthly cellular phone service for $0.50 a minute for the first 60 minutes but only $0.10 a minute for each minute thereafter. Quick-Talk charges for the exact amount of time used. Answer the following.
   a. Make one graph showing the cost per minute as a function of number of minutes and the other showing the total cost for calls as a function of the number of minutes up to 100 min.
   b. If you connect the points in the second graph in part (a), what kind of assumption needs to be made about the way the telephone company charges phone calls?
   c. Why does the total cost for calls consist of two line segments? Why is one part steeper than the other?
   d. The function representing the total cost for calls as a function of number of minutes talked can be represented by two equations. Write these equations.

10. For each of the following sequences (either arithmetic or geometric), find a possible function $f(n)$ whose domain is the set of natural numbers and whose outputs are the terms of the sequence.
    a. $3, 8, 13, 18, 23, \ldots$
    b. $3, 9, 27, 81, 243, \ldots$
    c. $3, 3, 3, 3, \ldots$
    d. $3, 3^{\frac{4}{3}}, 3^{\frac{5}{3}}, 3^2, \ldots$

11. Consider the following two function machines. Find the final output for each of the following inputs.
    a. 6
    b. 10
    c. $\sqrt{10}$
    d. 0
    e. $\frac{5}{8}$
    f. n

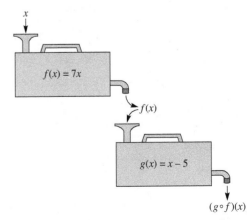

$(g \circ f)(x)$

165

12. In problem 11, find all inputs for which the final output equals twice the input.

13. **a.** Repeat problem 11 when the bottom machine $g(x) = x - 5$ is on top and the top machine $f(x) = 7x$ is at the bottom. (In this case, the final output is $(f \circ g)(x)$.)
   b. Find all x for which $(f \circ g)(x) = x$.

14. Consider the function $f(x) = {}^-x + b$, where b is a constant, and find the following.
   a. $f(f(0))$ **b.** $f(f(2))$
   c. All inputs x for which the final output is x, that is, $f(f(x)) = x$.

15. Let $t(n)$ represent the nth term of a sequence for $n \in N$. Answer the following.
   a. If $t(n) = 4n - 3$, determine which of the following are output values of the function:
      i. 1   **ii.** 385   **iii.** 389   **iv.** 392
   b. If $t(n) = n^2$, determine which of the following are output values of the function.
      i. 0   **ii.** 25   **iii.** 625   **iv.** 1000   **v.** 90
   c. If $t(n) = n(n - 1)$, determine which of the following are in the range of the function.
      i. 0   **ii.** 2   **iii.** 20   **iv.** 999

16. **a.** If $f(x) = x^2$ and the output is 2 find all possible inputs.
   b. Repeat (a) if $f(x) = x^3$

17. Consider a function machine that accepts inputs as ordered pairs. Suppose the components of the ordered pairs are natural numbers and the first component is the length of a rectangle and the second is its width. The following machine computes the perimeter (the distance around a figure) of the rectangle. Thus, for a rectangle whose length, l, is 3 and whose width, w, is 2, the input is $(3, 2)$ and the output is $2 \cdot 3 + 2 \cdot 2$, or 10.

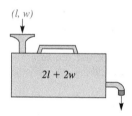

(l, w)

$2l + 2w$

   a. For each of the following inputs, find the corresponding output: $(1, 7), (2, 6), (6, 2), (\sqrt{5}, \sqrt{5})$.
   b. Find the set of all the inputs for which the output is 20.
   c. What is the domain and the range of the function?

18. The following graph shows the relationship between the number of cars on a certain road and the time of day for times between 5:00 A.M. and 9:00 A.M.:

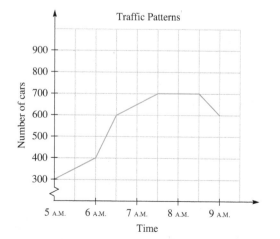

Traffic Patterns

   a. What was the increase in the number of cars on the road between 6:30 A.M. and 7:00 A.M.?
   b. During which half hour was the increase in the number of cars the greatest?
   c. What was the increase in the number of cars between 8:00 A.M. and 8:30 A.M.?
   d. During which half hour(s) did the number of cars decrease? By how much?
   e. The graph for this problem is composed of segments rather than just points. Why do you think segments are used here instead of just points?

19. A ball is shot out of a cannon at ground level. Its height H in feet after t sec is given by the function $H(t) = 128t - 16t^2$.
   a. Find $H(2), H(6), H(3)$, and $H(5)$. Why are some of the outputs equal?
   b. Graph the function and from the graph find at what instant the ball is at its highest point. What is its height at that instant?
   c. How long does it take for the ball to hit the ground?
   d. What is the domain of H?
   e. What is the range of H?

20. In the following sequence of matchstick figures assume a possible pattern and, let $S(n)$ be the function giving the total number of matchsticks in the nth figure. Find $S(n)$ in terms of n.

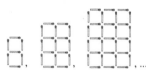

21. Assume the pattern continues for the following sequence of square tile figures; that is each square is divided into four squares in the subsequent figure. Let $S(n)$ be the function giving the total number of tiles in the nth figure. Find a formula for $S(n)$ in terms of n.

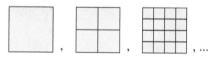

22. Which of the following equations or inequalities represent functions and which do not? In each case x and y are real numbers; x is in the domain and y in the range. If your answer is "not a function" explain why not.
   a. $x + y = 2$ **b.** $x - y < 2$
   c. $y = x^3 + x$ **d.** $xy = 2, x \neq 0$
   e. $y = |x|$ **f.** $|y| = x$
   g. $x^2 + y^2 = 1$ **h.** $y = \sqrt{{}^-x}$

23. Which of the following are graphs of functions and which are not? If a graph is not a graph of function explain why not.
   a.

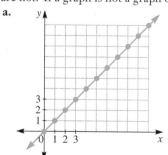

b. 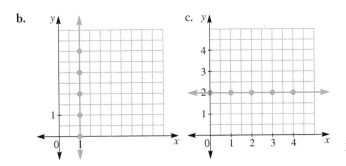 **c.**

24. Suppose each point and letter in the figure represents a child on a playground, and an arrow going from I to J means that I is the sister of J.

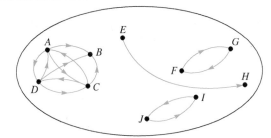

a. Based on the information in the figure, who are definitely girls and who are definitely boys?

b. Suppose we write "A is the sister of B" as an ordered pair (A, B). Based on the information in the diagram, write the set of all such ordered pairs.

c. Is the set of all ordered pairs in (b) a function with the domain equal to the set of all first components of the ordered pairs and with the range equal to the set of all second components?

25. **a.** Consider the relation consisting of ordered pairs (x, y) such that y is the biological mother of x. Is this a function whose domain is the set of all people born on January 1, 2015?

   b. Use the same information as in part (a) but now y is a brother of x. Is the relation a function from the set of all boys to the set of all boys?

26. Tell whether each of the following is reflexive, symmetric, or transitive on the set of all people. Which are equivalence relations?

   a. "Is a parent of"
   b. "Is the same age as"
   c. "Has the same last name as"
   d. "Is the same height as"
   e. "Is married to"
   f. "Lives within 10 mi of"
   g. "Is older than"

Assessment 4B

1. The following sets of ordered pairs are functions. Give a rule that could describe each function.
   a. $\{(^-1, 3), (0, 0), (1, ^-3), (3^{-\frac{1}{2}}, ^-3^{\frac{1}{2}})\}$
   b. $\{(^-5, 0), (0, 5), (5, 10), (\sqrt{5}, \sqrt{5} + 5)\}$
   c. $\{(0, 0), (\sqrt{3}, 3), (^-\sqrt{5}, 5), (\frac{1}{\sqrt{6}}, \frac{1}{6})\}$

2. Which of the following are functions from the set $\{1, 2, 3\}$ to the set $\{a, b, c, d\}$? If the set of ordered pairs is not a function, explain why not.
   a. $\{(1, c), (3, d)\}$ **b.** $\{(1, a), (1, b), (1, c)\}$
   c. $\{(1, b), (2, b), (3, b)\}$ **d.** $\{(1, a), (2, b), (2, c), (3, d)\}$

3. **a.** Draw an arrow diagram of a function with domain $\{1, 2, 3\}$ and range $\{a, b\}$.
   b. How many possible functions are there for part (a)?

4. Suppose $f(x) = 2(x - 1)$ and the domain is $\{0, 1, \sqrt{2}, \sqrt{3}, 4\}$. Describe the function in the following ways.
   a. Draw an arrow diagram involving two sets.
   b. Use ordered pairs.
   c. Make a table.
   d. Draw a graph to depict the function.

5. Determine which of the following are functions from the set of real numbers, R, or a subset of R, to R. If your answer is that it is not a function, explain why not.
   a. $f(x) = 0$ if $x \in \{0, 1, 2, 3\}$, and $f(x) = 3$ if $x \notin \{0, 1, 2, 3\}$
   b. $f(x) = 0$ for all $x \in R$ and $f(x) = 1$ if $x \in \{3, 4, 5, 6, \dots\}$
   c. $\{(x, y) \mid y = |x|\}$
   d. $\{(x, y) \mid x = \sqrt{y^2}\}$

6. Given the following arrow diagrams for functions from A to B, give a possible rule for the function.
   a.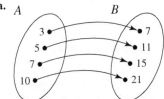
   b.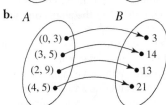

7. According to wildlife experts, the rate at which crickets chirp is a function of the temperature; specifically, $C = T - 40$, where C is the number of chirps every 15 sec and T is the temperature in degrees Fahrenheit.
   a. How many chirps does the cricket make per second if the temperature is 70°F?
   b. What is the temperature if the cricket chirps 40 times in 1 min?

8. For each of the following, guess what might be Latifah's rule. In each case, if n is your input and $L(n)$ is Latifah's answer, express $L(n)$ in terms of n.

a.

You	Latifah
6	42
0	0
8	72
2	6

b.

You	Latifah
0	1
1	2
5	32
6	64
10	1024

9. ChitChat charges $0.45 a minute for cellular phone calls. The cost per minute does not change, but the total cost changes as the telephone is used.

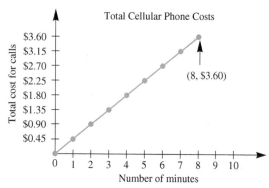

Cellular Phone Costs per Minute

Total Cellular Phone Costs

(8, $3.60)

a. When the number of minutes is 6, what do the values of the corresponding point on each graph represent?

b. What kind of assumption about the charges needs to be made to allow the connection of the points on each graph? Explain.

c. If the time in minutes is t and the cost in dollars for calls is c, write c as a function of t for each graph.

10. For each of the following (arithmetic or geometric) sequences, discover the pattern and find a function whose domain is the set of natural numbers and whose outputs are the terms of the sequence:

a. $2, 4, 6, 8, 10, \ldots$

b. $1, 3, 9, 27, 81, \ldots$

c. $\sqrt{3}, \sqrt[3]{3}, \sqrt[4]{3}, \sqrt[5]{3}, \ldots$

d. $3^{-1}, 3^{-\frac{1}{2}}, 1, 3^{\frac{1}{2}}, 3, \ldots$

11. Consider two function machines that are placed as shown. Find the final output for each of the following inputs.

a. 5 **b.** $\sqrt{3}$

c. 10 **d.** a

e. $\dfrac{7}{6}$

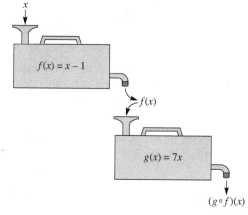

$f(x) = x - 1$

$f(x)$

$g(x) = 7x$

$(g \circ f)(x)$

12. In problem 11, find all inputs for which the final output equals twice the input.

13. a. Repeat problem 11 when the bottom machine $g(x) = 7x$ is on top and the top machine $f(x) = x - 1$ is at the bottom. (In this case, the final output is $(f \circ g)(x)$.)

b. Find all x for which $(f \circ g)(x) = x$.

14. Consider the function $f(x) = ^-(x + b)$, where b is a constant, and find the following (simplify your answers).

a. $f(f(0))$

b. $f(f(\sqrt{2}))$

c. All inputs x for which the final output is x, that is, $f(f(x)) = x$

15. Consider the function $f(x) = \dfrac{2x - 1}{2x + 1}$ and find, all possible, inputs for the following outputs.

a. 2 **b.** 0

c. $-\dfrac{1}{2}$ **d.** 1

16. Let $t(n)$ represent the nth term of a sequence for $n \in N$.

a. If $t(n) = n^2$, determine which of the following are output values of the function:

i. 1 **ii.** 4 **iii.** 9 **iv.** 10 **v.** 900

b. If $t(n) = n(n + 1)$, determine which of the following are in the range of the function:

i. 2 **ii.** 12 **iii.** 2550 **iv.** 2600

17. Consider a function machine that accepts inputs as ordered pairs. Suppose the components of the ordered pairs are natural numbers and the first component is the length of a rectangle and the second is its width. The following machine computes the perimeter (the distance around a figure) of the rectangle. Thus, for a rectangle whose length, l, is 3 and whose width, w, is 1, the input is (3, 1) and the output is $2 \cdot 3 + 2 \cdot 1$, or 8.

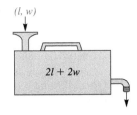

(l, w)

2l + 2w

a. For each of the following inputs, find the corresponding output: $(1, 4), (2, 1), (1, 2), (\sqrt{3}, \sqrt{3}), (x, y)$.
b. Find the set of all the inputs for which the output is 20.
c. Is $(2, 2)$ a possible output? Explain your answer.

18. A health club charges a one-time initiation fee of $100.00 plus a membership fee of $40.00 per month.
   a. Write an expression for the cost function $C(x)$ that gives the total cost for membership at the health club for x months.
   b. Draw the graph of the function in (a).
   c. The health club decided to give its members an option of a higher initiation fee but a lower monthly membership charge. If the initiation fee is $300 and the monthly membership fee is $30, use a different color and draw on the same set of axes the cost graph under this plan.
   d. Determine after how many months the second plan is less expensive for the member.

19. A ball is shot straight up at ground level. Its height H in feet after t sec is given by the function $H(t) = 128t - 16t^2$.
   a. Graph the function and from the graph find at what instant the ball is at its highest point. What is its height at that instant?
   b. Find from the graph all t such that $H(t) = H(1)$.
   c. Use your graph to find how long it takes the ball to hit the ground.
   d. What is the domain of H?
   e. What is the range of H?

20. In the following sequence of matchstick figures, assume that your discovered pattern continues and let $S(n)$ be the function giving the total number of matchsticks in the nth figure.
   a. Find the total number of matchsticks in the fourth figure.
   b. Find a formula for $S(n)$ in terms of n.

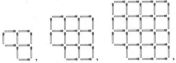

21. Assume the pattern continues for each of the following sequences of square tile figures. Let $S(n)$ be the function giving the total number of tiles in the nth figure. For each of the following, find a formula for $S(n)$ in terms of n.
   a.

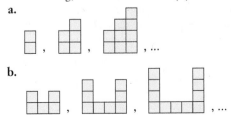

   b.

22. Which of the following equations or inequalities represent functions and which do not? In each case x and y are real numbers; x is in the domain and y in the range. If your answer is "not a function" explain why not.
   a. $x - y = 2$ b. $x + y < 20$
   c. $y = 2x^2$ d. $y = x^3 - 1$
   e. $y = {}^-|x|$ f. $|y| = |x|$
   g. $x^2 - y^2 = 1$ h. $y = {}^-\sqrt{{}^-x}$

23. Which of the following are graphs of functions and which are not? Justify your answers.
   a.

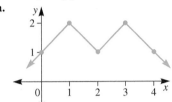

   b.   c.

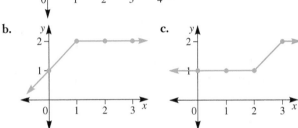

   d.   e.

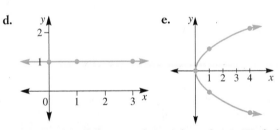

24. a. Which of the following relations from the set W of whole numbers to W have the symmetric property? Justify your answers.
   i. $x + y = 10$
   ii. $x - y = 100$
   iii. $xy = 100$
   iv. $y = x$
   v. $y = x^2$
   b. Which of the relations in part (a) are functions? Justify your answer.

25. Suppose each point and letter in the figure represents a child on a playground, and an arrow going from I to J means that I "is the sister of" J.

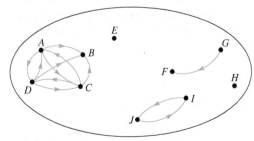

   a. Based on the information in the figure, who are definitely girls and who are definitely boys?

b. Suppose we write "*A* is the sister of *B*" as an ordered pair (A, B). Based on the information in the diagram, write the set of all such ordered pairs.

c. Is the set of all ordered pairs in (b) a function with the domain equal to the set of all first components of the ordered pairs and with the range equal to the set of all second components?

26. Which of the following are functions and which are relations but not functions from the set of first components of the ordered pairs to the set of second components?

a. {(Montana, Helena), (Oregon, Salem), (Illinois, Springfield), (Arkansas, Little Rock)}

b. {(Pennsylvania, Philadelphia), (New York, Albany), (New York, Niagara Falls), (Florida, Ft. Lauderdale)}

c. $\{(x, y) \mid x$ resides in Birmingham, Alabama, and x is the mother of y, where y is a U.S. resident$\}$

d. $\{(1, 1), (2, 4), (3, 9), (4, 16)\}$

e. $\{(x, y) \mid x$ and y are natural numbers and $x + y$ is an even number$\}$

27. Tell whether each of the following is reflexive, symmetric, or transitive on the set of subsets of a nonempty set. Which are equivalence relations?

a. "Is equal to"

b. "Is a proper subset of"

c. "Is not equal to"

d. "Has the same cardinal number as"

Mathematical Connections 4

Reasoning

1. Does the diagram define a function from *A* to *B*? Why or why not?

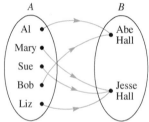

2. Is a one-to-one correspondence a function? Explain your answer and give an example.

3. Which of the following are functions from *A* to *B*? If your answer is "not a function," explain why not.

a. *A* is the set of mathematics faculty at the university. *B* is the set of all mathematics classes. To each mathematics faculty member, we associate a class that person is teaching during a given term.

b. *A* is the set of mathematics classes at the university. *B* is the set of mathematics faculty. To each mathematics class, we associate the teacher who is teaching the class.

c. *A* is the set of all U.S. senators and *B* is the set of all senate committees. We associate each senator to a committee of which the senator is chairperson.

4. If *S* is the set of students in Ms. Carmel's class, and *A* is any subset of *S*, we define: $f(A) = \overline{A}$ (where $\overline{A}$ is the complement of *A*). Notice that the input in this function is a subset of *S* and the output is a subset of *S*. Answer the following.

a. Explain why *f* is a function and describe the domain and the range of *f*.

b. If there are 20 children in the class, what are the number of elements in the domain and the number in the range? Explain.

c. Is the function in this question a one-to-one correspondence? Justify your answer.

5. Answer the following about $f(x) = 2^x$, an exponential function.

a. What do you think $f(x) = 2^{3.14}$ means?

b. What could $2^{\sqrt{3}}$ mean?

c. What is the domain of $f(x)$? Why?

d. What is the range of $f(x)$? Why?

6. A sum of money is invested for a certain length of time in an account earning interest at a certain rate. Explain how the balance in the account at the end of that time can be considered a function of three variables. Clearly identify the variables and derive a formula for the balance in terms of these three variables.

7. Is every set of ordered pairs a function whose domain is the set of first components and whose range is the set of second components? Justify your answer.

Open-Ended

8. Examine several newspapers and magazines and describe at least three examples of functions that you find. What is the domain and range of each function?

9. Give at least three examples of functions from *A* to *B*, where neither *A* nor *B* is a set of numbers.

10. Draw a sequence of matchstick figures and describe the pattern in words. Find as simple an expression as possible for $S(n)$, the total number of matchsticks in the *n*th figure.

11. A function whose output is always the same regardless of the input is a *constant function*. Give several examples of constant functions from real life.

12. A function whose output is the same as its input is an *identity function*. Give several concrete examples of identity functions.

13. Define three functions $f(x), g(x)$, and $h(x)$ that are placed in a way similar to the two machines in exercise 11 of Assessment 4B. Draw a figure depicting the machines and find $(h \circ g \circ f)(x)$ for the following inputs.

a. 1

b. $\sqrt{3}$

c. *n*

Cooperative Learning

14. Each person in a group picks a natural number and uses it as an input in the following function machine:

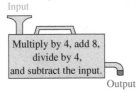

a. Compare your answers. Based on the answers, make a conjecture about the range of the function.

b. Based on your answer in (a), graph the function.

c. Write the function in the simplest possible way using $f(x)$ notation.

d. Justify your conjecture in (a).

e. Make up similar function machines and try different inputs in your group.

f. Devise a function machine in which the machine performs several operations but the output is always the same as the input. Exchange your answer with someone in the group and check that the other person's function machine performs as required.

15. In a group of four, work through the following. You will need a metric tape or meterstick.

a. Place your mathematics book on the edge of a desk and measure the distance (to the nearest centimeter) from the floor to the top of the book. Record the distance.

b. Place a second mathematics book on top of the first and measure the distance (to the nearest centimeter) from the floor to the top of the second book. Record the distance.

c. Continue this procedure for all four of your mathematics books and complete the following table and graph:

Number of books	Distance from floor
1	
2	
3	
4	

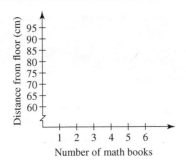

d. Without measuring, what is the distance from the floor with 0 books? 5 books?

e. Write a rule or function for $d(x)$, where $d(x)$ is the distance above the floor to the top of the stack of books and x is the number of books.

f. Suppose the distance from the floor to the ceiling is 2.5 m. If you stack the books as described above, how many books would be needed to reach the ceiling?

g. The function $h(x) = 34x + 70$ represents the height of another stack of x mathematics books (in centimeters) of

the same thickness in a cabinet. What does the function tell you about the height of the cabinet?

h. Suppose that a table with a stack of similar mathematics books (more than 10) is 200 cm high. If the top mathematics book is removed, the height is 197 cm. If a second book is removed, the height is 194 cm. What is the height if 5 books are removed?

i. Write a function $h(x)$ for the height of the stack in part (h) after x books are removed.

16. As a teacher you noticed that several students in your class assumed that if f is a function, then $f(a + b) = f(a) + f(b)$ whenever a, b, and $a + b$ are in the domain of the function. How do you respond?

Connecting Mathematics to the Classroom

17. A student claims that the following machine does not represent a function machine because it accepts two inputs at once rather than a single input. How do you respond?

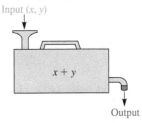

18. A student claims that the following does not represent a function, since all the values of x correspond to the same number.

x	0	1	2	3	4	5
y	1	1	1	1	1	1

How do you respond?

19. A student asks if the function $f(x) = 3x + 5$ with domain the set of real numbers is a one-to-one correspondence between the sets of real numbers. How do you respond?

20. A student wants to know why sometimes it is incorrect to connect points on the graph of a function. How do you respond?

21. A student does not understand why $\{(x, y) \mid y = x^2, x \in R\}$ is a function but $\{(x, y) \mid x = y^2, x \in R, x \geq 0\}$ is not. How do you respond?

Review Problems

22. Solve the following equations for x.

a. $2\sqrt{2} - \sqrt{2}x = x$ b. $\frac{3}{4}x = \frac{\sqrt{2}}{2}x + 3$

c. $(x - 1)^2 = 2$ d. $\sqrt{2}(2x - 3) = \sqrt{3}(2x - 3)$

e. $\sqrt{(x - 1)^2} = x - 1$ f. $\sqrt{(x - 1)^2} = 1 - x$

23. Solve the following problem by setting up an appropriate equation:

Two cars, each traveling at a constant speed—one 60 mph and the other 70 mph—start at the same time from the same point traveling in the same direction. After how many hours will the distance between them be 40 mi?

24. a. Find two rational numbers between $\sqrt{3}$ and 2.

b. Find two irrational numbers between $\frac{11}{13}$ and $\frac{12}{13}$.

25. Show that the set of irrational numbers is not closed under addition.

National Assessments

National Assessment of Educational Progress (NAEP) Questions

In	Out
2	5
3	7
4	9
5	11
15	31
38	

The table shows how the "In" numbers are related to the "Out" numbers. When 38 goes in, what number comes out?

A. 41
B. 51
C. 54
D. 77

NAEP, Grade 4, 2007

Each figure in the pattern below is made of hexagons that measure 1 centimeter on each side.

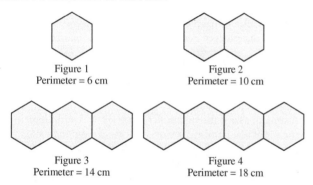

Figure 1
Perimeter = 6 cm

Figure 2
Perimeter = 10 cm

Figure 3
Perimeter = 14 cm

Figure 4
Perimeter = 18 cm

If the pattern of adding one hexagon to each figure is continued, what will be the perimeter of the 25th figure in the pattern? Show how you got your answer.

NAEP, Grade 8, 2007

Old Faithful is one of hundreds of geysers in Yellowstone National Park. Predicting when Old Faithful will erupt next can be done by timing the previous eruption.

If an eruption lasts t minutes, then the next eruption will occur approximately $12.5t + 33$ minutes after the eruption ends. If the previous eruption lasted 6 minutes and ended at 1:23 P.M., when is the next eruption expected to occur?

Answer: _____

Show how you found your answer.

NAEP, Grade 8, 2012

---

5 Objectives

5 Equations in a Cartesian Coordinate System

Students will be able to understand and explain

• Equations of lines.

• The slope of a line and the slope formula.

• Graphic and algebraic solutions for systems of linear equations.

• Ways to determine if a system of linear equations has a unique solution, infinitely many solutions, or no solution.

The Cartesian coordinate system (named for René Descartes) enables us to combine geometry and algebra. The **Cartesian coordinate system**, is constructed by placing two number lines perpendicular to each other, as shown in Figure 27. The intersection point of the two lines is the **origin**, the horizontal line is the x-axis, and the vertical line is the y-axis. The location of any point P can be described by an ordered pair of numbers (a, b), where a perpendicular from P to the x-axis intersects at a point with coordinate a and a perpendicular from P to the y-axis intersects at a point with coordinate b; the point is identified as $P(a, b)$. A line is **perpendicular** to another line if they form a 90° angle (right angle). There is a one-to-one correspondence between all the points in the plane and all the ordered pairs of real numbers. For example, in Figure 27, Q has coordinates $(^-4, ^-3)$, written $Q(^-4, ^-3)$.

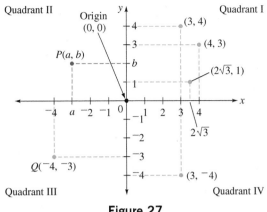

Figure 27

In Figure 27, the axes separate the plane into four **quadrants** numbered counterclockwise.

Equations of Vertical and Horizontal Lines

Every point on the x-axis has a y-coordinate of zero. Thus, the x-axis can be described as the set of all points (x, y) such that $y = 0$. The x-axis has the equation $y = 0$. Similarly, *the y-axis can be described as the set of all points (x, y) such that $x = 0$ and y is an arbitrary real number*. Thus, $x = 0$ is the equation of the y-axis. Using set notation, the x-axis is the set of points $\{(x, 0) \mid x \text{ is a real number}\}$ and the y-axis is the set of points $\{(0, y) \mid y \text{ is a real number}\}$.

Example 20

Sketch the graph for each of the following on a Cartesian coordinate system.

a. $x = 2$

b. $y = 3$

c. $\{(x, y) \mid x < 2 \text{ and } y = 3\}$

Solution

a. The equation $x = 2$ represents the set of all points (x, y) for which $x = 2$ and y is any real number, as in Figure 28(a).

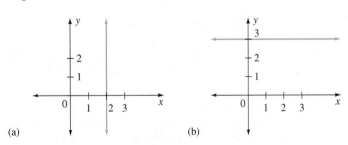

Figure 28

b. The equation $y = 3$ represents the set of all points (x, y) for which $y = 3$ and x is any real number, as in Figure 28(b).

c. The statements in part (c) represent the set of all points (x, y) for which $x < 2$, but $y = 3$. The set is part of a line, as shown in Figure 29. Note that the hollow dot at $(2, 3)$ indicates that this point is not included in the solution set.

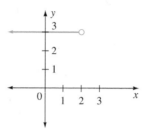

Figure 29

As seen in Example 20(a) and (b) *the graph of the equation* $x = a$, *where a is some real number, is the line perpendicular to the x-axis through the point with coordinates* $(a, 0)$. Similarly, *the graph of the equation* $y = b$ *is the line perpendicular to the y-axis through the point with coordinates* $(0, b)$.

Equations of Lines

The arithmetic sequence $4, 7, 10, 13, \ldots$ in Table 6 has xth term $3x + 1$. If the number of the term is the x-coordinate and the corresponding term the y-coordinate, the set of points appear to lie on a line that is parallel to neither the x-axis nor the y-axis, as in Figure 30.

Table 6	
Number of Term	**Term**
1	4
2	7
3	10
4	13
⋮	⋮
x	$3x + 1$

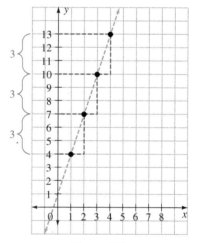

Figure 30

In Table 6, we see that there is a difference of 3 in the y-coordinates of the marked points. Correspondingly, there is a difference of 1 in the number of the term on the x-axis. Hence, we might say that the rate of change of the term with respect to the number of the term is 3, or the ratio is 3 to 1. Does something comparable happen with other arithmetic sequences?

To help answer this question, we consider the following sequences in Table 7.

Number of Term x	$1x = x$	$2x$	$\frac{1}{2}x$	$(^-1)x = {}^-x$	$(^-2)x = {}^-2x$
1	1	2	$\frac{1}{2}$	$^-1$	$^-2$
2	2	4	1	$^-2$	$^-4$
3	3	6	$\frac{3}{2}$	$^-3$	$^-6$
4	4	8	2	$^-4$	$^-8$
5	5	10	$\frac{5}{2}$	$^-5$	$^-10$
6	6	12	3	$^-6$	$^-12$
$\vdots$	$\vdots$	$\vdots$	$\vdots$	$\vdots$	$\vdots$
x	x	$2x$	$\frac{1}{2}x$	^-x	^-2x

Table 7

Figure 31 shows the sets of ordered pairs (x, y) in Table 7 plotted on a graph so that the number of the term is the x-coordinate and the corresponding term is the y-coordinate. Again the separate sets of points appear to lie on straight lines.

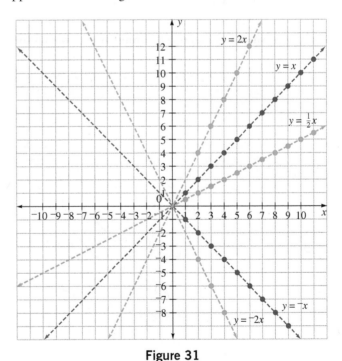

Figure 31

All dashed lines in Figure 31 have equations of the form $y = mx$, where m takes the values 1, 2, $\frac{1}{2}$, $^-1$, and $^-2$. If we consider the equations but allow x to be any real number, then all the points (x, y) that satisfy the equation lie along a given dashed line and all the points on that line satisfy the equation. The number m is a measure of steepness and is the **slope** of the line whose equation is $y = mx$. The graph goes up from left to right (y increases as x increases) if m is positive, and it goes down from left to right (y decreases as x increases) if m is negative.

a. In the equation $y = mx$, if m is 0, what happens to the line?

b. What happens to the line as m increases from 0?

c. What happens to the line when m decreases from 0?

All dashed lines in Figure 31 pass through the origin. This is true for any line whose equation is $y = mx$. If $x = 0$, then $y = m \cdot 0 = 0$, and $(0, 0)$ is a point on the graph of $y = mx$. Conversely, it is possible to show that any nonvertical line passing through the origin has an equation of the form $y = mx$ for some value of m.

Example 21

Find the equation of the line that contains $(0, 0)$ and $(2, 3)$.

Solution   The line goes through the origin so its equation has the form $y = mx$. To find the equation of the line, we find the value of m. The line contains $(2, 3)$, so we substitute 2 for x and 3 for y in the equation $y = mx$ to obtain $3 = m \cdot 2$, and thus $m = \dfrac{3}{2}$. The required equation is $y = \dfrac{3}{2}x$.

Next, we consider equations of the form $y = mx + b$, where b is a real number. We do this by first examining the graphs of $y = x$, $y = x + 2$ and $y = x - 2$. Given the graph of $y = x$, we obtain the graph of $y = x + 2$ by "raising" each point on the graph of $y = x$ by 2 units. This is shown in Figure 32(a). Similarly, to sketch the graph of $y = x - 2$, we first draw the graph of $y = x$ and then lower each point vertically by 2 units, as shown in Figure 32(a).

The graphs of $y = x$, $y = x + 2$, and $y = x - 2$ are parallel lines. In general, *for a given value of m, the graph of $y = mx + b$ is a straight line through $(0, b)$ and parallel to the line whose equation is $y = mx$.*

Thus, the graph of the line $y = mx + b$ can be obtained from the graph of $y = mx$ by sliding $y = mx$ up b units if $b > 0$ and down $|b|$ units if $b < 0$, as shown in Figure 32(b). In general, *any two parallel lines have the same slope it will be shown later in this section that* vertical lines have no slope.

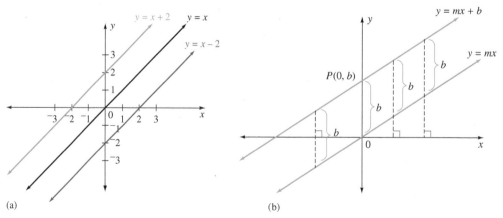

(a)   (b)

Figure 32

The graph of $y = mx + b$ in Figure 32(b) crosses the y-axis at point $P(0, b)$. The value of y at the point of intersection of any line with the y-axis is the **y-intercept**. Thus, b is the y-intercept of $y = mx + b$; this form of an equation of a straight line is the **slope-intercept form**. Similarly, the value of x at the point of intersection of a line with the x-axis is the **x-intercept**.

Example 22

Given the equation $y - 3x = {}^-6$, answer the following.

a. Find the slope of the line.
b. Find the y-intercept.
c. Find the x-intercept.
d. Sketch the graph of the equation.

Solution

a. We write the equation in the form $y = mx + b$ by adding $3x$ to both sides of the given equation: $y = 3x + ({}^-6)$. Hence, the slope is 3.
b. The form $y = 3x + ({}^-6)$ shows that $b = {}^-6$, which is the y-intercept. The y-intercept can also be found directly by substituting $x = 0$ in the equation and finding the corresponding value of y.
c. The x-intercept is the x-coordinate of the point where the graph intersects the x-axis. At that point, $y = 0$. Substituting 0 for y in $y = 3x - 6$ gives 2 as the x-intercept.
d. Knowing the y-intercept and the x-intercept gives us two points, $(0, {}^-6)$ and $(2, 0)$, on the line. We may plot these points and draw the line through them to obtain the desired graph in Figure 33.

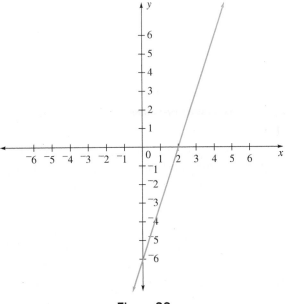

Figure 33

Any vertical line has equation $x = a$ for some real number a, and cannot be written in slope-intercept form. A horizontal line has slope of 0, and can be written in a slope intercept form as $y = 0 \cdot x + b = b$. In general, *every line has an equation of the form either* $y = mx + b$ *or* $x = a$. Any equation that can be put in one of these forms is a **linear equation**. Equations of the form $ax + by + c = 0$, where a, b, c are real numbers, are linear equations and may be written in slope intercept form if $b \neq 0$. (Why?) If $b = 0$ and $a \neq 0$, we get the equation $x = \dfrac{{}^-c}{a}$, which is an equation of a vertical line.

Theorem 7: Equation of a Line

Every line has an equation of the form either $y = mx + b$ or $x = a$, where m is the slope and b is the **y-intercept**. In the equation $x = a$, a is the **x-intercept**.

▶ NOW TRY THIS 11

The *n*th term of an arithmetic sequence is given as $a_n = a_1 + (n - 1)d$. Explain why this is considered a *linear relationship*.

Determining Slope

We defined the slope of a line with equation $y = mx + b$ to be m. The slope is a measure of steepness of a line. A different way to discuss the steepness of a line is to consider the rate of change in y-values in relation to their corresponding x-values. In Figure 34, line k has a greater rate of change than line ℓ. In other words, line k rises faster than line ℓ for the same horizontal run.

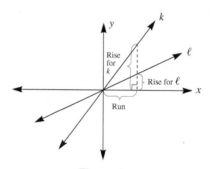

Figure 34

Thus, we could express the rate of change, or steepness, as the ratio $\dfrac{\text{change in } y\text{-values}}{\text{corresponding change in } x\text{-values}}$. The rate is frequently expressed as $\dfrac{rise}{run}$.

Given two points $A(x_1, y_1)$ and $B(x_2, y_2)$ the difference $x_2 - x_1$ is the *run*, and the difference $y_2 - y_1$ is the *rise*. The values of *rise* and *run* depend on the points chosen on the line and hence vary. However, the ratio $\dfrac{y_2 - y_1}{x_2 - x_1}$ is always the same, regardless of which two points on a given nonvertical line are chosen, and equals the slope of the line. This can be shown as follows:

$$
\begin{aligned}
\frac{y_2 - y_1}{x_2 - x_1} &= \frac{(mx_2 + b) - (mx_1 + b)}{x_2 - x_1} \\
&= \frac{mx_2 - mx_1 + b - b}{x_2 - x_1} \\
&= \frac{m(x_2 - x_1)}{x_2 - x_1} \\
&= m
\end{aligned}
$$

Thus, as seen in Figure 35, we can define the slope of a nonvertical line as $\dfrac{rise}{run}$.

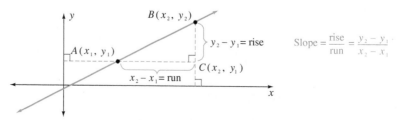

Figure 35

The discussion of slope is summarized in the following definition for the slope of a line.

Definition of Slope (Slope Formula)

Given two points $A(x_1, y_1)$ and $B(x_2, y_2)$ with $x_1 \neq x_2$, the slope m of the line through A and B is

$$m = \frac{y_2 - y_1}{x_2 - x_1}.$$

In the above definition, if we multiply both the numerator and the denominator on the right side of the slope formula by $^-1$, we obtain

$$m = \frac{y_2 - y_1}{x_2 - x_1} = \frac{(y_2 - y_1)(^-1)}{(x_2 - x_1)(^-1)} = \frac{y_1 - y_2}{x_1 - x_2}.$$

Thus, it does not matter which point is named (x_1, y_1) and which is named (x_2, y_2); *the order of the coordinates in the subtraction must be the same.*

▶ NOW TRY THIS 12

a. Use the slope formula to find the slope of any horizontal line.
b. What happens when we attempt to use the slope formula for a vertical line? What is your conclusion about the slope of a vertical line?

When a line is inclined downward from the left to the right, the slope is negative. This is illustrated in Figure 36, where the graph of the line $y = ^-2x$ is shown.

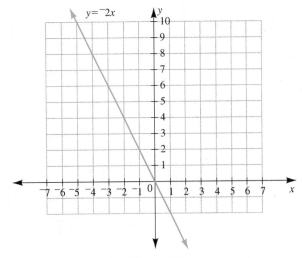

Figure 36

Example 23

a. Given $A(3, 1)$ and $B(5, 4)$, find the slope of $\overleftrightarrow{AB}$ (the line through A and B).
b. Find the slope of the line passing through the points $A(^-3, 4)$ and $B(^-1, 0)$.
c. In Figure 37, find the slope of $\overleftrightarrow{OA}$ (the line through O and A).

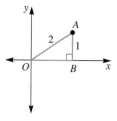

Figure 37

Solution

a. $m = \dfrac{4-1}{5-3} = \dfrac{3}{2}$

b. $m = \dfrac{4-0}{^-3-(^-1)} = \dfrac{4}{^-2} = {^-2}$

c. OB (the distance from O to B) is the run while AB, or 1, is the rise.

$(OB)^2 + 1^2 = 2^2$ in right triangle OAB, using the Pythagorean theorem.

$(OB)^2 + 1 = 4$

$(OB)^2 = 4 - 1 = 3$

$OB = \sqrt{3}$

The slope of $\overleftrightarrow{OA}$ (the line through O and A) is $\dfrac{1}{\sqrt{3}}$, which is sometimes written as

$\dfrac{1}{\sqrt{3}} \cdot \dfrac{\sqrt{3}}{\sqrt{3}} = \dfrac{\sqrt{3}}{3}.$

Given two points on a nonvertical line, we use the slope formula to find the slope of the line and its equation as demonstrated in the following example.

Example 24

In Figure 38, the points $(^-4, 0)$ and $(1, 4)$ are on the line ℓ. Find:

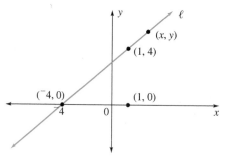

Figure 38

a. The slope of the line
b. The equation of the line

Solution

a. $m = \dfrac{4-0}{1-(^-4)} = \dfrac{4}{5}$

b. Any point (x, y) on ℓ different from $(^-4, 0)$ can be found using the slope $\dfrac{4}{5}$ determined by points $(^-4, 0)$ and (x, y). Thus,

$$\frac{y - 0}{x - (^-4)} = \frac{4}{5}$$

$$\frac{y}{x + 4} = \frac{4}{5}$$

$$y = \frac{4}{5}(x + 4).$$

The equation of the line is $y = \dfrac{4}{5}x + \dfrac{16}{5}$.

Systems of Linear Equations

The mathematical descriptions of many problems involve more than one equation, each having more than one unknown. To solve such problems, we must find a common solution to the equations, if it exists. An example is given below and on the student page shown on the next page.

Example 25

May Chin paid $18 for three soyburgers and twelve orders of fries. Another time she had paid $12 for four soyburgers and four orders of fries. Assume the prices have not changed. Set up a system of equations with two unknowns representing the prices of a soyburger and an order of fries, respectively.

Solution Let x be the price in dollars of a soyburger and y be the price in dollars of an order of fries. Three soyburgers cost $3x$ dollars, and twelve orders of fries cost $12y$ dollars. Because May paid $18 for her entire order, we have $3x + 12y = 18$, or, after dividing each side by 3, $x + 4y = 6$. Similarly, $4x + 4y = 12$ is equivalent to $x + y = 3$. The system of equations is $x + 4y = 6$ and $x + y = 3$.

An ordered pair satisfying the two linear equations in Example 25 is a point that belongs to each of the lines. Figure 39 shows the graphs of $x + 4y = 6$ and $x + y = 3$. The price x of the soyburger and the price y of an order of fries satisfy both equations; that is, (x, y) is a point on both lines. The two lines appear to intersect at $(2, 1)$. Thus, $(2, 1)$ seems to be the solution of the given system of equations. This solution can be checked by substituting 2 for x and 1 for y in each equation. Because two distinct lines intersect in only one point, $(2, 1)$ is the only solution to the system. Therefore, in Example 25 a soyburger costs $2 and fries cost $1.

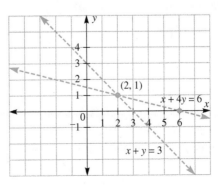

Figure 39

Because costs of the soyburger and an order of fries cannot be negative, parts of the lines are dashed.

School Book Page — Linear Functions

GPS Guided Problem Solving

Linear Functions

For each rental plan, represent the relationship between the number of miles (from 20 to 45) and the cost. Use a linear function, a table of ordered pairs, and a graph (using the same coordinate grid). What conclusions can you draw about these plans?

Car Rental Plan **1**
$15 per day plus
$.25 per mile

Car Rental Plan **2**
$8 per day plus
$.45 per mile

What You Might Think

What do I know? What do I want to find out?

How can I write a function rule for each plan?

How can I make a table and graph?

What conclusions can be stated?

What You Might Write

Plan 1 costs $15 plus $.25 per mile. Plan 2 costs $8 plus $.45 per mile. I want to compare the two plans using function rules, tables, and graphs.

Let m = the number of miles driven. Let C = the cost of the rental in dollars.

Plan 1: $C_1 = \$.25m + 15$

Plan 2: $C_2 = \$.45m + 8$

I can use the function rule to get data points for the table. Then I can graph those points.

m	C_1	C_2
20	20	17
30	22.5	21.5
35	23.75	23.75
45	26.25	28.25

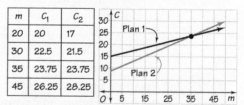

The lines intersect at (35, 23.75). Plan 2 is better if you drive less than 35 miles.

Plan 1 is better if you drive more than 35 miles. The costs of Plans 1 and 2 are equal if you drive exactly 35 miles.

Substitution Method

The graphing method for solving systems of equations is not practical when the point of intersection of the lines cannot be accurately identified. There are algebraic methods for solving systems of equations. One such method is the **substitution method**. The equations

$$x + 4y = 6 \quad \text{and} \quad x + y = 3$$

can be solved by finding x in terms of y (or vice versa) from one of the equations and substituting in the other. From the second equation, we have $x = 3 - y$. Substituting for x in the first equation we get the equivalent equations: $3 - y + 4y = 6, 3 + 3y = 6, 3y = 3, y = 1$. Substituting $y = 1$ in $x + y = 3$, we get $x + 1 = 3$ and hence $x = 2$. Thus, $x = 2$ and $y = 1$ is the solution to the system. Example 26 demonstrates the substitution method in another system of equations.

Example 26

Solve the following system using the substitution method.

$$3x - 4y = 5$$
$$2x + 5y = 1$$

Solution   First, rewrite one equation, expressing y in terms of x.

$$y = \frac{3x - 5}{4}$$

Because we are looking for x and y that satisfy each equation, we substitute $\dfrac{3x - 5}{4}$ for y in the other original equation and solve the resulting equation for x.

$$2x + 5\left(\frac{3x - 5}{4}\right) = 1$$
$$4\left[2x + 5\left(\frac{3x - 5}{4}\right)\right] = 4 \cdot 1$$
$$8x + 5(3x - 5) = 4$$
$$8x + 15x - 25 = 4$$
$$23x = 4 + 25$$
$$x = \frac{29}{23}$$

Substituting $\dfrac{29}{23}$ for x in $y = \dfrac{3x - 5}{4}$ gives $y = \dfrac{-7}{23}$. Hence, $x = \dfrac{29}{23}$ and $y = \dfrac{-7}{23}$. This can be checked by substituting the values for x and y in the original equations.

Elimination Method

The **elimination method** for solving two equations with two unknowns is based on eliminating one of the variables by adding or subtracting the original or equivalent equations. For example, consider the following system:

$$x - y = {}^{-}3$$
$$x + y = 7$$

By adding the two equations, we can eliminate the variable y. The resulting equation can then be solved for x.

$$\begin{array}{rcl} x - y &=& {}^{-}3 \\ \underline{x + y} &=& \underline{7} \\ 2x &=& 4 \\ x &=& 2 \end{array}$$

Substituting 2 for x in the first equation (either equation may be used) gives $y = 5$. Checking this result shows that $x = 2$ and $y = 5$, or $(2, 5)$, is the solution to the system.

Often, another operation is required before equations are added so that an unknown can be eliminated. For example, consider the following system:

$$\begin{array}{rcl} 3x + 2y &=& 5 \\ 5x - 4y &=& 3 \end{array}$$

Neither adding nor subtracting the equations eliminates an unknown. However, if the first equation contained $4y$ rather than $2y$, the variable y could be eliminated by adding. To obtain $4y$ in the first equation, we multiply both sides of the equation by 2 to obtain the equivalent equation $6x + 4y = 10$. Adding the equations in the equivalent system gives the following:

$$\begin{array}{rcl} 6x + 4y &=& 10 \\ \underline{5x - 4y} &=& \underline{3} \\ 11x &=& 13 \\ x &=& \dfrac{13}{11} \end{array}$$

To find the corresponding value of y, we substitute $\dfrac{13}{11}$ for x in either of the original equations and solve for y. We get $y = \dfrac{8}{11}$.

Consequently, $x = \dfrac{13}{11}$ and $y = \dfrac{8}{11}$, or equivalently $\left(\dfrac{13}{11}, \dfrac{8}{11} \right)$ is the solution of the original system. This solution, as always, should be checked by substitution in the original equations.

Solutions to Various Systems of Linear Equations

All examples thus far have had unique solutions. However, other situations may arise. Geometrically, a system of two linear equations can be characterized as follows:

1. *The system has a unique solution if, and only if, the graphs of the equations intersect in a single point.*
2. *The system has no solution if, and only if, the equations represent distinct parallel lines.* Two distinct lines in a plane are parallel if they do not intersect.
3. *The system has infinitely many solutions if, and only if, the equations represent the same line.* A line is considered parallel to itself.

Consider the following system and assume it has a solution.

$$\begin{array}{rcl} 2x - 3y &=& 1 \\ {}^{-}4x + 6y &=& 5 \end{array}$$

In an attempt to solve for x, we multiply the first equation by 2 and then add as follows:

$$\begin{array}{rcl} 4x - 6y &=& 2 \\ \underline{{}^{-}4x + 6y} &=& \underline{5} \\ 0 &=& 7 \end{array}$$

A false statement results from the assumption that the system had a solution. That assumption caused a false statement; therefore, the assumption itself must be false. Hence, the system has no solution. In other words, the solution set is $\emptyset$. This situation arises if, and only if, the corresponding lines are parallel and different. The lines are parallel because their equations can be written as $y = \frac{2}{3}x - \frac{1}{3}$ and $y = \frac{2}{3}x + \frac{5}{6}$, which shows that the slope of each line is $\frac{2}{3}$.

Next, consider the following system:

$$2x - 3y = 1$$
$$^{-}4x + 6y = {}^{-}2$$

To solve this system, we multiply the first equation by 2 and add as follows:

$$4x - 6y = 2$$
$$\underline{{}^{-}4x + 6y = {}^{-}2}$$
$$0 = 0$$

The resulting statement, $0 = 0$, is always true. In the original system, if we multiply by $^{-}2$ both sides of the first equation, the result would be the second equation. Thus, the graphs are exactly the same or the graph is a single line. All pairs of x and y that correspond to points on the line $2x - 3y = 1$ also satisfy the equivalent equation $^{-}4x + 6y = {}^{-}2$.

Thus, one way to determine that a system of two equations in two unknowns has infinitely many solutions is by checking whether each of the original equations represents the same line. It can be shown that a system has infinitely many solutions if, and only if, we get $0 = 0$ by trying to eliminate one of the variables and adding or subtracting the equations side by side. The statement $0 = 0$ originated from $0 \cdot x + 0 \cdot y = 0$, which is satisfied by all x and y.

Example 27

Identify each of the following systems as having a unique solution, no solution, or infinitely many solutions:

a. $2x - 3y = 5$
$\frac{1}{2}x - y = 1$

b. $\frac{x}{3} - \frac{y}{4} = 1$
$3y - 4x + 12 = 0$

c. $6x - 9y = 5$
$^{-}8x + 12y = 7$

Different methods are illustrated in the solutions.

Solution One method is to attempt to solve each system. Another method is to write each equation in the slope-intercept form and interpret the system geometrically.

a. *First method.* To eliminate x, multiply the second equation by $^{-}4$ and add the equations.

$$2x - 3y = 5$$
$$\underline{{}^{-}2x + 4y = {}^{-}4}$$
$$y = 1$$

Substituting 1 for y in either equation gives $x = 4$. Thus $x = 4$ and $y = 1$, or $(4, 1)$ is the unique solution of the system.

Second method. In slope-intercept form, the first equation is $y = \frac{2}{3}x - \frac{5}{3}$. The second equation is $y = \frac{1}{2}x - 1$. The slopes of the corresponding lines are $\frac{2}{3}$ and $\frac{1}{2}$, respectively. Consequently, the lines are distinct and are not parallel and, therefore, intersect in a single point whose coordinates are the unique solution to the original system.

b. *First method.* Multiply the first equation by 12 and rewrite the second equation as $^-4x + 3y = {}^-12$. Then, adding the resulting equations gives the following:

$$4x - 3y = 12$$
$$\underline{{}^-4x + 3y = {}^-12}$$
$$0 = 0$$

Hence, the two equations represent the same line, and the original system has infinitely many solutions (all the points on the line).

Second method. In slope-intercept form, both equations are

$$y = \frac{4}{3}x - 4.$$

Thus, the two lines are identical, so the system has infinitely many solutions.

c. *First method.* To eliminate y, multiply the first equation by 4 and the second by 3; then, add the resulting equations.

$$24x - 36y = 20$$
$$\underline{{}^-24x + 36y = 21}$$
$$0 = 41$$

This is a contradiction (no pair of numbers x and y satisfy $0 \cdot x + 0 \cdot y = 41$), so this equation has no solutions, and, consequently, the original system has no solutions.

Second method. In slope-intercept form, the first equation is $y = \frac{2}{3}x - \frac{5}{9}$. The second equation is $y = \frac{2}{3}x + \frac{7}{12}$. The corresponding lines have the same slope, $\frac{2}{3}$, but different y-intercepts.

Consequently, the lines are distinct and parallel, and the original system has no solution.

▶ **NOW TRY THIS 13**

Find all solutions (if any) of each of the following systems.

a. $x - y = 1$
$\quad 2x - y = 5$

b. $2x - y = 1$
$\quad 2y - 4x = 3$

c. $2x - y = 1$
$\quad 2y - 4x = {}^-2$

Substitution and elimination methods may be used to solve systems with 3 or more variables. Consider the problem in Example 28. We use the strategy of writing an equation.

Example 28

At a local farmer's market, three purchases were made for the following prices:

- cantaloupe and a vase for $8
- watermelon and an identical vase for $9
- same-priced watermelon and a same-priced cantaloupe for $7

What is the cost of each object?

Solution If the cost of the cantaloupe is c dollars, the cost of the vase is v dollars, and the cost of the watermelon is w dollars, we have the following system of 3 equations with 3 unknowns.

$$c + v = 8$$
$$w + v = 9$$
$$w + c = 7$$

We can eliminate the unknown w by subtracting the third equation from the second:
$(v + w) - (c + w) = 9 - 7$ or equivalently $v - c = 2$.

Now we have a system of two equations with two unknowns: $c + v = 8$ and $v - c = 2$. Adding the equations we get $2v = 10$ or $v = 5$. Substituting $v = 5$ into the first equation, we get $c + 5 = 8$ or $c = 3$. Substituting $v = 5$ into the second equation, we get $w + 5 = 9$ or $w = 4$. Thus, the vase costs $5, a cantaloupe $3, and a watermelon $4.

Assessment 5A

1. The graph of $y = mx$ is given in the following figure. Sketch the graphs for each of the following on the same figure. Explain your answers.
   a. $y = mx + 3$
   b. $y = mx - 3$
   c. $y = 3mx$
   d. $y = {}^-3mx$

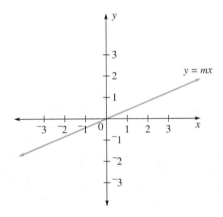

2. Sketch the graphs for each of the following equations:
   a. $y = \dfrac{{}^-3}{4}x + 3$
   b. $y = {}^-3$
   c. $y = 15x - 30$
3. Find the x-intercept and y-intercept for the equations in exercise 2, if they exist.
4. In the following figure, part (i) shows a dual-scale thermometer and part (ii) shows the corresponding points plotted on a graph.

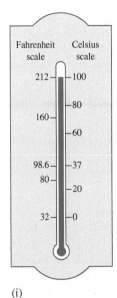

(i)

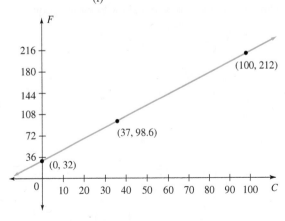

(ii)

a. Use the points $(0, 32)$ and $(100, 212)$ to develop a formula for conversion from degrees Celsius (C) to degrees Fahrenheit (F).

b. Use your answer in (a) to find a formula for converting from degrees F to degrees C.

c. Is there a point where degree Celsius and degree Fahrenheit are the same? If so, find it.

5. Write each of the following equations in slope-intercept form and identify the slope and y-intercept.

a. $3y - x = 0$ **b.** $x + y = 3$ **c.** $x = 3y$

6. For each of the following, write the equation of the line determined by the given pair of points in slope-intercept form or in the form $x = a$ or $y = b$.

a. $(^-4, 3)$ and $(1, ^-2)$

b. $(0, 0)$ and $(2, 1)$

c. $\left(0, \dfrac{^-1}{2}\right)$ and $\left(\dfrac{1}{2}, 0\right)$

d. $(0, ^-3)$ and $(^-1, ^-3)$

7. Find the coordinates of two other **collinear** points (on the same line) with each of the following pairs of given points.

a. $P(2, 2)$, $Q(4, 2)$ **b.** $P(0, 0)$, $Q(0, 1)$

8. For each of the following, give as much information as possible about x and y.

a. The ordered pairs $(^-2, 0)$, $(^-2, 1)$, and (x, y) represent collinear points.

b. The ordered pair (x, y) is in the fourth quadrant.

9. Consider lines through $P(2, 4)$ that form $90°$ angles with the x- and y-axes, respectively. Find the area and the perimeter of the rectangle formed by these lines and the axes.

10. Find the equations for each of the following lines.

a. The line containing $P(3, 0)$ and perpendicular to the x-axis

b. The line containing $P(^-4, 5)$ and parallel to the x-axis

11. For each of the following, find the slope, if it exists, of the line determined by the given pair of points.

a. $(4, 3)$ and $(^-5, 0)$ **b.** $(\sqrt{5}, 2)$ and $(1, 2)$

c. (a, a) and (b, b) **d.** $(\sqrt{5}, 2)$ and $(\sqrt{5}, ^-2)$

12. Write the equation of each line in exercise 11.

13. Wildlife experts found that the number of chirps a cricket makes in a 15-sec interval is related to the temperature T in degrees Fahrenheit, as shown in the following graph:

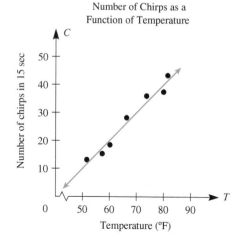

Number of Chirps as a Function of Temperature

a. If C is the number of chirps in 15 sec, write a formula for C in terms of T (temperature in degrees Fahrenheit) that seems to fit the data best.

b. Use the equation in (a) to predict the number of chirps in 15 sec when the temperature is $90°$.

c. If N is the number of chirps per minute, write a formula for N in terms of T.

14. The lines $\overleftrightarrow{AB}$ and $\overleftrightarrow{BC}$ shown in the figure are graphs of $y = 2x - 20$ and $y = 4 - 2x$. Through the point C, a vertical line (parallel to the y-axis) was drawn intersecting $\overleftrightarrow{AB}$ at D.

a. Which graph corresponds to which line? Justify your answer.

b. Find the coordinates of point D.

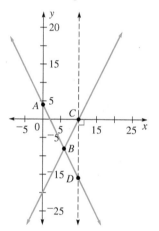

15. What do the graphs of the following equations have in common?

a. $y = m(x + 3)$ for different real number values of m?

b. $y = m(1 - x)$ for different real number values of m?

c. $\dfrac{x}{a} + \dfrac{y}{2a} = 1$ for different non-zero values of a?

d. $x + y = a$ for different values of a?

16. Suppose a car is traveling at a constant speed of 60 mph.

a. Draw a graph showing the relation between the distance traveled and the amount of time that it takes to travel the distance.

b. What is the slope of the line that you drew in part (a)?

17. Solve each of the following systems, if possible. Indicate whether the system has a unique solution, infinitely many solutions, or no solution.

a. $y = 3x - 1$
$y = x + 3$

b. $3x + 4y = ^-17$
$2x + 3y = ^-13$

c. $2x - 3y = ^-1$
$\dfrac{^-2}{3}x + y = \dfrac{1}{3}$

d. $y = 1 - x$
$y = x - 1$

18. The owner of a 5000-gal oil truck loads the truck with gasoline and kerosene. The profit on each gallon of gasoline is 13¢ and on each gallon of kerosene it is 12¢. How many gallons of each fuel did the owner load if the profit was $640.00?

19. Josephine's bank contains 27 coins. If all the coins are either dimes or quarters and the value of the coins is $5.25, how many of each kind of coin are there?

Assessment 5B

1. The graph of $y = mx + 5$ is given in the following figure. Sketch the graphs for each of the following equations on the same figure. Explain your answers.
   a. $y = mx$
   b. $y = mx - 5$
   c. $y = {}^-mx$
   d. $y = 2mx$

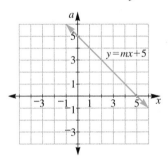

2. Sketch the graphs for each of the following equations:
   a. $x = {}^-2$
   b. $y = 3x - 1$
   c. $y = \dfrac{1}{20}x$

3. Find the x-intercept and y-intercept for the equations in exercise 2, if they exist.

4. On a ruler that measures both metric and English units, we see that $1\text{ m} = 39.37\text{ in.}$ Use this information to write an equation to convert x *m* to y *in.* meters.

5. Write each of the following equations in slope-intercept form and identify the slope and y-intercept.
   a. $\dfrac{x}{3} + \dfrac{y}{4} = 1$
   b. $3x - 4y + 7 = 0$
   c. $x - y = 4(x - y)$

6. For each of the following, write the equation of the line determined by the given pair of points in slope-intercept form or in the form $x = a$ or $y = b$.
   a. $(0, 1)$ and $(2, 1)$
   b. $(2, 1)$ and $(2, {}^-1)$
   c. $({}^-a, 0)$ and $(a, 0), a \neq 0$
   d. $(0, {}^-\sqrt{3})$ and $({}^-1, {}^-\sqrt{3})$

7. Find the coordinates of two other collinear points (on the same line) with each of the following pairs of given points:
   a. $P({}^-1, 0), Q({}^-1, 2)$ **b.** $P(0, 0), Q(1, 1)$

8. Give as much information as possible about x and y in the following.
   a. The ordered pairs $({}^-2, 1)$, $(0, 1)$, and (x, y) represent collinear points.
   b. (x, y), $(0, 0)$ and $({}^-1, {}^-1)$ are collinear

9. A rectangle has two vertices on the x-axis, two vertices on the y-axis, and one vertex at the point with coordinates $(4, 6)$.
   a. Make a sketch showing that there is a rectangle with these characteristics.
   b. Write the coordinates of each of the other three vertices.
   c. Write the equations of the diagonals of the rectangle.
   d. Find the coordinates of the point of intersection of the diagonals.

10. Find the equation for each of the following lines.
    a. The line containing $P(0, {}^-2)$ and parallel to the x-axis
    b. The line containing $P({}^-4, 5)$ and parallel to the y-axis

11. For each of the following, find the slope, if it exists, of the line determined by the given pair of points:
    a. $({}^-4, 1)$ and $(5, 2)$
    b. $({}^-3, 81)$ and $({}^-3, 198)$
    c. $(1.0001, 12)$ and $(1, 10)$
    d. $(2, \sqrt{5})$ and $({}^-2, \sqrt{5})$

12. Write the equation of each line in exercise 11.

13. At the end of 10 months, the balance of an account earning annual simple interest is $2100.
    a. If, at the end of 18 mo, the balance is $2180, how much money was originally in the account?
    b. What is the annual rate of interest?

14. The lines $\overleftrightarrow{AB}$ and $\overleftrightarrow{BC}$ shown in the figure are graphs of $y = 2 - 2x$ and $y = x - 4$, respectively. The line $\overleftrightarrow{CD}$ goes through $D(0, 5)$ and is parallel to the x-axis. Find the coordinates of $A, B,$ and C.

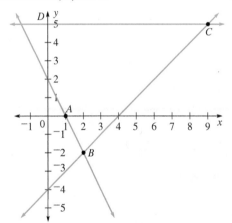

15. What do the graphs of the following equations under the given conditions in each part of the problem have in common?
    a. $y = m(x - 3)$, for different real number values of m?
    b. $y = m(3 - x)$, for different real number values of m?
    c. $x - y = a$, for different real number values of a?
    d. $y = m(x - 1) + 1$, for different real number values of m?

16. Suppose a car is traveling at a constant speed of 45 mph.
    a. Draw a graph showing the relation between the distance traveled and the amount of time that it takes to travel the distance.
    b. What is the slope of the line you drew in part (a)?

17. Solve each of the following systems, if possible. Indicate whether the system has a unique solution, infinitely many solutions, or no solution.
    a. $2x - 6y = 7$
    $3x - 9y = 10$
    b. $4x - 6y = 1$
    $6x - 9y = 1.5$
    c. $y = 2 - x$
    $y = x - 2$
    d. $3x - 2y = {}^-1$
    $\dfrac{{}^-3}{2}x + y = \dfrac{1}{2}$

18. The vertices of a triangle are given by $(0, 0)$, $(10, 0)$, and $(6, 8)$. Show that the segments connecting $(5, 0)$ and $(6, 8)$, $(10, 0)$ and $(3, 4)$, and $(0, 0)$ and $(8, 4)$ intersect at a common point.

Mathematical Connections 5

Reasoning

1. In this chapter, an arithmetic sequence was associated with a linear graph. Explain whether a geometric sequence should be associated with a linear graph.
2. Explain why two lines with the same slope and different y intercepts, are parallel.
3. Given the equations $y = mx + b$ and $y = nx + a$ answer the following.
   a. Assuming that the lines intersect in a single point, find the coordinates of this point in terms of $m, n,$ and a and b.
   b. Under what condition (in terms of m, n, a and b) do the lines intersect in a single point? Find the answer using part (a) and interpret it using the graphs of the lines.
4. Given the lines in problem 3, once x is found, y can be found by substituting the value of x into either equation. Explain why it does not matter which one.
5. Draw graphs for the following. Justify your solution.
   a. $(x + y)^2 = 4$
   b. $|x + y| = 1$
   c. $|x| = 1$ and y is any real number
   d. $|y| = 1$ and x is any real number
6. Explain why there exist lines with irrational numbers as slopes.

Open-Ended

7. Look for situations in books or the internet that can be modeled by equations whose graphs are straight lines.
8. a. Write equations of two lines that intersect but when graphed look parallel.
   b. At what point do those two lines intersect?

Cooperative Learning

9. Play the following game between your group and another group. Each group makes up four linear equations that have a common property and presents the equations to the other group. For example, one group could present the equations $2x - y = 0, 4x - 2y = 3, y - 2x = 3,$ and $3y - 6x = 5$. If the second group discovers a common property that the equations share, such as the graphs of the equations are four parallel lines, they get 1 point. Each group takes a specified number of turns.
10. Consider equations of the form $ax + by = c$, where not both a and b equal 0. Each group should choose three such equations so that $a, b,$ and c are consecutive terms in arithmetic sequence and answer the following.
    a. In your group, choose all pairs of your equations (there are 3 pairs) and solve each pair simultaneously. What do the solutions have in common?
    b. Compare the answers from different groups.
    c. Explain why what you discovered in parts (a) and (b) is always true. Compare the arguments from different groups and choose the best argument. What makes it best?

Connecting Mathematics to the Classroom

11. A student would like to know why it is impossible to find the slope of a vertical line. How do you respond?

12. Jonah tried to solve the equation $^-5x + y = 20$ by adding 5 to both sides. He wrote $5 - 5x + y = 5 + 20$ or $0 \cdot x + y = 25$ and finally $y = 25$. How would you help Jonah?
13. Jill would like to know why two lines with an undefined slope are parallel. How would you respond?
14. Janis noticed that in the simultaneous equations
$$2x - 3y - 5 = 0$$
$$^-4x + 6y + 10 = 0,$$
$\frac{2}{^-4} = \frac{^-3}{6} = \frac{^-5}{10}$ and the system has infinitely-many solutions. She would like to know whether, if a similar situation occurs in other systems of two equations in two unknowns, the corresponding system will have infinitely many solutions. How do you respond?

Review Problems

15. Write the following with algebraic expressions or equations.
    a. The cube root of a number is 3 less than its square.
    b. The sum of the squares of two numbers is 36.
    c. $\sqrt{0.\overline{9}}$ has 1 as its principal square root.
16. Give an approximation of $\sqrt{6}$ correct to hundredths.
17. Solve the following for x.
    a. $x\sqrt{2} = ^-3\sqrt{2}x + 2$
    b. $x^2 - 81 = 0$
    c. $3x < ^-\sqrt{7}$
18. Find $f(x)$ for each given value of x when $f(x) = x\sqrt{7} - \sqrt{7}$.
    a. 3
    b. $\sqrt{7}$
    c. $^-4$
19. If $f(x) = 12$ when $f(x) = 3x - \sqrt{2}$, find x.
20. What are the domains for each of the following functions?
    a. $f(x) = \sqrt{x + 1}$
    b. $f(x) = \sqrt{^-x}$

National Assessments

National Assessment of Educational Progress (NAEP) Questions

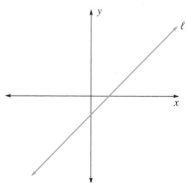

Which of the following statements is true about line ℓ shown above?

A. Line ℓ has a positive slope and a positive y-intercept.
B. Line ℓ has a positive slope and a negative y-intercept.
C. Line ℓ has zero slope and a negative y-intercept.
D. Line ℓ has a negative slope and a positive y-intercept.
E. Line ℓ has a negative slope and a negative y-intercept.

NAEP, Grade 8, 2013

Two large storage tanks, T and W, contain water. T starts losing water at the same time additional water starts flowing into W. The graph below shows the amount of water in each tank over a period of hours.

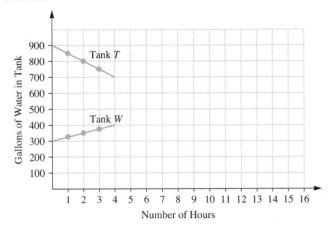

Assume that the rates of water loss and water gain continue as shown. At what number of hours will the amount of water in T be equal to the amount of water in W?

Show or explain how you found your answer.

NAEP, Grade 8, 2013

Hint for Solving the Preliminary Problem

Use Figure 40 to write a proportion and slove for $\dfrac{l}{w}$

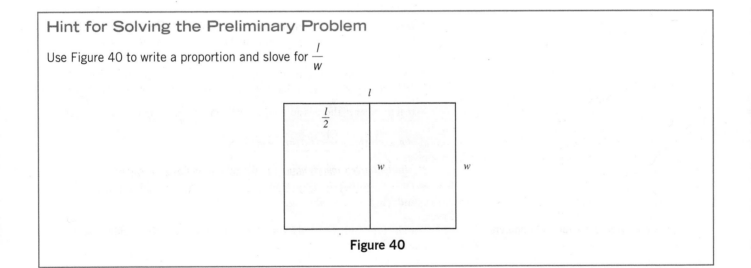

Figure 40

Chapter Summary

KEY CONCEPTS	DEFINITIONS, DESCRIPTIONS, AND THEOREMS
Section 1	
Irrational number	Any number that is not rational.
Real number	Any rational or irrational number. Every real number can be represented as a decimal.
Square root	If a is any nonnegative number, a *square root of a* is a number x such that $x^2 = a$. For example, 9 has square roots 3 and $^-3$. If a is any nonnegative number, the *principal square root of a* (denoted $\sqrt{a}$) is the nonnegative number x such that $x^2 = a$. For example, $\sqrt{9} = 3$.
Principal nth root	If n is even and b is any nonnegative real number, then the *principal nth root* of b (denoted as $\sqrt[n]{b}$) is the positive solution of $x^n = b$. If n is odd and b is any real number, the *nth root* of b (or $\sqrt[n]{b}$) is the unique solution of $x^n = b$.
Pythagorean Theorem	If a and b are the lengths of the shorter sides (legs) of a right triangle and c is the length of the hypotenuse (the side opposite the right angle), then $a^2 + b^2 = c^2$.
Fraction	Any real number of the form $\frac{a}{b}$, where a and b are real numbers with $b \neq 0$.
Addition and multiplication properties for real numbers	• *Closure*—for all real numbers a and b, $a + b$ and ab are unique real numbers. • *Commutative*—for all real numbers a and b, $a + b = b + a$ and $ab = ba$. • *Associative*—for all real numbers a, b, and c, $(a + b) + c = a + (b + c)$ and $(ab)c = a(bc)$. • *Identity*—for all real numbers a; 0 is the (unique) *additive identity* such that $a + 0 = 0 + a$, 1 is the (unique) *multiplicative identity* such that $a \cdot 1 = 1 \cdot a = a$. • *Inverse*—for every real number a, there is an unique real number $-a$, the *additive inverse of a*, such that $a + {}^-a = 0 = {}^-a + a$. For every nonzero real number a, there is an unique real number $\frac{1}{a}$, the *multiplicative inverse of a*, such that $a \cdot \frac{1}{a} = 1 = \frac{1}{a} \cdot a$. • *Multiplicative Property of 0*—for all real number a, $a \cdot 0 = 0 \cdot a = 0$. • *Distributive property of multiplication over addition*—for all real numbers a, b, and c, $a(b + c) = ab + ac$.
Density property for real numbers	For all real numbers a and b with $a < b$, there exists a real number c such that $a < c < b$.
Rational exponents	For any positive integer n and any integer m, $x^{1/n} = \sqrt[n]{x}$, if $\sqrt[n]{x}$ is a real number, and $x^{m/n} = \sqrt[n]{x^m}$, if $GCD(m, n) = 1$ and $\sqrt[n]{x^m}$ is a real number.

Section 1

Properties of exponents

Let r and s be any rational numbers, x and y be any real numbers, and n be any nonzero integer. (Assume the following expressions are meaningful.)

- $x^{-r} = \dfrac{1}{x^r}$, $x^{-1/n} = \dfrac{1}{x^{1/n}} = \dfrac{1}{\sqrt[n]{x}}$

- $(xy)^r = x^r y^r$, $(xy)^{1/n} = x^{1/n} y^{1/n}$ and $\sqrt[n]{xy} = \sqrt[n]{x}\,\sqrt[n]{y}$

- $\left(\dfrac{x}{y}\right)^r = \dfrac{x^r}{y^r}$, $\left(\dfrac{x}{y}\right)^{1/n} = \dfrac{x^{1/n}}{y^{1/n}}$ and $\sqrt[n]{\dfrac{x}{y}} = \dfrac{\sqrt[n]{x}}{\sqrt[n]{y}}$

- $(x^r)^s = x^{rs}$, $\left(x^{1/n}\right)^p = x^{p/n}$ and $\left(\sqrt[n]{x}\right)^p = \sqrt[n]{x^p}$ where p is an integer.

Section 2

Constant

A fixed number or other fixed mathematical object

Variable

A quantity that varies.

A variable may

(1) represent a missing element or an unknown,

(2) stand for more than one thing,

(3) be used in generalizations of patterns, and

(4) be an element of a set, or a set itself.

nth term of an arithmetic sequence

$a_n = a_1 + (n - 1)d$, where a_1 is the first term and d is the difference.

nth term of an geometric sequence

$a_n = a_1 r^{n-1}$, where a_1 is the first term and r is the ratio.

Fibonacci sequence

A sequence in which $F_1 = F_2 = 1$ and $F_n = F_{n-1} + F_{n-2}$ for $n \geq 3$.

Section 3

Properties of equality and equations

- *Addition*—for all real numbers a, b, and c, if $a = b$, then $a + c = b + c$.
- *Multiplication*—for all real numbers a, b, and c, if $a = b$, then $ac = bc$.
- *Cancellation*—For any real numbers a, b, and c,

    if $a + c = b + c$, then $a = b$.

    if $c \neq 0$ and $ac = bc$, then $a = b$.

- *Substitution*—equality is not affected if we substitute a number for its equal.

Section 4

Function

A correspondence from set A to set B in which each element of A is paired with one, and only one, element of B.

Let f be a function from A to B. If $x \in A$, then $f(x)$, the value of the function f at x (or the *image of x*) is the element in B that corresponds to x.

Set A is the *domain* of the function, and set B is the *codomain* (or the set of all possible outputs) of the function. The *range* of the function is the set of all outputs of the function.

Section 4

Function models	Functions may be modeled in various ways: • as a rule between two sets • as a machine relating inputs and outputs • as an equation relating two variables • as a table relating two variables • as an arrow diagram showing the correspondence between elements of two sets • as a set of ordered pairs • as a graph in two dimensions
Sum of the first n terms, $S(n)$, of an arithmetic sequence	$$S(n) = \left(\frac{a_1 + a_n}{2}\right)n \quad \text{or} \quad S(n) = a_1 n + \frac{n(n-1)d}{2},$$ where a_1 is the first term, a_n is the last term, d is the difference, and n is the number of terms.
Sum of the first n terms, $S(n)$, of a geometric sequence	$$S(n) = \frac{a_1(1 - r^n)}{1 - r},$$ where a_1 is the first term, r is the ratio ($r \neq 1$), and n is the number of terms.
Composition of functions	Given the functions f and g, the composition of f with g is the function $g \circ f$ such that $(g \circ f)(x) = g(f(x))$.
Relation	A *relation from set A to set B* is any set of ordered pairs; that is, a subset of $A \times B$. A *relation* is a *function* from set A to set B if for every $a \in A$, there is a unique $b \in B$ such that (a, b) is in the relation.
Properties of relations	*Reflexive*—a relation R on a set X is *reflexive* if, and only if, for every element $a \in X$, a is related to a; that is, for every $a \in X$, $(a, a) \in R$. *Symmetric*—a relation R on a set X is *symmetric* if, and only if, for all elements a and b in X, whenever a is related to b, then b also is related to a; that is, if $(a, b) \in R$, then $(b, a) \in R$. *Transitive*— a relation R on a set X is *transitive* if, and only if, for all elements a, b, and c in X, whenever a is related to b and b is related to c, then a is related to c; that is, if $(a, b) \in R$ and $(b, c) \in R$, then $(a, c) \in R$.
Equivalence relation	Any relation that has the reflexive, symmetric, and transitive properties.

Section 5

Cartesian coordinate system	A system constructed by placing two number lines perpendicular to each other. The intersection point of the two lines is the *origin*. The two perpendicular lines are commonly called the *x-axis*, and the *y-axis*.
Slope	The measure of steepness (denoted by m) of a line. Give two points $A(x_1, y_1)$ and $B(x_2, y_2)$ with $x_1 \neq x_2$, the *slope m of the line* through A and B is $$m = \frac{\text{rise}}{\text{run}} = \frac{y_2 - y_1}{x_2 - x_1} = \frac{y_1 - y_2}{x_1 - x_2}.$$
x-intercept and y-intercept	The value of x at the point of intersection of a line with the x-axis is the *x-intercept*. The value of y at the point of intersection of a line with the y-axis is the *y-intercept*.
Equation of a line	Every nonvertical line has an equation of the form $y = mx + b$ (*slope-intercept form*), where m is the *slope* and b is the *y-intercept*. A vertical line has undefined slope and the equation $x = a$. A horizontal line has 0 slope and the equation $y = b$.

Section 5

Solving a system of equations	A system of two equations in two unknowns may be solved using any of the following methods: • *Graphing* • *Substitution* • *Elimination*
Number of solutions of a system of two equations in two variables	The system has *a unique solution* if, and only if, the graphs of the equations intersect in a single point. The system has *no solution* if, and only if, the equations represent distinct parallel lines. The system has *infinitely many solutions* if, and only if, the equations represent the same line.

Chapter Review

1. Classify each of the following as rational or irrational (assume the patterns shown continue):
   a. 2.19119911999119999119 . . .
   b. $\dfrac{1}{\sqrt{2}}$
   c. $\dfrac{4}{9}$
   d. 0.0011001100110011 . . .
   e. 0.001100011000011 . . .

2. Write each of the following in the form $a\sqrt{b}$ or $a\sqrt[n]{b}$, where a and b are positive integers and b has the least value possible:
   a. $\sqrt{484}$ b. $\sqrt{288}$
   c. $\sqrt{180}$ d. $\sqrt[3]{162}$

3. Answer each of the following and explain your answers.
   a. Is the set of irrational numbers closed under addition?
   b. Is the set of irrational numbers closed under subtraction?
   c. Is the set of irrational numbers closed under multiplication?
   d. Is the set of irrational numbers closed under division?

4. Find an approximation for $\sqrt{23}$ correct to three decimal places without using the $\boxed{y^x}$ or the $\boxed{\sqrt{}}$ keys on a calculator.

5. Approximate $\sqrt[3]{2}$ to two decimal places by using the squeezing method.

6. Each of the following is a geometric sequence. Find the missing terms.
   a. 5, ____, 10
   b. 1, ____, ____, ____, 1/4

7. In a geometric sequence, if the nth term is $\sqrt{7}(^-1)^n$, what is the 10th term and what is the ratio?

8. If the first two terms of an arithmetic sequence are 1 and $\sqrt{2}$, what is an algebraic expression for the nth term?

9. There are 13 times as many students as professors at a college. Use S for the number of students and P for the number of professors to represent the given information.

10. Write a sentence that gives the same information as the following equation: $A = 103B$, where A is the number of girls in a neighborhood and B is the number of boys.

11. Write an equation to find the number of feet given the number of yards (let f be the number of feet and y be the number of yards).

12. The sum of n whole numbers is S. If each number is multiplied by 10 and then decreased by 10, what is the sum of the new numbers in terms of n and S?

13. I am thinking of a whole number. If I divide it by 13, then multiply the answer by 12, then subtract 20, and then add 89, I end up with 93. What was my original number?

14. a. Think of a number.
   > Add 17.
   > Double the result.
   > Subtract 4.
   > Double the result.
   > Add 20.
   > Divide by 4.
   > Subtract 20.
   Your answer will be your original number. Explain how this "trick" works.
   b. Fill in two more steps that will take you back to your original number.
   > Think of a number.
   > Add 18.
   > Multiply by 4.
   > Subtract 7.
   > .
   > .

15. Find all the values of x that satisfy the following equations write your answers in simplified form:
   a. $4(7x - 21) = 14(7x - 21)$
   b. $3(\sqrt{x} - 1) = \sqrt{9x} + 5$
   c. $2(3x + 5) = 6x + 11$
   d. $2(x + \sqrt{3}) = 3(x - \sqrt{3})$

16. Mike has 3 times as many baseball cards as Jordan, who has twice as many cards as Paige. Together, the three children have 999 cards. Find how many cards each child has.

17. Jeannie has 10 books overdue at the library. She remembers she checked out 2 science books two weeks before she checked out 8 children's books. The daily fine per book is $0.20. If her total fine was $11.60, how long was each book overdue?

18. Three children deliver all the newspapers in a small town. Jacobo delivers twice as many papers as Dahlia, who delivers 100 more papers than Rashid. If altogether 500 papers are delivered, how many papers does each child deliver?

19. Which of the following sets of ordered pairs are functions from the set of first components to the set of second components?
  a. $\{(a,b),(c,d),(e,a),(f,g)\}$
  b. $\{(a,b),(a,c),(b,b),(b,c)\}$
  c. $\{(a,b),(b,a)\}$
  d. $\{(x,y) \mid x \text{ is any real number}, y = 2\}$

20. Given the following function rules and the domains, find the associated ranges:
  a. $f(x) = x + 3$; domain $= \{0,1,2,3\}$
  b. $f(x) = 3x - 1$; domain is R (all real numbers)
  c. $f(x) = x^2$; domain is R (all real numbers)
  d. $f(x) = x^2 + 3x + 5$; domain $= \{0,1,2\}$

21. Which of the following correspondences from A to B describe a function? If a correspondence is a function, find its range. Justify your answers.
  a. A is the set of college students, and B is the set of majors. To each college student corresponds his or her major.
  b. A is the set of books in the library, and B is the set N of natural numbers. To each book corresponds the number of pages in the book.
  c. $A = \{(a,b) \mid a \in N \text{ and } b \in N\}$, and $B = N$. To each element (a,b) of A corresponds the number $4a + 2b$.
  d. $A = N$ and $B = N$. If x is even, then $f(x) = 0$, and if x is odd, then $f(x) = 1$.
  e. $A = N$ and $B = N$. To each natural number corresponds the sum of its digits.

22. A health club charges an initiation fee of $200, which gives 1 month of free membership, and then charges $55 per month.
  a. If $C(x)$ is the total cost of membership in the club for x months, express $C(x)$ in terms of x.
  b. Graph $C(x)$ for the first 12 months.
  c. Use the graph in (b) to find when the total cost of membership in the club will exceed $600.
  d. When will the total cost of membership exceed $6000?

23. For each of the following functions, find possible inputs x, if $f(x)$ is as given.
  a. $f(x) = 4x - 5; f(x) = 15$
  b. $f(x) = x^2 - 1; f(x) = 2$
  c. $f(x) = \sqrt{x}; f(x) = 3$
  d. $f(x) = \sqrt{x}; f(x) = {}^-3$
  e. $f(x) = \dfrac{x + 1}{x + 2}; f(x) = {}^-1$
  f. $f(x) = \dfrac{x + 1}{x + 2}; f(x) = 1$

24. Which of the following graphs represent functions? Tell why.

a.

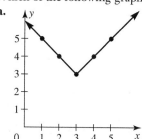

b.

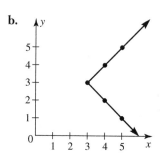

c.

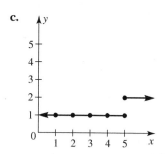

25. a. Jilly is building towers with cubes, placing one cube on top of another and painting the tower (including the top and the bottom, but not the faces touching each other). Find the number of square faces that Jilly needs to paint for towers made of 1, 2, 3, 4, 5, and 6 cubes by filling in the following table:

# of Cubes	# of Squares to Paint
1	6
2	10
3	
4	
5	
6	

  b. Graph the information you found in part (a) where the number of cubes in a tower is on the horizontal x-axis and the number of squares to be painted is on the vertical axis.
  c. If x is the number of cubes in a tower and y is the corresponding number of squares to be painted, write an equation that gives y as a function of x.
  d. Is the graph describing the number of squares as a function of the number of cubes used a straight line?

26. Graph each of the following equations:

   a. $y = {}^-2x + 5$

   b. $-\dfrac{x}{3} + \dfrac{y}{5} = 1$

   c. $y = {}^-x\sqrt{2}$

27. The following are graphs of $x - y - 1 = 0$ and of $4x + 3y - 12 = 0$. Answer the following.

   a. Which equation is the graph of $\overleftrightarrow{CD}$?

   b. If line $\overleftrightarrow{ED}$ is parallel to the x-axis, find the coordinates of E.

   c. If line $\overleftrightarrow{BF}$ is parallel to the x-axis, find the length of segment $\overline{BF}$.

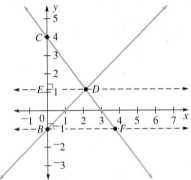

28. Solve the following equations if possible(s).

   a. ${}^-3x + 12 = 23$

   b. $\sqrt{2}x - 5 = \sqrt{8}x + 1$

   c. $x^3 = {}^-2$

   d. $4x^2 - 33 = 3$

   e. $(x - 1)^3 = 2$

   f. $(2x + 1)^4 = 5$

   g. $(2x - 1)(x - 1) = 0$

29. If we take the third root of every term of a geometric sequence is the resulting sequence also geometric? If so, what is its ratio? Justify your answer.

Answers to Problems

Answers to odd-numbered Mathematical Connections problems are available at www.pearsonhighered.com/mathstatsresources
<http://www.pearsonhighered.com/mathstatsresources>.

Assessment 1A

1. Answers vary $0.232232223\ldots$ **2. a.** $\sqrt{6}$ **b.** $2\sqrt{2}$ **c.** $\sqrt{21}$
3. $0.\overline{9}, 0.9\overline{98}, \sqrt{0.98}, 0.\overline{98}, 0.9, 0.\overline{898}$ **4. a.** Yes **b.** No **c.** No

d. Yes **e.** Yes **f.** Yes **5. a.** 15 **b.** 13 **c.** $^-9$ **d.** 25 **e.** $\dfrac{1}{2}$

f. 0.01 **6. a.** 2.65 **b.** 0.11 **7. a.** False: $\sqrt{2} + 0 = \sqrt{2}$
b. False: $^-\sqrt{2} + \sqrt{2} = 0$ **c.** False: $\sqrt{2} \cdot \sqrt{2} = 2$
d. True: $\sqrt{2} - \sqrt{2} = 0$ **8. a.** Answers vary; for example,
$\sqrt{2}, \sqrt{3},$ and $\sqrt{5}$. **b.** Answers vary. Three such numbers
are: $0.546010010001\ldots, 0.547010010001\ldots,$ and
$0.548010010001\ldots$. Then $0.\overline{54} < 0.546010010001\ldots <$
$0.547010010001\ldots < 00.548010010001\ldots < 0.\overline{55}$

c. Answers vary. $\dfrac{\sqrt{3}}{4}, \dfrac{\pi}{7},$ and $\dfrac{\sqrt{2}}{3}$ are three such irrational

numbers. **9.** Answers vary. For example, between any two
rational numbers we could find three irrational numbers. Because
there are infinitely many disjoint intervals bounded by rational
numbers, there must be infinitely many irrational numbers.
10. a. R **b.** $\varnothing$ **c.** Q **d.** $\varnothing$ **e.** R **f.** R
11. a. Q, R **b.** $N, I, Q R$ **c.** R, S **d.** I, Q, R **e.** Q, R
12. a. N, I, Q, R, S **b.** Q, R **c.** R, S **d.** None **e.** Q, R
13. a. 64 **b.** None **c.** $^-64$ **d.** None **e.** x 70, x is a real
number **f.** None **14. a.** $6\sqrt{5}$ **b.** $11\sqrt{3}$ **c.** $6\sqrt{7}$ **15. a.** $^-3\sqrt[3]{2}$
b. $2\sqrt[5]{3}$ **c.** $5\sqrt[3]{2}$ **d.** $^-3$ **16. a.** $5\sqrt[3]{2}, 5\sqrt[3]{4}$
b. $2^{3/4}, 2^{1/2}, 2^{1/4}$ or $^-2^{3/4}, 2^{1/2}, ^-2^{1/4}$
c. There are two possible geometric sequences.
$\dfrac{5\sqrt{15}}{3}, 5, \sqrt{15}, 3$
$-\dfrac{5\sqrt{15}}{3}, 5, ^-\sqrt{15}, 3$

d. There are two possible geometric sequences.
$\dfrac{2\sqrt{6}}{3}, ^-2, \sqrt{6}, ^-3$

$-\dfrac{2\sqrt{6}}{3}, ^-2, ^-\sqrt{6}, ^-3$

17. a. 2^{10} **b.** 2^{11} **c.** 2^{12} **18. a.** $\dfrac{1}{25}$ **b.** $\dfrac{125}{8}$ **c.** $\dfrac{729}{125}$

d. $\dfrac{1}{125}$ **e.** $\dfrac{1}{81}$ **f.** $-\dfrac{1}{81}$ **19. a.** 5 **b.** $-\dfrac{3}{2}$ **c.** $-\dfrac{5}{6}$
d. $^-18$ **e.** $2^{-\frac{4}{3}}$ **f.** $1 + \sqrt{2}$ or $1 - \sqrt{2}$ **20. a.** $x^5 - 20 = 0$
b. $x^3 + 2 = 0$ **c.** $(x + 1)^3 - 10 = 0$ **d.** $3x^2 - 2 = 0$
21. $4^3 = 64$
$4.6^3 \approx 97.3$
$4.7^3 \approx 103.8$
$5^3 = 125$
So, an integer approximation of $\sqrt[3]{103}$ is 5.
22. a. Rational **b.** Rational **c.** Rational **d.** Irrational

Assessment 2A

1. a. $10 + 3d$ **b.** $2n - 15$ **c.** $15n^2$ **d.** $n^2 - 2n$

2. a. $\dfrac{7(n + \sqrt{3}) - 14}{7} - n$ **b.** $\sqrt{3} - 2$ **3. a.** $2(n + 1)$

b. $(n + 2)^2 - 2(n + 1)$ or $n^2 + 2n + 2$ **4. a.** $50 + 60b$
dollars **b.** $250d$ cents **c.** $3x + 3$ **d.** $q \cdot 2^n$ **e.** $(40 - 3t)°F$
f. $4s + 15{,}000$ dollars **g.** $3x + 6$ **h.** $3m$
5. $S = 45P$ **6.** $g = b + 5$ **7.** $6n + 7$ **8. a.** $P = 12t$
b. $P = 12(t - 1) + 15$ **9.** $5x + 1300$ dollars **10. a.** Eldest
$3x$; middle $\dfrac{3}{2}x$; x **b.** Eldest $2y$; youngest $\dfrac{2}{3}y$ **c.** Middle $\dfrac{1}{2}z$;

youngest $\dfrac{1}{3}z$ **11. a.** $^-297; ^-3(n - 1)$ **b.** $1 + 197\sqrt{2}$;
$(1 - \sqrt{2}) + 2\sqrt{2}(n - 1)$ **c.** $\sqrt{3} + 198.5; (\sqrt{3} + 0.5) + 2(n - 1)$
12. Answers vary. **a.** $13{,}122; 2(\sqrt{3})^{n-1}$
b. $512; 2(^-\sqrt{2})^{n-1}$ **c.** $^-\sqrt{5} \cdot 5^8; (^-\sqrt{5})^n$

13. $d = \dfrac{\sqrt{3} - \sqrt{2}}{100}; a_1 = \sqrt{2} - \left(\dfrac{99}{100}\right)(\sqrt{3} - \sqrt{2})$

14. $^-4$ **15.** 3.3 ft **16.** Day 31 **17. a.** $\sqrt{2}, \sqrt{3}, \sqrt{2} + \sqrt{3},$
$\sqrt{2} + 2\sqrt{3}, 2\sqrt{2} + 3\sqrt{3}, 3\sqrt{2} + 5\sqrt{3}, 5\sqrt{2} + 8\sqrt{3},$
$8\sqrt{2} + 13\sqrt{3}, 13\sqrt{2} + 21\sqrt{3}, 21\sqrt{2} + 34\sqrt{3}$
b. i. $L_7 = 5\sqrt{2} + 8\sqrt{3} = F_5\sqrt{2} + F_6\sqrt{3}$
ii. $L_8 = F_6\sqrt{2} + F_7\sqrt{3}$
$L_9 = F_7\sqrt{2} + F_8\sqrt{3}$
$L_{10} = F_8\sqrt{2} + F_9\sqrt{3}$
iii. $L_n = F_{n-2}\sqrt{2} + F_{n-1}\sqrt{3}$

Assessment 3A

1. $\bigcirc = 3, \triangle = 8, \square = 4$ **2. a.** $\dfrac{\sqrt{3}}{2}$ **b.** $2(3 + \sqrt{2})$
c. $\dfrac{1 - \sqrt{2}}{2}$ **d.** 9 **e.** $\{4, 64\}$ **3.** 22 **4.** 524 student tickets

5. Let x be the amount the youngest receives. Then
$x + 3x + x + 14{,}000 = 486{,}000$, or $5x = 472{,}000$. Youngest
received \$94,400.00; oldest \$283,200.00; middle \$108,400.00.
6. 3 ft, 5 in, 3 ft 5 in, 3 ft 2 in **7.** Let x be the number of nickels.
Then $67 - x$ is the number of dimes. So $10(67 - x) + 5x$
$= 420, x = 50$. Thus, 50 nickels and 17 dimes. **8.** Ricardo, 4,
Miriam, 14 **9.** 1000 students **10.** $a = 300$ yd., $b = 600$ yd.
11. 298, 301, 304 **12.** $12.5\sqrt{10}$ ft

Assessment 4A

1. a. Multiply the input by $^-2$. **b.** Add 6 to the input.
c. Square the input. **2. a.** This is not a function, since the

input 1 is paired with two outputs (*a* and *d*). **b.** Function
c. Function **d.** Function **3. a.** Answers will vary. For example:

b. 30
4. a.

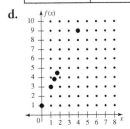

b. $(0, 1), (1, 3), (\sqrt{2}, 2\sqrt{2} + 1), (\sqrt{3}, 2\sqrt{3} + 1), (4, 9)$

c.

x	*f(x)*
0	1
1	3
$\sqrt{2}$	$2\sqrt{2} + 1$
$\sqrt{3}$	$2\sqrt{3} + 1$
4	9

d.

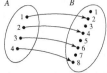

5. a. Function **b.** Function **c.** Not a function because $(4, {}^-2)$ and $(4, 2)$ both satisfy the relation, but inputs can have only one associated output. **d.** Function
6. a. i. **ii.**

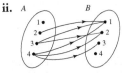

b. Part (i) is a function from A to B. For each element in A, there is a unique element in B. The range of the function is $\{2, 4, 6, 8\}$.

7.

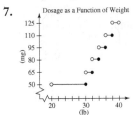

8. Answers vary.
a. $L(n) = 2n + (n - 1)$, or $3n - 1$
b. $L(n) = n^2 + 1$

9. a.

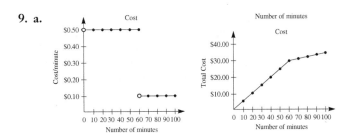

Notice that because we can't really depict 100 dots on the graphs a dot is drawn only for a multiple of 10 minutes. **b.** That the company charges for each part of a minute at the rate of $0.50 per minute **c.** The two segments represent different charges per minute. The one representing the higher cost is steeper.
d. $C(t) = 0.50t$ if $0 \leq t \leq 60$, $C(t) = 30 + 0.10(t - 60)$ if $t > 60$ **10. a.** $5n - 2$ **b.** 3^n **c.** $f(n) = 3$ **d.** $f(n) = 3^{\frac{n+2}{3}}$

11. a. 37 **b.** 65 **c.** $7\sqrt{10} - 5$ **d.** $^-5$ **e.** $\dfrac{^-5}{8}$ **f.** $7n - 5$ **12.** 1

13. a. (a) 7 **(b)** 35 **(c)** $7(\sqrt{10} - 5)$ **(d)** $^-35$ **(e)** $\dfrac{^-245}{8}$

(f) $7(n - 5)$ **b.** 1 **14. a.** 0 **b.** 2 **c.** All real numbers.
15. a. (i), (ii), and (iii) **b.** (ii) and (iii) **c.** (i), (ii), and (iii)
16. a. $\sqrt{2}$ or $^-\sqrt{2}$ **b.** $\sqrt[3]{2}$ **17. a.** 16; 16; 16; $4\sqrt{5}$
b. $\{(1, 9), (2, 8), (3, 7), (4, 6), (5, 5), (6, 4), (7, 3), (8, 2), (9, 1)\}$
c. The domain is $R^+ \times R^+$, and the range is R^+. **18. a.** 50 cars
b. Between 6 and 6:30 A.M. **c.** 0 **d.** Between 8:30 A.M. and 9 A.M., by 100 cars **e.** Segments are used because the data are continuous rather than discrete. For example, there are a number of cars at 5:20 A.M. **19. a.** $H(2) = 192$; $H(6) = 192$; $H(3) = 240$; $H(5) = 240$. Some of the heights correspond to the ball going up, some to the ball coming down.
b.

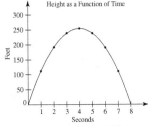

At $t = 4$ sec, the ball's height is $H(4) = 256$ ft above the ground.
c. 8 sec **d.** $0 \leq t \leq 8$ **e.** $0 \leq H(t) \leq 256$
20. $S(n) = (n + 1)^2 + (n + 2)n$ or $2n^2 + 4n + 1$
21. 4^{n-1} **22.** (a), (c), (d), (e), (h) are functions. (b) does not represent a function; if x, the input, is any given real number, then y is not unique, as it could be any real number y such that $y > x - 2$ **f.** Not a function; if $x = 1$ then $y = 1$ or $^-1$.
g. Not a function; if $x = 0$, $y = 1$ or $^-1$.
23. Only (b) is not. For $x = 1$ there are many values of y.
24. a. Boys: B, H; girls: A, C, D, G, I, J, E, F
b. $\{(A, B), (A, C), (A, D), (C, A), (C, B), (C, D), (D, A), (D, B), (D, C), (F, G), (G, F), (I, J), (J, I), (E, H)\}$ **c.** No

25. a. Yes **b.** No **26. a.** None **b.** Reflexive, symmetric, and transitive (and so an equivalence relation) **c.** Reflexive, symmetric, and transitive (and so an equivalence relation) **d.** Reflexive, symmetric, and transitive (and so an equivalence relation) **e.** Symmetric **f.** Reflexive and symmetric **g.** Transitive

Assessment 5A

1. a. and b. The graph of $y = mx + 3$ contains the point $(0, 3)$ and is parallel to the line $y = mx$. Similarly, the graph of $y = mx - 3$ contains the point $(0, ^-3)$ and is parallel to $y = mx$.

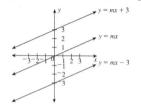 **c. and d.**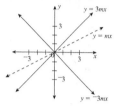

2. a. 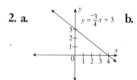 **b.** **c.**

3.

	x-intercept	y-intercept
a.	4	3
b.	None	$^-3$
c.	2	$^-30$

4. a. Using $(0, 32)$ and $(100, 212)$, the slope is $(212 - 32)/(100 - 0) = \dfrac{9}{5}$. So $F = \left(\dfrac{9}{5}\right)C + b$.

Substitute in the point $(0, 32)$. Thus, $b = 32$, and the equation is $F = \left(\dfrac{9}{5}\right)C + 32$. **b.** $C = \dfrac{5}{9}(F - 32)$ **c.** $(^-40°, ^-40°)$

5. a. $y = \left(\dfrac{1}{3}\right)x$; slope $\dfrac{1}{3}$, y-intercept 0 **b.** $y = ^-x + 3$; slope $^-1$, y-intercept 3 **c.** $y = \left(\dfrac{1}{3}\right)x$; slope $\dfrac{1}{3}$, y-intercept 0

6. a. $y = ^-x - 1$ **b.** $y = \left(\dfrac{1}{2}\right)x$ **c.** $y = x - \dfrac{1}{2}$ **d.** $y = ^-3$

7. Answers vary. **8. a.** $x = ^-2$; y is any real number. **b.** $x > 0, y < 0$ **9.** Perimeter: 12 units Area: 8 sq. units

10. a. $x = 3$ **b.** $y = 5$ **11. a.** $\dfrac{1}{3}$ **b.** 0 **c.** 1

d. Slope does not exist. **12. a.** $y = \dfrac{1}{3}x + \dfrac{5}{3}$ **b.** $y = 2$

c. $y = x$ **d.** $x = \sqrt{5}$ **13.** Answers vary, depending on estimates from the fitted line; for example: **a.** From the fitted line, estimate point coordinates of $(50, 8)$ and $(60, 18)$; the slope is $\dfrac{10}{10} = 1$. Use the point $(50, 8)$ and substitute $T = 50$ and $C = 8$ into $C = 1T + b$ (i.e., an equation of the form $y = mx + b$), so $8 = 1(50) + b; b = ^-42$; the equation is then $C = T - 42$. **b.** Answers vary. 48 chirps in 15 sec. **c.** Answers vary. $N = 4T - 168$ **14. a.** $y = 2x - 20$ is line BC and $y = 4 - 2x$ is line AB. **b.** $(10, ^-16)$ **15. a.** The lines have the same x-intercept, $^-3$. **b.** The lines have the same x-intercept, 1.

c. The lines have the same slope, $^-2$. **d.** The lines have the same slope, $^-1$.

16. a. 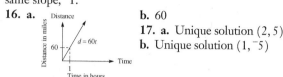 **b.** 60

17. a. Unique solution $(2, 5)$ **b.** Unique solution $(1, ^-5)$

c. Infinitely-many solutions of the form $\left(x, \dfrac{2}{3}x + \dfrac{1}{3}\right)$

d. Unique solution $(1, 0)$ **18.** 4000 gal of gasoline; 1000 gal of kerosene **19.** 17 quarters, 10 dimes

Chapter Review

1. a. Irrational **b.** Irrational **c.** $\dfrac{4}{9}$ **d.** Rational **e.** Irrational

2. a. 22 **b.** $12\sqrt{2}$ **c.** $6\sqrt{5}$ **d.** $3\sqrt[3]{6}$ **3. a.** No, $\sqrt{2} + (^-\sqrt{2})$ is rational **b.** No **c.** No, $\sqrt{2} \cdot \sqrt{2}$ rational **4.** 4.796 **5.** 1.26 **6. a.** $5\sqrt{2}$ or $^-5\sqrt{2}$

b. $\dfrac{1}{\sqrt[4]{4}}, \dfrac{1}{\sqrt[4]{16}}, \dfrac{1}{\sqrt[4]{64}}$ or $\dfrac{^-1}{\sqrt[4]{4}}, \dfrac{1}{\sqrt[4]{16}}, \dfrac{^-1}{\sqrt[4]{64}}$ **7.** $\sqrt{7}; r = ^-1$

8. $1 + (n - 1)(\sqrt{2} - 1)$ **9.** $S = 13P$ **10.** There are 103 times as many girls as boys. **11.** $f = 3y$ **12.** $10S - 10n$
13. 26 **14. a.** If n is the original number, then each of the following lines shows the result of performing the instruction:

$$n$$
$$n + 17$$
$$2(n + 17) = 2n + 34$$
$$2n + 30$$
$$4n + 60$$
$$4n + 80$$
$$n + 20$$
$$n$$

b. Answers will vary. For example, the next two lines could be subtract 65 and then divide by 4. **15. a.** 3 **b.** No solutions **c.** No solutions **d.** $5\sqrt{3}$ **16.** Paige 111, Jordan 222, and Mike 666 **17.** Science books 17 days, other books 3 days **18.** Rashid 50, Dahlia 150, Jacobo 300 **19. a.** Function **b.** Not a function **c.** Function **d.** Function **20. a.** Range = $\{3, 4, 5, 6\}$ **b.** All real numbers **c.** $\{x \mid x \geq 0, x$ any real number$\}$ **d.** Range = $\{5, 9, 15\}$ **21. a.** This is not a function, since one student can have two majors. **b.** This is a function. The range is the subset of the natural numbers that includes the number of pages in each book in the library. **c.** This is a function. The range is $\{6, 8, 10, 12, \dots\}$. **d.** This is a function. The range is $\{0, 1\}$. **e.** This is a function. The range is N. **22. a.** $C(x) = 200 + 55(x - 1)$

b.

c. In the ninth month, the cost exceeds $600. **d.** in the 107th month **23. a.** 5 **b.** $\pm\sqrt{3}$ **c.** $^-9$

d. No such input   **e.** $-\dfrac{3}{2}$ **f.** No such input   **24.**   **a.** Yes, each input has exactly one output.   **b.** No, for $x = 4$, there are two values for y.   **c.** No, for $x = 5$, there are two values for y.
25. a. $14, 18, 22, 26$ **b.** The graph consists of points on the line $y = 4x + 2$ for $x = 1, 2, 3, 4, \ldots$.

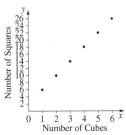

c. $y = 4x + 2$ **d.** The graph does not contain all the points on the line, and hence is not a straight line. The points lie along a line.

26. a.
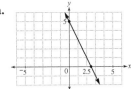   **b.**
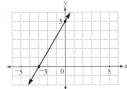

c.

27. a. Line CD has equation $4x + 3y - 12 = 0$.
b. $\left(0, \dfrac{8}{7}\right)$ **c.** $\dfrac{15}{4}$ **28. a.** $\dfrac{-11}{3}$ **b.** $-\dfrac{6}{\sqrt{2}} = {}^{-}3\sqrt{2}$
c. $\sqrt[3]{-2} = {}^{-}\sqrt[3]{2}$ **d.** 3 or ${}^{-}3$ **e.** $1 + \sqrt[3]{2}$ **f.** $\dfrac{\sqrt[4]{5} - 1}{2}$
g. $\dfrac{1}{2}$ or 1 **29.** Yes. The new ratio is the cube root of the original ratio, i.e., $\sqrt[3]{(r^n)} = (r^n)^{\frac{1}{3}} = \left(r^{\frac{1}{3}}\right)^n$.

Answers to Now Try This

1. a. Let g_k be the kth approximation. Then if $g_1 = 4$ then
$g_2 = \dfrac{1}{2}\left(\dfrac{13}{4} + 4\right) \doteq 3.625, g_3 = \dfrac{1}{2}\left(\dfrac{13}{3.625} + 3.625\right) \doteq 3.605$.
Because $g_4 \doteq 3.605$, 3.605 is accurate to 3 decimal places.
b. The algorithm for finding $\sqrt{a}$ is given by the recursive formula
$g_{n+1} = \dfrac{1}{2}\left(\dfrac{a}{g_n} + g_n\right)$, where g_1 is the initial guess.
2. a. The approach works as shown.
$$\sqrt{\sqrt{\sqrt{a}}} = \left(\left(a^{1/2}\right)^{1/2}\right)^{1/2} = \left(a^{1/4}\right)^{1/2}$$
$$= a^{1/8}$$
$$= \sqrt[8]{a}$$
b. For $n = 2^k$, where k is a positive integer. As shown in part (a), by repeatedly applying the square-root function we get $\sqrt[2^k]{a}$.
3. For a number like $8^{0.\overline{3}}$, one meaning is $8^{1/3}$ or $\sqrt[3]{8}$. Any repeating or terminating decimal can be converted to a number in

$\dfrac{a}{b}$ form where a, b are integers and $b \neq 0$. For a number like $8^{0.101001\cdots}$, one interpretation is as $8^{\left(\frac{1}{10} + \frac{0}{100} + \frac{1}{1000} + \frac{0}{10000} + \frac{0}{100000} + \frac{1}{1000000} + \cdots\right)}$ or $8^{\frac{1}{10}} \cdot 8^0 \cdot 8^{\frac{1}{1000}} \cdot 8^0 \cdot 8^0 \cdot 8^{\frac{1}{1000000}} \cdots$. Each part could be evaluated and an approximation of the total value could be obtained.
4. a. 206 **b.** $2n + 6$ **5. a.** After 10 hours, there are $2 \cdot 3^{10} = 118{,}098$ bacteria, and after n hours, there are $2 \cdot 3^n$ bacteria.   **b.** After 10 hours, there are $2 + 10 \cdot 3 = 32$ bacteria, and after n hours, there are $2 + 3n$ bacteria. We can see that after only 10 hours each term of the geometric sequence is greater than the corresponding term of the arithmetic sequence, in general when $r > 1$ and the first term is positive the terms of a geometric sequence eventually increase faster than the corresponding terms of any arithmetic sequence.   **6. a.** $\square = 3, \triangle = 9$ **b.** $\square = 4, \triangle = 2$
7. If Bob delivered b papers then Abby delivered $3b$ papers and Connie $3b + 13$ papers.
$$b + 3b + 3b + 13 = 496$$
$$b = 69$$
$$a = 3b = 207$$
$$c = 3b + 13 = 220$$

8. a. It is a function from the set of natural numbers to $\{0, 1\}$, because for each natural number there is a unique output in $\{0, 1\}$.   **b.** It is a function from the set of natural numbers to $\{0, 1\}$, because for each natural number there is a unique output in $\{0, 1\}$.   **9. a.** Girls: A, C, D, F, G, I; boys: B, J **b.** E and H
10. a. If $m = 0$, the line is the x-axis.   **b.** As m increases from 0, the slope is positive and the graph of the line becomes steeper as m becomes larger.   **c.** As m decreases from 0, the slope is negative and the graph of the line becomes steeper as the absolute value of m becomes larger.   **11.** If there were no restriction on the domain, a_n is replaced by y, and n is replaced by x, the equation becomes $y = a_1 + (x - 1)d$ or $y = dx + (a_1 - d)$. The slope of this line is d and the y-intercept is $a_1 - d$.   **12. a.** All the points on a horizontal line have the same y-coordinate. Thus, two points on a horizontal line have the form (x_1, y_1) and (x_2, y_2), where $y_2 = y_1$. The slope is $\dfrac{y_2 - y_1}{x_2 - x_1} = \dfrac{0}{x_2 - x_1} = 0$.   **b.** For any vertical line, $x_2 = x_1$ and therefore $x_2 - x_1 = 0$. If we attempted to find the slope, we would have to divide by 0, which is impossible. Hence, the slope of a vertical line is not defined.
13. a. The graphs are lines that intersect at $x = 4$ and $y = 3$.   **b.** The lines are parallel and not equal and hence the system has no solution. Algebraic approach: Assuming that there is a solution x and y, we multiply the first equation by 2 and add it side-by-side to the second. Therefore, x and y must satisfy $0 \cdot x + 0 \cdot y = 5$. However, no x and y satisfies this equation (a solution would imply $0 = 5$). This contradicts our assumption that the original system has a solution.   **c.** The equations represent the same line. If we divide both sides of the second equation by ${}^{-}2$ we get the first equation. Hence the system has infinitely many solutions: x is any real number and $y = 2x - 1$.

Answer to the Preliminary Problem

a. If the length of the sheet of paper is l and the width is w, then the ratio of length to width is $\dfrac{l}{w}$. The ratio of length to width of the half sheet is $\dfrac{w}{l/2} = \dfrac{2w}{l}$. Because the ratios need to be equal, we have:

$$\frac{l}{w} = \frac{2w}{l}$$

$$\frac{l^2}{w^2} = 2$$

$$\left(\frac{l}{w}\right)^2 = 2, \quad \frac{l}{w} = \sqrt{2}.$$

b. When two sheets are joined along their lengths, the ratio of the length of the longer side to the shorter is $\frac{2w}{l}$. We have seen in part (a) that $\frac{l}{w} = \frac{2w}{l}$. Hence $\frac{2w}{l} = \sqrt{2}$.

Credits

Credits are listed in the order of appearance.

Text Credits

388 Excerpt from Grade 8, The Number System, Standards For Mathematics. Copyright by Common Core State Standards Initiative. Used by permission of Common Core State Standards Initiative. Excerpt from Grade 8, Standards For Mathematics. Copyright by Common Core State Standards Initiative. Used by permission of Common Core State Standards Initiative.

Excerpt from Grade 8, Operations and Algebraic Thinking, Standards For Mathematics. Copyright by Common Core State Standards Initiative. Used by permission of Common Core State Standards Initiative. Excerpt from Grade 6, Expressions and Equations, Standards For Mathematics. Copyright by Common Core State Standards Initiative. Used by permission of Common Core State Standards Initiative.

enVisionMATH Common Core, Grade 4, © 2012. Printed and Electronically reproduced by permission of Pearson Education, Inc., Upper Saddle River, New Jersey.

MATHEMATICS Common Core, Course 1, © 2013. Printed and Electronically reproduced by permission of Pearson Education, Inc., Upper Saddle River, New Jersey.

Excerpt from Grade 8, Standards For Mathematics. Copyright by Common Core State Standards Initiative. Used by permission of Common Core State Standards Initiative.

MATHEMATICS Common Core, Course 1, © 2013. Printed and Electronically reproduced by permission of Pearson Education, Inc., Upper Saddle River, New Jersey.

MATHEMATICS Common Core, Course 3, © 2013. Printed and Electronically reproduced by permission of Pearson Education, Inc., Upper Saddle River, New Jersey.

Image Credits

Elenathewise/Fotolia

Pearson Education

Orphan Work

Pearson Education

top, middle, and bottom, Pearson Education

Pearson Education

Pearson Education

Index